# THE COMPLETE
## ENCYCLOPEDIA OF
# HUNTING RIFLES

# THE COMPLETE ENCYCLOPEDIA OF

# HUNTING RIFLES

A comprehensive guide to shotguns and other game guns
from around the world

## A.E. HARTINK

REBO
PUBLISHERS

© 1997 Rebo International b.v., Lisse, The Netherlands

Text: A.E. Hartink
Translation by: Stephen Challacombe
Cover design: Minkowsky Graphics, The Netherlands
Coordination and production: TextCase, Groningen, The Netherlands
Typesetting: de Zrij, The Netherlands

ISBN 90 366 1588 7

Because the introduction of new proof regulations and markings does not of itself render invalid earlier proof marks, guns may bear valid proof marks impressed under Rules of Proof of 1986, 1954, 1925 or even earlier. The majority of British proved shotguns in use at the present time have been proved or reproved since 1925. Marks are normally impressed on the flats of shotgun barrels or otherwise near the breech and upon the action.

## Under 1989 Rules of Proof

The proof marks at present (1993) impressed by the London and Birmingham Proof Houses are as follows:-

| | London | Birmingham |
|---|---|---|
| 1 Provisional proof |  |  |
| 2 Definitive proof for nitro powders | | |
| on action | |  |
| on barrel | | |
| 3 Definitive proof for Black Powder only |  |  |
| and the words    NOT NITRO | | BLACK POWDER |
| 4 Ammunition Inspection |  |  |

# Contents

# 1. The history of shotguns

Mankind has invented, made, and used weapons since the beginning of time. At first they were instruments of survival: man had to hunt in order to eat. The hunting territory had also to be defended against competitors: both other humans and prey animals. Until the Middle Ages these weapons consisted of knives, spears, slings, and clubs, plus the bow and arrow. Weapons that fired projectiles by means of an explosive charge first appeared in the western world in the fifteenth century. A form of gunpowder had been known to the Chinese in Asia since earlier times. The Chinese principally used this powder for their fireworks. There are various theories about the emergence of gunpowder in Europe. One of these is that the Venetian merchant venturer Marco Polo returned from China with the formula for gunpowder. He was part of a trading mission to China that managed to reach the Imperial City of Beijing during its travels across Asia between 1271 and 1292. Other stories propose one Roger Bacon, or the monk Berthold Schwarz from Freiburg in Germany. Black powder derives its name from Schwarz, whose name means "black" in German. Black powder is generally composed of 75% saltpetre, 15% sulphur, and 10% charcoal. It was discovered that, in addition to making fine fireworks, heavy projectiles could also be shot into the air using black powder. The first hand cannon appeared in the fifteenth century. These were a short metal tube attached to a long wooden pole that acted as a butt. At first the technology was very primitive. One end of the tube or barrel was closed off and a small hole was made in this closed end which was the flash hole or pan. Gunpowder was fed into the open end of the tube and then the projectile – usually a stone, lead or metal ball – was rammed back against the gunpowder. To fire the projectile, the powder had to be ignited so that a source of fire was needed. At first, this was done using glowing cinders or wood chips; these were later replaced by a slow burning fuse. The firing hole was filled with finely-ground powder.

*Beretta S06 shotgun*

*Fuselock gun by Hege with a flintlock and two ignition pistols in foreground.*

*Old type of wheel-lock combined with a fuselock.*

By bringing the slow-burning fuse onto the powder by means of a hinged lever, the powder was ignited. The powder in the pan set off the main charge in the barrel. The gases generated from the combustion of the gunpowder expand so quickly and at such high pressures that the projectile or bullet is ejected from the barrel. There were a number of disadvantages to ignition with a smouldering fuse. When it was windy and especially if raining, achieving ignition could be a problem. Ignition with the fuse was a problem for military purposes, particularly in the dark, when the glowing end would betray the position of the person firing the weapon. This led to the development of the wheel-lock. This is a metal disc combined with a coil spring, that is wound up with a key and then secured or "locked". When the wheel-lock is released by pressing

*Flintlock pistol.*

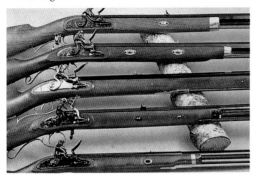

*Flintlock guns.*

was the true flintlock. Because the snaphaunce lock was rather sensitive to weather conditions, a cover was devised to protect the flash hole. This cover's vertical metal plate also acted as the steel for the flint. A major breakthrough in the development of firearms was made in Great Britain. A British chemist named Howard discovered explosive mercury in 1799 and a Scottish priest, Alexander Forsyth was granted a patent in 1807 for the principles of the percussion primer. In 1808 Forsyth developed a chemical compound, known as fulminate, that could be enclosed in a small cap. The problem of using a naked flame for ignition was a thing of the past. The chamber (the place in the barrel where the charge was placed) still had to be loaded with both the powder and the ball through the muzzle. For ignition, however, the percussion cap was fixed by a small attachment to the flash hole. This attachment is known as the nipple or piston. To hit the percussion cap really hard, a hammer mechanism was developed similar to the flintlock. This hammer was located immediately behind the barrel chamber. The hammer (or cock) was drawn backwards against the pressure of a spring and locked in position. By pulling the trigger, the hammer was released to hit the percussion cap

*Set of Hege percussion pistols.*

*Model 1777 musket by Hege with percussion lock.*

the trigger, the tension of the spring causes the metal disc to spin backwards, scraping against a flint as it does. This causes a shower of sparks that ignites the fine gunpowder in the pan. Because the wheel-lock system was complicated and expensive to make, a simpler, cheaper alternative was sought after. This was the flintlock. The flint was secured in the jaws of a kind of hammer. This hammer or cock , as it is called, was fixed to the side of the weapon and could be drawn backwards (cocked) against the tension of the spring and locked into position. When the trigger was pressed, the flint struck a metal plate close to the flash hole. The resulting sparks ignited the gunpowder in the flash hole. The flintlock system took several centuries of development. During the course of its development, one of its variations was the snaphaunce lock. This system consisted of two hammers. The first had a kind of screw claw into which a flint could be fixed. This hammer could be drawn back against the pressure of the hammer spring. The second hammer was a sort of anvil or steel situated just above the flash hole. When the trigger was pulled, the hammer with the flint struck against the steel. This produced sparks that fell into the flash hole. The fine gunpowder in the flash hole was ignited which, in turn, set off the main charge in the barrel. A further development so forcibly that it exploded. The resulting flash passed through the nipple to ignite the gunpowder charge in the chamber. This percussion system was used for a long time for rifles, pistols, and later in more modern five and six-shot black powder revolvers. The next important step in the evolution of firearms was the creation of the cartridge. At first this was simply a case of paper or cardboard, and later of brass. The components of the cartridge – gunpowder, percussion cap and case – were assembled in one unit. The Swiss gunmaker, Johann Samuel Pauly, experimented in 1812 with a brass cartridge with a central firing position. This cartridge could no longer be loaded via the muzzle but had to be placed in the chamber of the barrel through the back of the firearm. This meant that the rear of the barrel had to be open to load the weapon. After loading, the barrel then had to be strong enough and securely closed to prevent it from splitting or springing open when the charge exploded. The renowned weapon maker Lefaucheux created the first pelleted shot cartridge in 1832. He improved it in 1840 and introduced the first metal pin-fire cartridge. The history of the shotgun runs broadly parallel with that of military weapons and began in the sixteenth century. In those times, leaded shot or scrap metal was not used for shooting game but for defence. The arquebus was a gun that was loaded via the muzzle with gunpowder and small stones or bits of metal. The closed end of the tube or barrel had a flash hole. The shooter ignited the charge by pressing a glowing fuse or match to the hole. An interesting example of this type of weapon is the blunderbuss, which was a short gun or pistol with a funnel-shaped muzzle. This weapon was also developed for military purposes such as battles at sea and the protection of valuable coach or wagon loads. The present-day shotgun was invented in Britain in 1758. According to an old patent, the shot was first moulded and

*Painting of roe deer (Zoli).*

*Hege percussion guns: Great Plains, Hawks, and Hawks hunting gun.*

then rounded off in a drum that was turned round and round. The method of producing lead shot is also a British invention, dating from 1782. Molten lead was poured through sieves from a height of about 100ft (30m) onto cold water. The lead formed a round shape during its fall. The size of the shot could be varied by using sieves of different diameter mesh. Over the years various methods of producing shot have been developed, such as pressing shot from lead wire. The nobility used guns firing bullets for hunting as early as the sixteenth century. The first report of a gun firing multiple shot comes from a German engraving of 1545, which portrays a Duck hunt. In those times hunting for game was restricted solely to the nobility. For this reason, the numbers of shotguns produced was never comparable to the production of military weapons. Even though farmers had problems with wild animals, they were not permitted to hunt them. In many kingdoms, dukedoms, and other fiefdoms, farmers and citizens were strictly forbidden to own weapons to prevent poaching of "noble game". An example of this is the Act of Parliament of 1542 which forbids ownership of guns except for landowners and wealthy individuals with an income in excess of £100 per annum.

Farmers were required to act as beaters and attendants during shooting parties. It was not unusual for several hundred farmers to be rounded up to drive the game so that the elegantly clad nobility could shoot it with the superbly engraved guns. The hunting of smaller game, such as rabbits, hares, pheasants, and other fowl was generally performed with less spectacle. Before the development of the shotgun, this sort of hunt was mainly carried out with birds of prey such as falcons. From 1600 onwards the gentry increasingly used smooth-bore shotguns. A complete hunting outfit from those days consisted of a rifle for hunting deer, a shotgun, and one or more pistols. These hunting sets were often highly decorated with the engraving of firearms becoming very fashionable in the sixteenth and seventeenth centuries. The gunsmiths of the Brescia region of Italy developed engraving to a high art form. Names from this period became renowned, such as that of Matteo Acqua Fresca, who made superb weapons for Cosimo the Third, Duke of Tuscany. Books were even published containing designs for firearm engravings. Firearms developed rapidly between 1800–1900. Many new ignition and cartridge developments were achieved, such as the percussion cap of Forsyth, previously referred to. He founded Forsyth & Company as an armaments maker in 1808. In addition to rifles and pistols, some fine shotguns with damask designs on the barrels have been preserved.

The invention in 1850 of the English T-form locking system for breech-loading shotguns led to many new developments. Until that time the shotgun had two external hammers which fired percussion caps. Following the development of the pivoting breech, the percussion cap was replaced by cartridges containing the charge, which could be inserted into the breech for pin-fire ignition, and later to the complete cartridge with both charge and load that was fired by the firing pin. In 1875, Anson & Deely of Birmingham were granted a patent for a hammer-less gun. This shotgun had an internal cock and self-cocking mechanism. This was a very important step forward: many modern shotguns are still based on this principle.

**Measurements and weights used in this book are expressed in both metric and Imperial units. The source dimension is given first with the conversion in brackets. This results in metric figures sometimes appearing first and elsewhere in brackets.**

*Hand-crafted gunsmith's workshop (Arrieta).*

*Bernardelli shotgun with external hammers.*

*Cut-away view of the action of a modern shotgun (Browning Model B25).*

# 2. Technical terminology for shotguns and combination guns

## Shotgun

The term shotgun refers to a group of weapons and it refers to the type of barrel. Shotguns have one or more barrels of smooth bore without any rifling. These weapons are principally used for firing cartridges containing pelleted shot. Shotguns can in turn be sub-divided into:

**Single-barrelled shotguns**
1. single shot breech-loading
2. semi-automatic gas-pressure repeaters
3. semi-automatic recoil-operated repeaters
4. pump-action repeaters
5. bolt-action repeaters

**Double-barrelled shotguns**
1. barrels side-by-side
2. barrels over-and-under

**Combination gun**
A combination gun has one or more smooth barrels combined with one or more rifled barrels.

1. double-barrelled smooth-bore/bullet side-by-side
2. double-barrelled smooth-bore/bullet over-and-under
3. triple-barrelled firearm
4. quadruple-barrelled firearm

### *Single-barrelled shotgun*

#### I. SINGLE-SHOT BREECH-LOADING
The centre of the firearm is hinged, so that access to the chamber is possible for loading of cartridges. The opening is referred to as the breech and not as a hinge. When the breech of a gun is open, the gun is referred to as "broken" which does not mean that it is in need of repair. The locking mechanisms for breech-loaders vary but is mainly by means of a swivel catch across the breech. There are also alternative methods using a

*Single-barrel breech-loading shotgun: Harrington & Richardson's Pardner.*

*This Beretta A303 semi-automatic shotgun is stripped down into its main groups.*

press button and other catches mounted on the action or close to the trigger guard.

#### 2. GAS-OPERATED SEMI-AUTOMATIC REPEATING
With this system some of the gas from the fired cartridge is utilised for the repeating mechanism. While the plug and shot are exiting the barrel, some of the gas-pressure is vented off. This is fed to a pressure-cylinder with a piston beneath the barrel which forces the piston back as a kind of pneumatic hammer. The piston lever unlocks the firearm, pulls the spent cartridge from the chamber and ejects it from the gun. The continued rearwards motion cocks the weapon to fire the subsequent shot. Once the backward motion is ended, the return spring, which has been compressed, presses for-

*Cut-away diagram of the Browning gas-pressure repeating system. Browning produces a self-regulating mechanism for light to heavy calibre shotgun cartridges.*

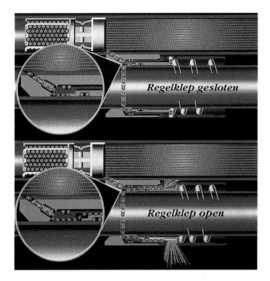

Regelklep gesloten

Regelklep open

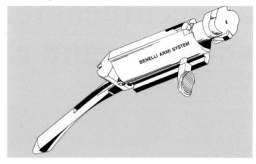

ward, pushing the bolt or receiver forward and feeds a new cartridge into the chamber from the magazine. The final stage of the forward movement is the locking of the chamber and breech. With most systems this is performed by a rotating bolt head. The firearm is ready to be discharged. This method cannot be used to fire the first round since there is no gas-pressure so that the gun must be cocked manually. This is done with the right hand pulling back a cocking lever. This cocks the gun and then during the forward motion caused by the return spring, a cartridge is taken from the magazine and pushed into the chamber.

### 3. RECOIL-OPERATED SEMI-AUTOMATIC REPEATING

With this type of semi-automatic gun, the repeating mechanism is operated by the recoil or blow back. It is not venting off of gas-pressure but the recoil action which drives back a slider. Two different types of forces are created when a cartridge is fired: a forward force which propels the projectile or shot through the barrel and an backwards force in the opposite direction against the weight of the firearm itself and ultimately against the shooter's shoulder. This recoil provides the energy required to move the bolt or slider and this in turn cocks the weapon. The rest of the action of this system is the same as gas-operated systems.

### 4. PUMP-ACTION REPEATER

The manual operation of this type of repeater is the simplest to understand. This system is not driven by either gas-pressure or recoil forces but by hand. The front hand grip on the stock of the firearm is mounted on a slide and can be pulled back and pushed forward to operate the mechanism. The hand grip is linked to the slider. This type of repeating action is usually combined with falling block locking but rotating bolt heads are also used. When the hand grip is pulled backwards, the bar linked to the

*The Browning BPS (Browning Pump Shotgun) is an example of a pump-action gun.*

receiver or slider ensures that this moves too. The action pulls the spent cartridge from the chamber and ejects it. The gun is cocked. When the handle is pushed forward, the slider is also pushed forwards, pushing a new cartridge into the chamber. This mechanism is fairly noisy and there is no effort made with riot guns used by police forces in some countries to diminish this sound because of the intimidating effect it can have. Riot guns are single-barrelled shotguns with a short barrel. Most of them are pump-action repeaters but semi-automatic mechanisms are also used. These are typically defensive weapons with a broad spread of shot. The cartridges used are normally shotgun cartridges with coarse shot of 5-7mm ($^{3}/_{16}$-$^{1}/_{4}$in). A hit at close quarters up to about 30m (100ft) is normally catastrophic.

### 5. BOLT-ACTION REPEATER

A shotgun can be equipped with a bolt just like a rifle. The bolt is manually unlocked and pulled to the rear which causes the cartridge extractor to remove the spent cartridge and also cocks the firing pin. When the bolt is pushed forward again, a new cartridge is taken from the magazine and pressed into the chamber. Once the bolt is fully pressed home the final action of pressing down the bolt handle locks the firearm. This ensures that one or more lugs on the bolt engage with cams in the end of the barrel. This system is fairly unusual for shotguns.

## *Double-barrelled shotgun*

Double-barrelled shotguns are almost always of the breech-loading type, with barrels that hinge open at the stock. The shooter operates the locking mechanism by means of a catch mounted on the neck of the stock. Some breech-loading shotguns have a cocking and locking lever incorporated with the trigger guard or a locking push-button or locking lever at the rear of

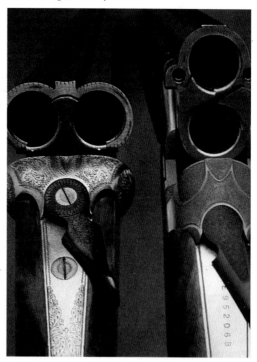

*The clear difference between side-by-side (left) with the barrels arranged next to each other and over-and-under (right) with the barrels on top of each other. Both these guns are by Beretta.*

the action or beside an external cocking mechanism.

Double-barrelled shotgun can be subdivided into two different types.

1. **Side-by-side:** with which the barrels are next to each other.
2. **Over-and-under:** with which the barrels are placed one on top of the other.

*A bolt-action shotgun: the Marlin Slugmaster.*

*An example of a side-by-side combination gun by Gaucher: the right-hand barrel is rifled but the left-hand barrel is smooth-bore.*

# Combination gun

A combination gun is composed of one or more smooth-bore barrels and one or more rifled barrels for cartridges with bullets or slugs. These can be grouped as follows.

### 1. Double-barrelled side-by-side shotgun and rifle

with the smooth-bore and rifled barrels arranged side-by-side, sometimes both in 12 bore with one barrel being rifled for use with slugs.

*A Ferlach combination gun with smooth-bore barrel above and rifled barrel below.*

*Ferlach drilling gun with a single smooth-bore barrel above and two rifled barrels below.*

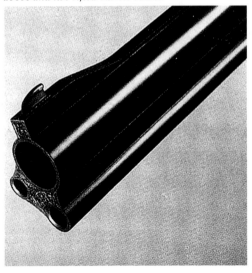

### 2. Double-barrelled over-and-under shotgun and rifle

with combined smooth-bore and rifled barrels placed on top of each other.

### 3. Triple-barrelled gun with single or double smooth-bore barrels and single or double rifled barrels.

### 4. Quadruple-barrelled gun with various combinations of rifled and smooth-bore barrels.

These guns are most popular for use in extensive hunting areas with a variety of terrain in which the hunter might shoot a

*Ferlach Drilling gun with twin smooth-bore barrels above for shotgun cartridges and a single rifled barrel beneath for cartridges with bullets.*

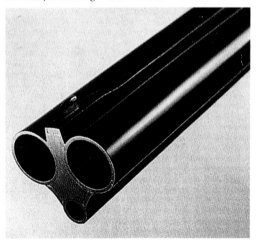

*A different type of Ferlach Drilling gun with twin rifled barrels uppermost and a single smooth-bore barrel for shotgun cartridges below.*

*Ferlach Quad gun with double over-and-under smooth-bore barrels and double rifled barrels side-by-side*

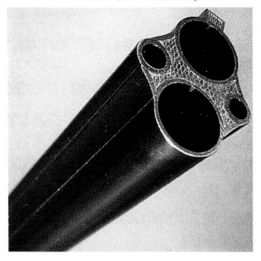

*An overview of the barrel production stages for a Heym combined gun*

*Two barrels being soldered together to create an over-and-under Browning gun*

*Ferlach Quad gun with double rifled barrels over-and-under and double smooth-bore barrels side-by-side*

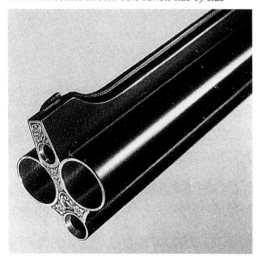

# Gun parts and production processes

A breech-loading shotgun consists of the following parts:

1. the barrel with pivot, locking lever, and choke
2. the action with the firing mechanism,
3. the stock including the fore-end or hand-grip.

Certain techniques are required to produce double-barreled shotguns and these are described below.

## 1. The barrel

The smooth-bore barrels of shotguns used to be hand-forged. Iron and steel was heated and then wrought around a steel rod. By forging the iron and steel together a particular texture was created in the metal. These barrels are sometimes referred to as "damask" barrels from this texture and these were principally used with black powder.

Modern shotguns are equipped with steel barrels because the iron and steel forged types are unable to withstand the high gas-pressures of modern munitions. Since the

which the hunter might shoot a pheasant one moment with the smooth-bore and a shot cartridge and then perhaps ten minutes later come face to face with a deer for which the rifled barrel would be needed. Combination guns avoid the need to carry more than one gun.

*The busy barrel production shop of Fabarm.*

*Mass production of actions at Fabarm.*

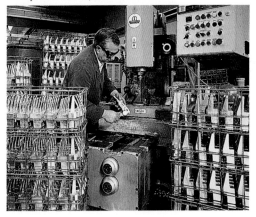

*Stages in the production of shotgun actions with the single block and other smaller components.*

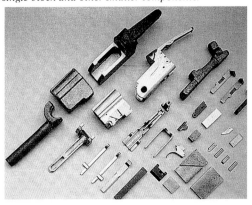

barrels are forged from steel or turned from steel rod which is subsequently bored out. Two barrels are needed, of course, for a double-barrelled gun. Most gunsmiths or makers acquire their barrels from highly specialised firms that produce barrels to size on order or by the metre. Two barrels of approximately the correct length are then joined together by the gunsmith. The gunmaker solders a block of steel to the chamber end of the barrel which will be machined to form the hinged breech. Between the barrels spot solders are performed at intervals but these will not be seen once the stock is added with its front hand grip. About half-way along the barrel, the gunmaker welds a lug to which the stock can be attached. The spot welds have to be carefully and specifically performed because they have a considerable influence on the vibrations that occur in the barrels and consequently on the direction of the shot pellets when they exit the muzzle. The two barrels

*Stages in the production of Heym actions.*

*Polishing the double-barrels of a Browning.*

*Alignment of barrels is a highly-skilled art.*

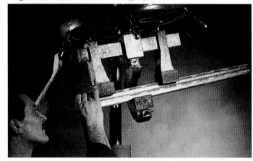

*Ensuring the perfect fit for action and barrel of a Browning.*

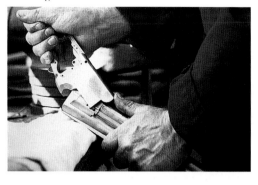

*The perfect fit of action and barrel without play is always done by hand.*

must also be perfectly aligned with each other so that the central axis of each barrel converges at about 102 in (2.6m) from the muzzle. The two barrels can be joined together at the chamber end by various types of blocks. The barrels can be joined together as one piece with one block or one block can be used per barrel. These are then later soldered together. Tin or copper used to be used as solder but this is nowadays usually a silver-copper alloy.

The next stage in the production is the precise boring of the barrels. These already have internal diameters that are approximately the right size. These have to be machined to the precise bore and polished. The cartridge chambers are also bored in the rear of the barrels to the correct length for the intended cartridge calibre. Some older shotguns have chambers of $2^{11}/_{16}$in (67.5mm).

Modern shotguns have a chamber length of $2^{3}/_{4}$in (70 mm). Cartridge manufacturers denote both the gauge (bore) and length of their cartridges, such as 12/70. American shotguns generally have a larger cartridge length of 3in (76mm) which is also known as 12-gauge Magnum. It is obvious that a longer cartridge cannot be fired in a chamber that is shorter than intended because the gas pressure will be too great. The chamber has a larger diameter than the barrel itself. The projectile or shot is contained within the cartridge and this is of smaller diameter than the cartridge. The transition from chamber to barrel must not be too abrupt or the recoil of the firearm will be greatly increased. This is why a conical form is preferred.

Rifled barrels also generally have a transition cone in the chamber. During the process of making a gun, the barrel is tested or proved to ensure that it can withstand the

| Choke | Designation | Reduction | % of shot on target [1] |
|---|---|---|---|
| Cylindrical | C or CL | none | 30 |
| Improved cylinder or ¹/₄ choke | IC or **** | 0.33mm | 35–40 |
| Modified or ¹/₂ choke | M or *** | 0.56mm | 60 |
| Improved modified or ³/₄ choke | IM or ** | 0.79mm | 70 |
| Full choke | F or * | 1.02mm | 75–80 |
| | | | |
| Special sporting chokes | | | |
| Skeet | S, Sk, or ***** | 0.10mm | – |
| Sporting 1 | SC1 | 0.18mm | – |
| Sporting 2 | SC2 | 0.41mm | – |

[1] Percentage of shot hitting target of 75cm (29¹/₂in) diameter at 35m (115ft) from the muzzle

considerable gas pressures. Finally, the gunsmith ensures that the barrel and action are perfectly united with the stock and that they operate effectively.

An important part of a shotgun barrel is the choke or narrowing of the diameter of the barrel. A barrel will be cylindrical from the

*A set of interchangeable chokes by Fair. The chokes are screwed and unscrewed using the special*

*A complete set of interchangeable chokes.*

chamber to within approximately 5cm (2in) from the end of the barrel. The choke applied to the end of the barrel is a conical reduction which has a certain influence on the spread of shot. Shotguns that have no choke produce an irregular spread of shot resulting in an uneven and unpredictable coverage of the target. The purpose of the choke is to determine the extent of spread of the shot and by so doing, it also influences the effective range of the shot. The percentage cover of a specific choke is measured by determining the number of hits of a 12 gauge cartridge on a 75cm (29¹/₂in) target at 35m (115ft) from the muzzle. A 12 gauge cartridge with a 36g (1¹/₄oz) load comprises approximately 770 pellets of 2mm (³/₃₂in). With a wholly cylindrical barrel, only 30 percent of these pellets will hit the target.

There are different types of choke. The table above lists them together with the extent of their reduction and general percentage of pellets on target.

Skeet chokes are a slightly improved cylindrical bore with a cone that widens towards the muzzle. The shot is therefore first forced together and then given extra space. This has the effect of the spread of shot becoming greater in direct proportion to the distance travelled but also produces a cluster of shot that is more compact from front to rear. Not all pellets have the same velocity since air resistance can work on them differently. Some pellets may be slightly misshapen causing greater air resistance. This causes the column of shot to have a certain depth. The centre of a column of shot pellets of 3.5mm ($^5/_{32}$in) will be about 2m (79in) deep at a range of 35m (115ft) and have a diameter of about 75cm (29$^1/_2$in). Skeet chokes favourably influence the breadth or diameter of the column of shot to improve the chances of hitting the fast moving clay pigeon. Most double-barrelled shotguns have different chokes in each barrel. A widely used combination is Improved Cylinder or $^1/_4$ choke with Improved Modified or $^3/_4$ choke. The broader choke is best for targets at closer range and the narrower choke for those at a greater ranger. In addition to fixed chokes, there are interchangeable or variable choke systems. The Vari-choke or Poly-choke comprises an outer casing that can be rotated with a number of individual internal elements. By turning the adjustment ring of the outer casing, the choke can be made narrower or wider. Interchangeable chokes are tubes which can be screwed into the barrel or added to the end of the barrel, each with a different extent of reduction. The different makes of these systems have their own brand names, such as Beretta's Mobil-choke, the Invector chokes of Browning, and Winchester's Winchoke.

## 2. The action or breech

The action or breech is the heart of the gun. All the mechanical elements of the gun such as the cocking, firing, and safety mechanisms are located within the action. The most usual types of mechanisms are those of Anson & Deeley, the side-lock of Holland & Holland, and the Blitz lock.

This explanation of how shotguns work refers to the mechanisms most usually found. The terminology used in describing shotguns and their mechanisms is dealt with in Chapter 8.

### THE ANSON & DEELY SYSTEEM
The British gunmakers Anson and Deeley of Birmingham developed a locking mechanism together in 1875. This is the most widely used principle in which all the mechanical elements are housed together within the action or action body.

The main parts of this system are:
- the hammer or internal firing pin
- the hammer or firing pin spring
- the trigger lever
- the trigger spring
- the cocking lever

*The A&D locking mechanism of a Browning Citori.*

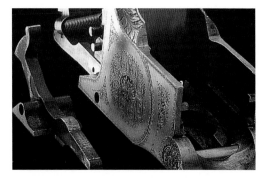

*An example of a Browning cocking lever beside an action.*

With double-barrelled shotguns, two sets of these mechanisms are next to each other within the action. The working of a breech-loading shotgun depends on the cocking levers which are connected to a lug attached to the barrels within the front hand grip. When the breech is opened by "breaking" the gun, the levers are pressed downwards as the barrel pivots on the action. The cocking levers act somewhat like see-saws in which the rear part of the levers are tipped upwards. The rear section of the cocking levers engage beneath the hammers or firing pin mechanisms, pushing them to the rear against the pressure of the firing springs. At the end of their travel, the hammers or firing pin mechanisms engages with notches in the trigger mechanisms. The hammers or firing pins are now cocked but locked. Some gunmakers incorporate indicator pins which are pressed up into view on the action so that the shooter can see that the gun is cocked. This type of locking is often combined with automatic safety devices , whereby once the firing pins are cocked, a safety lever also engages. To fire these systems, the safety catch first has to be pushed or pressed. Other safety systems lock the trigger mecha-

*An Anson & Deely lock by Heym. The cocked hammer pushes the cocking indicator upwards through the action body and the safety disc blocks the trigger.*

*Krieghoff side-lock.*

nism by means of a safety catch or even by means of automatic safety so that both barrels cannot be fired. An explanation of the different safety systems is dealt with in the next chapter.

## THE HOLLAND & HOLLAND SIDE-LOCKING SYSTEM

The locking mechanism with this system is not housed within the action but separately mounted on side-plates screwed to either side of the action. This system is used in particular with very expensive hand-made guns, although the notable exception to this generalization are the Spanish gunmakers who make superb side-lock guns at modest prices. The metal-work and screws on a gun with these plates often indicate that the gun is side-locking. This type of lock generally has the same components as an Anson & Deely type mechanism.

Components for each barrel are mounted on the side plates with the exception of the cocking lever which is attached between the action, fore-end, and firing mechanism. Older side-lock guns did not have internal firing mechanisms, because they had external hammers or cocks rather like old percussion firearms. Guns with side-plates that are not side-locking came into being in the era when only expensive side-locking guns were available. These appear to be side-locks with their screws and swivels but they are merely imitations.

## THE BLITZ SYSTEM

The German Blitz system can be regarded as a variation of the Anson & Deely principles. However this mechanism is so much of an improvement that it deserves consideration as an apart system. With this locking mechanism, almost all the components are incorporated within one action block and this can often be fitted as one unit to a gun and also removed in one piece. By unscrewing the trigger guard and both triggers (or disengaging them) the entire locking mechanism can be easily removed from the action in one go.

*This Beretta has a different type of side-lock.*

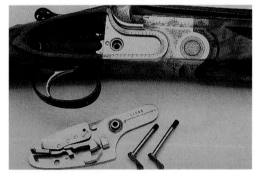

*A Krieghoff Blitz lock, combined with the special Krieghoff hand-cocking mechanism.*

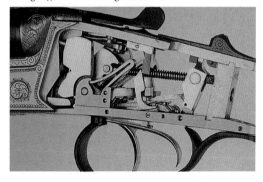

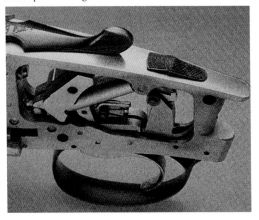

*The Rottweil Blitz lock with coil springs in their telescopic housings.*

The only components which remain in the action are both cocking levers which link the lock and fore-end. Makers such as Sauer and Merkel have developed superb Blitz locking mechanisms. The Sauer Blitz locks are equipped with leaf springs, whilst those of Merkel have coiled springs. The Blitz lock of Rottweil should not be overlooked. This has a coil spring in a telescopic housing which prevents dust or other dirt from impairing its operation.

The Italian firm of Beretta have developed a further variation of the Blitz system with a single trigger which first operates the firing mechanism and firing pin of one barrel and then the other.

The Rottweil Blitz lock that is used in the Paragon gun is a more compact version. All

*The unusual and very compact Blitz lock of the Rottweil Paragon shotgun.*

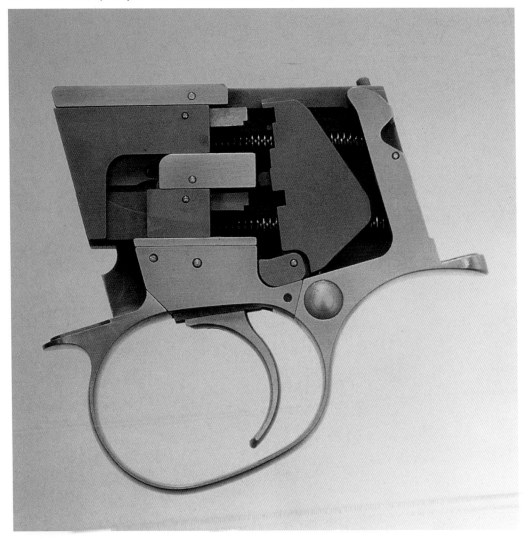

A one-piece extractor of an American Arms Basque side-by-side

Double-barreled shotguns usually have a single extractors for both barrels while ejectors are per barrel.

## b. Ejector

With an ejector, the spent shells are automatically ejected when the weapon is broken or cocked but this is selectively done since if only one barrel is fired, a shooter would not wish to eject both cartridges. The front of the cocking lever, which is also responsible for cocking the firing pin, engages the forward part of the ejector levers that are mounted along both barrels.

When the gun is broken or cocked, both ejector levers are also cocked. If one barrel is fired, the ejector lever is released by the operation of the trigger and the ejector lever rises up to come into operation. When the gun is broken or cocked, the ejector lever strikes the spent shell to eject it from the chamber. The ejector lever for the other barrel which has not been fired remains disengaged so that this unused cartridge is not ejected.

The shell is pushed out of the chamber a little so that it can be removed by hand if required. Those not engaged in field sports

The Browning ejector system. Note the spring-loaded ejector hammers

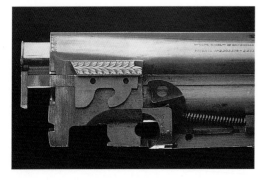

may not appreciate the value of this system. The shooter (or gun as most field shooters are termed) may have to cross a ditch or stile and it is an absolute rule that the gun should be both broken before doing so. It would be a nuisance to have an unused cartridge fly out over the shoulder in the process.

## 3. The stock

Hopefully the different parts of a gun are now becoming clearer in the reader's mind. The barrel, its manufacture, and the action or breech at the heart of the gun have now been dealt with but not the "rear end" of the gun. The stock is often one of the most problematical parts of a shotgun in contrast to a rifle.

Many theories have been developed and countless books written about shotgun stocks and this is perhaps less surprising when you consider that a target rifle is rarely aimed and fired under such hectic circumstances as a shotgun.

During a hunt or shoot a hare or other game can suddenly scamper out of cover or a wild duck fly up suddenly. A moment's hesitation can result in the game being more than 100 ft (30 m) away. The gun therefore has to be shouldered, aimed, and fired with lightning speed. The same is equally true of clay pigeon shooting. For this reason, the stock of a shotgun has to be made to measure the person who uses it. It is even so that a stock may be slightly off line with the barrel in order to compensate for the distance between right eye and shoulder.

A number of measurements need to be taken very carefully in order to adjust the length of the stock. A stock that is too long can easily be shortened but one that is too

Various stages in the making of a Heym gun-stock

*Chequering a Browning gun-stock.*

## 3. The stock

Hopefully the different parts of a gun are now becoming clearer in the reader's mind. The barrel, its manufacture, and the action or breech at the heart of the gun have now been dealt with but not the "rear end" of the gun. The stock is often one of the most problematical parts of a shotgun in contrast to a rifle. Many theories have been developed and countless books written about shotgun stocks and this is perhaps less surprising when you consider that a target rifle is rarely aimed and fired under such hectic circumstances as a shotgun. During a hunt or shoot a hare or other game can suddenly scamper out of cover or a wild duck fly up suddenly. A moment's hesitation can result in the game being more than 100 ft (30 m) away. The gun therefore has to be shouldered, aimed, and fired with lightning speed. The same is equally true of clay pigeon shooting. For this reason, the stock of a shotgun has to be made to measure the person who uses it. It is even so that a stock may be slightly off line with the barrel in order to compensate for the distance between right eye and shoulder

A number of measurements need to be taken very carefully in order to adjust the length of the stock. A stock that is too long can easily be shortened but one that is too short has to be extended by adding spaces between the butt and the stock.

A gunsmith takes measurements related to the trigger for the position of the stock. These are:

a. from the trigger to the upper rear or heel of the stock;
b. from the trigger to the centre of the butt;
c. from the trigger to the lower rear or toe of the stock.

The incline from a continuation of the sighting line for the stock must also be accurately determined by measuring from this horizontal to the comb and heel. Stocks are made from all sorts of type of wood but walnut is

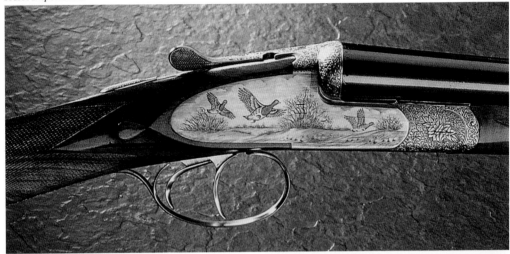

used for the more expensive guns. Walnut from mature trees is used to ensure the finest grain and figuring, and this in turn influences the price. Wood such as maple, birch, beech, elm, cherry, and peach are also used for making gun stocks. The use of plastic for pump-action and repeating shotguns is becoming more common. This type of gun often has a magazine incorporated into the fore-end or hand-grip. Some parts of the stock must have a texture or rough finish so that the person shooting the gun can hold it firmly. This is true of the fore-end and the neck, and/or pistol-grip. The wood is usually finished with a chequered finish rather like fish scales.

## SIGHTS
The sights of shotguns are quite primitive in comparison with those of rifles and pistols. Some who use them might dispute this but shotguns are principally used in a reactive mode. When a shooter calls "pull" on a clay pigeon shoot, a clay flies with great speed into the air so that there is no time for getting the aim absolutely on target. The shooter must also "aim off" or shoot ahead of the target so that his shot will not pass behind the rapidly moving target. The same is more or less true of a hare that is running away, or of a rabbit, or pheasant that has been put up. Sights with precise adjustment serve little purpose for a shotgun.

## ENGRAVING
The extent of the engraving on a gun is dependent on the make but above all the

*Engraving the action of a Browning.*

*A fine example of engraving on a Ferlach gun.*

price of the gun. The tradition of decorating guns has a long history but some modern guns can be works of art too. Many gunmakers provide an extensive "collection" of engravings.

## SHOTGUN
The term shotgun is used in this book for guns with smooth-bore barrels as opposed to the machined "fields" of a rifle's barrel. The book also includes combination guns that have both smooth-bore and rifled barrels, and certain specialist rifles that are made solely for hunting game. Some call this

*Another example of Ferlach engraving.*

*Superb artistry by Browning.*

*A fine hunting scene on the action of a CZ gun.*

*A museum piece by Merkel.*

*Brace of Arrieta model 875.*

*This Winchester 101 is hand engraved by FN Browning. It is the competition gun of Diana van der Valk, European and Dutch Skeet and Double-Trap champion.*

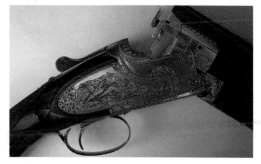

group of guns field sports guns but although they are extensively used for field sports, they are also used for shooting at clay pigeons and also by police forces as public order weapons. Rifles too have the same range of uses for shooting game, target shooting, and military purposes.

Both shotguns and rifles are shoulder arms. With a rifle, however, the internal rifling of the barrel has the purpose of rotating the bullet for stability in flight or trajectory. The rifling of a barrel forms a spiral in the barrel which runs from the chamber to the muzzle. The companion book The Encyclopaedia of Rifles and Carbines deals with rifles that are used for target shooting and hunting. This book centres its attention on shotguns and those specialist guns which have both shotgun and rifle characteristics.

# 3. Safety systems

The purpose of a safety system is to prevent the firearm from being accidentally discharged. Double-barrel shotguns also need a mechanism to prevent both barrels from being fired at the same time.

The safety of both shotguns and combination guns can be provided by a number of methods, such as a sliding lever on the top of the action or breech, behind the locking lever. This sliding-lever catch sometimes also acts as barrel selector. A second switch is provided which enables the smooth-bore or rifled barrels to be selected. Such systems are widely used with triple and quadruple barrelled guns. The selector can also be an entirely separate catch as in the case of the Krieghoff K 80.

Krieghoff has an automatic safety system by which the gun is not automatically cocked when the breech is broken. To make the gun "live" a large slider has to be pushed forwards on the neck of the stock. Krieghoff has an additional safety catch to enable the gun to be uncocked. A further example of a safety system is the push-button safety catch in the trigger guard, sometimes placed in front of the guard, sometimes behind.
An unusual safety system with shotguns is the finger catch in the front of the trigger guard. Such systems are common with rifles but the mechanism is to be found on some of the French Verney-Carron shotguns.

There are seven safety systems that can generally be found with shotguns, sometimes in combinations.

a. trigger safety
b. firing lever or tumbler safety
c. firing pin or hammer safety
d. cocking safety
e. dropped-gun safety
f. closing safety
g. load indicator

### a. Trigger safety
With trigger safety. the trigger is locked to prevent its operation. This type of safety system is also known as Greener safety.

*Merkel Drilling gun*

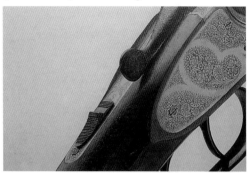

*Safety-catch slider on the neck of the stock. This system is widely used on shotguns.*

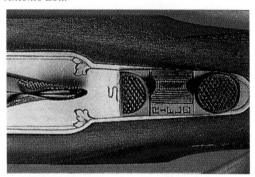

*Safety-catch slider combined with barrel selector by Antonio Zoli.*

### b. Firing lever or tumbler safety
When the safety catch is operated, the firing lever or tumbler is locked. Another safety system that is similar is where a firing lever is automatically blocked by a safety lever. This prevents both barrels from being discharged. Shotguns that have only single triggers yet do not have barrel selectors use this method, whereby the recoil from the first shot brings the lever into operation. The sequence for this type of gun is:

- side-by-side: right-hand barrel then left-hand;
- over-and-under: top barrel then bottom.

### c. Firing pin or hammer safety
The firing pin or hammer is blocked by means of the safety catch (see drawing on p 31).

29

*Barrel selector from a Krieghoff K80 gun. The lever just in front of the trigger operates the firing mechanism between either barrel.*

*Krieghoff hand cocking system with safety catch next to locking lever.*

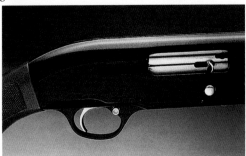

*Push-button safety catch at the front of the trigger guard.*

*Push-button safety catch at the rear of the trigger guard (Browning Auto 5).*

*The push-button safety catch on this Verney-Carron gun is hard to see: look at the triangle at the front of the trigger guard.*

### d. Automatic or cocking safety

A firearm with automatic safety is sometimes termed a "safe gun." When the breech is opened and the gun loaded, the firearm remains uncocked and has to be cocked by hand using the cocking lever or knob. The cocking lever is often positioned on the neck of the stock, where the safety catch is located on other guns. Combination rifle and shotguns usually have this type of system. The gun is cocked once more by pushing the lever backwards.

### e. Dropped-gun safety

This type of safety incorporates a moveable weight which when the gun is dropped swings down to block the firing mechanism or automatically uncocks the gun.

### f. Closing safety

Closing safety prevents a gun from being discharged if the gun is not fully closed and locked. This could have fatal consequences for the person holding the gun. Most

breech-opening guns incorporate closing safety as part of the gun's mechanism. If the breech does not close properly, the firing pins are prevented from being able to reach the firing caps of the cartridges in the chamber so that they cannot be fired, however if the gun is closed but not properly locked this could happen. This is prevented in many guns by the firing mechanism being blocked.

### g. Load indicator

Double-barrel combination guns and triple- and quadruple-barrel guns often have one or more load indicators on the action. This enables the shooter to see or feel if one or more barrels are cocked:

for the smooth-bore barrel or barrels and for one or more rifled barrels, depending on the type of gun.

*Diagram of one of the Krieghoff safety systems:*
*1. Trigger block*
*2. Trigger lever block*

*3. Firing mechanism block*
*A. Trigger; B. Trigger lever; C. Firing spring*
*D. Firing mechanism; E. Firing pin*

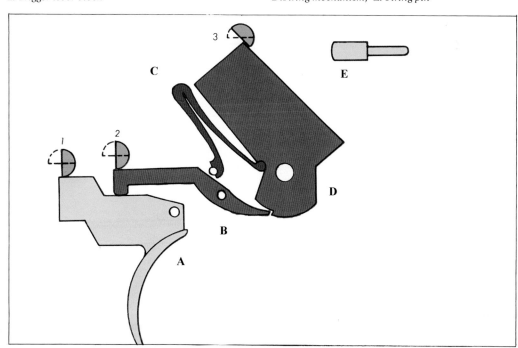

# 4. Locking systems in shotguns

This chapter provides an overview of the different types of locking mechanisms use in shotguns.

*The most common types are:*

- barrel-block locking

- Greener locking

- Kersten locking or double Greener locking

- pin locking

- semi-automatic action: falling block and rotation locking

- pump-action.

Enormous forces are unleashed with the barrel chamber when a shot cartridge is fired. The gas pressure reaches as high as 1,200 kg per cubic metre.

This is not high by comparison with the pressure produced by a bullet cartridge, where pressures can reach 2,000–4000 kg per cubic metre, depending on the calibre of the cartridge. Because the pressures are so much lower, the barrel and chamber walls are thinner than those of a rifle. A shotgun does need to be locked though to ensure that the shot exits the chamber in the only safe direction – the open barrel. The force which propels the shot forward also works in the opposite direction as recoil. The breech, which is required to enable new cartridges to be inserted, needs to be safely closed during the firing process until the pressure has been dissipated through the barrel. This is known as locking.

With semi-automatic guns the locking is provided by a solid steel block known as the slider or bolt. The slider is driven backwards by a part of the gas pressure or the recoil so that the chamber is open. When the slider is driven backwards, a spring is compressed and this return spring presses the slider forward again to close the chamber. The true locking of the slider or bolt occurs when the bolt head rotates to engage with locking lugs. An alternative to a rotating bolt head is a moveable lever on the underside or top of the action which engages a recess when the slider is pressed forward against the chamber. This is known as falling block locking. Breech-opening guns cannot have such a mechanism. With breech-opening guns, the rear part of the breach mechanism (on the stock side) has to ensure for good closing or locking. When the gun has been broken to insert new cartridges, the barrel or barrels are once more re-aligned with the rear of the breech but it is not sufficient for the barrels merely to be aligned with the rear of the breech. The barrels must be locked in position to prevent them flying open when gas pressure is released when a shot is fired. The locking of the barrel or barrels can be done by various means. The most commonly found methods are described.

*Single barrel-block locking of a Rottweil 770 shotgun.*

*Left: Merkel Drilling gun.*

## Barrel-catch locking

Barrel-catch locking is the most generally used locking mechanism for double-barrels shotguns. There are one or two large lugs on the underside of the barrel block which have recesses machined into them on the front edge. These lugs are the barrel blocks which engage with precisely machined recesses in the rear of the breech. By means of the locking lever, a horizontal slider engages the recesses on the barrel block to lock the firearm.

This type of locking can withstand considerable pressure. When a shot is fired, the recoil force mainly travels straight back along an imaginary line in the centre of the barrel. This force is therefore above the locking line because the locking lugs are under the barrel. The recoil therefore has a tendency to pivot the barrel but the strong barrel block lock prevents this. Some gunmakers even use two barrel block locks, one behind the other, known as double barrel-block locking. This type of locking can also be used in combination with other locking mechanisms such as Greener locking or double Greener locking.

*Barrel-catch locking (Browning).*

*Clear example of double barrel-block locking used for Zabala Hermanos shotguns.*

*Greener locking of Ferlach.*

## Greener locking

With Greener locking, the rib on the upper barrel of over-and-under guns or centre of side-by-side guns is extended to form a vertical plate with a hole which fits precisely into a recess in the upper side of the rear of the breech. The locking is performed when a transverse bolt is pushed through the hole in the barrel plate by means of the locking lever.

Greener locking is sometimes combined with single or double barrel-block locking. A wide variation has developed in the form of Greener locking systems.

## Kersten locking

The locking mechanism sometimes referred to as double Greener locking was developed by Kersten of Strasbourg in France. This type of locking is principally used with over-and-under and triple- and quadruple-barrel guns.
Two locking plates are found on either side of the upper barrel which fit precisely in recesses in the rear of the breech. The transverse bolt that locks though the plates is operated by the locking lever. This method is often used in combination with single or double barrel-block locking with triple- and quadruple-barrel guns.

*Combined barrel block lock and Kersten locking.*

*Combined barrel block lock and Kersten locking.*

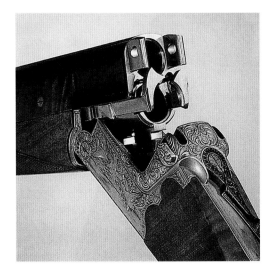

*Pin locking of a side-by-side gun by Verney-Carron.*

The Czech maker CZ uses first-class variations of the Kersten or double Greener locking system. Two half plates with half holes are found on either side of the upper barrel of over-and-under guns.

The advantage of this method is that it is cheaper to make. The locking mechanism is also easily adjustable after many years of reliable use.

There is also no need to machine recesses in the rear of the breech; two grooves in the closing plate suffice.

pins engage with the grooves on the barrel block.

Other fine examples of pin locking are the Sagittaire over-and-under guns by Verney-Carron of France. Both the similarity and the differences with the Beretta system can be seen in the form of the barrel grooves. Verney-Carron have another surprising technical variation in their range of guns. This is a combination of pin locking with a reverse Greener locking. Instead of extended barrel ribs serving as catch plates, Verney-Carron machine a hole in the barrel block, between the barrels. A pin is pushed into this hole from the rear of the breach by means of the locking lever. These Verney-Carron guns also have barrel-block locking so that the barrels are locked from above and below to hold them rigid.

## Pin locking

Good examples of pin locking can be found with Beretta guns. Two grooves are machined in either side of the upper barrel of over-and-under guns. In the corresponding position in the rear part of the breech there are pins which are operated by the locking lever. When the gun is locked, both

## Semi-automatic action

Semi-automatic shotguns are operated by either gas pressure or recoil energy. With a gas-pressure operated gun, some of the gas is vented off the barrel into a cylinder where a piston pushes the slider backwards. The actual locking by the falling block mecha-

*An example of pin locking by Verney-Carron.*

*Diagrams showing the working of a Browning A 500 semi-automatic gun with rotating locking.*

nism can be compared with an old-fashioned WC door catch. When the door is locked, the catch rests in the corresponding recess on the door post. To open the door, the catch has to be lifted to open it. This is the principle applied for this type of locking. When locked, the catch on the slider engages with a recess in the action body or action. When the cartridge is fired, the vented gas pressure drives the piston and piston lever back. This also lifts the catch from the recess and releases the locking so that the slider is free to move back.

Another type of semi-automatic locking is found with shotguns which operate by recoil energy, such as the Browning Auto 5. The forces which propel the shot from the cartridge are also applied in the opposite direction. This recoil is harnessed to operate the mechanism. A semi-automatic shotgun with rotating locking works in a similar manner but with a falling block. Instead the rotating head of the slider or bolt head has lugs which engage with recesses in the action end of the chamber. The repeating mechanism is driven by the recoil. Rotating locking can also be found with gas-pressure repeating mechanisms.

## Pump-action

The locking with pump-action repeating guns is similar in principle to that of semi-automatic shotguns. Here too falling-block or rotating locking is found except the locking mechanism is not operated by either gas pressure or recoil energy, instead it is manually-operated by pulling and pushing the hand-grip on the fore-end backwards and forwards – hence the term "pump" action.

## UNUSUAL LOCKING MECHANISMS

There are two unusual locking mechanisms that may be encountered: Breton and Darne. These are interesting because of the way in which these systems differ from the "usual" locking systems previously described.

## Breton locking

With the Breton double-barrels shotgun of Atamec C. Fourneyron of St. Etienne in France, the locking lever is on the right-hand side of the action body. When this is turned, the entire stock moves back on two stout runners. This opens the chambers so that the gun can be loaded and unloaded. The extractors are also mounted on the runners. The gun is closed by turning the locking lever once more, when two locking lugs engage in recesses in the runners.

## Darne locking

Darne double-barrels shotguns have a sliding rather than hinged breech opening, rather like that of the Breton gun. The locking lever of the Darne gun is located on the top of the action. When the lever is pushed downwards, the upper part of the action slides back slightly on runners to give access to the chambers. When the lever is pushed downwards, the action moves forward to close the chamber and a locking lug engages with a projection between the two barrels.

*Breton locking in the closed position.*

*Darne locking in the closed position.*

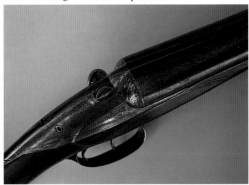

# 5. Safety in the use of shotguns

Previous chapters have dealt with the various parts of a shotgun and the terms used for them. This chapter turns its attention to safety in the use and handling of firearms. There are a number of golden rules for the safe use of firearms.

**1. Treat every firearm as if it is loaded.**
This is the most important rule. If someone hands you a gun to look at and says that the weapon is not loaded, do not take their word for it. Check for yourself. This may save you a great deal of misery in the end.

**2. Never play with a gun.**
A firearm may be a technically and aesthetically pleasing object but it can also be extremely dangerous. A firearm deserves respect and to be handled very carefully. It is certainly not a toy.

**3. Always point the barrel in a safe direction**
and never point it in a direction you do not want to shoot at! Never wave a weapon around.

**4. Keep your finger away from the trigger**
and use the safety catch, even if you are sure the weapon is not loaded. Only move your finger to the trigger on the firing range and only then in the firing position and when the weapon is aiming at the intended target.

**5. Practise loading and unloading**
a new weapon in a safe place until you have perfected the drill.

**6. Never leave a loaded or unloaded gun unattended.**
This is vitally important, especially where there are children. Children love to imitate adults and they could be waving your gun around before you know it.

**7. Keep your weapons and ammunition separate from each other**
and out of reach of your own or anyone else's children. Lock your weapons and ammunition securely away. This will also prevent a burglar from having instant access to a loaded firearm.

**8. Service your weapons regularly.**
Check before you service your gun that it really is not loaded. If you intend using your gun after is has not been used for some time, make sure that the barrel is not blocked, for example, by a wad of cleaning cloth.
If this should prove to be the case, you will need a new weapon after taking the first shot.

**9. Always wear ear protection and shooting or safety glasses.**
A significant proportion of all shooting accidents are caused by technical defects in the guns or ammunition of the person injured or in the guns and ammunition of people shooting nearby.
Make sure your eyes are protected from powder debris, escaping gas pressure, or ejected cartridge cases.

**10. Do not leap or jump during a shoot.**
If it is necessary to cross an obstacle or ditch while shooting do not rely upon the safety

catch. Always unload your gun and carry it "broken." Not only is the safest conduct, it gives your companions confidence in you.

## 11. NEVER combine shooting with alcohol

or, even worse, with drugs in whatever form, or strong medicines (check the instructions for the medicine's use first). Alcohol or drugs will disturb your perception, judgement, and behaviour. Drink your beer or dram after shooting and after you have unloaded and stored your guns safely. And of course, at the end of a shooting session if you have to drive yourself home, don't drink and drive!

## 12. Point out any unsafe behaviour to fellow shooters.

Beginners never learn unless someone tells them what to do or what not to do. Try to explain the proper use of guns in a polite way.

*Proefbanktekens op een Browning dubbelloops hagelgeweer*

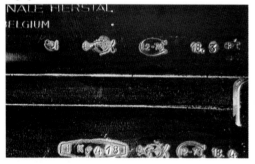

Even experienced shooters make mistakes. Avoid the company of "know-it-alls" who think they know better than anyone else. They are a source of potential danger.

## *Proof marks*

All small arms sold in the United Kingdom have first to be proved and then marked with a proof mark. Until 1980, there was a reciprocal recognition between the British Proof Houses of London and Birmingham and certain foreign proof houses. Britain became a member of the International Proof Commission (Commission Internationale Permanente or CIP) based in Liège in Belgium. All member countries recognise each others marks. The current member countries are Austria, Belgium, Chile, the Czech Republic, Finland, France, Germany, Hungary, Italy, Spain, and the United Kingdom. Britain also has reciprocal arrangements with Eire which is not a member. Guns also should be reproved after alterations to the action or barrel, and require reproving for steel shot before its use if the gun is not already proof marked for this more demanding shot.

1. Provisional proof
On action
2. Definitive proof for nitro powders

On barrel
3. Definitive proof for black powder only with the words NOT NITRO
– Ammunition inspection

In addition to these marks, there may also be special definitive proof marks and reproofing marks. A gun will also bear markings to indicate the maximum mean pressure of cartridges for which the gun has been proved together with the nominal gauge in a diamond with figure (e.g. 12), chamber length, or nominal calibre and case length. Shotguns also bear marks to indicate the nominal bore diameter 9in (23cm) from the breech, expressed in millimetres, e.g. 18.5.

# 6. Maintenance of shotguns

It almost goes without saying that good maintenance of a gun extends its life. It is not a difficult matter either and all that is required is oil, wadding, some brushes, and a cleaning rod. Dirt and moisture are not only potential sources of faults, they can also cause rust.

*Browning gun cleaning kit.*

The different maintenance requirements of the parts of a gun are dealt with under each of the main parts.

## 1. The stock

It is best to carefully wipe the stock of a gun dry after use. Varnished stocks may need any damage promptly dealt with to prevent water and dirt from entering the wood. Stocks that are coated with oil need to be re-coated from time to time with the correct oil, using a soft cloth. The oil should not be

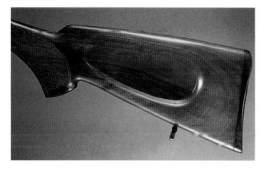

*Regular care is needed to keep a stock in good condition.*

applied to any chequered part of the stock because if the grooves become filled with oil it will not be possible to hold the gun so firmly. If necessary, the chequered part of the stock can be lightly brushed with a little furniture wax on a toothbrush.

## 2. The action, or action body

The action or mechanism of a gun is located at the breech of guns that open, or within the action body of semi-automatic guns. It is important to clean this part of the gun thoroughly after shooting to remove any moisture, dirt, and above all powder residue. An old toothbrush is an ideal tool and can be used if required with a little diesel oil. After scrubbing, the action should be carefully dried and then smeared with a little oil. The moving parts such as the breech pivot, cocking levers, locking lever, and locks should be given a few drops of oil. This servicing needs to be more thorough at the end of the season or if the gun has not been used for a time. In this case, the mechanism within the casing also needs to be given some attention. The firing mechanism needs to be cleaned and lightly lubricated, with particular care given to the firing pins, firing pin springs, and safety mechanisms. Residues of dirt can cause faults and lead to corrosion. If the dismantling of your gun frightens you, take it to a gun dealer.

## 3. The barrel or barrels

First of all, the inside of the barrels must be thoroughly cleaned.
This is best done using a cleaning rod. Sets of brushes can be bought to use with cleaning rods, consisting of a copper brush to remove the first layer of dirt and residue and a nylon brush to remove loosened dirt. Once this is done, the barrel needs to be pulled through a number of times with pieces of wadding, until the wadding comes out clean. Finally, a felt brush is used to lightly oil the barrels.

One thing that must not be forgotten is to clean the rib between the barrels. Barrels get rather hot during shooting and this can lead to vibrations. A ventilated rib provides a vibration-free sighting line but these are places for dirt to get trapped.

The rib should therefore be cleaned well. This is best done with an old toothbrush and some gun oil or diesel oil. Once cleaned, wipe carefully and dry before lightly smearing with oil on a cloth. Interchangeable chokes should be unscrewed from the muzzle and thoroughly cleaned after a shooting session.

Considerable residue can accumulate around chokes and if left they will become stuck fast. Failure to perform this maintenance task is likely to lead to corrosion.

Once the chokes have been cleaned they can be threaded back into the barrel but do not lubricate the thread because such a film of oil can be heated during shooting and become a hard residue.

Guns should be properly stored after use and that means in a safe place but also unloaded and uncocked. Not only is this the safest policy, it prevents springs from being compressed too long so that they can lose their tension.

However, I have an absolute hatred of guns being fired "dry" because this can cause damage to the firing pin. It is therefore best to use "buffer" cartridges with a sprung pin instead of the normal percussion cap. These are not expensive and are certainly cheaper than the price of new firing pins. The best of these dummy cartridges are made of aluminium rather than plastic which tend to crumble due to the effect of gun oil.

*It is best to remove chokes and clean them after each shooting session.*

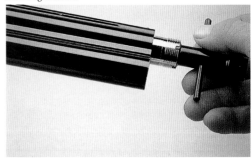

# 7. Shotgun cartridges

*This chapter deals in turn with:*

– how a cartridge works

– the components of a cartridge

– cartridge gauges

– chamber length

– shot velocity

– delay to target

– shot pellets

– slugs

– overview of shotgun cartridges.

## How a shotgun cartridge works

The sequence of events when a shotgun cartridge is fired are as follows: the firing pin strikes the percussion cap fixed in the centre of the cartridge head; this is filled with a small quantity of detonating compound which burns almost instantaneously when struck lightly. In milliseconds the ignition of the compound causes a brief but fierce flame which passes through the opening in the cap to ignite the powder in the base of the cartridge. In a fraction of a second the powder burns fiercely, creating high gas pressure. The pressure of the gas is restricted because the cartridge is closely surrounded on almost all sides: at the rear against the action or receiver, and at the side by the chamber of the barrel.

The cartridge head (or base) is usually made of brass, which is a soft and pliable material. Because the cartridge case is pressed against the chamber by the gas pressure, this makes a gas-tight seal, ensuring that the gas pressure is wholly available for propelling the projectiles or shot through the barrel. The only outlet for the gas is forwards but the load of pellets is in the way. There is also a closure or crimped end to seal the cartridge. The pressure forces the shot out of the cartridge. Between the powder and the shot there is a wad, made of felt or plastic, which

pushes the shot ahead of it. Plastic wads are more or less like little baskets containing the shot.

## Components of a shotgun cartridge

Shotgun cartridges are made from a number of components, such as:
1. the head (or base)
2. the percussion cap
3. the case or shell
4. the powder charge
5. the wad
6. the shot
7. the closure

*Cross-section of a shotgun cartridge with felt wad (Rottweil Weidsmannsheil). From left to right: closure or crimping, shot, felt wad, powder charge, head (or base) with percussion cap.*

1. *The head (or base):*
with shotgun cartridges this is usually made of brass, which is pressed onto the end of the shell or case. The heat of the ignition deforms the brass sufficiently to hermetically seal the chamber so that all the gas pressure is available to propel the shot out of the cartridge.

*Cross-section of a shotgun cartridge with plastic air wad which also acts as a shock absorber (Rottweil Weidsmannsheil).*

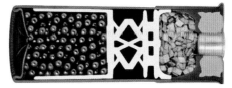

2. *The percussion cap:*
the percussion cap is held fast in the centre of the brass head (or base). Inside the brass cap is a detonating chemical compound which burns when hit by the firing pin. The

compound produces a fierce flame which is required to ignite the powder charge of the cartridge. The ignition time of the compound is of the order of 0.0001–0.0002 seconds. The percussive compound was discovered in the nineteenth century when it originally consisted of a mixture of fulminate of mercury, antimony sulphide, and potassium chlorate to which trinitrotoluene (TNT) was subsequently added. Unfortunately this resulted in potassium chloride being formed which had serious results for the barrels of guns. Modern non-rusting percussive compound consists of TNT, lead oxide, barium nitrate, calcium silicide, and antimony sulphide.

### 3. *The case or shell*
of a shotgun cartridge has the same function as that of a rifle cartridge: to hold all the components together. The case may be made of cardboard, plastic, or aluminium, although the last of these is fairly uncommon. Immediately inside the brass head (or base) is a base wad and the bottom of the case is often strengthened with a liner of cardboard, or plastic. Liners were once of iron.

### 4. *The powder charge*:
shotguns use a powder charge that burns very rapidly in order to create high volume and pressure of gas. This causes rapid acceleration of the shot pellets. The pressure produced rises very quickly, depending on the gauge and type of powder charge. With a shotgun cartridge, the maximum pressure is achieved when the shot is about 130mm (5$^1/_8$in) along the barrel and has halved by the time the shot has travelled 150–170mm (5$^7/_8$–6$^7/_8$in). By the time the shot has travelled 400mm (15$^3/_4$in) the entire powder charge has burned and been converted into gas pressure. This rapid ignition is essential to overcome the resistance the wad and shot encounter in the smooth barrel.

### 5. *The wad*
is located between the powder charge and the shot pellets. Wads were once almost exclusively made of felt but modern shotgun cartridges often have a plastic wad, often combined with a tub containing the shot. In more expensive cartridges the base of these plastic wads may have a shock absorber incorporated, which momentarily absorbs the impact. The advantage of this is that it reduces the deformation of shot against the barrel wall. Deformed shot has a more irregular trajectory on leaving the barrel than shot which is not deformed. With modern steel shot, the plastic container holding the shot also protects the barrel. The wad must make a good seal so that all the gas pressure is used to propel the shot. The wad also protects the shot from the hot gases to prevent any risk of the lead partially melting and welding together. The wad also prevents lead deposits on the barrel. When the shot exits the barrel, the column of shot continues on its trajectory but the wadding quickly falls to the ground. Plastic wads were dominant until recently but the present day trend among shooters is for a return to cardboard cases with felt and/or cardboard wads to protect the environment from waste plastic.

### 6. *The shot load*:
these were mainly made of lead until the late 1980's but since then there has been a debate about the harmful effects of lead on the natural environment. This led to legislation in many countries, banning lead shot. This had already occurred in North Amer-

*Cross-section of a Rottweil spreading-shot cartridge. The plastic cross among the pellets helps to spread the shot more widely.*

ica. Lead is still permitted, for clay pigeon and target shooting, with certain provisions regarding the shooting range. Lead shot is made of lead with antimony added to harden the shot. Molten lead is dropped in a tower from a height of about 100ft (30m) through mesh which determines the size of the shot. As the lead falls, it forms into balls and cools. The shot then plunges into water at the bottom of the tower. The pellets are sorted, polished, and coated to prevent corrosion. Centrifuges are also used to produce shot; lead is forced through mesh by centrifugal force before dropping into water. Steel shot is mainly produced by the centrifugal method. In countries which ban lead shot, it has been replaced by steel, zinc, bismuth, or tin. Zinc and bismuth are relatively expensive so many shooters have switched to steel. This has its consequences though.

The first is weight: the specific gravity of lead is 11.34 and of iron 7.2–7.8. The specific gravity of zinc is 7.2, while that of bismuth is closer to lead at 9.8. A cartridge with a 1oz (28g) load of size 6 shot 2.75mm (.0108in) has 220 lead pellets. The same weight of iron or zinc shot consists of 300 pellets or 250 bismuth pellets. One advantage of steel shot is that it is harder and is virtually free from deformities so that there are therefore fewer stray pellets to ensure better coverage. The matter of "coverage" is dealt with later in this chapter.

7. *The closure*:
the open end of a shotgun cartridge is crimped or rolled inwards. There are two types of closure used for shotgun cartridges: with one a closing plate is placed above the shot and the case is crimped over to seal it in; with the other, no closure is used, instead the case is crimped over itself to form the closure.

## Gauge designation

The size of the bore of shotguns are derived from the number of pellets of pure lead to a pound (1lb/453.59g) that will precisely fit the bore. For 12 gauge this is 12 pellets and the actual bore is .729in (18.52mm). For 16 gauge there would be 16 pellets or .662in (16.81mm) and 20 pellets for 20 gauge with

*Cross-section of a Rottweill Express cartridge with large pellets. The case is closed with a closing plate and crimped over.*

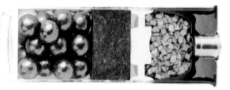

*Winchester cartridge with "star" closure.*

an actual bore of .615 (15.62mm). The most widely used gauges are 12, 16, and 20. Other less common gauges include 24, 28, and 32, with bores of .579in (14.70mm), .550in

(13.97mm), .526in (13.56mm). A gauge that has largely fallen into disuse is .410in (10.4mm) which was a popular gauge for youth. A gauge that is widely used for shooting goose and hunting wild turkey in North America is gauge 10 which is .775in (19.7mm). This gauge is banned for hunting use in a number of European countries.

## Chamber length

The length of a shotgun chamber is indicated in inches or millimetres. The current standard length for 12 gauge is 2³⁄₄in (70mm). American shotguns and particularly semi-automatic and pump-action guns often have a longer chamber of 3in (76mm) which is also known as 12 gauge Magnum. The length is important when buying cartridges because it is dangerous to place too long a cartridge in a chamber because this can lead to gas pressures that are too high. There is a conical reduction between the chamber and barrel which centres the wad and shot. If a 3in (76mm) cartridge is fired from a 2³⁄₄in (70mm) chamber, the closure on the cartridge has insufficient space to open and the propulsion of the shot is impeded. At this point, the gas pressure is at its highest and if obstructed can become far too high. The shooting of shorter cartridges from a longer chamber is not dangerous. The popular American gauge 10 has a 3¹⁄₂in (89mm) Magnum chamber size. Other cartridge lengths are 65mm (approx. 2¹⁄₂in) and 2⁵⁄₈in (67.5mm).

## Shot velocity

The velocity of a column of shot is often underestimated. The velocity is expressed in metres per second. With rifle bullets the velocity is expressed in terms of muzzle velocity and velocity at 25m (82ft), 50m (164ft), 100m (328ft) or more. This is indicated with V for velocity followed by the range so that muzzle velocity is V0 and V50 is the velocity at 50m from the muzzle and so on. With shotguns the velocity is give as V12.5 because the column of shot has its best form at 12.5m (41ft). Not all the pellets have the same velocity due to deformation, the fanning out effect, and the density of the column of shot. These factors can also be influenced by the choke. A column of lead shot at 30m (100ft) from the muzzle has a front to back spread of about 3–5m (9.8–16.4ft). With steel shot this is more compact – 1.5–2.5m (4.92–8.2ft). There are different cartridges for different types of

| Type | shot weight g | shot size mm | Gas pressure bar | V12.5 m/s |
|---|---|---|---|---|
| Kettner Skeet 24 | 24 | 2.0 | 580 | 330 |
| Kettner Skeet 28 | 28 | 2.0 | 600 | 370 |
| Kettner Skeet 32 | 32 | 2.0 | 620 | 360 |
| Kettner Field 32 | 32 | 2.0–4.0 | 620 | 360–380 |
| Kettner Nickel 32 | 32 | 2.3–3.2 | 560 | 330 |
| Kettner Nickel 36 | 36 | 2.5–3.2 | 600 | 310 |
| Rottweil Field | 36 | 2.5–3.5 | 600 | 370–385 |
| Rottweil Sport | 28 | 2.0 | 600 | 380 |
| Rottweil Steel | 30 | 3.0–3.7 | 740 | 320 |
| Fiocchi Field 28 | 28 | 2.7 | 600 | 270 |
| Fiocchi Trap 24 | 24 | 2.41 | 600 | 330 |
| Fiocchi Skeet 28 | 2.8 | 2.0 | 620 | 370 |

V12.5 = velocity measured at 12.5m from the muzzle

game and shooting sports. For clarification, a number of different types and makes are shown below in 12 gauge.

Because of the lower specific gravity (or mass) of steel and zinc, the velocity falls off more quickly than with lead shot. Rottweil has calculated velocity for lead and steel. The findings were that lead shot of 2.7mm (.010in) diameter and a weight of 0.116g

| | Shot diameter mm | Distance Velocity V0 | V12.5 | V25 | V35 | V50 |
|---|---|---|---|---|---|---|
| lead | 2.7 | 400 | 310 | 245 | 200 | 175 |
| steel | 3.2 | 400 | 290 | 225 | 175 | 150 |

V12.5 = shot velocity at 12.5m from the muzzle
V25 = shot velocity at 25m
V35 = shot velocity at 35m
V50 = shot velocity at 50m

(.0040oz) has more or less the same velocity as a steel pellet of 3.2mm (.0126in) and a weight of 0.134g (.0047oz).

**DELAY TO TARGET**

The shot velocity is an important consideration when shooting at a moving target, such as a clay pigeon or wild game. Although the velocity depends on the size and type of shot, and the powder charge, shot velocity can generally be reckoned as follows:

– shot reaches 10m (33ft) in 0.029 seconds after firing
– shot reaches 20m (65ft) in 0.063 seconds after firing
– shot reaches 30m (98ft) in 0.1 seconds after firing
– shot reaches 40m (131ft) in 0.143 seconds after firing
– shot reaches 50m (164ft) in 0.2 seconds after firing.

The speed of the game or clay pigeon also needs to be considered. These are generally considered as follows:

| | mph | (km/hour) | fps | (m/s) |
|---|---|---|---|---|
| small clay pigeon | 75 | (120) | 107 | (33) |
| fleeing wild game bird | 56 | (90) | 81 | (25) |
| medium-sized clay pigeon | 55 | (88) | 78 | (24) |
| fast flying wild game bird | 44 | (70) | 62 | (19) |
| fleeing deer | 31 | (50) | 46 | (14) |
| fleeing hare | 22 | (35) | 32 | (10) |
| deer trotting | 9 | (15) | 13 | (4) |

mph = miles per hour (km/hour) = kilometres per hour
fps = feet per second (m/s) = metres per second

The shooter needs to master the art of swinging with and in front of the target to avoid the shot sailing past behind the target. This lead or aiming off to allow for delay to target is essential to hit fast moving targets.

## Shot pellets

The choice of the correct shotgun cartridge depends on a number of factors, including:

– the gauge of the gun
– the chokes of the barrels and desired shot pattern
– the spread and coverage of the shot
– the type of game being shot or type of sport shooting
– the range (distance)
– the sensitivity of the shooter to recoil.

The designations of shotgun pellets needs some explanation. The size of shot is sometimes given in millimetres but can also be a number.

The diameter of the shot plays a role in relation to the type of game being shot. The range at which the game is likely to be shot is also a consideration. Cartridge manufacturers take these factors into consideration. The average range for shooting rabbits is about 65ft (20m). For hares and pheasants this is 81–97ft (25–30m) and for waterfowl this is about 113ft (35m). This factor is important for the coverage of the shot.

This coverage is measured with test targets at 15m (48.75ft).

The number of pellets that hit the target is important. The even distribution of the pellets over the target is also important.

The density of shot in the centre of the column is compared with the hits on the edge of the target. The hits in the main area of the target are counted and the percentage on target is calculated. Chokes of course play a major role in the spread of shot. The most appropriate shot diameter for different game is indicated.

Here it is essential to allow for the difference between lead and steel shot. This difference has already been dealt with. To generalize, steel shot needs to be twice the size of lead shot. If size 5 lead shot (3mm) was used then size 3 (3.5mm) will be required in steel.

**LEAD SHOT CARTRIDGE DATA**

| Shot number | Diameter in mm | weight in grams | Recommended for |
|---|---|---|---|
| 9 | 2.0 | 0.05 | clay pigeon |
| 7¹/₂ | 2.4 | 0.08 | clay pigeon, snipe, partridge, pigeon |
| 7 | 2.5 | 0.09 | partridge, pigeon, rabbit |
| 6 | 2.7 | 0.12 | pigeon, rabbit, pheasant, duck, hare |
| 5 | 3.0 | 0.16 | duck, goose, hare |
| 4 | 3.3 | 0.20 | goose, hare, fox |
| 3 | 3.5 | 0.25 | goose, fox |
| 2 | 3.8 | 0.30 | goose, fox |
| 1 | 4.0 | 0.37 | goose, fox |

Shotgun cartridges can be purchased in a variety of gauges, lengths, and sizes. It has not been possible to include every type of cartridge in this book.

The assortment is so enormous that a selection has been made of different makers and types.

*These are sub-divided as follows:*

- Overview of shotgun cartridges for game shooting:

  • bismuth
  • lead
  • Molyshot
  • steel
  • tin
  • zinc.

- Overview of shotgun cartridges for sporting use.

- Unusual cartridges.

# Overview of cartridges for game shooting

There is an enormous range of shotgun cartridges. Quite apart from the various types for shooting in the field at game and for sport shooting at targets, there are also different types and versions. An overview follows but with the following remark: the United Kingdom government is seeking to prevent the use of lead shot over wetlands and may introduce legislation. Elsewhere in Europe various levels of bans from total to partial exist on the use of lead shot. National organizations for field sports will be able to advise the position for a given country.

### Bismuth cartridges for shooting game

Bismuth is a metal that is a by-product of refining copper, gold, lead, tin, and silver. This metal has a high specific gravity which can be seen from the table below, in which it is compared with iron, steel, zinc, and lead.

| Type of metal | Specific gravity |
|---|---|
| lead | 11.34 |
| bismuth | 9.8 |
| steel | 7.8 |
| tin | 7.3 |
| iron | 7.2–7.8 |
| zinc | 7.2 |
| Molyshot | 10.2 |

| Gauge | Cartridge | | | Shot | | |
|---|---|---|---|---|---|---|
| | length | | weight | diameter | Velocity V1 | |
| | in | mm | gram | in mm | fps | m/s |
| 10 | 3½ | 89 | 53 | 3.3–3.8 | 1,218 | 375 |
| 12 | 2½ | 63.5 | 28 | 2.5–3.3 | 1,235 | 380 |
| 12 | 2¾ | 70 | 32 | 2.5–2.7 | 1,244 | 383 |
| 12 | 2¾ | 70 | 35 | 2.7–3.3 | 1,209 | 372 |
| 12 | 2¾ | 70 | 35 | 2.7, 3.0, 3.3 | 1,316 | 405 |
| 12 | 2¾ | 70 | 39 | 2.7, 3.0, 3.3, 3.8 | 1,267 | 390 |
| 12 | 3 | 76 | 46 | 2.7, 3.0, 3.3, 3.8 | 1,235 | 380 |
| 12 | 3½ | 89 | 53 | 3.3–3.8 | 1,218 | 375 |
| 16 | 2¾ | 70 | 32 | 3.0–3.3 | 1,186 | 365 |
| 20 | 2¾ | 70 | 28 | 2.7–3.3 | 1,186 | 365 |
| 20 | 3 | 76 | 30 | 2.7, 3.0, 3.3, 3.8 | 1,235 | 380 |
| 28 | 2¾ | 70 | 18 | 2.5, 2.7, 3.3 | 1,235 | 380 |
| .410 | 2½ | 63.5 | 12 | 2.5 | 1,235 | 380 |
| .410 | 3 | 76 | 16 | 2.5, 2.7, 3.3 | 1,235 | 380 |

V1 = shot velocity at 1m (39³/₈in) from the muzzle in fps (feet per second) and m/s (metres per second)

Bismuth shot is made from an alloy of 97 percent bismuth and 3 percent tin. Bismuth is the only heavy metal that is non toxic, whereas lead is toxic. A further advantage of bismuth is that it is relatively soft. On the Brinell scale of hardness, bismuth is a mere 18 compared with 12 for lead and steel varying between 290 and 310. The use of bismuth does not increase wear of the barrels and chokes. Tests have shown that bismuth shot has fewer wayward shots than lead. The coverage of shot is measured by firing at test targets. In American tests various cartridges and different types of shot were fired at a 30in (76cm) diameter target at ranges of 40 and 60 yards (36.5 and 55m). The shot used was of the same diameter and the tests showed that bismuth performed as well as or slightly better than steel.

## Bismuth Cartridge Company

This company is a subsidiary of Winchester and makes cartridges in the following gauges, with a plastic wad.

*Bismuth cartridges from the Bismuth Cartridge Company.*

## Eley Alphamax

Alphamax cartridges have a red plastic case and an environmentally-friendly felt wad. Cartridges are available in the following gauge and shot sizes:

| Gauge | Cartridge | | | Shot |
|---|---|---|---|---|
| | length | | weight | diameter |
| | in | mm | gram | in mm |
| 12 | 2¾ | 70 | 36 | 2.4, 2.6, 2.8, 3.1 |

*Eley Alphamax bismuth shotgun cartridge.*

## Eley Crown Squire

This cartridge has a red plastic case with a felt wad. Cartridges are available in the following gauge and shot sizes

| Gauge | Cartridge | | | Shot |
|---|---|---|---|---|
| | length | | weight | diameter |
| | in | mm | gram | in mm |
| 12 | 2⅝ | 67.5 | 28 | 2.0, 2.6, 2.8, 3.1 |

*Eley Crown Squire bismuth shotgun cartridge.*

*Eley Grand Prix HV bismuth cartridge.*

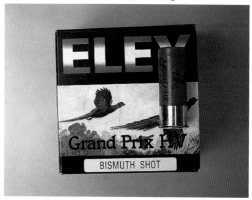

## Eley Field Special

The Field Special has a yellow plastic case with a felt wad. Cartridges are available in the following gauge and shot sizes

| Gauge | Cartridge | | Shot |
|---|---|---|---|
| | length | | weight | diameter |
| | in | mm | gram | in mm |
| 20 | 2¾ | 70 | 28,5 | 2.4, 2.6, 2.8, 3.1 |

*Eley Field Special bismuth cartridge.*

## Eley Grand Prix HV

The Grand Prix HV (High Velocity) has a velocity of approx. 1,300 ft per second (400 m per second) in 12 gauge. The case is of yellow plastic and the cartridge has a felt wad. Cartridges are available in the following gauge and shot sizes

| Gauge | Cartridge | | Shot |
|---|---|---|---|
| | length | | weight | diameter |
| | in | mm | gram | in mm |
| 12 | 2⅝ | 67,5 | 32 | 2.0, 2.6, 2.8, 3.1 |

# Lead shot cartridges for shooting game

## Rottweil Jagd (Hunter) brown cardboard

This cartridge is specially developed for shotguns with ¼ and ¾ choke combinations. The cardboard case and greased felt wad are quickly biodegradable. Cartridges are available in the following gauges and shot sizes

| Gauge | Cartridge | | weight | Shot diameter |
|---|---|---|---|---|
| | length | | | |
| | in | mm | gram | in mm |
| 12 | 23/4in | 70 | 36 | 2.5, 2.7, 3.0, 3.5 |
| 16 | 23/4in | 70 | 31 | 2.5, 2.7, 3.0, 3.5 |
| 12* | 23/4in | 70 | 34 | 2.75 |
| 16* | 23/4in | 70 | 34 | 2.75 |

*Rottweil Jagd brown cardboard cased cartridge.*

## Rottweil Magnum, black plastic case

A true 3in (76mm) magnum cartridge with a heavy 52 gram shot load. This cartridge is mainly intended for wildfowling. Guns need to be able to withstand the higher gas pressures of approx. 900 bar. The shot is loaded in a plastic wad which also serves as a shock absorber. Cartridges are available in the following gauges and shot sizes.

| Gauge | Cartridge | | weight | Shot |
|---|---|---|---|---|
| | length | | | diameter |
| | in | mm | gram | in mm |
| 12 | 3in | 76 | 52 | 2.7, 3.0, 3.2 3.7 |
| 20 | 3in | 76 | 52 | 2.7, 3.0, 3.2 3.7 |

*Rottweil Magnum cartridge with 52g shot load.*

### Rottweil Semi-Magnum, black plastic case

This cartridge has an extra heavy shot load but is suitable for all types of shotgun. The shot is loaded in a plastic wad. The maximum gas pressure is 650 bar. Cartridges are available in the following gauge and shot sizes.

| Gauge | Cartridge | | weight | Shot |
|---|---|---|---|---|
| | length | | | diameter |
| | in | mm | gram | in mm |
| 12 | 2³/₄in | 70 | 540 | 2.7, 3.0, 3.2 3.7 4,0 |

*Rottweil Semi-Magnum cartridge with 40g shot load.*

### Rottweil Tiger, red plastic case

This cartridge is not intended for tiger hunting. It is an all-round cartridge particularly intended for the traditional shotgun. The cartridge has a plastic wad and is available in the following gauges and shot sizes.

| Gauge | Cartridge | | weight | Shot |
|---|---|---|---|---|
| | length | | | diameter |
| | in | mm | gram | in mm |
| 12 | 2⁵/₈in | 67.5 | 32 | 2.5, 2.7, 3.0 3.3 3.5 |
| 16 | 2⁵/₈ | 67.5 | 27 | 2.5, 2.7, 3.0 3.3 3.5 |
| 20 | 2⁵/₈ | 67.5 | 25.5 | 2.5, 2.7, 3.0 |

*Rottweil Tiger cartridge.*

### Rottweil Weidmannsheil with black cardboard case

This cartridge has a high brass base. The shot is separated from the powder charge by a greased felt wad. The card case is waterproofed with paraffin wax but is easily biodegradable and therefore environmentally-friendly. The greased wad also helps to clean the barrel. Cartridges are available in the following gauges and shot sizes

| Gauge | Cartridge | | weight | Shot |
|---|---|---|---|---|
| | length | | | diameter |
| | in | mm | gram | in mm |
| 12 | 2³/₄in | 70 | 36 | 2.5 2.7 3.0 3.2 3.5 4.0 |
| 16 | 2³/₄in | 70 | 31 | 2.5, 3.0, 3.5 4.0 |

*Rottweil Weidmannsheil cartridge with black cardboard case.*

### Rottweil Weidmannsheil with black plastic case

This cartridge is primarily intended for use during months when the air is moist and for wildfowling. The shot is contained in a plastic wad and cartridges are available in the following gauges and shot sizes

| Gauge | Cartridge | | weight | Shot |
|---|---|---|---|---|
| | length | | | diameter |
| | in | mm | gram | in mm |
| 12 | 2³/₄in | 70 | 36 | 2.5, 2.7, 3.0 3.2 3.5 3.7 4.0 4.2 |
| 16 | 2³/₄in | 70 | 31 | 2.5, 2.7, 3.0 3.2 3.5 |
| 20 | 2³/₄in | 70 | 27 | 2.5, 2.7, 3.0 |

*Rottweil Weidmannsheil cartridge with black plastic case.*

## Molyshot of Kent Cartridge Company

Molyshot is not derived from the metal molybdenum used to create steel alloys. Molyshot is a new type of shot that is much softer than molybdenum and has a high specific gravity of 10.2, which is reasonably similar to that of lead which is 11.4. The penetration force of Molyshot is therefore greater than that of bismuth, steel, or zinc. The shot retaining wad is biodegradable and therefore termed "Biowad". Molyshot is not toxic. A big advantage of Molyshot is that chokes do not have to be changed.

## Molyshot Hunter Eco

This cartridge has a black plastic case and a Biowad wad. Hunter Eco cartridges are available in the following gauge and shot sizes:

| Gauge | Cartridge length | | Shot weight | diameter |
|---|---|---|---|---|
| | in | mm | gram | in mm |
| 12 | 2³/₄in | 70 | 32 | 3.0-3.3 |

*The Hunter Eco Molyshot cartridge with Biowad.*

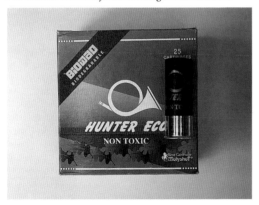

## Molyshot Hunter Ecomag

A fine cartridge with a yellow plastic case and Biowad. Cartridges are available in the following gauges and shot sizes:

| Gauge | Cartridge length | | Shot weight | diameter |
|---|---|---|---|---|
| | in | mm | gram | in mm |
| 12 | 2³/₄in | 70 | 36 | 3.0-3.3 |
| 16 | 2³/₄in | 70 | 28 | 3.0-3.3 |

*The Hunter Ecomag Molyshot cartridge with Biowad.*

# Steel shot cartridges for game shooting

Steel was the first replacement for lead shot. The shot was developed in the 1970's in the USA where the first measures were taken to restrict the use of lead shot for game shooting. This was first a restriction on lead for wildfowling and in most states this followed for other game. Because of its lower specific gravity, steel shot needs to be a different shot size to achieve the same penetration. The guiding rule is to use shot three sizes larger: e.g. steel shot 3 (3.5mm) or 4 (3.3mm) to replace lead shot 6 (2.7mm). Shooters who switch over to use of steel shot are advised to first have their gun checked by a gunsmith and then proved for steel if it does not already bear a steel shot proof mark. The chokes have to be altered for many shotguns. Older guns which cannot withstand higher gas pressures are also less suitable for use with steel shot, although some cartridge manufacturers play down this aspect. Apart from the problems that steel shot can cause for the gun itself, there are other disadvantages.
Game containing steel shot can cause problems when cooked in a microwave oven and it also needs to be eaten with greater caution. Steel is far more likely to damage your teeth than other shot.

## Gamebore Pure Gold

The Gamebore Cartridge Company of Hull, England, makes steel shot cartridges for both field and sport shooting. Most types of cartridge are available with either plastic or

*Gamebore Pure Gold steel shot cartridge.*

## Gamebore Traditional Game

This cartridge has a yellow plastic case and plastic wad. The 20 gauge Traditional has a very light shot load for "lady's guns" Cartridges are available in the following gauges and shot sizes:

| Gauge | Cartridge | | | Shot |
|---|---|---|---|---|
| | length in | mm | weight gram | diameter in mm |
| 12 | 2⁵/₈in | 67.5 | 32 | 2.4, 2.6, 2.8 |
| 20 | 2³/₄in | 70 | 21 | 2.6, 2.8, 3.0, 3.3 |

*Gamebore Traditional Game steel shot cartridge.*

felt wads. Pure Gold cartridges have a red plastic case and are available in the following gauges and shot sizes:

| Gauge | Cartridge | | | Shot |
|---|---|---|---|---|
| | length in | mm | weight gram | diameter in mm |
| 12 | 2⁵/₈in | 67.5 | 28 | 2.6 |
| 16 | 2⁵/₈in | 67.5 | 26 | 2.6, 2.8, 3.0, 3.3 |
| 20 | 2³/₄in | 70 | 28 | 2.6, 2.8, 3.0, 3.3 |

## Gamebore Super Steel

De Super Steel heeft een groene kunststof huls met een kunststof schotelprop en is geschikt voor vederwild en voor kleiduiven. De patroon is verkrijgbaar in de volgende kalibers en hagelmaten:

| Gauge | Cartridge | | | Shot |
|---|---|---|---|---|
| | length in | mm | weight gram | diameter in mm |
| 12 | 2⁵/₈in | 67.5 | 24 | 2.0-2.4 |
| 12 | 2⁵/₈in | 67.5 | 28 | 2.0-2.4 |

## Rottweil Steel-X-range with red plastic case

Rottweill developed these steel cartridges for countries where lead shot is forbidden or restricted.
To provide a similar result to lead, the shot sizes are slightly larger. To protect the barrel, the shot is housed in a plastic wad. Car-

*Gamebore Super Steel cartridge.*

*Rottweil Steel-X-Range hagelpatroon*

tridges are available in the following gauge and shot sizes

| Gauge | Cartridge | | weight | Shot diameter |
|---|---|---|---|---|
| | length in | mm | gram | in mm |
| 12 | 2³/₄in | 70 | 28 3.5, 3.8 |

| Gauge | Cartridge | | Shot |
|---|---|---|---|
| | length in | mm | weight gram | diameter in mm |
| 12 | 3in | 76 | 39 | 2.8, 3.3, 3.5, 3.8, 4.0, 4.5 |
| 20 | 3in | 76 | 28 | 2.8,-3.3 |

### Rottweil Weidmannsheil Steel, green cardboard

This is an exceptionally environmentally-friendly cartridge. The cardboard case and felt prop are biodegradable. The maximum gas pressure is 740 bar and the shot has a velocity at 2.5m (8ft) of 400m per second (1,300 ft per second). Cartridges are currently only available in 12/70 (12/3in).

| Gauge | Cartridge | | Shot |
|---|---|---|---|
| | length in | mm | weight gram | diameter in mm |
| 12 | 2³/₄in | 70 | 30 | 3.2, 3.5, 3.7 |

*Rottweil Weidmannsheil steel-shot cartridge.*

### Winchester Super-X

Winchester make a special steel shot Magnum cartridge for game shooting with a red plastic 3in (76mm) case with a heavy shot load. Cartridges are available in the following gauges and shot sizes:

*Winchester Super-X steel-shot cartridge.*

# Tin

Tin is a silver-coloured soft metal which makes it easy to shape. It has a low specific gravity of 7.3 and therefore is considered a medium-heavy metal. An advantage of tin is that it can be shot without the need for any modification to a gun. Tin is not toxic: a great deal of food is packed in tin, such as fruit and fish. The metal is also widely used in the creation of alloys.

### Gamebore Tin Shot

The English makers Gamebore developed tin shot cartridges in their quest for a first-class replacement for lead shot. By increasing the size of shot, sufficient penetration power is achieved. Cartridges have a transparent plastic case and plastic wad and are available in the following gauge and shot sizes:

| Gauge | Cartridge | | Shot |
|---|---|---|---|
| | length in | mm | weight gram | diameter in mm |
| 12 | 2⁵/₈in | 67.5 | 23 | 3.3, 3.5, 3.8 |

*Winchester Super-X steel-shot cartridge.*

# Zinc

Cartridges with zinc shot are particularly environmentally-friendly and provide a good alternative to steel shot up to a range of about 104ft (32m). With its specific gravity of 7.2, zinc has similar penetration power to iron. The shot is ideal for use with older guns because the soft metal does not require chokes or barrels to be adapted, which is usually necessary with steel shot.
Cartridges have a shot velocity at V12.5 of 1,007 ft per second (310m per second).

## *Hubertus Zinc*

Hubertus Zinc cartridges have a heavy-duty black cardboard case and felt shot-retaining wad. Because zinc is non toxic, the materials are environmentally friendly, except for the brass base which does not readily biodegrade. Because the specific gravity of 7.2 is low, the shot pellets have to be larger than those of heavier metals to maintain penetration power. Cartridges are available in the following gauges and shot sizes:

| Gauge | Cartridge | | weight | Shot diameter |
| | length in | mm | gram | in mm |
|---|---|---|---|---|
| 12 | 2³/₄in | 70 | 28 | 3.0-3.5 |
| 12 | 2³/₄in | 70 | 30 | 3.0-3.5 |
| 16 | 2³/₄in | 70 | 30 | 3.0-3.5 |
| 20 | 2³/₄in | 70 | 28 | 3.0-3.5 |

*Hubertus Zinc cartridge.*

# Overview of cartridges for sport shooting

The use of lead shot for sport shooting is still permitted in most countries although the shooting terrain usually is required to meet strict environmental requirements. This may include protective membranes laid under the grass to prevent contamination leaching into the ground. If the top soil subsequently has to be removed, it is treated as chemical waste. Some countries and also certain shooting clubs require steel shot to be used on shooting ranges..

## *Geco Special 24, red plastic case*

This cartridge, sold under the Geco name, has been specially developed for sport shooting and is available in both Skeet and Trap. Cartridges have a plastic cross and wad and are only available in 12 gauge.

| Gauge | Cartridge | | weight | Shot diameter |
| | length in | mm | gram | in mm |
|---|---|---|---|---|
| 12-Skeet | 2⁵/₈in | 67.5 | 24 | 2.0 |
| 12-Trap | 2⁵/₈in | 67.5 | 24 | 2.4 |

*Geco Special 24 lead-shot cartridge.*

## *Geco Special 28, red plastic case*

This cartridge is a top quality product from Dynamite Nobel, developed for sporting clays. the shot is packed in a plastic wad and is only available in 12 gauge.

*Geco Special 28 lead-shot cartridge.*

| Gauge | length in | Cartridge mm | weight gram | Shot diameter in mm |
|---|---|---|---|---|
| 12-Skeet | 2⁵/₈in | 67.5 | 28 | 2.0 |
| 12-Trap | 2⁵/₈in | 67.5 | 28 | 2.4 |

### Geco Special 28 spreading, red plastic case

This cartridge is equally developed for sporting shooting and intended for use with guns with narrower chokes. Cartridges have a felt wad but plastic cross to spread the shot when it leaves the barrel; and are only available in 12 gauge.

| Gauge | length in | Cartridge mm | weight gram | Shot diameter in mm |
|---|---|---|---|---|
| 12 | 2⁵/₈in | 67.5 | 28 | 2.0 |

Geco Special 28 Spreading cartridge.

### Maionchi Skeet Gold

A special skeet shooting cartridge that is widely used by many clay pigeon shooters. Cartridges are available in 12 gauge and have a plastic shot-retaining wad.

| Gauge | length in | Cartridge mm | weight gram | Shot diameter in mm |
|---|---|---|---|---|
| 12 | 2⁵/₈in | 67.5 | 24 | 2.0 |

Maionchi Skeet Gold cartridge, used by sporting shooters.

### Rottweil Club 28 spreading, black plastic case

A special skeet cartridge in 16 gauge for guns with a narrow choke. The plastic cross ensures greater spread of the shot than normal and removes the disadvantage of narrower chokes. This applies to full and ³/₄chokes. Cartridges are available in the following gauge and shot size.

| Gauge | length in | Cartridge mm | weight gram | Shot diameter in mm |
|---|---|---|---|---|
| 16 | 2⁵/₈in | 67.5 | 28 | 2.0 |

Rottweil Club 28 Spreading cartridge.

### Rottweil Steel-X-Range Trap or Skeet

Rottweil has developed this special sporting cartridge for countries which ban the use of lead shot for clay pigeon shooting. In a red plastic case, the shot is held in a plastic retaining wad to protect the barrel. Cartridges are available in the following gauge and shot sizes.

| Gauge | length in | Cartridge mm | weight gram | Shot diameter in mm |
|---|---|---|---|---|
| 12 Skeet | 2³/₄in | 70 | 28 | 2.3 |
| 12 Trap | 2³/₄in | 70 | 28 | 2.6 |

Rottweil Steel-X-range Trap steel shot cartridge.

### Rottweil Subsonic Trap 28, green plastic case

A cartridge developed to reduce noise disturbance from clay pigeon shooting grounds. The velocity of the shot remains under the sound barrier at approx. 1,105 ft per second (340m per second). Aiming requires extra care due to the greater delay to target. The cartridge has a plastic shot-retaining wad

*Rottweil Subsonic Trap 28 cartridge.*

and is only available in 12 gauge.

| Gauge | | Cartridge | | | Shot |
| | length | | weight | | diameter |
| | in | mm | gram | | in mm |
|---|---|---|---|---|---|
| 12 | 2⁵/₈in | 67,5 | 24 | | 2.0 |

## Rottweil Superskeet 24, red plastic case

A special skeet cartridge with a reduced shot load. The shot is packed in a shot-retaining wad to virtually eliminate wayward shot. Cartridges are only available in 12 gauge.

| Gauge | | Cartridge | | | Shot |
| | length | | weight | | diameter |
| | in | mm | gram | | in mm |
|---|---|---|---|---|---|
| 12 | 2⁵/₈in | 67,5 | 24 | | 2.0 |

*Rottweil Superskeet 28 cartridge.*

## Rottweil Superskeet 28 Spreading, red plastic case

The Superskeet spreading cartridge has a plastic cross that helps to spread the shot when it leaves the barrel. The cartridge have a felt wad and are only available in 12 gauge.

| Gauge | | Cartridge | | | Shot |
| | length | | weight | | diameter |
| | in | mm | gram | | in mm |
|---|---|---|---|---|---|
| 12 | 2⁵/₈in | 67,5 | 28 | | 2.0 |

*Rottweil Superskeet 28 Spreading cartridge.*

## Rottweil Supersport 24, green plastic case

The Supersport is developed for double trap shooting and gives high coverage. It is a cartridge that falls between normal Skeet and Trap cartridges. Cartridges are also suitable for sporting clays. Cartridges have a plastic shot-retaining wad and are only available in 12 gauge.

| Gauge | | Cartridge | | | Shot |
| | length | | weight | | diameter |
| | in | mm | gram | | in mm |
|---|---|---|---|---|---|
| 12 | 2⁵/₈in | 67,5 | 24 | | 2.2 |

*Rottweil Supersport 24 cartridge.*

## Rottweil Supertrap 24, blue plastic case

This sports cartridge is specially developed for trap shooting. The shot is extra hard and the column of shot remains concentrated over a longer range. Cartridges have a plastic shot-retaining wad and are only available in 12 gauge.

| Gauge | | Cartridge | | | Shot |
| | length | | weight | | diameter |
| | in | mm | gram | | in mm |
|---|---|---|---|---|---|
| 12 | 2⁵/₈in | 67,5 | 24 | | 2.4 |

*Rottweil Supertrap 24 cartridge.*

## Rottweil Supertrap 28, red plastic case

Red Supertrap 28 cartridges have an ideal shot distribution and the right shot velocity for trap shooting. Cartridges have a plastic shot retaining wad and are only available in 12 gauge.

| Gauge | | Cartridge | | | Shot |
| | length | | weight | | diameter |
| | in | mm | gram | | in mm |
|---|---|---|---|---|---|
| 12 | 2⁵/₈in | 67,5 | 28 | | 2.4 |

# Special cartridges

Red Supertrap 28 cartridges have an ideal shot distribution and the right shot velocity for trap shooting. Cartridges have a plastic shot-retaining wad and are only available in 12 gauge.

## *Rottweil Express Transparent*

This cartridge is filled with buckshot (large diameter shot). Such cartridges were once commonly used for game shooting. A number of European countries ban the use of buckshot. The cartridge has a transparent plastic case and plastic case reinforcing, between the shot and felt wad. Cartridges are available in the following gauges and shot sizes:

| Gauge | Cartridge | | | Shot |
|-------|-----------|---|--------|------|
| | length | | weight | diameter |
| | in | mm | gram | in mm |
| 12 | 2⁵/₈in | 67,5 | 70 | 4,5 |
| 12 | 2⁵/₈in | 67,5 | 43 | 5,2 |
| 12 | 2⁵/₈in | 67,5 | 27 | 6,2 |
| 12 | 2⁵/₈in | 67,5 | 12 | 7,5 |
| 12 | 2⁵/₈in | 67,5 | 9 | 8,6 |
| 12 | 2⁵/₈in | 67,5 | 9 | 7,9 |

*Rottweil Express buckshot cartridge.*

## *Slugs*

Another type of cartridge for shooting larger game is the slug or bullet for use in a smooth-bore barrel. This type of ammunition is forbidden in a few European coun-

tries but is permissible in most European countries and in North America. The best known type is Brenneke by Rottweil which is so well known that the name has become widely used as a description. Most other cartridge manufacturers have a similar type of cartridge.

Slugs are mainly used for shooting larger game, such as deer and wild boar, although may not be used for this purpose in the United Kingdom under the Deer Act and other legislation. They are most commonly used with smooth-bore guns rather than rifles but their use is not covered by a United Kingdom shotgun certificate. A number of countries, including those in North and South America have sporting competitions for slug guns with rifled barrels at ranges of 100–300m (approx. 100–300 yds). These projectiles do, however need some of the stability of a rifle bullet. This is provided by putting a kind of rifling onto the projectile itself. Flutes are machine at an angle onto the side of the slug to impart spin on the projectile during its trajectory. Below is a table of certain "Brenneke" cartridges. The data was supplied by Rottweil/Dynamit Nobel.

| Gauge | Weight | Gaspressure | | Velocity in fps/m/s | | | |
|-------|--------|-------------|-----|------|------|------|------|
| | gram | bar | V0 | V25 | V50 | V75 | V100 |
| 12 | 31.5 | 650 | 430 | 370 | 330 | 300 | 275 |
| 12/76 | 39 | 900 | 460 | 400 | 350 | 315 | 290 |
| 16 | 27 | 680 | 430 | 370 | 330 | 300 | 275 |
| 20 | 24 | 720 | 430 | 370 | 330 | 300 | 275 |

V0 = projectile velocity at muzzle
V25 = projectile velocity at 25m from muzzle
V50 = projectile velocity at 50m from muzzle
V75 = projectile velocity at 75m from muzzle
V100 = projectile velocity at 100m from muzzle

*Rottweil Brenneke slug cartridge.*

*Cross-section of a Rottweil Brenneke slug cartridge.*

# 8 Law regarding hunting, shooting, and shotguns

Many countries ban the use of lead shot for game shooting and a few ban its use entirely. The government in the United Kingdom is expected to introduce legislation shortly to ban the use of lead shot over wetlands and all shooting organizations have promoted a voluntary code so that lead shot generally has not been used over wetlands for some time. Lead shot was first banned in the USA in 1983.

In general terms, deer can only be shot with rifles, with certain exceptions related to crops, deer culling, and in the event of the need to humanely kill an injured deer.

The Deer Act 1991 sets out these rare exceptions. Both buckshot/AAA shot and slugs are not of themselves banned for game shooting in the United Kingdom but use of slugs requires a Firearms Permit instead of a Shotgun Certificate.

Generally no more than 2 rounds are permitted in magazines, though guns with a greater capacity may be used provided their magazine capacity is permanently restricted to 2 cartridges. Where sufficient cause can be shown for requiring say a 5-round magazine, police firearms officers may permit this and this might include a permit for use in Practical Shotgun sport. A gun with at least one rifled barrel requires a Firearms Permit. Your local firearms officer can advise and certificates or permits must always be obtained before a gun or firearm is acquired.

## Sport shooting

Clay pigeon shooting is a growing sport. In general terms, clay pigeons are shot at from fixed positions, with the object being to shatter the clay disc or "pigeon".

The clays are launched into the air by a machine at different angles and speeds; sometimes two are fired into the air together, known as double rise. There are a number of disciplines in the sport and the main ones are described here.

*Wild boar in a wood (Photograph by Browning).*

– Trap
– Skeet
– English Sporting (Sporting Clays/Parcours de Chasse)
– Practical shotgun

## Trap

Olympic Trap grounds have five shooting stands, each with a clay ejector in a trench 16m (52ft) wide and 15m (approx. 50ft) in front of the shooting stands.

The clays are launched at different angles and speeds in a random sequence. Shooters may shoulder their guns and then shout "pull" to launch the clay. The English "pull" has become international in use wherever clay pigeon shooters enjoy their sport. After five clays, the shooter moves up one position until all five stands have been shot.

The shooter or gun is allowed to fire twice at one clay. One round consists of 25 clays. International competitions consist of five series of 25 clays plus a further round of 25. The sport is quite demanding in terms of concentration. Trap shotguns are specially adapted with long barrels (76 or 81cm/30 or 32in) and narrow chokes.

A variation on Trap shooting is Double Trap, which was first seen at the Olympic Games in 1966. In this discipline double clays only are launched in the same sequence as Trap. Women shoot at 120 clays

*Diagram of an Olympic Trap ground (Browning).*

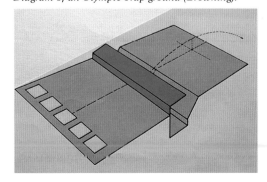

in three series of 20 pairs of clays. Men shoot at 150 clays in three series of 25 pairs. Both men and women have a final round of 25 clays.

A third form of Trap shooting that is popular in Britain is Down The Line. This is popular with beginners because the clays are launched at a moderate speed and fly at low angle that does not exceed 22 degrees.
The shooting stands are arranged in a quarter circle at 15m (50ft). Each stand has one machine that ejects clays at a fixed angle. There are five stands in the quarter circle.
The five guns shoot five clays in turn but at one clay only each call. After five clays have been shot, the guns all move up one stand until all 25 clays have been shot at. The shooting stands are sometimes set up in a straight line for this discipline.

A forth variation of Trap shooting is Ball Trap in which just one machine launches the clays. The launcher is of special construction and can launch clays with great variety of angles and speed, within an arc of 90 degrees horizontally and 35 degrees in elevation. The single machine is located in a dug-out bunker at 50ft (15m) from the shooting stands. One clay is launched per turn and the guns move up a stand each shot.

## Skeet

Skeet is an old form of shooting sport.
The first rules for the sport were laid down in the USA in 1926. Seven shooting stands or posts are formed in a semi-circle with a eighth post situated at the centre of an imaginary line between the two ends of the semi-circle.
A machine is located in a protective hut on either side of the semi-circle:

*Hunting scene (photo by Browning).*

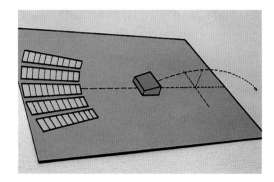

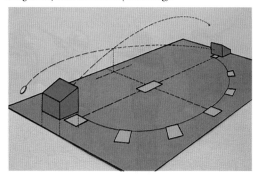

the left-hand machine being raised 10ft (305cm) off the ground and on the opposite side the machine is mounted at 42in (107cm). The trajectory of the clays must cross each other in the centre of the semi-circle at about 15ft (approx. 4.5m). The clays are launched to call but not necessarily straight away. The difference may vary by 1–3 seconds. The gun may not be shouldered beforehand, only when the clays are launched. The range to target is relatively close, therefore skeet guns have a wide choke. Standard shot size for skeet shooting is 2mm.

The sequence of skeet shooting and numbers of clays is as follows:
Post 1: at the extreme right-hand post three clays are launched, first a single clay from the elevated hut, followed by two clays simultaneously from both huts. These double rising clays must be shot in sequence: first the clay from the elevated hut and then the other. This sequence is repeated at posts 2 and 3. At post 4, guns shoot at a single clay from each of the huts in sequence. Post 5 and 6 are a repeat of posts 1–3. At the extreme left post 7, double rising clays are shot, this time with the first target being the clay from the lower hut.

At post 8 in the centre of the line between the two huts, one clay is shot from the elevated hut and then one from the other hut. The gun may only be loaded with one cartridge per clay at this post. The complete round consists of 25 clays. An Olympic series comprises five rounds each of 25 clays plus a final round of 25 clays.

## Jachtparcours, Parcours de Chasse of Sporting Clays.

Sporting Clays is not a rigidly prescribed discipline. The different elements of the competition are laid down but there may be many variations in the sequence and design of the course.

This form of shooting seeks to imitate shooting in the field. The clays are launched at a wide variety of angles, from many different positions, and with different speeds. Many gunmakers have developed special guns for the discipline, which is becoming increasingly popular. It provides the nearest equivalent to a day's shooting in the field for those unable to enjoy the real thing as often as they would like. If rabbit is on the menu in the club restaurant afterwards, the substitute is total.

The purpose of each of the different posts is described below.

Post 1:
Crossing Shot – the clays come from left and right, singly, close together, or in pairs. This post attempts to imitate the flight pattern of woodcock.

Post 2: Driven Shot – the clays imitate grouse and other game birds that fly high over the guns when they are driven towards

*Diagram of a sporting clays course (Browning).*

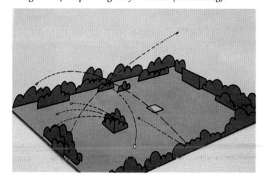

*Wildfowling.*

the guns by beaters. The clays are mainly launched as simultaneous pairs.

## Post 3:

Going Away Shot – single clays or simultaneous pairs (doublets) that fly high up over the gun and away from them. This mimics the flight of pheasants.

*Sporting Clays, post 1: Crossing Shot (a Beretta illustration).*

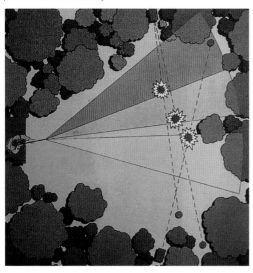

## Post 4:

Incoming Tower Shot – the clays are launched from a height of about 100ft (25–30m) to imitate incoming wildfowl and

*Sporting Clays, post 2: Driven Shot (a Beretta illustration).*

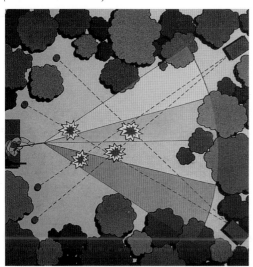

pheasants. The clays can be launched together as pairs or in close succession and at different angles.

*Sporting Clays, post 3: Going Away Shot (a Beretta illustration).*

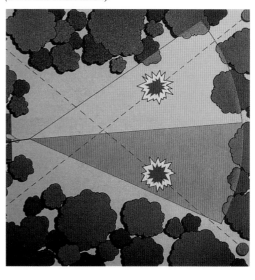

## Post 5:

Fur and Feather Shot – two clays are ejected in close succession. One flies up at an angle to mimic a game bird and the other is bounced along the ground to imitate a running rabbit.

*Sporting Clays, post 4: Incoming Tower Shot (a Beretta illustration).*

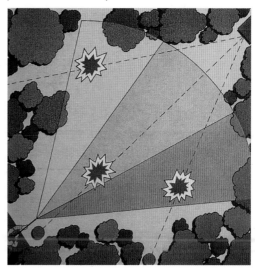

*Sporting Clays, post 5: Fur & Feather Shot (a Beretta illustration).*

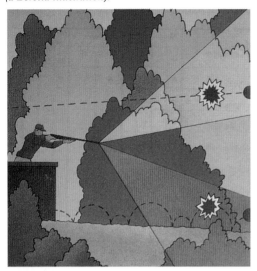

*Sporting Clays, post 6: Springing Teal Shot (a Beretta illustration).*

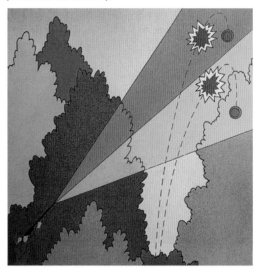

Post 6:
Springing Teal – the clay flies very steeply away from the gun at an angle of 70 degrees. This is intended to imitate a teal. The shot is made more difficult because two clays are launched together.

Post 7:
Overhead Shot – simultaneous pairs of clays are launched high over the heads of the gun to mimic high-flying wood pigeons.

*Russian clay pigeon shooting ground (photo Izhevsky/Baikal).*

*Post 7: Overhead Shot (a Beretta illustration).*

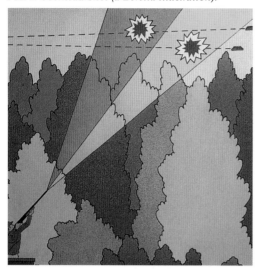

The illustrations to help explain the different clay-shooting disciplines originate from the catalogues of Beretta and Browning and are reproduced here with their permission.

## *Practical Shotgun*

The sport of shooting around a set course with a semi-automatic shotgun originates like so many other shooting sports activities from North America. The sport has also taken root in certain European countries, including Britain, Austria, France, Germany, Spain, and Switzerland.

The course is set out with different stages at which various types of target have to be fired on. These include pop-up discs, bowling pins, "pepper-poppers" (steel discs which fall down when hit), and cardboard target discs. The course has to be completed in a certain time and the points are awarded for a combination of hits and time.

The most popular classes are those for 12 bore or 12 gauge which are often termed "major classes" with 20 gauge being known as "minor classes". Commercial interests constantly bring pressure to develop further classes such as semi-automatic with aim and point sights, laser sights, barrel compensators etc. The sceptical may see this as a game for people who want to find an outlet for their aggression but it is taken just as seriously as other shooting disciplines and there has even been talk of it being included as an Olympic sport. Countries such as those in North and South America, and Austria, Spain, and Switzerland hold national and international matches, usually on outdoor ranges.

**REMARK:** many European countries, including the United Kingdom, do not permit the use of semi-automatic shotguns with a magazine capacity in excess of two cartridges. A permit may be granted in the United Kingdom for a higher capacity where good cause is shown in an application.

The internationally established sequence for Practical Shotgun is described below.

Stage 1:
shoot at 5 cardboard targets at three different ranges – (1A) at a range of 20m (21.83yds); (1B) – at a range of 15m (16.40yds); (1C) at a range of 10m (10.93yds).

Stage 2:
shoot at 5 cardboard targets with gun loaded with 5 cartridges then quickly reload and fire at a second set of 5 targets at a range of 15m (16.40yds).

Stage 3:
shoot at 5 cardboard targets at a range of 15m (16.40yds) from left to right.

Stage 4:
5 steel targets have to be knocked down at ranges of 10–13m (10.93–14.21yds).

Stage 5:
5 steel targets have to be knocked down at ranges of 10–15m (10.93–16.40yds) at stand A. The shooter then runs with an empty gun to stand B where the gun is reloaded quickly with 4 cartridges and then 4 more steel targets have to be knocked down. The shooter reloads again fires on 2 cardboard targets. The shooter then proceeds to stand C and fires at 5 cardboard discs. Finally, the shooter runs to stand D, fires at a bowling pin at 10m (10.93) and the clock stops when the pin is hit. Each target that is not hit receives 20 penalty points. Variations in both the sequence and composition of the course described are possible.

# 9 Explanation of exploded drawings

Exploded drawings have nothing to do with explosions! The term means a dimensional drawing of all the parts that are assembled in a gun. In this encyclopaedia a lot of words are used that might confuse the reader. Most shotguns have more or less the same technical basis. These drawings provide a guide to both the parts and the functioning of these guns.
Not every nut, bolt, or screw has been named in these drawings but all the important parts are named.

*Left: Bernardelli Dream.*

*Engraving on a Browning Ducks Unlimited.*

The drawing on the following page is of a Bernardelli Vincent semi-automatic shotgun.

| Part no. | Name |
| --- | --- |
| 1 | breech block carrier |
| 2. | gas cylinder housing |
| 3 | breech block return spring |
| 7 | housing tube return spring |
| 11 | barrel |
| 12 | gas-tight seal (with piston, 66 and closing ring 67) |
| 13 | breech block |
| 14 | breech block rear stop |
| 17/18/19 | cartridge elevating unit |
| 35 | disengagement lever |
| 36 | extractor claw |
| 39 | cartridge feed bar |
| 40 | firing pin |
| 42 | firing pin spring |
| 43 | fore-end |
| 44 | securing plate for fore-end |
| 45 | bead |
| 48 | hammer |
| 51 | hammer spring tube |
| 52 | hammer spring |
| 54 | action catch spring |
| 55 | action catch |
| 56 | return spring tail guide, for breech block carrier (1) |
| 57 | locking block breech block |
| 58 | magazine cover |
| 60 | magazine spring end cap (see *) |
| 61 | magazine spring |
| 62 | magazine spring tube |
| 63 | cocking lever |
| 66 | piston ring |
| 67 | cylinder closing ring |
| 68 | action body (receiver) |
| 69 | butt pad |
| 70 | butt plate screw |

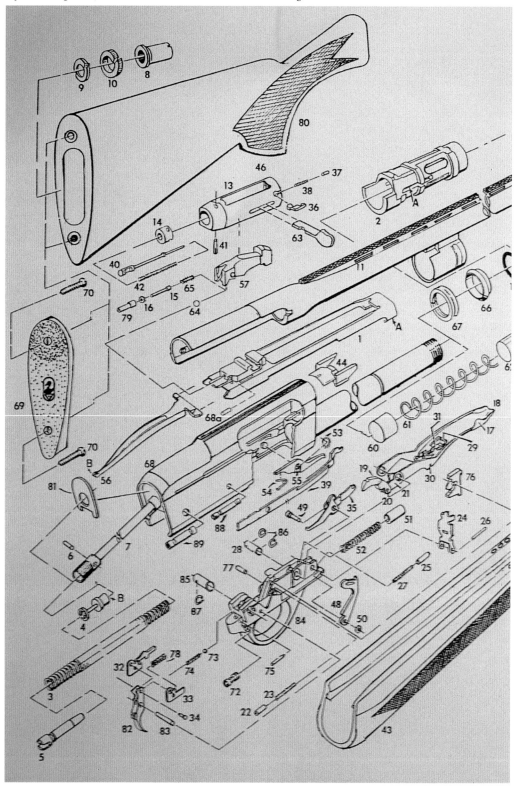

| 72 | push-button safety-catch |
|---|---|
| 74 | safety-catch spring |
| 76 | tumbler |
| 77 | tumbler spindle |
| 78 | tumbler spring |
| 80 | stock butt |
| 81 | recoil plate |
| 82 | trigger |
| 84 | trigger guard and trigger action body unit |
| 88/89 | pins for fixing trigger mechanism |

(* The capacity of the magazine can be varied by changing the length of this part or by adding a wooden plug).

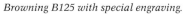
*Browning B125 with special engraving.*

The cut-away drawing of a Benelli semi-automatic shotgun below gives some idea of how all the parts are fitted together.

*Drawing of a Benelli semi-automatic shotgun.*

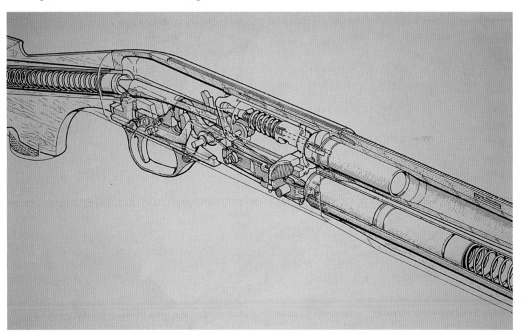

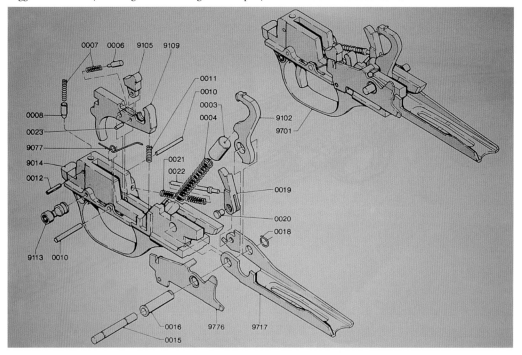

The firing mechanism of a shotgun consists of one or two triggers. The illustration above of a Benelli semi-automatic shotgun is provided as an example.

The illustration on p69 gives an overview of the parts of a breech-loading shotgun, using a Bernardelli Dream over-and-under as an example.

| Part no. | Name |
|---|---|
| 1 | action body |
| 2 | top lever locking |
| 5 | locking lever spring |
| 7 | barrel-locking block |
| 9 | safety-catch |
| 10 | safety-catch spring |
| 12 | trigger guard for single trigger |
| 14 | trigger (single) |
| 18 | barrel selector |
| 19 | inertia block (to switch barrels after first shot) |
| 21 | tumbler (one per barrel) |
| 22 | tumbler spring |
| 24 | trigger spring or springs |
| 27 | hammer spring guide rods |
| 28 | hammer springs |
| 29 | left hammer |
| 30 | right hammer |
| 32 | firing pins |
| 33 | firing pin springs |
| 35 | right ejector bar |
| 36 | left ejector bar |
| 37 | ejector for bottom barrel |
| 38 | ejector for top barrel |
| 39 | ejector spring guide bar |
| 40 | ejector spring |
| 41 | right ejector tumbler for bottom barrel |
| 42 | left ejector tumbler for top barrel |
| 45 | fore-end |
| 46 | hinge for fore-end iron |
| 47 | fore-end iron |
| 50 | fore-end retaining catch housing |
| 51 | fore-end retaining catch |
| 54 | barrels |
| 55 | cocking lever |
| 56 | cocking lever spring |
| 57 | cocking lever spring guide rod |
| 59 | action cover plate |
| 60 | stock butt |
| 64 | stock retaining bolt |
| 65 | butt screw |
| 66 | butt pad |
| 67 | trigger guard for twin triggers |
| 68 | front trigger |
| 69 | rear trigger |
| 71 | trigger operating lever |

*Overview of the parts of a Bernardelli Dream double-barrelled shotgun.*

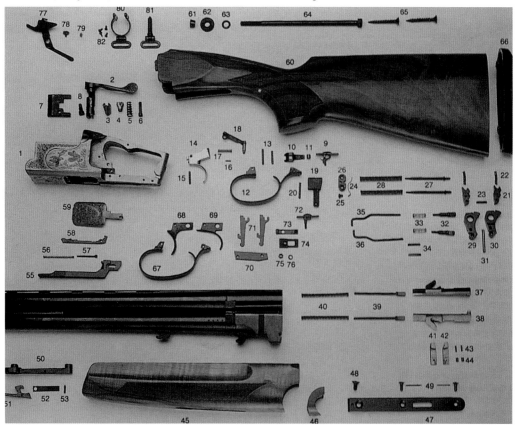

| 72 | safety catch for twin triggers |
|---|---|
| 77 | automatic safety lever (gun remains safe after opening and reclosing) |
| 78/79 | sight bead |
| 80/81 | sling swivels |

# Symbols of use

Symbols are used beside each gun in this book to indicate the type of use for which it is suitable. These indications are not hard and fast rules; a superb traditional side-by-side gun with gold inlaid engraving of animals on its side-lock plates is not per se a clay pigeon shooting gun but if I were to say so didactically I can imagine piles of angry letters proving me wrong. The gun, however, is not made for that specific purpose. These symbols should only be taken as a general guide for the average shooter.

## Symbols

Shotgun and combination gun for field shooting

Shotgun for sports shooting – Skeet, Trap, and Sporting Clays

Shotgun for Practical Shotgun

Slug-gun or shotgun for use with slugs

Shotgun with short barrel and/or stock for defence and police use

# 10 An A–Z of shotguns and combination rifles

## American Arms

American Arms is based in Kansas City, Missouri. The specialist company imports and distributes a number of European makes. The company's under-and-over shotgun stems from factories in Brescia in Italy while the more traditional side-by-side gun originates from the Basque region of Spain. The shotguns are chiefly intended for the US market chamber lengths for the over-and-under for 12 gauge of 3in (76mm) or $3^1/_2$ in (89mm). The company has a large share of the US market for both imported European shotguns small calibre pistols, such as Erma, and single-action revolvers by Sauer and Uberti. The company also sells the superb replica black powder Colt and Remington revolvers by Uberti.

| | |
|---|---|
| Safety | : sliding catch on neck of stock, also barrel choice switch |

**CHARACTERISTICS**

| | |
|---|---|
| – material | : steel |
| – finish | : entirely blued or blued barrel with plain metal action body with engraving |
| – stock | : walnut with pistol-grip or straight English stock |

The Basque range consists of the following models:

– The Specialty in 12/89 calibre with extractor, walnut stock with pistol-grip;
– The Gentry in all the above calibres with extractor, walnut stock and pistol-grip
– The Brittany in calibre 12, and 20+, with ejector and a straight English stock
☞

### American Arms Basque

**TECHNICAL DETAILS**

| | |
|---|---|
| Gauge/calibre | : 12, 20, 28, or .410 |
| Chamber length | : $2^3/_4$, 3, or 3 $^1/_2$in (70, 76, or 89mm) |
| Number of barrels | : double barrels side-by-side |
| Action | : breech-loading |
| Locking | : barrel-block locking |
| Trigger | single or twin triggers |
| Weight | : 6lb 6oz–7lb 8 oz (2.9–3.4kg) |
| Length | : $42^{15}/_{16}$ or $44^7/_8$in (109 or 114cm) |
| Barrel length | : 26 or 28in (66 or 71cm) |
| Ejector | : extractor or ejector |
| Choke | interchangeable chokes |
| Sight | bead |

### American Arms Silver

**TECHNICAL DETAILS**

| | |
|---|---|
| Gauge/calibre | : 10, 12, 20, 28, or .410 |
| Chamber length | : $2^3/_4$, 3, or 3 $^1/_2$in (70, 76, or 89mm) |
| Number of barrels | : double barrels over-and-under |
| Action | : breech-loading |
| Locking | : barrel-block locking |
| Trigger | single trigger |
| Weight | : 6lb 6oz–9lb1/4oz (2.9–4.2kg) |
| Length | : $41^3/_4$–$47^5/_8$in (106–121cm) |
| Barrel length | : 24–30in (61–76cm) |
| Ejector | : extractor or ejector |
| Choke | fixed or interchangeable chokes |
| Sight | ventilated rib and bead |
| Safety | : sliding catch on neck of stock |

## CHARACTERISTICS
- material : steel
- finish : blued barrels and plain metal action body or entirely blued
- stock : walnut with pistol-grip or plastic stock in camouflage colours

The Silver range consists of the following models:
- Silver Upland Lite in 12 or 20 gauge, light alloy breech, 6lbs 7oz (2.9kg);
- Silver I in above gauges, fixed choke to choice, extractor;
- Silver II as Silver I, with ejectors and interchangeable chokes;
- Silver Sporting in 12/3in (12/76) and 20/3in (20/76), interchangeable chokes, compensator vents in both barrels, ejectors;
- Silver Magnum in 10 or 12 gauge, extractor or ejector, matt blue barrel and breech or camouflage finish.

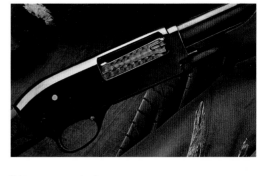

Sight : bead
Safety : push button at front of trigger guard

## CHARACTERISTICS
- material : steel
- finish : blued
- stock : hardwood

# Armscor/KBI

Arms Corporation, or Armscor for short, is based in The Philippines, where it produces both weapons and munitions .
The guns produced by Armscor are imported into the USA by KBI Inc of Harrisburg, Pennsylvania.
This company also imports the Sabatti sporting rifles and shotguns from the Brescia region of Italy. KBI also imports Feg pistols from Hungary such as the PJK-9HP which is a copy of the famous FN-Browning High Power 9mm Para pistol. Feg also produces a copy of the Walther PPK 9mm short and .22 LR.

## Armscor Field

### TECHNICAL DETAILS
Gauge/calibre : 12
Chamber length : 3in (76mm)
Number of barrels : single barrel
Magazine : tubular magazine for 2 or 5 cartridges
Action : pump-action
Locking : falling block locking
Trigger single trigger
Weight : 7lb 11¼oz (3.5kg)
Length : 47¼in (120cm)
Barrel length : 28in (71cm)
Ejector : extractor
Choke interchangeable chokes or fixed: ½

## Armscor Riotgun

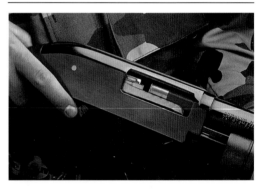

### TECHNICAL DETAILS
Gauge/calibre : 12
Chamber length : 76mm (3in)
Number of barrels : single barrel
Magazine : tubular magazine for 5 cartridges
Action : pump-action
Locking : falling-block locking
Trigger single trigger
Weight : 7lb or 7lb 4oz (3.2 or 3.3kg)
Length : 37¾ or 39¼in (96 or 99.7cm)
Barrel length : 18½ or 20in (47 or 50.8cm)
Ejector : extractor
Choke cylindrical
Sight bead
Safety : push button at front of trigger guard

### CHARACTERISTICS
- material : steel
- finish : blued
- stock : hardwood

Possession of this firearm is not permitted for hunting or other sporting purposes in a number of European countries because of the magazine capacity and short barrel-length. To hold a gun on a shotgun certificate in the United Kingdom the magazine capacity must not exceed 2 cartridges and the barrel must not shorter than 24in (61cm).

## Armscorp Special Purpose

**TECHNICAL DETAILS**

| | |
|---|---|
| Gauge/calibre | : 12 |
| Chamber length | : 3in (76mm) |
| Number of barrels | : single barrel |
| Magazine | : tubular magazine for 2 or 7 cartridges |
| Action | : pump-action |
| Locking | : falling-block locking |
| Trigger | single trigger |
| Weight | : 7lb 8oz (3.4kg) |
| Length | : 39¹/₄in (99.7cm) |
| Barrel length | : 20in (50.8cm) |
| Ejector | : extractor |
| Choke | cylindrical |
| Sight | bead |
| Safety | : push button at front of trigger guard |

**CHARACTERISTICS**

| | | |
|---|---|---|
| — material | : | steel |
| — finish | : | matt black |
| — stock | : | black plastic |

This model is based on the fighting weapon of the SAS (Special Air Services) special forces unit of the British Army. The gun can be loaded rapidly with a 4-round "Speed-feed" clip through the right-hand side of the stock. Possession of this firearm is not permitted for hunting or other sporting purposes in a number of European countries because of the magazine capacity and short barrel-length. To hold a gun on a shotgun certificate in the United Kingdom the magazine capacity must not exceed 2 cartridges and the barrel must not shorter than 24in (61cm).

# Arrieta

The Spanish firm of Arrieta has been making exceptional quality side-by-side shotguns with side-locking for more than 80 years. Avelino Arrieta began his career at Eibar in the renowned Spanish armaments region. He established himself as an independent gunsmith in 1916, producing hand-made guns. Both his sons, José and Victor entered the business in 1940. The company became a limited company under the name Manufacturas Arrieta in 1970. The present company only produces side-lock side-by-side guns by traditional methods with a work-force of 20 highly-trained craftsmen. Arrieta exports widely to countries which include Great Britain, USA, Italy, and Germany.

At the present time the company is run by the grandsons of the founder, Juan Carlos and Asier Arrieta. Every gun is made to the customer's order and individual specification. These specify the overall and barrel lengths, choke, and engraving. The stocks are made by hand and polished with oil. An expert from the company selects walnut from mature trees in the Pyrenees, Galicia, and Andalusia. Only high-quality Bellota steel is used for making the guns and they can be inlaid with gold if required. The company uses modern communications techniques and Arrieta, with Manuel Santos as its general manager, has a web site on the Internet. It is sufficient to type "Arrieta" in your Internet search request. Enthusiasts for traditional hand-made side-lock side-by-side barrelled shotguns make an excellent choice when they select Arrieta, although understandably these guns are fairly expensive.

## Arrieta Model 557 Side-lock

**TECHNICAL DETAILS**

| | |
|---|---|
| Gauge/calibre | : 12, 16, 20, 28, or .410 |
| Chamber length | : 70 or 76mm (2³/₄ or 3in) |
| Number of barrels | : double-barrels side-by-side |
| Action | : breech-loading |
| Locking | : barrel block lock |
| Trigger | twin triggers |
| Weight | : 3.1–3.3kg (6lb 13oz–7lb 4oz) |
| Length | : to choice |

Barrel length    : to choice
Ejector          : automatic (Holland & Holland)
Choke            : to choice
Sight            bead
Safety           : sliding catch on neck of stock, gas relief vents in undersides of barrel

**CHARACTERISTICS**
— material       : steel
— finish         : blued barrels, plain metal action body with engraved side-lock plates, spring-loaded breech
— stock          : straight English stock of specially selected walnut

## Arrieta Model 570 Side-lock

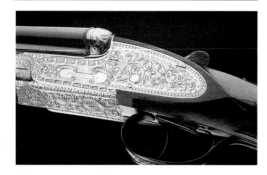

**TECHNICAL DETAILS**
Gauge/calibre     : 12, 16, 20, 28, or .410
Chamber length    : 70 or 76mm (2³/₄ or 3in)
Number of barrels : double-barrels side-by-side
Action            : breech-loading
Locking           : barrel block lock
Trigger           twin triggers
Weight            : 3.1–3.3kg (6lb 13oz–7lb 4oz)
Length            : to choice
Barrel length     : to choice
Ejector           : automatic (Holland & Holland)
Choke             to choice
Sight             bead
Safety            : sliding catch on neck of stock, gas relief vents in undersides of barrel

**CHARACTERISTICS**
— material       : steel

— finish         : blued barrels, plain metal action body with engraved side-lock plates
— stock          : straight English stock of specially selected walnut

## Arrieta Model 578 Side-lock

**TECHNICAL DETAILS**
Gauge/calibre     : 12, 16, 20, 28, or .410
Chamber length    : 70 or 76mm (2³/₄ or 3in)
Number of barrels : double-barrels side-by-side
Action            : breech-loading
Locking           : barrel block lock
Trigger           twin triggers
Weight            : 3.1–3.3kg (6lb 13oz–7lb 4oz)
Length            : to choice
Barrel length     : to choice
Ejector           : automatic (Holland & Holland)
Choke             to choice
Sight             bead
Safety            : sliding catch on neck of stock, gas relief vents in undersides of barrel

**CHARACTERISTICS**
— material       : steel
— finish         : blued barrels, plain metal action body with engraved side-lock plates
— stock          : straight English stock of specially selected walnut

## Arrieta Model 600 Side-lock

## TECHNICAL DETAILS

| | |
|---|---|
| Gauge/calibre | : 12, 16, 20, 28, or .410 |
| Chamber length | : 70 or 76mm (2³/₄ or 3in) |
| Number of barrels | : double-barrels side-by-side |
| Action | : breech-loading |
| Locking | : barrel block lock |
| Trigger | single or twin triggers |
| Weight | : 3.1–3.3kg (6lb 13oz–7lb 4oz) |
| Length | : to choice |
| Barrel length | : to choice |
| Ejector | : automatic (Holland & Holland) |
| Choke | to choice |
| Sight | bead |
| Safety | : sliding catch on neck of stock, gas relief vents in undersides of barrel |

## CHARACTERISTICS

| | |
|---|---|
| — material | : steel |
| — finish | : blued barrels, plain metal action body with engraved side-lock plates, spring-loaded breech |
| — stock | : straight English stock of specially selected walnut |

# Arrieta Model 601 Side-lock

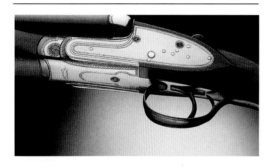

## TECHNICAL DETAILS

| | |
|---|---|
| Gauge/calibre | : 12, 16, 20, 28, or .410 |
| Chamber length | : 70 or 76mm (2³/₄ or 3in) |
| Number of barrels | : double-barrels side-by-side |
| Action | : breech-loading |
| Locking | : barrel block lock |
| Trigger | single trigger |
| Weight | : 3.2–3.3kg (7lb–7lb 4oz) |
| Length | : to choice |
| Barrel length | : to choice |
| Ejector | : automatic (Holland & Holland) |
| Choke | to choice |
| Sight | bead |
| Safety | : sliding catch on neck of stock |

## CHARACTERISTICS

| | |
|---|---|
| — material | : steel |
| — finish | : blued barrels, plain metal action body with lightly engraved side-lock plates, spring-loaded breech |
| — stock | : stock with pistol-grip of specially selected walnut |

# Arrieta Model 801 Side-lock

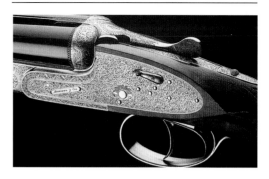

## TECHNICAL DETAILS

| | |
|---|---|
| Gauge/calibre | : 12, 16, 20, 28, or .410 |
| Chamber length | : 70 or 76mm (2³/₄ or 3in) |
| Number of barrels | : double-barrels side-by-side |
| Action | : breech-loading |
| Locking | : barrel block lock |
| Trigger | twin triggers |
| Weight | : 3.1–3.3kg (6lb 13oz–7lb 4oz) |
| Length | : to choice |
| Barrel length | : to choice |
| Ejector | : automatic (Holland & Holland) |
| Choke | to choice |
| Sight | bead |
| Safety | : sliding catch on neck of stock |

## CHARACTERISTICS

| | |
|---|---|
| — material | : steel |
| — finish | : blued barrels, plain metal action body with removable engraved side-lock plates, spring-loaded breech |
| — stock | : straight English stock of specially selected walnut |

# Arrieta Model 802 Side-lock

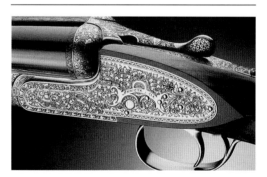

## TECHNICAL DETAILS

| | |
|---|---|
| Gauge/calibre | : 12, 16, 20, 28, or .410 |
| Chamber length | : 70 or 76mm (2³/₄ or 3in) |
| Number of barrels | : double-barrels side-by-side |
| Action | : breech-loading |
| Locking | : barrel block lock |

| Trigger | twin triggers |
| Weight | : 3.1–3.3kg (6lb 13oz–7lb 4oz) |
| Length | : to choice |
| Barrel length | : to choice |
| Ejector | : automatic (Holland & Holland) |
| Choke | to choice |
| Sight | bead |
| Safety | : sliding catch on neck of stock |

**CHARACTERISTICS**
| – material | : steel |
| – finish | : blued barrels, plain metal action body with engraved side-lock plates, spring-loaded breech |
| – stock | : straight English stock of specially selected walnut |

## *Arrieta Model 803 Side-lock*

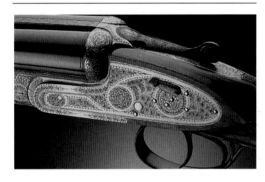

**TECHNICAL DETAILS**
| Gauge/calibre | : 12, 16, 20, 28, or .410 |
| Chamber length | : 70 or 76mm (2¾ or 3in) |
| Number of barrels | : double-barrels side-by-side |
| Action | : breech-loading |
| Locking | : barrel block lock |
| Trigger | twin triggers |
| Weight | : 3.1–3.3kg (6lb 13oz–7lb 4oz) |
| Length | : to choice |
| Barrel length | : to choice |
| Ejector | : automatic (Holland & Holland) |
| Choke | to choice |
| Sight | bead |
| Safety | : sliding catch on neck of stock |

**CHARACTERISTICS**
| – material | : steel |
| – finish | : blued barrels, plain metal action body with removable engraved side-lock plates, spring-loaded breech |
| – stock | : straight English stock of specially selected walnut |

## *Arrieta Model 871 Side-lock*

**TECHNICAL DETAILS**
| Gauge/calibre | : 12, 16, 20, 28, or .410 |

| Chamber length | : 70 or 76mm (2¾ or 3in) |
| Number of barrels | : double-barrels side-by-side |
| Action | : breech-loading |
| Locking | : barrel block lock |
| Trigger | twin triggers |
| Weight | : 3.1–3.3kg (6lb 13oz–7lb 4oz) |
| Length | : to choice |
| Barrel length | : to choice |
| Ejector | : automatic (Holland & Holland) |
| Choke | to choice |
| Sight | bead |
| Safety | : sliding catch on neck of stock |

**CHARACTERISTICS**
| – material | : steel |
| – finish | : blued barrels, plain metal action body with engraved side-lock plates |
| – stock | : straight English stock of specially selected walnut |

## *Arrieta Model 872 Side-lock*

**TECHNICAL DETAILS**
| Gauge/calibre | : 12, 16, 20, 28, or .410 |
| Chamber length | : 70 or 76mm (2¾ or 3in) |
| Number of barrels | : double-barrels side-by-side |
| Action | : breech-loading |
| Locking | : barrel block lock |
| Trigger | twin triggers |
| Weight | : 3.1–3.3kg (6lb 13oz–7lb 4oz) |
| Length | : to choice |
| Barrel length | : to choice |
| Ejector | : automatic (Holland & Holland) |
| Choke | to choice |

Sight            bead
Safety           : sliding catch on neck of stock

**CHARACTERISTICS**
— material       : steel
— finish         : blued barrels, plain metal action body with remov-
                   able engraved side-lock plates, spring-loaded breech
— stock          : straight English stock of specially selected walnut
👆

## *Arrieta Model 873 Side-lock*

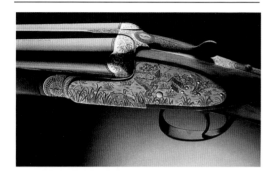

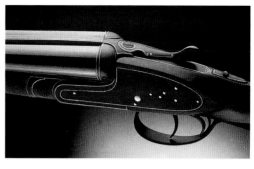

Ejector          : automatic (Holland & Holland)
Choke            to choice
Sight            bead
Safety           : sliding catch on neck of stock

**CHARACTERISTICS**
— material       : steel
— finish         : blued barrels, side-lock plates lined with gold
— stock          : straight English stock of specially selected walnut
👆

## *Arrieta Model 875 Side-lock*

**TECHNICAL DETAILS**
Gauge/calibre    : 12, 16, 20, 28, or .410
Chamber length   : 70 or 76mm (2³/₄ or 3in)
Number of barrels : double-barrels side-by-side
Action           : breech-loading
Locking          : barrel block lock
Trigger          twin triggers
Weight           : 3.2–3.4kg (7lb–7lb 8oz)
Length           : to choice
Barrel length    : to choice
Ejector          : automatic (Holland & Holland)
Choke            to choice
Sight            bead
Safety           : sliding catch on neck of stock

**CHARACTERISTICS**
— material       : steel
— finish         : blued barrels, plain metal action body with
                   engraved side-lock plates
— stock          : specially selected walnut stock, with pistol-grip
👆

## *Arrieta Model 874 Side-lock*

**TECHNICAL DETAILS**
Gauge/calibre    : 12, 16, 20, 28, or .410
Chamber length   : 70 or 76mm (2³/₄ or 3in)
Number of barrels : double-barrels side-by-side
Action           : breech-loading
Locking          : barrel block lock
Trigger          twin triggers
Weight           : 3.1–3.3kg (6lb 13oz–7lb 4oz)
Length           : to choice
Barrel length    : to choice

**TECHNICAL DETAILS**
Gauge/calibre    : 12, 16, 20, 28, or .410
Chamber length   : 70 or 76mm (2³/₄ or 3in)
Number of barrels : double-barrels side-by-side
Action           : breech-loading
Locking          : barrel block lock
Trigger          twin triggers
Weight           : 3.1–3.3kg (6lb 13oz–7lb 4oz)
Length           : to choice
Barrel length    : to choice
Ejector          : automatic (Holland & Holland)
Choke            to choice
Sight            bead
Safety           : sliding catch on neck of stock

**CHARACTERISTICS**
  material        : steel
— finish          : blued barrels, plain metal removable side-lock
                   plates, engraved and inlaid with gold

- stock    : straight English stock of specially selected walnut

A "pair" of Model 875 guns are shown with consecutive serial numbers.

## Arrieta Model 931 Side-lock

**TECHNICAL DETAILS**
Gauge/calibre    : 12, 16, 20, 28, or .410
Chamber length   : 70 or 76mm (2³/₄ or 3in)
Number of barrels : double-barrels side-by-side
Action           : breech-loading
Locking          : barrel block lock
Trigger          twin triggers
Weight           : 3.1–3.3kg (6lb 13oz–7lb 4oz)
Length           : to choice
Barrel length    : to choice
Ejector          : automatic (Holland & Holland)
Choke            to choice
Sight            bead
Safety           : sliding catch on neck of stock

**CHARACTERISTICS**
— material    : steel
— finish      : blued barrels, removable plain metal engraved side-lock plates, spring-loaded breech
— stock       : straight English stock of specially selected walnut

## Arrieta Express R-1

**TECHNICAL DETAILS**
Gauge/calibre    : 7 x 65R, 8 x 57JRS, or 9.3 x 74R
Chamber length   : not applicable
Number of barrels : double-barrels side-by-side

Action      : breech-loading
Locking     : double barrel-block locking
Trigger     twin triggers
Weight      : 3.3–3.5kg (7lb 4oz–7lb 11oz))
Length      : 104 or 108cm (41 or 42¹/₄in)
Barrel length : 60 or 65cm (23⁵/₈ or 25⁵/₈in)
Ejector     : automatic
Choke       not applicable (rifled barrel)
Sight       notched sight and bead
Safety      : sliding catch on neck of stock

**CHARACTERISTICS**
— material    : steel
— finish      : blued barrels, engraved plain metal action and side-lock plates
— stock       : straight English stock of specially selected walnut

## Arrieta Express R-2

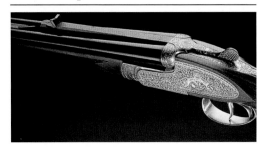

**TECHNICAL DETAILS**
Gauge/calibre    : 7 x 65R, 8 x 57JRS, or 9.3 x 74R
Chamber length   : not applicable
Number of barrels : double-barrels side-by-side
Action           : breech-loading
Locking          : double barrel-block locking
Trigger          twin triggers
Weight           : 3.4–3.6kg (7lb 8oz–7lb 14oz))
Length           : 108cm (42¹/₂in)
Barrel length    : 63.5cm (25in)
Ejector          : automatic
Choke            not applicable (rifled barrel)
Sight            notched sight and bead
Safety           : sliding catch on neck of stock

**CHARACTERISTICS**
— material    : steel
— finish      : blued barrels, engraved plain metal action and side-lock plates
— stock       : stock of specially selected walnut stock, with pistol-grip

## Arrieta Express R-3

**TECHNICAL DETAILS**
Gauge/calibre    : 7 x 65R, 8 x 57JRS, or 9.3 x 74R
Chamber length   : not applicable

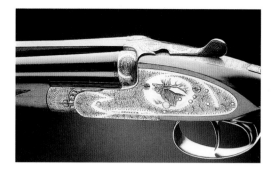

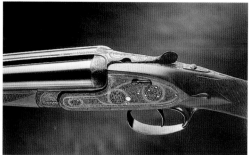

| | |
|---|---|
| Number of barrels | : double-barrels side-by-side |
| Action | : breech-loading |
| Locking | : double barrel-block locking |
| Trigger | twin triggers |
| Weight | : 3.3–3.5kg (7lb 4oz–7lb 11oz)) |
| Length | : to choice |
| Barrel length | : to choice |
| Ejector | : automatic |
| Choke | not applicable (rifled barrel) |
| Sight | notched sight and bead |
| Safety | : sliding catch on neck of stock |

**CHARACTERISTICS**

| | |
|---|---|
| — material | : steel |
| — finish | : blued barrels, engraved plain metal action and side-lock plates, special hunting engravings to choice |
| — stock | : pistol-grip and cheek plate or straight English stock of specially selected walnut |

# Aya

The gunmakers Aya have been in existence in the Basque region of Spain since 1917 when the business was founded by Nicolás Aranzábal and Miguel Aguirre. The firm is based in Eibar, which is renowned for production of armaments. Aya chiefly produces traditional side-by-side shotguns and its side-lock guns are world famous. The majority of models have double barrel block lock, sometimes combined with Kersten locking. More recently, Aya has also produced three over-and-under guns for sports shooting.

## Aya No. 1

**TECHNICAL DETAILS**

| | |
|---|---|
| Gauge/calibre | : 12 or 20 |
| Chamber length | : 70 or 76mm (2³/₄ or 3in) |
| Number of barrels | : double-barrels side-by-side |
| Action | : breech-loading |

| | |
|---|---|
| Locking | : double barrel block lock |
| Trigger | twin triggers |
| Weight | : 3.1–3.4kg (6lb 13oz–7lb 8oz) |
| Length | : 109 or 114cm (43 or 45in) |
| Barrel length | : 66 or 71cm (26 or 28in) |
| Ejector | : automatic |
| Choke | to choice |
| Sight | bead |
| Safety | : automatic safety after cocking, sliding catch on neck of stock, load indicators beside locking lever |

**CHARACTERISTICS**

| | |
|---|---|
| — material | : steel |
| — finish | : blued barrels, tempered action with floral engravings, side-lock plates can be removed by hand |
| — stock | : straight English stock of walnut |

## Aya No. 2

**TECHNICAL DETAILS**

| | |
|---|---|
| Gauge/calibre | : 12, 16, 20, 28, or .410 |
| Chamber length | : 70–76mm (2³/₄–3in) |
| Number of barrels | : double-barrels side-by-side |
| Action | : breech-loading |
| Locking | : double barrel block lock |
| Trigger | twin triggers |
| Weight | : 3.1–3.8kg (6lb 13oz–8lb 6oz) |
| Length | : 109–124cm (43–48³/₄in) |
| Barrel length | : 66–76cm (26 or 30in) |
| Ejector | : automatic |
| Choke | to choice |
| Sight | bead |

Safety            : automatic safety after cocking, sliding catch on neck of stock

**CHARACTERISTICS**
— material        : steel
— finish          : blued barrels, tempered action and side-lock plates with decorative engravings, side-lock plates can be removed by hand
— stock           : straight English stock of walnut
∽

## Aya No. 4

Trigger           single or twin triggers
Weight            : 3.1—3.8kg (6lb 13oz—8lb 6oz)
Length            : 109—124cm (43—48³/₄in)
Barrel length     : 66—76cm (26—30in)
Ejector           : automatic
Choke             to choice
Sight             bead
Safety            : automatic safety after cocking, sliding catch on neck of stock

**CHARACTERISTICS**
— material        : steel
— finish          : blued barrels, tempered action with decorative engravings
— stock           : straight English stock of walnut
∽

**TECHNICAL DETAILS**
Gauge/calibre     : 12, 16, 20, 28, or .410
Chamber length    : 70 or 76mm (2³/₄ or 3in)
Number of barrels : double-barrels side-by-side
Action            : breech-loading
Locking           : double barrel block lock
Trigger           twin triggers
Weight            : 3.1—3.8kg (6lb 13oz—8lb 6oz)
Length            : 109—124cm (43—48³/₄in)
Barrel length     : 66—76cm (26 or 30in)
Ejector           : automatic
Choke             to choice
Sight             bead
Safety            : automatic safety after cocking, sliding catch on neck of stock

**CHARACTERISTICS**
— material        : steel
— finish          : blued barrels, tempered action
— stock           : walnut stock: either straight English or with pistol-grip
∽

## Aya XXV/BL

## Aya No. 4 Deluxe

**TECHNICAL DETAILS**
Gauge/calibre     : 12, 20, 28, or .410
Chamber length    : 70 or 76mm (2³/₄ or 3in)
Number of barrels : double-barrels side-by-side
Action            : breech-loading
Locking           : double barrel block lock

**TECHNICAL DETAILS**
Gauge/calibre     : 12 or 20
Chamber length    : 70 (12) or 76mm (20) (2³/₄ or 3in)
Number of barrels : double-barrels side-by-side
Action            : breech-loading
Locking           : double barrel block lock
Trigger           twin triggers
Weight            : 3.1kg (6lb 13oz)
Length            : 109cm (43in)
Barrel length     : 63.5cm (25in)
Ejector           : automatic
Choke             to choice
Sight             bead
Safety            : automatic safety after cocking, sliding catch on neck of stock

## CHARACTERISTICS

- material : steel
- finish : blued barrels, tempered action with floral engraving
- stock : straight English stock of walnut

## Aya XXV/SL

## TECHNICAL DETAILS

Gauge/calibre : 12 or 20
Chamber length : 70 (12) or 76mm (20) (2³/₄ or 3in)
Number of barrels : double-barrels side-by-side
Action : breech-loading
Locking : double barrel block lock
Trigger : twin triggers
Weight : 3.1kg (6lb 13oz)
Length : 109cm (43in)
Barrel length : 63.5cm (25in)
Ejector : automatic
Choke : to choice
Sight : bead
Safety : automatic safety after cocking, sliding catch on neck of stock, load indicators next to locking lever

## CHARACTERISTICS

- material : steel
- finish : blued barrels, tempered action and side-lock plates with floral engravings, side-lock plates can be removed by hand
- stock : straight English stock of walnut

## Aya No. 37/Super

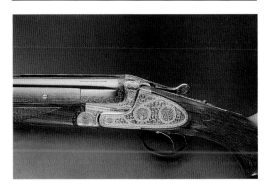

## TECHNICAL DETAILS

Gauge/calibre : 12
Chamber length : 70mm (2³/₄in)
Number of barrels : double-barrels over-and-under
Action : breech-loading
Locking : double barrel block lock and Kersten locking
Trigger : single or twin triggers
Weight : 3.7kg (8lb 3oz)
Length : 113cm (44¹/₂in)
Barrel length : 71cm (28in)
Ejector : automatic
Choke : to choice
Sight : ventilated rib and bead
Safety : sliding catch on neck of stock

## CHARACTERISTICS

- material : steel
- finish : blued barrels, plain metal action and side-lock plates with decorative engravings (Model 37/Super A) or with hunting motifs (Model 37/Super B or C)
- stock : walnut stock with pistol-grip

## Aya No. 53

## TECHNICAL DETAILS

Gauge/calibre : 12, 16, or 20
Chamber length : 70 or 76mm (2³/₄ or 3in)
Number of barrels : double-barrels side-by-side
Action : breech-loading
Locking : double barrel block lock
Trigger : twin triggers
Weight : 3.1–3.8kg (6lb 13oz–8lb 6oz)
Length : 109–124cm (43–48³/₄in)
Barrel length : 66–76cm (26–30in)
Ejector : automatic
Choke : to choice
Sight : bead
Safety : automatic safety after cocking, sliding catch on neck of stock, load indicators beside locking lever

## CHARACTERISTICS

- material : steel
- finish : blued barrels, tempered action and side-lock plates with floral engravings which are removable by hand
- stock : straight English stock of walnut

## Aya No. 56

**TECHNICAL DETAILS**

| | |
|---|---|
| Gauge/calibre | : 12 |
| Chamber length | : 70mm (2³/₄in) |
| Number of barrels | : double-barrels side-by-side |
| Action | : breech-loading |
| Locking | : double barrel block lock |
| Trigger | single or twin triggers |
| Weight | : 3.1–3.4kg (6lb 13oz–7lb 8oz) |
| Length | : 109 or 114cm (43 or 45in) |
| Barrel length | : 66 or 71cm (26 or 28in) |
| Ejector | : automatic |
| Choke | to choice |
| Sight | bead |
| Safety | : automatic safety after cocking, sliding catch on neck of stock |

**CHARACTERISTICS**

| | |
|---|---|
| — material | : steel |
| — finish | : blued barrels, tempered action and side-lock plates with decorative engravings |
| — stock | : straight English or pistol-grip walnut stocks |

## Aya Augusta

**TECHNICAL DETAILS**

| | |
|---|---|
| Gauge/calibre | : 12 |
| Chamber length | : 70mm (2³/₄in) |
| Number of barrels | : double-barrels over-and-under |
| Action | : breech-loading |
| Locking | : double barrel block lock |

| | |
|---|---|
| Trigger | single or twin triggers |
| Weight | : 3.1–3.4kg (6lb 13oz–7lb 8oz) |
| Length | : 109 or 114cm (43 or 45in) |
| Barrel length | : 66 or 71cm (26 or 28in) |
| Ejector | : automatic |
| Choke | to choice |
| Sight | ventilated rib and bead |
| Safety | : sliding catch on neck of stock |

**CHARACTERISTICS**

| | |
|---|---|
| — material | : steel |
| — finish | : blued, side-lock plates with decorative engravings |
| — stock | : walnut stock with pistol-grip |

## Aya Coral Skeet, Sporting or Trap

**TECHNICAL DETAILS**

| | |
|---|---|
| Gauge/calibre | : 12 or 20 |
| Chamber length | : 76mm (3in) |
| Number of barrels | : double-barrels over-and-under |
| Action | : breech-loading |
| Locking | : double barrel block lock and Kersten locking |
| Trigger | single or twin triggers |
| Weight | : 3.3–3.7kg (7lb 4oz–8lb 2¹/₄ oz) |
| Length | : 111–125cm (44–49in) |
| Barrel length | : 66–76cm (26–30in) |
| Ejector | : automatic or with extractor |
| Choke | set of interchangeable chokes: full, ³/₄, ¹/₂, ¹/₄, cylindrical |
| Sight | ventilated rib and bead |
| Safety | : sliding catch on neck of stock |

**CHARACTERISTICS**

| | |
|---|---|
| — material | : steel |
| — finish | : blued barrels, plain metal action |
| — stock | : walnut stock with pistol-grip |

## Aya Coral Deluxe Sporting or Trap

**TECHNICAL DETAILS**

| | |
|---|---|
| Gauge/calibre | : 12 or 20 |
| Chamber length | : 76mm (3in) |

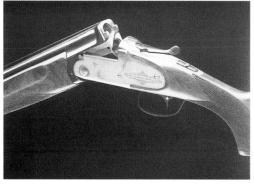

Ejector           : automatic
Choke             to choice
Sight             bead
Safety            : automatic safety after cocking, sliding catch on
                  neck of stock

**CHARACTERISTICS**
— material         : steel
— finish           : blued barrels, tempered action and side-lock plates
                  with decorative engravings
— stock            : straight English or pistol-grip walnut stocks

Number of barrels : double-barrels over-and-under
Action            : breech-loading
Locking           : double barrel block lock and Kersten locking
Trigger           single or twin triggers
Weight            : 3.3–3.7kg (7lb 4oz–8lb 2$^1$/$_4$oz)
Length            : 111–125cm (44–49in)
Barrel length     : 66–76cm (26–30in)
Ejector           : automatic
Choke             set of interchangeable chokes: full, $^3$/$_4$, $^1$/$_2$, $^1$/$_4$,
                  cylindrical
Sight             ventilated rib and bead
Safety            : sliding catch on neck of stock

**CHARACTERISTICS**
— material         : steel
— finish           : blued barrels, plain metal action body and decora-
                  tive panels (no side-lock)
— stock            : walnut stock with pistol-grip

# Aya Countryman

**TECHNICAL DETAILS**
Gauge/calibre     : 12 or 20
Chamber length    : 70mm/2$^3$/$_4$ in (12) or 76mm/3in) (20)
Number of barrels : double-barrels side-by-side
Action            : breech-loading
Locking           : double barrel block lock
Trigger           twin triggers
Weight            : 3.1–3.3kg (6lb 13oz–7lb 4oz)
Length            : 109 or 114cm (43 or 45in)
Barrel length     : 66 or 71cm (26 or 28in)

# Aya Excelsior Skeet, Sporting or Trap

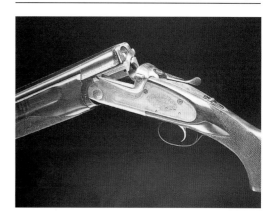

**TECHNICAL DETAILS**
Gauge/calibre     : 12 or 20
Chamber length    : 76mm (3in)
Number of barrels : double-barrels over-and-under
Action            : breech-loading
Locking           : double barrel block lock and Kersten locking
Trigger           single or twin triggers
Weight            : 3.3–3.7kg (7lb 4oz–8lb 2$^1$/$_4$oz)
Length            : 111–125cm (43$^3$/$_4$–49$^1$/$_4$in)
Barrel length     : 66–76cm (26–30in)
Ejector           : automatic or alternatively with extractor
Choke             set of interchangeable chokes: full, $^3$/$_4$, $^1$/$_2$, $^1$/$_4$,
                  cylindrical
Sight             ventilated rib and bead
Safety            : sliding catch on neck of stock

**CHARACTERISTICS**
— material         : steel
— finish           : blued barrels, plain metal action and side-lock
                  plates with decorative engravings
— stock            : walnut stock with pistol-grip

# Aya Iberia

**TECHNICAL DETAILS**
Gauge/calibre     : 12
Chamber length    : 70mm (2$^3$/$_4$in)

Weight          : 2.7–3.4kg (6lb–7lb 8oz)
Length          : 109–122cm (43–48in)
Barrel length   : 66 or 71cm (26 or 28in)
Ejector         : automatic
Choke             to choice
Sight             bead
Safety          : automatic safety after cocking, sliding catch on
                  neck of stock

**CHARACTERISTICS**
— material       : steel
— finish         : blued, with tempered action
— stock          : straight English stock of walnut
ᵥᵥ

Number of barrels : double-barrels side-by-side
Action            : breech-loading
Locking           : double barrel block lock and Kersten locking
Trigger             twin triggers
Weight            : 2.7–3.4kg (6lb–7lb 8oz)
Length            : 109–122cm (43–48in)
Barrel length     : 66 or 71cm (26 or 28in)
Ejector           : extractor
Choke               to choice
Sight               bead
Safety            : automatic safety after cocking, sliding catch on
                    neck of stock

**CHARACTERISTICS**
— material       : steel
— finish         : blued, tempered action with decorative engravings
— stock          : straight English stock of walnut
ᵥᵥ

### Aya Yeoman

**TECHNICAL DETAILS**
Gauge/calibre     : 12
Chamber length    : 70mm (2³/₄in)
Number of barrels : double-barrels side-by-side
Action            : breech-loading
Locking           : double barrel block lock
Trigger             twin triggers

# Baikal / Izhevsky Mekhanichesky Zavod

The production of sporting and hunting firearms by the Russian Izhevsk factory dates from 1885. The government of the day gave orders to the armaments works in Tula, Izhevsk, and Sestroretsk to make civilian as well as military firearms. The Russian Revolution of 1917 were turbulent times. The new Red Army modernised the weaponry of the Tsar's army but there were great shortages of both weapons and munitions. The factory in Izhevsky produced almost 1,3 million guns, 15,000 machine-guns, and 175,000 Nagant revolvers between 1918 and 1920. The factory also produced in the region of 840 million cartridges of different calibres for these weapons. The production capacity was also used for military purposes during World War II. The Izhevsky Mekhanichesky Zavod started making sporting firearms including shotguns once more in 1949. The double-barrelled Izh-49 was based on the Sauer Model 9. Baikal introduced the Izh 54 double-barrelled shotgun in 1954 that was designed by the engineers Leonid Pugachyev and Anatoly Klimov. The most popular Baikal shotgun was introduced in 1973. This is the Izh 27. Currently the factory produces a range of shotguns and combination sporting guns under the Izh name that are better known in the west under the Baikal brand name. Izhevsky also make air weapons, including the futuristic Izh 62 with its skeletal stock and Red Point sights. The Baikal firearms are always remarkably inexpensive, very robust, and reliable. Izhevsky can also

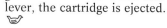
gun is broken to cock and by pulling the lever, the cartridge is ejected.

make some extremely fine guns too, as can be seen from the photographs. The finely crafted stocks and superb engraving speak for themselves.

## Baikal IZH-18M-M single-barrel

**TECHNICAL DETAILS**
| | |
|---|---|
| Gauge/calibre | : 12, 20, 28, 32, and .410 |
| Chamber length | : 70 or 76mm (2³/₄ or 3in) |
| Number of barrels | : single barrels |
| Action | : breech-loading |
| Locking | : locking lugs with cocking lever behind trigger guard |
| Trigger | single trigger |
| Weight | : 2.6–2.8kg (5lb 11¹/₂ oz–6lb 2¹/₂ oz) |
| Length | : 109 or 114cm (43 or 48 ³/₄in) |
| Barrel length | : 67.5 or 72.5cm (26¹/₂ or 28 ¹/₂in) |
| Ejector | : extractor |
| Choke | to choice, ¹/₂, ³/₄, or full |
| Sight | bead |
| Safety | : push-button above trigger |

**CHARACTERISTICS**
| | |
|---|---|
| — material | : steel |
| — finish | : blued with decorative engraving |
| — stock | : beech stock |

## Baikal IZH-18EM-M single-barrel

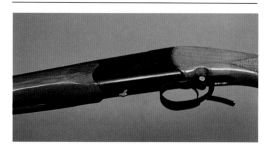

**TECHNICAL DETAILS**
| | |
|---|---|
| Gauge/calibre | : 12, 20, 28, 32, and .410 |
| Chamber length | : 70 or 76mm (2³/₄ or 3in) |
| Number of barrels | : single barrel |
| Action | : breech-loading |
| Locking | : locking lugs with cocking lever behind trigger guard |
| Trigger | single trigger |
| Weight | : 2.6–2.8kg (5lb 11¹/₂ oz–6lb 2¹/₂oz) |
| Length | : 109 or 114cm (43 or 48 ³/₄in) |
| Barrel length | : 67.5 or 72.5cm (26¹/₂ or 28 ¹/₂in) |
| Ejector | : ejector lever in bottom of action in front of trigger guard (gold-coloured lever in illustration) |
| Choke | to choice, ¹/₂, ³/₄, or full |
| Sight | bead |
| Safety | : push-button above trigger |

**CHARACTERISTICS**
| | |
|---|---|
| — material | : steel |
| — finish | : blued with decorative engraving |
| — stock | : beech stock |

This is an interesting gun for its locking mechanism and ejector lever.
The ejector works as an extractor when the

## Baikal IZH-18MN single-barrel

**TECHNICAL DETAILS**
| | |
|---|---|
| Gauge/calibre | : see below |
| Chamber length | : smooth-bore barrel 76mm (3in) |
| Number of barrels | : single barrel |
| Action | : breech-loading |
| Locking | : locking lugs with cocking lever behind trigger guard |
| Trigger | single trigger |

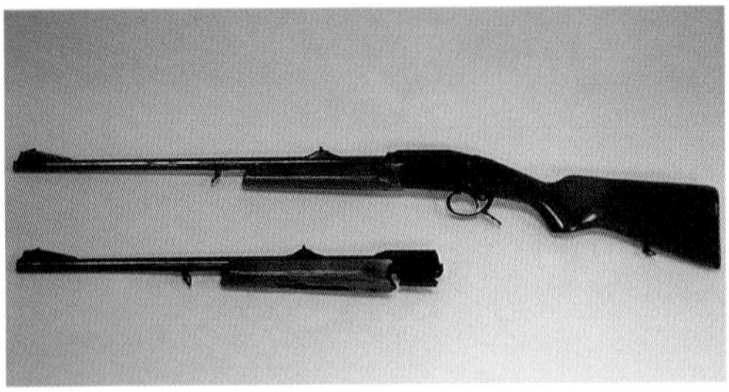

Weight : 3.2kg (7lb)
Length : 104cm (41in)
Barrel length : 60cm (23$^{5}/_{8}$in)
Ejector : extractor
Choke not applicable
Sight bead and notch
Safety : push-button above trigger

**CHARACTERISTICS**
– material : steel
– finish : blued with decorative engraving
– stock : beech stock

Available calibres/gauges: .222Rem., 5.6 x 50R Mag., 7 x 57R, 7 x 65R, 7.62 x 39mm, .308 Win., 7.62 x 53R, 9.3 x 74R; smoothbore barrel: exchangeable 12 gauge barrels for shotgun pellets or slugs (with rifling).

## *Baikal IZH-27E-CTK*

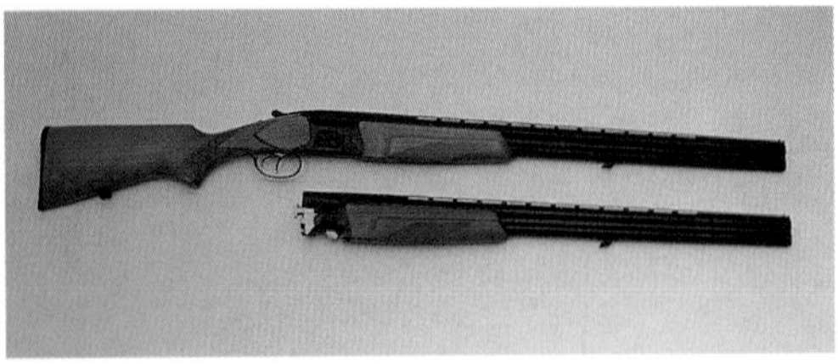

**TECHNICAL DETAILS**
Gauge/calibre : 12
Chamber length : 76mm (3in)
Number of barrels : double-barrels over-and-under
Action : breech-loading
Locking : locking lugs
Trigger twin triggers
Weight : 3.4kg (7lb 8oz)
Length : 115cm (45$^{1}/_{4}$in)
Barrel length : 72.5cm (28$^{1}/_{2}$in)
Ejector : extractor
Choke full, $^{1}/_{2}$, or interchangeable Skeet barrel
Sight ventilated rib with bead
Safety : automatic safety and sliding catch on neck of stock, dropped-gun safety

**CHARACTERISTICS**
– material : steel
– finish : blued
– stock : walnut stock

## *Baikal IZH-27EM-1C*

**TECHNICAL DETAILS**
Gauge/calibre : 12, or 16
Chamber length : 70 (2$^{3}/_{4}$) or 76mm (3in)
Number of barrels : double-barrels over-and-under
Action : breech-loading
Locking : locking lugs
Trigger single trigger
Weight : 3.4kg (7lb 8oz)
Length : 115cm (45$^{1}/_{4}$in)
Barrel length : 72.5cm (28$^{1}/_{2}$in)
Ejector : automatic
Choke full, $^{1}/_{2}$
Sight bead
Safety : sliding catch on neck of stock

**CHARACTERISTICS**
– material : steel
– finish : blued
– stock : beech or walnut stock

## *Baikal IZH-27EM-1C-M*

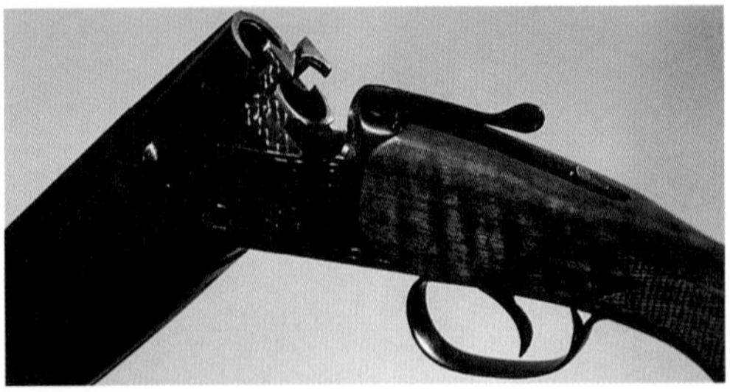

**TECHNICAL DETAILS**
Gauge/calibre : 12, or 16
Chamber length : 70 (2$^{3}/_{4}$) or 76mm (3in)
Number of barrels : double-barrels over-and-under
Action : breech-loading
Locking : locking lugs
Trigger single trigger

Weight        : 3.4kg (7lb 8oz)
Length        : 115cm (45¹/₄in)
Barrel length : 72.5cm (28¹/₂in)
Ejector       : automatic
Choke         full, ¹/₂
Sight         bead
Safety        : sliding catch on neck of stock

**CHARACTERISTICS**
— material    : steel
— finish      : blued
— stock       : beech or walnut stock

## Baikal IZH-27M

**TECHNICAL DETAILS**
Gauge/calibre      : 12, 16, or 20
Chamber length     : 70 (2³/₄) or 76mm (3in)
Number of barrels : double-barrels over-and-under
Action             : breech-loading
Locking            : locking lugs
Trigger            twin triggers
Weight             : 3.4kg (7lb 8oz)
Length             : 115cm (45¹/₄in)
Barrel length      : 72.5cm (28¹/₂in)
Ejector            : extractor
Choke              full, ¹/₂
Sight              ventilated rib with bead
Safety             : automatic safety and sliding catch on neck of stock, dropped-gun safety

**CHARACTERISTICS**
— material    : steel
— finish      : blued
— stock       : walnut stock

## Baikal IZH-27M-1C-M

**TECHNICAL DETAILS**
Gauge/calibre      : 12, 12 Magnum, or 16
Chamber length     : 70mm (2³/₄) or 76mm (3in)
Number of barrels : double-barrels over-and-under
Action             : breech-loading
Locking            : locking lugs
Trigger            single trigger
Weight             : 3.4kg (7lb 8oz)
Length             : 115cm (45¹/₄in)
Barrel length      : 72.5cm (28¹/₂in)
Ejector            : extractor
Choke              full, ¹/₂
Sight              ventilated rib with bead
Safety             : automatic safety and sliding catch on neck of stock, dropped-gun safety

**CHARACTERISTICS**
— material    : steel
— finish      : blued
— stock       : beech or walnut stock

## Baikal IZH-39 Sport

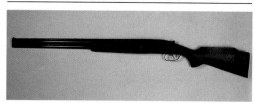

**TECHNICAL DETAILS**
Gauge/calibre      : 12
Chamber length     : 70mm (2³/₄in)
Number of barrels : double-barrels over-and-under
Action             : breech-loading
Locking            : locking lugs
Trigger            single trigger
Weight             : Skeet: 3.65 (8lb ¹/₂oz); Trap: 3.7kg (8lb 2¹/₄oz)
Length             : Skeet 110 (43¹/₄); Trap: 117.5cm (46¹/₄in)
Barrel length      : Skeet: 67.5 (26¹/₂); Trap: 75cm (29¹/₂in)
Ejector            : extractor
Choke              Skeet or Trap
Sight              ventilated rib with bead
Safety             : automatic safety and sliding catch on neck of stock, dropped-gun safety

**CHARACTERISTICS**
— material    : steel
— finish      : blued
— stock       : walnut stock

## Baikal IZH-39E Sport

**TECHNICAL DETAILS**
Gauge/calibre      : 12
Chamber length     : 70mm (2³/₄in)

Number of barrels : double-barrels over-and-under
Action : breech-loading
Locking : locking lugs
Trigger single trigger
Weight : 3.65kg (8lb ¹/₂oz) Skeet or 3.7kg (8lb 2¹/₄oz) Trap
Length : 110 (43¹/₄) Skeet or 117.5cm (46¹/₄in) Trap
Barrel length : 67.5 (26¹/₂) Skeet or 75cm (29¹/₂ in) Trap
Ejector : extractor
Choke Skeet or Trap
Sight ventilated rib with bead
Safety : automatic safety and sliding catch on neck of stock, dropped-gun safety

**CHARACTERISTICS**
— material : steel
— finish : blued
— stock : walnut stock

## *Baikal IZH-43*

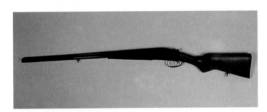

**TECHNICAL DETAILS**
Gauge/calibre : 12, or 16
Chamber length : 70mm (2³/₄in)
Number of barrels : double-barrels side-by-side

Action : breech-loading
Locking : double barrel-block locking
Trigger twin triggers
Weight : 3.4kg (7lb 8oz)
Length : 110 (43¹/₄) Skeet or 117.5cm (46¹/₄in) Trap
Barrel length : 72.5cm (28¹/₂ in)
Ejector : extractor
Choke ¹/₂ and full
Sight raised solid rib and bead
Safety : automatic safety and sliding catch on neck of stock

characteristics
— material : steel
— finish : blued
— stock : birch, beech, or walnut stock

This gun is also available with a smooth-bore barrel for slugs, with a notched sight, as Model IZH-43-1C.

## *Baikal IZH-43E*

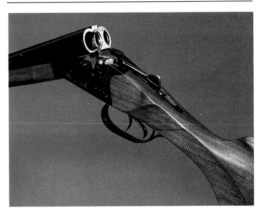

**TECHNICAL DETAILS**
Gauge/calibre : 12, or 16
Chamber length : 70mm (2³/₄in)
Number of barrels : double-barrels side-by-side
Action : breech-loading
Locking : double barrel-block locking
Trigger twin triggers
Weight : 3.4kg (7lb 8oz)
Length : 110 (43¹/₄) Skeet or 117.5cm (46¹/₄in) Trap
Barrel length : 72.5cm (28¹/₂ in)
Ejector : extractor
Choke ¹/₂ and full
Sight raised solid rib and bead
Safety : automatic safety and sliding catch on neck of stock

**CHARACTERISTICS**
— material : steel
— finish : blued
— stock : birch, beech, or walnut stock

## Baikal IZH-81KM Pump–action

**TECHNICAL DETAILS**

Gauge/calibre : 12
Chamber length : 76mm (3in)
Number of barrels : single barrel
Magazine : detachable magazine for 5 cartridges
Action : pump-action
Locking : falling-block locking
Trigger single trigger
Weight : 3.4kg (7lb 8oz)
Length : 109, 113, or 123cm (43, 44$^1$/$_2$, or 48$^1$/$_2$ in )
Barrel length : 56, 60, or 70cm (22, 23$^1$/$_2$, or 27$^1$/$_2$in)
Ejector : extractor
Choke full, cylindrical, or interchangeable chokes
Sight bead
Safety : push-button at rear of trigger guard

**CHARACTERISTICS**

— material : light alloy action, steel barrel
— finish : blued
— stock : birch, beech, or walnut stock

This gun is also available with a pistol-grip. Possession of this firearm is not permitted for hunting or other sporting purposes in a number of European countries because of the magazine capacity and short barrel-length. To hold a gun on a shotgun certifi-cate in the United Kingdom the magazine capacity must not exceed 2 cartridges and the barrel must not shorter than 24in (61cm).

## Baikal IZH-81M pump-action

**TECHNICAL DETAILS**

Gauge/calibre : 12
Chamber length : 76mm (3in)
Number of barrels : single barrel
Magazine : tubular magazine for 4 or 6 cartridges
Action : pump-action
Locking : falling block locking
Trigger single trigger
Weight : 3.4kg (7lb 8oz)
Length : 109, 113, or 123cm (43, 44$^1$/$_2$, or 48$^1$/$_2$ in )
Barrel length : 56, 60, or 70cm (22, 23$^1$/$_2$, or 27$^1$/$_2$ in)
Ejector : extractor
Choke interchangeable chokes
Sight bead
Safety : push-button at rear of trigger guard

**CHARACTERISTICS**

— material : light alloy action, steel barrel
— finish : blued
— stock : birch, beech, or walnut stock

This gun is also available with a pistol-grip. Possession of this firearm is not permitted for hunting or other sporting purposes in a number of European countries because of the magazine capacity and short barrel-length. To hold a gun on a shotgun certifi-cate in the United Kingdom the magazine capacity must not exceed 2 cartridges and the barrel must not shorter than 24in (61cm).

## Baikal IZH-94 combination gun

**TECHNICAL DETAILS**

Gauge/calibre : see below
Chamber length : smooth-bore: 12/70 (2$^3$/$_4$in), 20/76 (3in)
Number of barrels : double-barrels over-and-under
Action : breech-loading
Locking : locking lugs
Trigger twin triggers
Weight : 3.5kg (7lb 11oz)
Length : 105cm (41$^1$/$_4$in)
Barrel length : 60cm (23$^1$/$_2$ in)
Ejector : extractor
Choke bottom barrel to choice: $^1$/$_4$, $^1$/$_2$, $^3$/$_4$, or full
Sight bead, adjust. rack sight, mounting for telescopic sight
Safety : sliding catch on neck of stock which is also barrel selector

— material    : steel
— finish      : blued
— stock       : walnut stock

Available calibres for rifled barrel: .222Rem., 5.6 x 50R Mag., 6.5 x 55SE, 7 x 57R, 7 x 65R, .308 Win., 7.62 x 39mm, 7.62 x 53R, 7.62 x 54R. This gun cannot be held in the United Kingdom on a shotgun certificate.

## Baikal MP-251

**TECHNICAL DETAILS**
Gauge/calibre     : 7.62 x 51mm
Chamber length    : not relevant
Number of barrels : double-barrels over-and-under
Action            : breech-loading
Locking           : transverse Greener locking
Trigger           twin triggers
Weight            : 3.8kg (8lb 6oz)
Length            : 105cm (41¹/₄in)
Barrel length     : 60cm (23¹/₂ in)
Ejector           : extractor
Choke             not applicable
Sight             adjustable rack sight, mounting for telescopic sight
Safety            : automatic safety after cocking/breaking barrel, sliding catch on neck of stock, firing-pin safety

**CHARACTERISTICS**
— material    : steel
— finish      : blued
— stock       : beech or walnut stock

## Baikal Sever combination gun

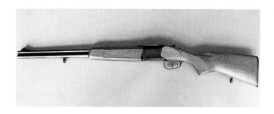

**TECHNICAL DETAILS**
Gauge/calibre     : see below
Chamber length    : bottom barrel: 12/70 (2³/₄in), 20/76 (3in)

Number of barrels : double-barrels over-and-under
Action            : breech-loading
Locking           : locking lugs
Trigger           twin triggers
Weight            : 3 or 3.2kg (6 lb 10oz or 7lb)
Length            : 105 or 115cm (41¹/₄ or 45¹/₄in)
Barrel length     : 50 or 60cm (19³/₄ or 23¹/₂ in)
Ejector           : extractor
Choke             bottom barrel ¹/₂
Sight             rack and bead sight, mounting for telescopic sight
Safety            : automatic safety, sliding catch on neck of stock

**CHARACTERISTICS**
— material    : steel
— finish      : blued
— stock       : beech or walnut stock

Available calibres/gauges for top rifled barrel: .22 LR or .22 WMR; bottom barrel: gauge 12/70mm (2³/₄in), or 20/76mm (3in). This gun cannot be held in the United Kingdom on a shotgun certificate.

# Benelli

The Italian firm of Benelli is based in the town of Urbino. Filippo and Giovanni Benelli founded their company at the beginning of the twentieth century. The company was at first best known for its mopeds but Benelli also produced machines and tools.
The company has been making firearms since 1967. In addition to the pistols for which the company is renowned, it also makes a wide range of semi-automatic shotguns.
The most technically interesting of these is the M-3 Super 90. This gun can easily be switched from semi-automatic to pump-action or vice-versa by simply twisting a steel ring on the front hand-grip a half turn.
Most Benelli shotguns are equipped with interchangeable chokes, known as "Vari-choke".
This can cause some confusion since other makers use the term for a single choke system with adjustable rings. Benelli's "Vari-choke" is supplied with five different screw-in chokes of ¹/₄, ¹/₂, ³/₄, full, and cylindrical.

## Benelli Executive I Standard

**TECHNICAL DETAILS**
Gauge/calibre     : 12

CHARACTERISTICS
— material : steel
— finish : blued barrel, plain metal action
with hunting motifs
— stock : stock of selected walnut with pistol-grip

Chamber length : 76mm (3in)
Number of barrels : single barrel
Magazine : tubular magazine for 2 or 5 cartridges
Action : semi-automatic
Locking : recoil-driven rotational locking
Trigger single trigger
Weight : 3.25kg (7 lb 2oz)
Length : 126cm (49⁵/₈in)
Barrel length : 70cm (27¹/₂ in)
Ejector : extractor
Choke interchangeable chokes
Sight ventilated rib with bead
Safety : safety catch in rear of trigger guard with red indi-
cator on the right above the trigger; closing safety

CHARACTERISTICS
— material : steel
— finish : blued barrel, plain metal action
— stock : stock of selected walnut with pistol-grip

## Benelli Executive I Varichoke

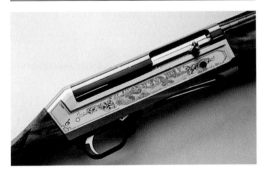

TECHNICAL DETAILS
Gauge/calibre : 12
Chamber length : 76mm (3in)
Number of barrels : single barrel
Magazine : tubular magazine for 2 or 5 cartridges
Action : semi-automatic
Locking : recoil-driven rotational locking
Trigger single trigger
Weight : 3.25kg (7 lb 2oz)
Length : 126cm (49⁵/₈in)
Barrel length : 70cm (27¹/₂ in)
Ejector : extractor
Choke Varichoke choke system
Sight ventilated rib with bead
Safety . safety catch in rear of trigger guard with red indi
cator on the right above the trigger; closing safety

## Benelli Executive II Varichoke

TECHNICAL DETAILS
Gauge/calibre : 12
Chamber length : 76mm (3in)
Number of barrels : single barrel
Magazine : tubular magazine for 2 or 5 cartridges
Action : semi-automatic
Locking : recoil-driven rotational locking
Trigger single trigger
Weight : 3.25kg (7 lb 2oz)
Length : 126cm (49⁵/₈ in)
Barrel length : 70cm (27¹/₂ in)
Ejector : extractor
Choke Varichoke choke system
Sight ventilated rib with bead
Safety : safety catch in rear of trigger guard with red indi-
cator on the right above the trigger; closing safety

CHARACTERISTICS
— material : steel
— finish : blued barrel, plain metal action engraved with
hunting motif
— stock : stock of selected walnut with pistol-grip

## Benelli Executive III Varichoke

TECHNICAL DETAILS
Gauge/calibre : 12
Chamber length : 76mm (3in)
Number of barrels : single barrel
Magazine : tubular magazine for 2 or 5 cartridges
Action : semi-automatic
Locking : recoil-driven rotational locking
Trigger single trigger
Weight : 3.25kg (7 lb 2oz)

Length            : 126cm (49⁵/₈in)
Barrel length     : 70cm (27¹/₂ in)
Ejector           : extractor
Choke             Varichoke choke system
Sight             ventilated rib with bead
Safety            : safety catch in rear of trigger guard with red indi-
                    cator on the right above the trigger; closing safety

**CHARACTERISTICS**
— material        : steel
— finish          : blued barrel, plain metal action engraved with
                    hunting motif and inlaid with gold
— stock           : stock of selected walnut with pistol-grip
🦆 🦃

## *Benelli M-1 Super 90 Hunter*

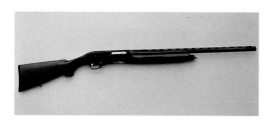

**TECHNICAL DETAILS**
Gauge/calibre     : 12
Chamber length    : 76mm (3in)
Number of barrels : single barrel
Magazine          : tubular magazine for 2 or 5 cartridges
Action            : semi-automatic
Locking           : recoil-driven rotational locking
Trigger           single trigger
Weight            : 3.1kg (6 lb 13oz)
Length            : 126cm (49⁵/₈ in)
Barrel length     : 70cm (27¹/₂in)
Ejector           : extractor
Choke             interchangeable chokes
Sight             ventilated rib with bead
Safety            : safety catch in rear of trigger guard with red
                    indicator on the right above the trigger;
                    closing safety

**CHARACTERISTICS**
— material        : steel

— finish          : matt black
— stock           : walnut stock with pistol-grip
🦆 🦃

## *Benelli M-1 Super 90 Hunter 'All Weather'*

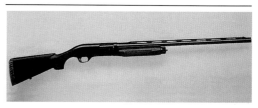

**TECHNICAL DETAILS**
Gauge/calibre     : 12
Chamber length    : 76mm (3in)
Number of barrels : single barrel
Magazine          : tubular magazine for 2 or 5 cartridges
Action            : semi-automatic
Locking           : recoil-driven rotational locking
Trigger           single trigger
Weight            : 3.1kg (6 lb 13oz)
Length            : 126cm (49⁵/₈in)
Barrel length     : 70cm (27¹/₂ in)
Ejector           : extractor
Choke             interchangeable chokes
Sight             ventilated rib with bead
Safety            : safety catch in rear of trigger guard with red indi-
                    cator on the right above the trigger; closing safety

**CHARACTERISTICS**
— material        : steel
— finish          : matt black
— stock           : black plastic stock with pistol-grip
🦆 🦃

## *Benelli M-1 Super 90 Standard*

**TECHNICAL DETAILS**
Gauge/calibre     : 12
Chamber length    : 76mm (3in)
Number of barrels : single barrel
Magazine          : tubular magazine for 2–6 cartridges
Action            : semi-automatic
Locking           : recoil-driven rotational locking
Trigger           single trigger
Weight            : 3.2kg (7 lb)
Length            : 106cm (41³/₄in)

| | |
|---|---|
| Barrel length | : 50cm (19³/₄in) |
| Ejector | : extractor |
| Choke | cylindrical |
| Sight | rack and bead sight |
| Safety | : safety catch in rear of trigger guard with red indicator on the right above the trigger; closing safety |

### CHARACTERISTICS

| | |
|---|---|
| — material | : steel |
| — finish | : matt black |
| — stock | : black plastic stock |

The Benelli M-1 Super 90 Standard is illustrated above in versions with a standard stock and also with a pistol-grip. Possession of this firearm is not permitted for hunting or other sporting purposes in a number of European countries because of the magazine capacity and short barrel-length. To hold a gun on a shotgun certificate in the United Kingdom the magazine capacity must not exceed 2 cartridges and the barrel must not shorter than 24in (61cm).

## Benelli M-3 Super 90 Hunter Varichoke

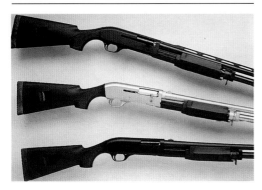

### TECHNICAL DETAILS

| | |
|---|---|
| Gauge/calibre | : 12 |
| Chamber length | : 76mm (3in) |
| Number of barrels | : single barrel |
| Magazine | : tubular magazine for 2, 4, or 6 cartridges |
| Action | : semi-automatic and pump-action |
| Locking | : recoil-driven rotational locking or pump-action |
| Trigger | single trigger |
| Weight | : 3.4kg (7 lb 8oz) |
| Length | : 122cm (48in) |
| Barrel length | : 66cm (26in) |
| Ejector | : extractor |
| Choke | interchangeable chokes |
| Sight | ventilated rib and bead |
| Safety | : safety catch in rear of trigger guard with red indicator on the right above the trigger; closing safety |

### CHARACTERISTICS

| | |
|---|---|
| — material | : steel |
| — finish | : matt black |
| — stock | : black plastic stock |

The unusual combination of cocking mechanisms on this gun can be switched between semi-automatic and pump-action by turning the ring on the front hand grip (by the sling swivel) Pictured above are the Benelli M-3 Super 90 Hunter Varichoke, M-3 Super 90 Chrome, and M-3 Super 90 Standard. The 4, or 6 cartridge magazines are not permitted for use in the U.K. To hold a gun on a shotgun certificate in the U.K. the magazine capacity must not exceed 2 cartridges and the barrel must not shorter than 24in (61cm).

## Benelli M-3 Super 90 Chrome

### TECHNICAL DETAILS

| | |
|---|---|
| Gauge/calibre | : 12 |
| Chamber length | : 76mm (3in) |
| Number of barrels | : single barrel |
| Magazine | : tubular magazine for 2–6 cartridges |
| Action | : semi-automatic and pump-action |
| Locking | : recoil-driven rotational locking or pump-action |
| Trigger | single trigger |
| Weight | : 3.3kg (7 lb 4oz) |
| Length | : 106cm (41³/₄in) |
| Barrel length | : 50cm (19³/₄ in) |
| Ejector | : extractor |
| Choke | cylindrical |
| Sight | rack and bead |
| Safety | : safety catch in rear of trigger guard with red indicator on the right above the trigger; closing safety |

### CHARACTERISTICS

| | |
|---|---|
| — material | : steel |
| — finish | : matt chrome (stainless-steel look) |
| — stock | : black plastic stock, with pistol-grip |

The unusual combination of cocking mechanisms on this gun can be switched between semi-automatic and pump-action by turning the ring on the front hand grip (by the sling swivel) Possession of this firearm is not permitted for hunting or other sporting purposes in a number of European countries because of the magazine capacity and short barrel-length. To hold a gun on a shotgun certificate in the United Kingdom the magazine capacity must not exceed 2 cartridges and the barrel must not shorter than 24in (61cm).

## Benelli M-3 Super 90 Standard

**TECHNICAL DETAILS**

| | |
|---|---|
| Gauge/calibre | : 12 |
| Chamber length | : 76mm (3in) |
| Number of barrels | : single barrel |
| Magazine | : tubular magazine for 2–6 cartridges |
| Action | : semi-automatic and pump-action |
| Locking | : recoil-driven rotational locking or pump-action |
| Trigger | single trigger |
| Weight | : 3.3kg (7 lb 4oz) |
| Length | : 106cm (41³/₄in) |
| Barrel length | : 50cm (19³/₄in) |
| Ejector | : extractor |
| Choke | cylindrical |
| Sight | rack and bead |
| Safety | : safety catch in rear of trigger guard with red indicator on the right above the trigger; closing safety |

**CHARACTERISTICS**

| | |
|---|---|
| — material | : steel |
| — finish | : matt black |
| — stock | : black plastic stock |

The unusual combination of cocking mechanisms on this gun can be switched between semi-automatic and pump-action by turning the ring on the front hand grip (by the sling swivel) Possession of this firearm is not permitted for hunting or other sporting purposes in a number of European countries because of the magazine capacity and short barrel-length. To hold a gun on a shotgun certificate in the United Kingdom the magazine capacity must not exceed 2 cartridges and the barrel must not shorter than 24in (61cm).

## Benelli Mancino, left-handed version

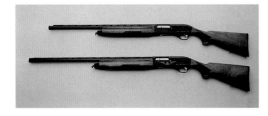

**TECHNICAL DETAILS**

| | |
|---|---|
| Gauge/calibre | : 12 |

| | |
|---|---|
| Chamber length | : 76mm (3in) |
| Number of barrels | : single barrel |
| Magazine | : tubular magazine for 2 or 5 cartridges |
| Action | : semi-automatic |
| Locking | : recoil-driven rotational locking |
| Trigger | single trigger |
| Weight | : 3.1–3.3kg (6lb 13oz–7 lb 4oz) |
| Length | : 116 or 126cm (45³/₄–49⁵/₈in) |
| Barrel length | : 61 or 70cm (24 or 27¹/₂ in) |
| Ejector | : extractor |
| Choke | fixed chokes: ¹/₂ or ³/₄, or interchangeable chokes |
| Sight | ventilated rib and bead |
| Safety | : safety catch in rear of trigger guard with red indicator on the right above the trigger; closing safety |

**CHARACTERISTICS**

| | |
|---|---|
| — material | : steel barrel, light alloy action |
| — finish | : blued |
| — stock | : walnut left-handed stock with pistol-grip |

## Benelli Montefeltro 20E

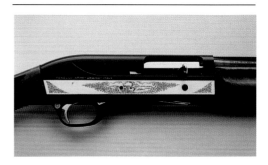

**TECHNICAL DETAILS**

| | |
|---|---|
| Gauge/calibre | : 20 |
| Chamber length | : 76mm (3in) |
| Number of barrels | : single barrel |
| Magazine | : tubular magazine for 2 or 5 cartridges |
| Action | : semi-automatic |
| Locking | : recoil-driven rotational locking |
| Trigger | single trigger |
| Weight | : 3.2kg (7 lb) |
| Length | : 121cm (47⁵/₈in) |
| Barrel length | : 65cm (25⁵/₈in) |
| Ejector | : extractor |
| Choke | interchangeable chokes |
| Sight | ventilated rib and bead |
| Safety | : safety catch in rear of trigger guard with red indicator on the right above the trigger; closing safety |

**CHARACTERISTICS**

| | |
|---|---|
| — material | : steel barrel, light alloy action |
| — finish | : blued, silver-coloured banding on action |
| — stock | : walnut stock with pistol-grip |

## Benelli Raffaello SL121 Varichoke

### TECHNICAL DETAILS
Gauge/calibre : 12
Chamber length : 70mm (2³/₄in)
Number of barrels : single barrel
Magazine : tubular magazine for 2 or 5 cartridges
Action : semi-automatic
Locking : recoil-driven rotational locking
Trigger single trigger
Weight : 3.1kg (6lb 13oz)
Length : 116cm (45³/₄in)
Barrel length : 61cm (24in)
Ejector : extractor
Choke interchangeable chokes
Sight ventilated rib and bead
Safety : safety catch in rear of trigger guard with red indicator on the right above the trigger; closing safety

### CHARACTERISTICS
— material : steel
— finish : blued
— stock : walnut stock with pistol-grip

## Benelli Raffaello SL123 Slug

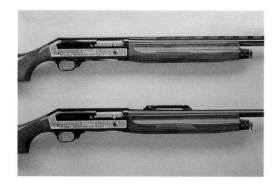

### TECHNICAL DETAILS
Gauge/calibre : 12
Chamber length : 76mm (3in)
Number of barrels : single barrel
Magazine : tubular magazine for 2 or 5 cartridges
Action : semi-automatic
Locking : recoil-driven rotational locking
Trigger single trigger
Weight : 3.2kg (7lb)
Length : 106cm (41³/₄in)

Barrel length : 50cm (19³/₄in)
Ejector : extractor
Choke cylindrical
Sight fold-down rack sight and rail for telesc. sight mounting
Safety : safety catch in rear of trigger guard with red indicator on the right above the trigger; closing safety

### CHARACTERISTICS
— material : steel
— finish : blued barrel, plain metal action with floral engraving
— stock : walnut stock with pistol-grip

Illustrated from top to bottom: Raffaello SL123 Varichoke and Raffaello SL123 Slug. Possession of this firearm is not permitted for hunting or other sporting purposes in a number of European countries because of the magazine capacity and short barrel-length. The 5 cartridge magazine is not permitted for use under a shotgun certificate in the United Kingdom. Shotguns are not permitted to exceed a magazine capacity of 2 in the magazine and 1 in the barrel.

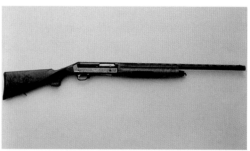

## Benelli Raffaello SL123 Varichoke

### TECHNICAL DETAILS
Gauge/calibre : 12
Chamber length : 70mm (2³/₄in)
Number of barrels : single barrel
Magazine : tubular magazine for 2 or 5 cartridges
Action : semi-automatic
Locking : recoil-driven rotational locking
Trigger single trigger
Weight : 3.1kg (6lb 13oz)
Length : 116cm (45³/₄in)
Barrel length : 61cm (24in)
Ejector : extractor
Choke interchangeable chokes
Sight ventilated rib and bead
Safety : safety catch in rear of trigger guard with red indicator on the right above the trigger; closing safety

### CHARACTERISTICS
— material : steel
— finish : blued barrel, plain metal action with floral engraving
— stock : walnut stock with pistol-grip

## Benelli Raffaello Special Lusso Varichoke

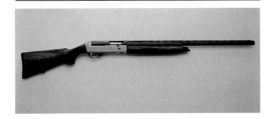

### TECHNICAL DETAILS

Gauge/calibre : 12
Chamber length : 70mm (2³/₄in)
Number of barrels : single barrel
Magazine : tubular magazine for 2 or 5 cartridges
Action : semi-automatic
Locking : recoil-driven rotational locking
Trigger single trigger
Weight : 3.1kg (6lb 13oz)
Length : 112cm (44¹/₄in)
Barrel length : 61cm (24in)
Ejector : extractor
Choke interchangeable chokes
Sight ventilated rib and bead
Safety : safety catch in rear of trigger guard with red indicator on the right above the trigger; closing safety

### CHARACTERISTICS

— material : steel
— finish : blued barrel, nickel-coated action with floral engraving
— stock : walnut stock with pistol-grip

## Benelli Raffaello Special Magnum

### TECHNICAL DETAILS

Gauge/calibre : 12
Chamber length : 76mm (3in)
Number of barrels : single barrel
Magazine : tubular magazine for 2 or 5 cartridges
Action : semi-automatic
Locking : recoil-driven rotational locking
Trigger single trigger
Weight : 3.3kg (7lb 4oz)
Length : 126cm (49⁵/₈in)
Barrel length : 75cm (29¹/₂in)
Ejector : extractor

Choke full choke
Sight ventilated rib and bead
Safety : safety catch in rear of trigger guard with red indicator on the right above the trigger; closing safety

### CHARACTERISTICS

— material : steel
— finish : blued barrel, nickel coated action
— stock : walnut stock with pistol-grip

## Benelli Super Black Eagle

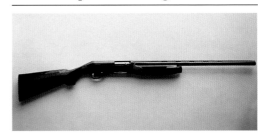

### TECHNICAL DETAILS

Gauge/calibre : 12
Chamber length : 89mm (3¹/₂ in)
Number of barrels : single barrel
Magazine : tubular magazine for 2 or 5 cartridges
Action : semi-automatic
Locking : recoil-driven rotational locking
Trigger single trigger
Weight : 3.1–3.3kg (6lb 13oz–7lb 4oz)
Length : 106, 111, or 116cm (41³/₄, 43³/₄, or 45³/₄in)
Barrel length : 61, 66, or 71cm (24, 26, or 28in)
Ejector : extractor
Choke interchangeable chokes
Sight ventilated rib and bead
Safety : safety catch in rear of trigger guard with red indicator on the right above the trigger; closing safety

### CHARACTERISTICS

— material : steel
— finish : blued
— stock : walnut stock with pistol-grip

# Beretta

Beretta is one of Europe's oldest gunmakers. Bartolomeo Beretta had a small gunsmith's workshop at Gardone in the Valle Trompia region of Italy, in the fifteenth century. Beretta mainly produced barrels for other gunsmiths. His son Giovannino followed in his father's footsteps and became a

renowned master gunsmith. Under his hand, the firm turned to making complete rifles and shotguns. By the late eighteenth century, the company was in the hands of Pietro Beretta who won huge orders to make guns for Napoleon's army. After the Battle of Waterloo, the demand for weapons was significantly reduced and so Pietro switched per force to making sporting and hunting guns. Pietro's son, Giuseppe, developed the firm into a substantial business between 1840–1865 and at the beginning of the twentieth century, his son, also named Pietro, introduced modern production techniques. Subsequent generations of the family in the form of Giuseppe and Carlo Beretta turned the business into a multinational enterprise with a subsidiary in the United States of America, France, Brazil, and Greece. Currently the business is headed by Ugo Gussalli Beretta. The company is renowned for production of military firearms, shotguns, sporting rifles, and pistols. A major breakthrough for the company was the choice by the US Army of the 9mm Para calibre Beretta M92-F pistol. To overcome the objections to the award being made to a foreign company, Beretta USA was established at Accokeek in Maryland. Most Beretta shotguns are equipped with a set of interchangeable chokes from full, through 3/4, 1/2, 1/4, and cylindrical. The sporting shotguns are also equipped with a Skeet choke tube. All modern Beretta chokes are suitable for use with steel shot.

**CHARACTERISTICS**
- material : steel
- finish : blued, with choice of engraving
- stock : walnut stock with pistol-grip

This gun is also available in Trap, Mono-Trap (single-barrel), Skeet, and Sporting models.

## Beretta Model ASE 90 Sporting

**TECHNICAL DETAILS**

| | |
|---|---|
| Gauge/calibre | : 12 |
| Chamber length | : 70mm (2³/₄in) |
| Number of barrels | : double-barrels over-and-under |
| Action | : breech-loading |
| Locking | : locking lugs on either side of top barrel with bolt in action |
| Trigger | single trigger |
| Weight | : 3.6–4kg (7lb 14³/₄oz–8lb 12³/₄oz) |
| Length | : 119–131cm (46⁷/₈, 51⁵/₈ in) |
| Barrel length | : 71–86cm (28–33⁷/₈in) |
| Ejector | : automatic |
| Choke | Mobil-choke interchangeable chokes |
| Sight | ventilated rib and bead |
| Safety | : sliding catch on neck of stock |

## Beretta A302

**TECHNICAL DETAILS**

| | |
|---|---|
| Gauge/calibre | : 12 |
| Chamber length | : 70 or 76mm (2³/₄ or 3in) |
| Number of barrels | : single-barrel |
| Magazine | : tubular magazine for 2 cartridges |

| | |
|---|---|
| Action | : semi-automatic (gas-operated) |
| Locking | : falling block locking |
| Trigger | single trigger |
| Weight | : 2.9–3.1kg (6lb 6oz–6lb 13oz) |
| Length | : 111–121cm (43³/₄–47⁵/₈ in) |
| Barrel length | : 66–76cm (26–30in) |
| Ejector | : extractor |
| Choke | Mobil-choke interchangeable chokes |
| Sight | ventilated rib and bead |
| Safety | : push-button safety catch in front of trigger guard |

**CHARACTERISTICS**

| | |
|---|---|
| — material | : steel barrel, light alloy action |
| — finish | : blued |
| — stock | : walnut stock with pistol-grip |

Illustrated from top to bottom: the A302 and A302 Supper Lusso with additional engraving.

## Beretta A303 Deluxe

**TECHNICAL DETAILS**

| | |
|---|---|
| Gauge/calibre | : 12 |
| Chamber length | : 70 or 76mm (2³/₄ or 3in) |
| Number of barrels | : single-barrel |
| Magazine | : tubular magazine for 2 cartridges |
| Action | : semi-automatic (gas-operated) |
| Locking | : falling block locking |
| Trigger | single trigger |
| Weight | : 2.7–3.4kg (6lb–7lb 8oz) |
| Length | : 106–126cm (41³/₄–49⁵/₈ in) |
| Barrel length | : 61–81cm (24–32in) |
| Ejector | : extractor |
| Choke | Mobil-choke interchangeable chokes |
| Sight | ventilated rib and bead |
| Safety | : push-button safety catch in front of trigger guard |

**CHARACTERISTICS**

| | |
|---|---|
| — material | : steel |

| | |
|---|---|
| — finish | : blued |
| — stock | : walnut stock with pistol-grip |

## Beretta A303 Field

**TECHNICAL DETAILS**

| | |
|---|---|
| Gauge/calibre | : 12 |
| Chamber length | : 70 or 76mm (2³/₄ or 3in) |
| Number of barrels | : single-barrel |
| Magazine | : tubular magazine for 2 cartridges |
| Action | : semi-automatic (gas-operated) |
| Locking | : falling block locking |
| Trigger | single trigger |
| Weight | : 3.3kg (7lb 4oz) |
| Length | : 111 or 116cm (43³/₄–45⁵/₈ in) |
| Barrel length | : 66–71cm (26–28in) |
| Ejector | : extractor |
| Choke | Mobil-choke interchangeable chokes |
| Sight | ventilated rib and bead |
| Safety | : push-button safety catch in front of trigger guard |

**CHARACTERISTICS**

| | |
|---|---|
| — material | : steel |
| — finish | : blued |
| — stock | : walnut stock with pistol-grip |

## Beretta A303 Slug

**TECHNICAL DETAILS**

| | |
|---|---|
| Gauge/calibre | : 12 or 20 |
| Chamber length | : 70 or 76mm (2³/₄ or 3in) |
| Number of barrels | : single-barrel |
| Magazine | : tubular magazine for 2 cartridges |
| Action | : semi-automatic (gas-operated) |
| Locking | : falling block locking |
| Trigger | single trigger |
| Weight | : 3.2kg (7lb) |
| Length | : 104cm (41in) |
| Barrel length | : 56cm (22in) |
| Ejector | : extractor |
| Choke | cylindrical for slugs |
| Sight | rack and bead |

| Safety | : push-button safety catch in front of trigger guard |

**CHARACTERISTICS**
| — material | : steel |
| — finish | : blued |
| — stock | : walnut stock with pistol-grip |

Possession of this firearm is not permitted for hunting or other sporting purposes in a number of European countries because of the short barrel-length. The law in United Kingdom requires the barrel of a shotgun to be a minimum of 24in (61cm).

## Beretta A303 Skeet

**TECHNICAL DETAILS**
| Gauge/calibre | : 12 or 20 |
| Chamber length | : 70mm (2³/₄in) |
| Number of barrels | : single-barrel |
| Magazine | : tubular magazine for 2 cartridges |
| Action | : semi-automatic (gas-operated) |
| Locking | : falling block locking |
| Trigger | single trigger |
| Weight | : 2.8–3.2kg (6lb 2¹/₂ oz–7lb) |
| Length | : 111 or 116cm (43³/₄–45⁵/₈ in) |
| Barrel length | : 66–71cm (26–28in) |
| Ejector | : extractor |
| Choke | Skeet choke |
| Sight | ventilated rib and bead |
| Safety | : push-button safety catch in front of trigger guard |

**CHARACTERISTICS**
| — material | : steel |
| — finish | : blued |
| — stock | : walnut stock with pistol-grip |

## Beretta A303 Trap

**TECHNICAL DETAILS**
| Gauge/calibre | : 12 |
| Chamber length | : 70mm (2³/₄in) |
| Number of barrels | : single-barrel |
| Magazine | : tubular magazine for 2 cartridges |
| Action | : semi-automatic (gas-operated) |
| Locking | : falling block locking |
| Trigger | single trigger |
| Weight | : 3.5–3.6kg (7lb 11oz–7lb 14³/₄oz) |
| Length | : 120 or 126cm (47¹/₄–49⁵/₈ in) |
| Barrel length | : 76 or 81cm (30 or 32in) |
| Ejector | : extractor |
| Choke | Full or special Trap choke |
| Sight | ventilated rib and bead |
| Safety | : push-button safety catch in front of trigger guard |

**CHARACTERISTICS**
| — material | : steel |
| — finish | : blued |
| — stock | : walnut stock with pistol-grip |

## Beretta A303 Youth

**TECHNICAL DETAILS**
| Gauge/calibre | : 20 |
| Chamber length | : 70mm (2³/₄in) |
| Number of barrels | : single-barrel |
| Magazine | : tubular magazine for 2 cartridges |
| Action | : semi-automatic (gas-operated) |
| Locking | : falling block locking |
| Trigger | single trigger |
| Weight | : 2.7kg (6lb) |
| Length | : 104cm (41in) |
| Barrel length | : 61cm (24in) |
| Ejector | : extractor |
| Choke | Mobil-choke interchangeable chokes |
| Sight | ventilated rib and bead |
| Safety | : push-button safety catch in front of trigger guard |

**CHARACTERISTICS**
| — material | : steel |
| — finish | : blued |
| — stock | : walnut stock with pistol-grip |

## Beretta A304

**TECHNICAL DETAILS**
| Gauge/calibre | : 12 |
| Chamber length | : 70 or 76mm (2³/₄ or 3in) |
| Number of barrels | : single-barrel |

Magazine              : tubular magazine for 2 cartridges
Action                : semi-automatic (gas-operated)
Locking               : falling block locking
Trigger               single trigger
Weight                : 2.9–3.3kg (6lb 6oz–7lb 4oz)
Length                : 111–126cm (43³/₄–49⁵/₈ in)
Barrel length         : 61–76cm (24–30in)
Ejector               : extractor
Choke                 Mobil-choke interchangeable chokes
Sight                 ventilated rib and bead
Safety                : push-button safety catch in front of trigger guard

**CHARACTERISTICS**
— material            : steel
— finish              : blued
— stock               : walnut stock with pistol-grip

## Beretta A304 Gold Lark

**TECHNICAL DETAILS**
Gauge/calibre         : 12
Chamber length        : 70 or 76mm (2³/₄ or 3in)
Number of barrels : single-barrel
Magazine              : tubular magazine for 2 cartridges
Action                : semi-automatic (gas-operated)
Locking               : falling block locking
Trigger               single trigger
Weight                : 2.9–3.3kg (6lb 6oz–7lb 4oz)
Length                : 111–126cm (43³/₄–49⁵/₈ in)
Barrel length         : 61–76cm (24–30in)
Ejector               : extractor
Choke                 Mobil-choke interchangeable chokes
Sight                 ventilated rib and bead
Safety                : push-button safety catch in front of trigger guard

**CHARACTERISTICS**
— material            : steel
— finish              : blued, with inlaid gold engravings on action
— stock               : walnut stock with pistol-grip

## Beretta A390 Gold Mallard

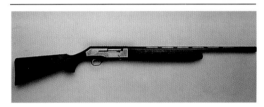

**TECHNICAL DETAILS**
Gauge/calibre         : 12
Chamber length        : 70 or 76mm (2³/₄ or 3in)
Number of barrels : single-barrel
Magazine              : tubular magazine for 2 cartridges
Action                : semi-automatic (gas-operated)
Locking               : falling block locking
Trigger               single trigger
Weight                : 3.3–3.4kg (7lb 4oz–7lb 8oz)
Length                : 111–126cm (43³/₄–49⁵/₈ in)
Barrel length         : 61–76cm (24–30in)
Ejector               : extractor
Choke                 Mobil-choke interchangeable chokes
Sight                 ventilated rib and bead
Safety                : push-button safety catch in front of trigger guard

**CHARACTERISTICS**
— material            : steel
— finish              : blued, with plain metal side-plates on action or
                        entirely blued with inlaid gold engravings on action
— stock               : walnut stock with pistol-grip

The A390 is also available in Sport Trap, Sport Super Trap, Sport Skeet, Sport Super Skeet, Sport Sporting, and Sport Super Sporting versions.

## Beretta A390 Hunter Camo

### TECHNICAL DETAILS

Gauge/calibre : 12
Chamber length : 76mm (3in)
Number of barrels : single-barrel
Magazine : tubular magazine for 2 cartridges
Action : semi-automatic (gas-operated)
Locking : falling block locking
Trigger single trigger
Weight : 3.3 or 3.4kg (7lb 4oz or 7lb 8oz)
Length : 116 or 126cm (45³/₄ or 49⁵/₈ in)
Barrel length : 66 or 76cm (26 or 30in)
Ejector : extractor
Choke Mobil-choke interchangeable chokes
Sight ventilated rib and bead
Safety : push-button safety catch in front of trigger guard

### CHARACTERISTICS

— material : steel
— finish : special camouflage coating
— stock : plastic stock with coating of camouflage colours and pistol-grip

## Beretta Collection '95/'96

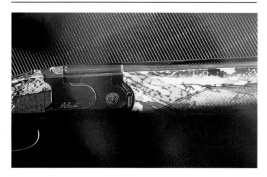

### TECHNICAL DETAILS

Gauge/calibre : 12
Chamber length : 70 or 76mm (2³/₄ or 3in)
Number of barrels : double-barrels over-and-under
Action : breech loading
Locking : conical lugs (Beretta patent)
Trigger single trigger
Weight : 3.5 or 3.6kg (7lb 11oz or 7lb 14³/₄oz)
Length : 116 or 120cm (45³/₄ or 47¹/₄in)
Barrel length · 71 or 76cm (28 or 30in)
Ejector : automatic
Choke Mobil-choke interchangeable chokes

Sight ventilated rib and bead
Safety : sliding catch on neck of stock

### CHARACTERISTICS

— material : steel
— finish : blued
— stock : brightly-coloured walnut stock and fore-end, with pistol-grip

## Beretta 426E

### TECHNICAL DETAILS

Gauge/calibre : 12 or 20
Chamber length : 70 or 76mm (2³/₄ or 3in)
Number of barrels : double-barrels side-by-side
Action : breech-loading
Locking : barrel-block locking
Trigger single trigger
Weight : 3—3.3kg (6lb 9¹/₂ oz—7lb 4oz)
Length : 111—121cm (43³/₄—47⁵/₈ in)
Barrel length : 67, 71, or 76cm (26³/₈, 28, or 30in)
Ejector : automatic
Choke ³/₄ and ¹/₄, ³/₄and ¹/₂, full and ¹/₂, or ¹/₂ and ¹/₄ chokes
Sight bead
Safety : sliding catch on neck of stock

### CHARACTERISTICS

— material : steel
— finish : blued, with chrome-plated and engraved action
— stock : walnut stock with pistol-grip

# Beretta 451 EELL

**TECHNICAL DETAILS**

Gauge/calibre : 12
Chamber length : 70mm (2³/₄in)
Number of barrels : double-barrels side-by-side
Action : breech-loading
Locking : double barrel-block locking
Trigger single or twin triggers
Weight : 3–3.3kg (6lb 9¹/₂oz–7lb 4oz)
Length : 111–121cm (43³/₄–47⁵/₈ in)
Barrel length : 66–75cm (26–29¹/₂ in)
Ejector : automatic
Choke fixed chokes to choice
Sight bead
Safety : sliding catch on neck of stock

**CHARACTERISTICS**

— material : steel
— finish : blued, with silvered and engraved action and side-lock plates
— stock : walnut with pistol-grip or straight English stock

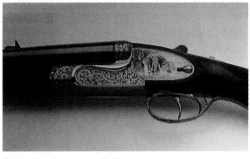

# Beretta 452 EELL

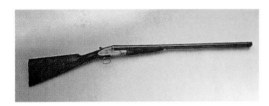

**TECHNICAL DETAILS**

Gauge/calibre : 12
Chamber length : 70mm (2³/₄in) or 76mm (3in) on request
Number of barrels : double-barrels side-by-side
Action : breech-loading
Locking : double barrel-block locking
Trigger twin triggers
Weight : 3–3.2kg (6lb 9¹/₂ oz–7lb)
Length : 111–120cm (43³/₄–47¹/₄in)
Barrel length : 67, 71, or 75cm (26³/₈, 28, or 29¹/₂ in)
Ejector : automatic
Choke fixed chokes to choice
Sight bead
Safety : sliding catch on neck of stock

**CHARACTERISTICS**

— material : steel
— finish : blued barrels, plain metal action with engraved side-lock plates
— stock : straight English stock of specially-selected walnut

# Beretta 455 EELL Express

**TECHNICAL DETAILS**

Gauge/calibre : see below

Chamber length : not applicable
Number of barrels : double-barrels side-by-side
Action : breech-loading
Locking : double barrel-block locking and Greener locking
Trigger twin triggers
Weight : 5 or 5.1kg (11lb–11lb 4oz)
Length : 101 or 106cm (39³/₄–41³/₄in)
Barrel length : 60 or 65cm (23⁵/₈ or 25⁵/₈ in)
Ejector : extractor
Choke not applicable, rifled barrels
Sight fold-down rack and bead
Safety : sliding catch on neck of stock

**CHARACTERISTICS**

— material : steel
— finish : blued barrels, plain metal action with engraved side-lock plates
— stock : walnut stock, with pistol-grip

Available calibres: .375 H&H Mag., .416 Rigby, .470 NE, or .500 NE (Nitro Express

# Beretta Model 470 Silver Hawk

**TECHNICAL DETAILS**

Gauge/calibre : 12 or 20
Chamber length : 70mm (2³/₄in) or 76mm (3in)
Number of barrels : double-barrels side-by-side
Action : breech-loading
Locking : barrel-block locking
Trigger single or twin triggers
Weight : 2.7–3.2kg (6lb–7lb)

| Length | : 108 or 121cm (42$^1/_2$ or 47$^5/_8$in) |
|---|---|
| Barrel length | : 62–76cm (24$^3/_8$–30in) |
| Ejector | : automatic |
| Choke | fixed: $^1/_2$ and full, or $^1/_4$ and $^3/_4$ |
| Sight | bead |
| Safety | : sliding catch on neck of stock |

### CHARACTERISTICS

| — material | : steel |
|---|---|
| — finish | : blued barrels and silvered action with decorative engraving |
| — stock | : straight English stock of walnut |

## Beretta 626E

### TECHNICAL DETAILS

| Gauge/calibre | : 12 or 20 |
|---|---|
| Chamber length | : 70mm (2$^3/_4$in) or 76mm (3in) |
| Number of barrels | : double-barrels side-by-side |
| Action | : breech-loading |
| Locking | : barrel-block locking |
| Trigger | single or twin triggers |
| Weight | : 2.7–3.2kg (6lb–7lb) |
| Length | : 112 or 117cm (44$^1/_8$–46in) |
| Barrel length | : 66 or 71cm (26 or 28in) |
| Ejector | : automatic |
| Choke | fixed: $^1/_2$ and full, or $^1/_4$ and $^3/_4$, or Mobil-choke set |
| Sight | bead |
| Safety | : sliding catch on neck of stock |

### CHARACTERISTICS

| — material | : steel |
|---|---|
| — finish | : blued barrels and engraved plain metal action |
| — stock | : straight English stock of walnut |

The Beretta 626E and 626 Onyx are illustrated.

## Beretta 626 Onyx

### TECHNICAL DETAILS

| Gauge/calibre | : 12 or 20 |
|---|---|
| Chamber length | : 70mm (2$^3/_4$in) or 76mm (3in) |

| Number of barrels | : double-barrels side-by-side |
|---|---|
| Action | : breech-loading |
| Locking | : barrel-block locking |
| Trigger | single trigger |
| Weight | : 2.7–3.2kg (6lb–7lb) |
| Length | : 112cm (44$^1/_8$ in) |
| Barrel length | : 66cm (26in) |
| Ejector | : automatic |
| Choke | Mobil-choke interchangeable chokes |
| Sight | bead |
| Safety | : sliding catch on neck of stock |

### CHARACTERISTICS

| — material | : steel |
|---|---|
| — finish | : blued |
| — stock | : walnut stock with pistol-grip |

## Beretta 627 EELL

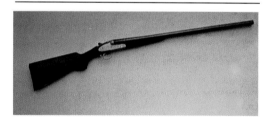

### TECHNICAL DETAILS

| Gauge/calibre | : 12 |
|---|---|
| Chamber length | : 70mm (2$^3/_4$in) |
| Number of barrels | : double-barrels side-by-side |
| Action | : breech-loading |
| Locking | : barrel-block locking |
| Trigger | single trigger |
| Weight | : 2.7–3.2kg (6lb–7lb) |
| Length | : 112 or 117cm (44$^1/_8$–46in) |
| Barrel length | : 66 or 71cm (26 or 28in) |
| Ejector | : automatic |
| Choke | fixed: $^1/_2$ and full, or $^1/_4$ and $^3/_4$ |
| Sight | bead |
| Safety | : sliding catch on neck of stock |

### CHARACTERISTICS

| — material | : steel |
|---|---|
| — finish | : blued barrels and engraved plain metal action and side-plates (not a side-lock) |
| — stock | : stock of specially selected walnut stock. |

## Beretta 627 EL Sporting Clays

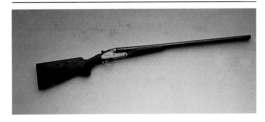

**TECHNICAL DETAILS**

Gauge/calibre : 12
Chamber length : 70mm (2³/₄in)
Number of barrels : double-barrels side-by-side
Action : breech-loading
Locking : barrel-block locking
Trigger single trigger
Weight : 3.2kg (7lb)
Length : 112 or 117cm (44¹/₈–46in)
Barrel length : 71cm (28in)
Ejector : automatic
Choke fixed: ¹/₂ and full
Sight bead
Safety : sliding catch on neck of stock

**CHARACTERISTICS**

— material : steel
— finish : blued barrels and engraved plain metal action and side-plates (not a side-lock)
— stock : walnut stock, with pistol-grip

## Beretta S680 Sporting

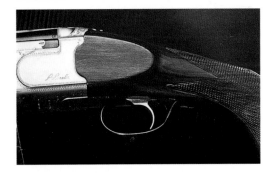

**TECHNICAL DETAILS**

Gauge/calibre : 12
Chamber length : 70mm (2³/₄in)
Number of barrels : double-barrels over-and-under
Action : breech-loading
Locking : conical lugs locking (Beretta patent)
Trigger single trigger
Weight : 3.45kg (7lb 9¹/₂ oz)
Length : 111–121cm (43³/₄–47⁵/₈ in)
Barrel length : 67, 71, or 75cm (26³/₈, 28, or 29¹/₂ in)
Ejector : automatic
Choke fixed: ³/₄ and ¹/₄, ¹/₂ and ¹/₄, or full and ¹/₂

Sight ventilated rib and bead
Safety : sliding catch on neck of stock

**CHARACTERISTICS**

— material : steel
— finish : blued barrels, plain metal action
— stock : walnut stock, with pistol-grip

This gun is made in S680 Trap, S680 Skeet, and S680 Sporting versions

## Beretta S682 Gold Sporting

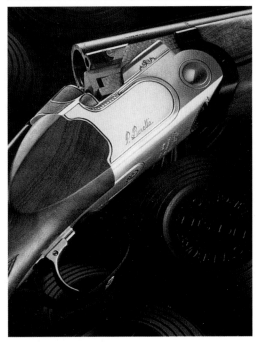

**TECHNICAL DETAILS**

Gauge/calibre : 12 or 20
Chamber length : 70mm (2³/₄in) or 76mm (3in) for 20 gauge
Number of barrels : double-barrels over-and-under
Action : breech-loading
Locking : conical lugs locking (Beretta patent)
Trigger single trigger, adjustable for travel
Weight : 3.45kg (7lb 9¹/₂oz)
Length : 116 or 121cm (45 ³/₄ or 47⁵/₈in)
Barrel length : 71 or 76cm (28 or 30in)
Ejector : automatic
Choke Mobil-choke interchangeable chokes
Sight ventilated rib and bead
Safety : sliding catch on neck of stock

**CHARACTERISTICS**

— material : steel
— finish : matt black barrels, plain metal or matt black action
— stock : walnut stock, with pistol-grip

## Beretta S682 Gold Super Trap New Model

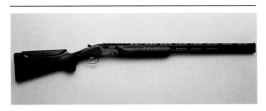

**TECHNICAL DETAILS**

Gauge/calibre : 12
Chamber length : 70mm (2³/₄in)
Number of barrels : double-barrels over-and-under (with compensator slots)
Action : breech-loading
Locking : conical lugs locking (Beretta patent)
Trigger : single trigger
Weight : 3.85kg (8lb 7¹/₂oz)
Length : 120cm (47¹/₄in)
Barrel length : 76cm (30in)
Ejector : automatic
Choke : Mobil-choke interchangeable chokes
Sight : ventilated rib and bead
Safety : sliding catch on neck of stock

**CHARACTERISTICS**

— material : steel
— finish : matt black barrels, grey action
— stock : walnut stock, with pistol-grip and adjustable stock comb

## Beretta S682 Gold Super Trap Old Model

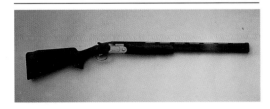

**TECHNICAL DETAILS**

Gauge/calibre : 12
Chamber length : 70mm (2³/₄in)
Number of barrels : double-barrels over-and-under (with compensator slots)

Action : breech-loading
Locking : conical lugs locking (Beretta patent)
Trigger : single trigger
Weight : 3.85kg (8lb 7¹/₂oz)
Length : 120cm (47¹/₄in)
Barrel length : 76cm (30in)
Ejector : automatic
Choke : Mobil-choke interchangeable chokes
Sight : ventilated rib and bead
Safety : sliding catch on neck of stock

**CHARACTERISTICS**

— material : steel
— finish : matt black barrels, plain metal action
— stock : walnut stock, with pistol-grip and adjustable stock comb

## Beretta S682 Gold Trap Combo 12/20

**TECHNICAL DETAILS**

Gauge/calibre : 12 and 20
Chamber length : 70mm (2³/₄in)
Number of barrels : double-barrels over-and-under
Action : breech-loading
Locking : conical lugs locking (Beretta patent)
Trigger : single trigger
Weight : 3.65kg (8lb)
Length : 120cm (47¹/₄in)
Barrel length : 76cm (30in)
Ejector : automatic
Choke : Fixed: Trap
Sight : ventilated rib and bead
Safety : sliding catch on neck of stock

**CHARACTERISTICS**

— material : steel
— finish : matt black barrels, plain metal action
— stock : walnut stock, with pistol-grip

This gun is supplied with two barrel sets, one for 12 gauge and the other for 20 gauge.

## Beretta S682 Gold X Trap Combo

**TECHNICAL DETAILS**

Gauge/calibre : 12

Chamber length : 70mm (2³/₄in)
Number of barrels : double-barrels over-and-under
Action : breech-loading
Locking : conical lugs locking (Beretta patent)
Trigger single trigger
Weight : 3.7–4kg (8lb 2¹/₄oz–8lb 12³/₄oz)
Length : 120–131cm (47¹/₄–51⁵/₄in)
Barrel length : 76, 81, or 86cm (30, 32, or 33⁷/₈ in)
Ejector : automatic
Choke Mobil-choke interchangeable chokes
Sight ventilated rib and bead
Safety : sliding catch on neck of stock

**CHARACTERISTICS**
— material : steel
— finish : blued
— stock : walnut stock, with pistol-grip

This gun is supplied with an interchangeable single barrel.

## Beretta S686 Essential New Silver

**TECHNICAL DETAILS**
Gauge/calibre : 12
Chamber length : 70mm (2³/₄in) or 76mm (3in)
Number of barrels : double-barrels over-and-under
Action : breech-loading
Locking : conical lugs locking (Beretta patent)
Trigger single or twin triggers
Weight : 3.05 or 3.1kg (6lb 11¹/₄oz–6lb 13oz)
Length : 112 or 116cm (44¹/₈–45⁵/₄in)
Barrel length : 67 or 71cm (26³/₈ or 28in)
Ejector : automatic
Choke Mobil-choke interchangeable chokes set
Sight ventilated rib and bead
Safety : sliding catch on neck of stock

**CHARACTERISTICS**
— material : steel

— finish : blued barrels, nickel-plated action
— stock : walnut stock, with pistol-grip

## Beretta S686 Silver Pigeon Sporting

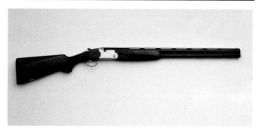

**TECHNICAL DETAILS**
Gauge/calibre : 12 or 20
Chamber length : 70mm (2³/₄in) or 76mm (3in)
Number of barrels : double-barrels over-and-under
Action : breech-loading
Locking : conical lugs locking (Beretta patent)
Trigger single or twin triggers
Weight : 3.5 or 3.6kg (7lb 11¹/₄oz–7lb 14³/₄oz)
Length : 116.5 or 120cm (45⁵/₈–47¹/₄in)
Barrel length : 71 or 75cm (28 or 29¹/₂in)
Ejector : automatic
Choke Mobil-choke interchangeable chokes set
Sight ventilated rib and bead
Safety : sliding catch on neck of stock

**CHARACTERISTICS**
— material : steel
— finish : blued barrels, silvered action with decorative
engravings
— stock : walnut stock, with pistol-grip

## Beretta S686 Ultralight

**TECHNICAL DETAILS**
Gauge/calibre : 12
Chamber length : 70mm (2³/₄in)
Number of barrels : double-barrels over-and-under
Action : breech-loading
Locking : conical lugs locking (Beretta patent)
Trigger single or twin triggers
Weight : 2.6 or 2.7kg (5lb 11¹/₂ oz – 6lb)
Length : 112 or 116cm (44¹/₈ – 45³/₄in)

| Barrel length | : 67 or 71cm (26³/₈ or 28in) |
|---|---|
| Ejector | : automatic |
| Choke | Mobil-choke interchangeable chokes set |
| Sight | ventilated rib and bead |
| Safety | : sliding catch on neck of stock |

**CHARACTERISTICS**

| — material | : steel barrels, light alloy action |
|---|---|
| — finish | : blued |
| — stock | : walnut stock, with pistol-grip |

🐓

## *Beretta S687 EELL Diamond Pigeon*

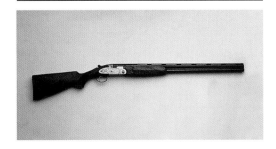

**TECHNICAL DETAILS**

| Gauge/calibre | : 12, 20, or 28 |
|---|---|
| Chamber length | : 70mm (2³/₄in) or 76mm (3in) |
| Number of barrels | : double-barrels over-and-under |
| Action | : breech-loading |
| Locking | : conical lugs locking (Beretta patent) |
| Trigger | single trigger |
| Weight | : 3.1 or 3.2kg (6lb 13oz³/₄7lb) |
| Length | : 112 or 116cm (44¹/₈–45³/₄in) |
| Barrel length | : 66 or 71cm (26 or 28in) |
| Ejector | : automatic |
| Choke | fixed to choice or Mobil-choke interchangeable chokes |
| Sight | ventilated rib and bead |
| Safety | : sliding catch on neck of stock |

**CHARACTERISTICS**

| — material | : steel |
|---|---|
| — finish | : blued barrels, silvered and engraved side-plates (no side-lock) |
| — stock | : selected walnut stock, with pistol-grip |

🐓

## *Beretta S687 EELL Diamond Pigeon Skeet Combo*

**TECHNICAL DETAILS**

| Gauge/calibre | : 12, 20, 28, or .410 |
|---|---|
| Chamber length | : 70mm (2³/₄in) |
| Number of barrels | : double-barrels over-and-under |
| Action | : breech-loading |
| Locking | : conical lugs locking (Beretta patent) |
| Trigger | single trigger |
| Weight | : 3.3 or 3.4kg (7lb 4oz 7lb 8oz) |
| Length | : 116cm (45³/₄in) |

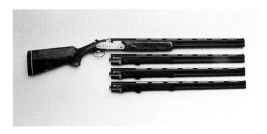

| Barrel length | : 71cm (28in) |
|---|---|
| Ejector | : automatic |
| Choke | fixed to choice |
| Sight | ventilated rib and bead |
| Safety | : sliding catch on neck of stock |

**CHARACTERISTICS**

| — material | : steel |
|---|---|
| — finish | : blued barrels, silvered and engraved side-plates (no side-lock) |
| — stock | : selected walnut stock, with pistol-grip |

Available with additional interchangeable barrels for 20 and 28 gauge and .410 calibre.
🐓

## *Beretta Model S687 EL Gold Pigeon*

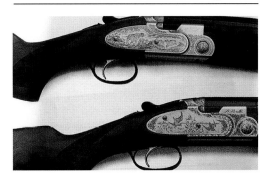

**TECHNICAL DETAILS**

| Gauge/calibre | : 12, 20, 28, or .410 |
|---|---|
| Chamber length | : 70mm (2³/₄in), 76mm (3in), or 89mm (3¹/₂in) |
| Number of barrels | : double-barrels over-and-under |
| Action | : breech-loading |
| Locking | : conical lugs locking (Beretta patent) |
| Trigger | single trigger |
| Weight | : 3.1kg (7lb) |
| Length | : 116–126cm (45³/₄–49⁵/₈in) |
| Barrel length | : 67–75cm (26³/₈–29¹/₂in) |
| Ejector | : automatic |
| Choke | Mobil-choke interchangeable chokes |
| Sight | ventilated rib and bead |
| Safety | : sliding catch on neck of stock |

**CHARACTERISTICS**

| — material | : steel |
|---|---|
| — finish | : blued barrels, silvered side-locks with inlaid gold animal figures |

– stock        : selected walnut stock, with pistol-grip

The S687 EL Gold Pigeon and S687 EELL
Diamond Pigeon are illustrated

## *Beretta Model S687 Golden Onyx*

Barrel length  : 66 or 71cm (26 or 28in)
Ejector        : automatic
Choke            fixed to choice or Mobil-choke interchangeable chokes
Sight            ventilated rib and bead
Safety         : sliding catch on neck of stock

**CHARACTERISTICS**
– material      : steel
– finish        : blued barrels, silvered action with decorative
                  engraving and Beretta insignia
– stock         : selected walnut stock, with pistol-grip

**TECHNICAL DETAILS**
Gauge/calibre   : 12 or 20
Chamber length  : 70mm (2³/₄in) or 76mm (3in)
Number of barrels : double-barrels over-and-under
Action          : breech-loading
Locking         : conical lugs locking (Beretta patent)
Trigger           single trigger
Weight          : 3 or 3.1kg (6lb 9¹/₂oz–6lb 13oz)
Length          : 112 or 116cm (44¹/₈–45³/₄in)
Barrel length   : 66 or 71cm (26 or 28in)
Ejector         : automatic
Choke             fixed to choice or Mobil-choke interchangeable
                  chokes
Sight             ventilated rib and bead
Safety          : sliding catch on neck of stock

**CHARACTERISTICS**
– material      : steel
– finish        : blued, action is engraved with bird motifs and
                  inlaid with gold
– stock         : specially selected walnut stock, with pistol-grip

## *Beretta S687 Sporting Deluxe*

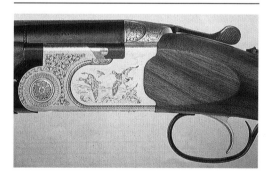

**TECHNICAL DETAILS**
Gauge/calibre   : 12
Chamber length  : 70mm (2³/₄in)
Number of barrels : double-barrels over-and-under
Action          : breech-loading
Locking         : conical lugs locking (Beretta patent)
Trigger           single trigger
Weight          : 3.4 or 3.5kg (7lb 8oz–7lb 11oz)
Length          : 116 or 120cm (45³/₄–47¹/₄in)
Barrel length   : 71 or 76cm (28 or 30in)
Ejector         : automatic
Choke             Mobil-choke interchangeable chokes
Sight             ventilated rib and bead
Safety          : sliding catch on neck of stock
**CHARACTERISTICS**
– material      : steel
– finish        : blued barrels, plain metal action with engraving of
                  hunting motifs
– stock         : walnut stock, with pistol-grip

## *Beretta S687 Silver Pigeon Special*

**TECHNICAL DETAILS**
Gauge/calibre   : 12 or 20
Chamber length  : 70mm (2³/₄in) or 76mm (3in)
Number of barrels : double-barrels over-and-under
Action          : breech-loading
Locking         : conical lugs locking (Beretta patent)
Trigger           single trigger
Weight          : 3 or 3.1kg (6lb 9¹/₂ oz–6lb 13oz)
Length          : 112 or 116cm (44¹/₈–45³/₄in)

## Beretta S687 Ultralight

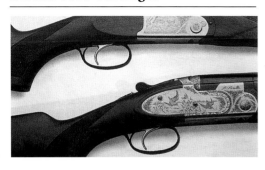

### TECHNICAL DETAILS

| | |
|---|---|
| Gauge/calibre | : 12 |
| Chamber length | : 70mm (2³/₄in) |
| Number of barrels | : double-barrels over-and-under |
| Action | : breech-loading |
| Locking | : conical lugs locking (Beretta patent) |
| Trigger | single trigger |
| Weight | : 2.6kg (5lb 11¹/₂ oz) |
| Length | : 116 or 120cm (45³/₄–47¹/₄in) |
| Barrel length | : 67 or 71cm (26³/₈ or 28in) |
| Ejector | : automatic |
| Choke | fixed to choice or Mobil-choke interchangeable chokes |
| Sight | ventilated rib and bead |
| Safety | : sliding catch on neck of stock |

### CHARACTERISTICS

| | |
|---|---|
| — material | : steel barrels, light alloy action |
| — finish | : blued barrels, nickel-plated action with engraving |
| — stock | : walnut stock, with pistol-grip |

The S687 Ultra Light and S687 EELL Diamond Pigeon are illustrated.

## Beretta SO3 EELL

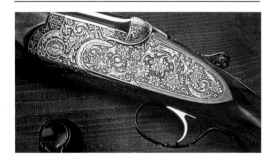

### TECHNICAL DETAILS

| | |
|---|---|
| Gauge/calibre | : 12 |
| Chamber length | : 70mm (2³/₄in) |
| Number of barrels | : double-barrels over-and-under |
| Action | : breech-loading |
| Locking | : locking lugs on both sides of upper barrel with transverse lock in breech |
| Trigger | single trigger |

| | |
|---|---|
| Weight | : 3.25kg (7lb 2oz) |
| Length | : 111–121cm (43³/₄–47⁵/₈in) |
| Barrel length | : 66–75cm (26–30in) |
| Ejector | : automatic |
| Choke | Mobil-choke interchangeable chokes |
| Sight | ventilated rib and bead |
| Safety | : sliding catch on neck of stock |

### CHARACTERISTICS

| | |
|---|---|
| — material | : steel |
| — finish | : matt black with engraved plain metal action and side-lock plates |
| — stock | : walnut stock, with pistol-grip |

The S03 EELL model illustrated has optional engravings of floral motifs.

## Beretta SO4 Trap/Skeet

### TECHNICAL DETAILS

| | |
|---|---|
| Gauge/calibre | : 12 |
| Chamber length | : 70mm (2³/₄in) |
| Number of barrels | : double-barrels over-and-under |
| Action | : breech-loading |
| Locking | : locking lugs on both sides of upper barrel with transverse lock in breech |
| Trigger | single trigger |
| Weight | : 3.4kg (7lb 8oz) |
| Length | : 115–120cm (45¹/₄–47¹/₄in) |
| Barrel length | : Trap: 71 or 75cm (28 or 29¹/₂ in); Skeet: 68 or 71cm (28 or 29¹/₂ in) |
| Ejector | : automatic |
| Choke | fixed: ³/₄ and ¹/₄, or ¹/₂ and ¹/₄, or Skeet choke |
| Sight | ventilated rib and bead |
| Safety | : sliding catch on neck of stock |

### CHARACTERISTICS

| | |
|---|---|
| — material | : steel |
| — finish | : blue barrels with engraved plain metal action and side-lock plates |
| — stock | : walnut stock, with pistol-grip |

## Beretta SO5 Gold Sporting

### TECHNICAL DETAILS

| | |
|---|---|
| Gauge/calibre | : 12 |

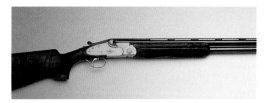

Chamber length     : 70mm (2³/₄in)
Number of barrels : double-barrels over-and-under
Action             : breech-loading
Locking            : locking lugs on both sides of upper barrel with transverse lock in breech
Trigger              single trigger
Weight             : 3.4kg (7lb 8oz)
Length             : 115cm (45¹/₄in)
Barrel length      : 71cm (28in)
Ejector            : automatic
Choke               Mobilchoke interchangeable chokes
Sight               ventilated rib and bead
Safety             : sliding catch on neck of stock

**CHARACTERISTICS**
— material         : steel
— finish           : blue barrels with engraved plain metal action and side-lock plates
— stock            : walnut stock, with pistol-grip

## Beretta SO5 Gold Trap

**TECHNICAL DETAILS**
Gauge/calibre      : 12
Chamber length     : 70mm (2³/₄in)
Number of barrels : double-barrels over-and-under
Action             : breech-loading
Locking            : locking lugs on both sides of upper barrel with transverse lock in breech
Trigger              single trigger
Weight             : 3.7kg (8lb 2¹/₄oz)
Length             : 119cm (46⁷/₈in)
Barrel length      : 76cm (30in)
Ejector            : automatic
Choke               fixed Trap choke
Sight               ventilated rib and bead
Safety             : sliding catch on neck of stock

**CHARACTERISTICS**
— material         : steel
— finish           : blued barrels with engraved plain metal action and side-lock plates
— stock            : walnut stock, with pistol-grip

## Beretta SO6

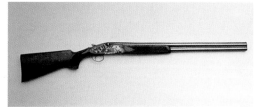

**TECHNICAL DETAILS**
Gauge/calibre      : 12
Chamber length     : 70mm (2³/₄in) or 76mm (3in)
Number of barrels : double-barrels over-and-under
Action             : breech-loading
Locking            : locking lugs on both sides of upper barrel with transverse lock in breech
Trigger              single trigger
Weight             : 3.3 or 3.4kg (7lb 4oz or 7lb 8oz)
Length             : 111–121cm (43³/₄–46⁵/₈in)
Barrel length      : 67, 71, or 76cm (26³/₄, 28, or 30in)
Ejector            : automatic
Choke               fixed to choice or Mobilchoke set of interchangeable chokes
Sight               ventilated rib and bead
Safety             : sliding catch on neck of stock

**CHARACTERISTICS**
— material         : steel
— finish           : blued barrels with tempered action and side-lock plates
— stock            : walnut stock, with pistol-grip, or straight English stock

## Beretta SO6 EL

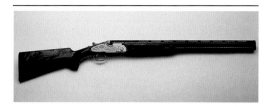

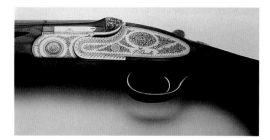

**TECHNICAL DETAILS**
Gauge/calibre      : 12
Chamber length     : 70mm (2³/₄in) or 76mm (3in)
Number of barrels : double-barrels over-and-under
Action             : breech-loading

| Locking | : locking lugs to upper barrel with transverse lock in breech |
|---|---|
| Trigger | single trigger |
| Weight | : 3.3 or 3.4kg (7lb 4oz or 7lb 8oz) |
| Length | : 111–121cm (43³/₄–46⁵/₈ in) |
| Barrel length | : 67, 71, or 76cm (26³/₈, 28, or 30in) |
| Ejector | : automatic |
| Choke | Mobilchoke set of interchangeable chokes |
| Sight | bead |
| Safety | : catch on neck of stock |

### CHARACTERISTICS

| — material | : steel |
|---|---|
| — finish | : blued barrels with silvered and engraved action and side-lock plates |
| — stock | : walnut stock, with pistol-grip, or straight English stock |

## Beretta SO6 EELL

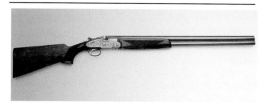

### TECHNICAL DETAILS

| Gauge/calibre | : 12 |
|---|---|
| Chamber length | : 70mm (2³/₄in) or 76mm (3in) |
| Number of barrels | : double-barrels over-and-under |
| Action | : breech-loading |
| Locking | : locking lugs to upper barrel with transverse lock in breech |
| Trigger | single or twin triggers |
| Weight | : 3.3 or 3.4kg (7lb 4oz or 7lb 8oz) |
| Length | : 111–121cm (43³/₄–46⁵/₈ in) |
| Barrel length | : 67, 71, or 76cm (26³/₈, 28, or 30in) |
| Ejector | : automatic |
| Choke | fixed choke to choice or set of Mobilchoke interchangeable chokes |
| Sight | raised solid rib or ventilated rib and bead |
| Safety | : sliding catch on neck of stock |

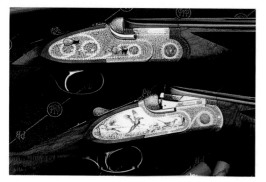

### CHARACTERISTICS

| — material | : steel |
|---|---|
| — finish | : blued barrels with silvered and engraved action and side-lock plates; side-plates can be removed by hand |
| — stock | : walnut stock, with pistol-grip, or straight English stock |

The close-up photograph shows details from (top) the SO6 EELL and (bottom) the SO9.

## Beretta Model SO9

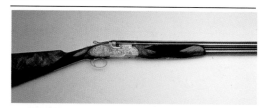

### TECHNICAL DETAILS

| Gauge/calibre | : 12, 20, 28, or .410 |
|---|---|
| Chamber length | : 70mm (2³/₄in) or 76mm (3in) |
| Number of barrels | : double-barrels over-and-under |
| Action | : breech-loading |
| Locking | : locking lugs to upper barrel with transverse lock in breech |
| Trigger | single or twin triggers |
| Weight | : 3.25–3.4kg (7lb 2oz–7lb 8oz) |
| Length | : 111–121cm (43³/₄–46⁵/₈ in) |
| Barrel length | : 67, 71, or 76cm (26³/₈, 28, or 30in) |
| Ejector | : automatic |
| Choke | fixed to choice or Mobilchoke set of interchangeable chokes (12 gauge only) |
| Sight | solid ridge or ventilated rib and bead |
| Safety | : sliding catch on neck of stock |

### CHARACTERISTICS

| — material | : steel |
|---|---|
| — finish | : blued barrels with silvered action and side-lock plates, engraved with hunting scenes |
| — stock | : specially selected walnut stock, with pistol-grip, or straight English stock |

## Beretta SO9/20

### TECHNICAL DETAILS

| Gauge/calibre | : 20 |
|---|---|

Chamber length        : 76mm (3in)
Number of barrels : double-barrels over-and-under
Action                : breech-loading
Locking               : locking lugs to upper barrel with transverse lock in breech
Trigger               single or twin triggers
Weight                : 3.2–3.4kg (7lb–7lb 8oz)
Length                : 111–121cm (43³/₄–46⁵/₈ in)
Barrel length         : 67, 71, or 76cm (26³/₈, 28, or 30in)
Ejector               : automatic
Choke                 fixed to choice
Sight                 ventilated rib and bead
Safety                : sliding catch on neck of stock

**CHARACTERISTICS**
— material            : steel
— finish              : blued barrels with silvered action and side-lock plates, engraved with hunting scenes
— stock               : specially selected walnut stock, with pistol-grip, or straight English stock

## Beretta SSO6 Express

**TECHNICAL DETAILS**
Gauge/calibre         : .375 H&H Mag., 9.3 x 74R, .458 Win. Mag.
Chamber length        : not applicable
Number of barrels : double-barrels over-and-under
Action                : breech-loading
Locking               : locking lugs to upper barrel with transverse lock in breech
Trigger               twin triggers
Weight                : 5kg (11lb)
Length                : 108cm (42¹/₂ in)
Barrel length         : 65cm (25⁵/₈ in)
Ejector               : automatic
Choke                 rifled barrel, not applicable
Sight                 fold-down rack and bead
Safety                : automatic safety after cocking and sliding catch on neck of stock

**CHARACTERISTICS**
— material            : steel

— finish              : blued barrels with tempered action and side-lock plates
— stock               : walnut stock, with pistol-grip and cheek plate

## Beretta SSO6 EELL Express

**TECHNICAL DETAILS**
Gauge/calibre         : .375 H&H Mag., 9.3 x 74R, .458 Win. Mag.
Chamber length        : not applicable
Number of barrels : double-barrels over-and-under
Action                : breech-loading
Locking               : locking lugs to upper barrel with transverse lock in breech
Trigger               twin triggers
Weight                : 5kg (11lb)
Length                : 108cm (42¹/₂ in)
Barrel length         : 65cm (25⁵/₈in)
Ejector               : automatic
Choke                 rifled barrel, not applicable
Sight                 fold-down rack and bead
Safety                : automatic safety after cocking and sliding catch on neck of stock

**CHARACTERISTICS**
— material            : steel
— finish              : blue barrels with tempered action and side-lock plates, with gold inlay animal figures
— stock               : walnut stock, with pistol-grip and cheek plate

## Beretta RS202

**TECHNICAL DETAILS**
Gauge/calibre         : 12
Chamber length        : 70mm (2³/₄in)
Number of barrels : single barrel
Magazine              : tubular magazine for 2 cartridges

| | |
|---|---|
| Action | : pump-action |
| Locking | : falling block locking |
| Trigger | single trigger |
| Weight | : 3.2kg (7lb) |
| Length | : 112–126cm (44¹/₈–49⁵/₈in) |
| Barrel length | : 61–76cm (24–30in) |
| Ejector | : extractor |
| Choke | to choice |
| Sight | ventilated rib and bead |
| Safety | : push-button at front of trigger guard |

**CHARACTERISTICS**

| | |
|---|---|
| — material | : steel, light alloy action |
| — finish | : matt black |
| — stock | : walnut stock, with pistol-grip |

The RS202P and 1201FP are illustrated above.
☝ 🦃 ♠

## Beretta 1200 F

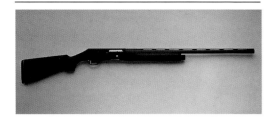

**TECHNICAL DETAILS**

| | |
|---|---|
| Gauge/calibre | : 12 |
| Chamber length | : 70mm (2³/₄in) |
| Number of barrels | : single barrel |
| Magazine | : tubular magazine for 2 cartridges |
| Action | : semi-automatic, recoil operated |
| Locking | : rotating block locking |
| Trigger | single trigger |
| Weight | : 3.25kg (7lb 2¹/₂ oz) |
| Length | : 107cm (42¹/₈in) |
| Barrel length | : 71cm (28in) |
| Ejector | : extractor |
| Choke | fixed to choice: full, ³/₄, or ¹/₂ |
| Sight | ventilated rib and bead |
| Safety | : push-button at front of trigger guard |

**CHARACTERISTICS**

| | |
|---|---|
| — material | : steel, light alloy action |
| — finish | : matt black |
| — stock | : black plastic stock, with pistol-grip |

☝ 🦃 ♠

## Beretta 1201FP

**TECHNICAL DETAILS**

| | |
|---|---|
| Gauge/calibre | : 12 |
| Chamber length | : 70mm (2³/₄in) or 76mm (3in) |
| Number of barrels | : single barrel |
| Magazine | : tubular magazine for 2 or 6 cartridges |

| | |
|---|---|
| Action | : semi-automatic, recoil operated |
| Locking | : rotating block locking |
| Trigger | single trigger |
| Weight | : 2.85kg (6lb 4oz) |
| Length | : 106cm (42in) |
| Barrel length | : 51cm (20in) |
| Ejector | : extractor |
| Choke | cylindrical |
| Sight | adjustable rack and bead |
| Safety | : push-button at rear of trigger guard |

**CHARACTERISTICS**

| | |
|---|---|
| — material | : steel, light alloy action |
| — finish | : matt black |
| — stock | : black plastic stock, with pistol-grip |

Illustrated: Beretta RS202P and Beretta 1201 FP. Possession of this firearm is not permitted for hunting or other sporting purposes in a number of European countries because of the short barrel-length. The law in United Kingdom requires the overall length of a gun to be a minimum of 40in (101.5cm) with a barrel not shorter than 24in (61cm). Guns are also not permitted to have a magazine capacity exceeding 2 cartridges in the magazine and 1 in the barrel.
☝ 🦃 ♠

# Bernardelli

The gunmakers Bernardelli of Gardone in the Valle Trompia, Italy, originate from 1721

when the business was established by the Bernardelli brothers. After the unification of Italy in 1865, the company was officially registered by Vincenzo Bernardelli.

The company is renowned for superb shotguns that often bear wonderful examples of engraving and evocative names like Saturno, Hemingway, and Holland. Much of the range consists of traditional side-by-side double-barrelled shotguns and Bernardelli still make two models – the Italia and Italia Extra – with external hammers.

A number of the guns are provided with false side-plates which given an impression of side-locks. Those guns with true side-locks, such as the Holland range, are clearly indicated in the data that follows. The company also produce a number of specialist field, police, and sporting pistols in various calibres. There are also large calibre double-barrelled rifles for hunting big game and these are indicated as "Express" rifles.

## Bernardelli Comb 2000 combination gun

**TECHNICAL DETAILS**

| | |
|---|---|
| Gauge/calibre | : see below |
| Chamber length | : smooth-bore barrel: 70mm (2³/₄in) |
| Number of barrels | : double-barrels over-and-under |
| Action | : breech-loading |
| Locking | : double barrel-block locking |
| Trigger | twin triggers; front trigger with pre-set for rapid reaction |
| Weight | : 3.1kg (6lb 13oz) |
| Length | : 104cm (41in) |
| Barrel length | : 60cm (23⁵/₈in) |
| Ejector | : extractor |
| Choke | smooth-bore barrel: interchangeable chokes |
| Sight | rack and bead, plus mounting for telescopic sight |
| Safety | : sliding catch on neck of stock |

**CHARACTERISTICS**

| | |
|---|---|
| — material | : steel |
| — finish | : blued barrels, plain metal action with light engraving. |
| — stock | : walnut stock, with pistol-grip and cheek plate |

Available calibres/gauge (smooth-bore): 12 or 16 gauge; (rifled): .22 Hornet, .222 Rem., 5.6x50R, .243 Win., 6.5x55, 6.5x57R, .270 Win., 7X57R, 7X65R, .308 Win., .30-06 Spr., 8x57JRS, 9.3x74R.

## Bernardelli Dream Field

**TECHNICAL DETAILS**

| | |
|---|---|
| Gauge/calibre | : 12 or 20 |
| Chamber length | : 70mm (2³/₄in) or 76mm (3in) |
| Number of barrels | : double-barrels over-and-under |
| Action | : breech-loading |
| Locking | : barrel-block locking |
| Trigger | single trigger |
| Weight | : 3–3.2kg (6lb 8oz–7lb) |
| Length | : 112, 117, or 122cm (44, 46, or 48in) |
| Barrel length | : 66, 71, or 76cm (26, 28, or 30in) |
| Ejector | : automatic |
| Choke | fixed to choice or multichoke |
| Sight | ventilated rib and bead |
| Safety | : automatic safety after cocking, sliding catch on neck of stock |

**CHARACTERISTICS**

| | |
|---|---|
| — material | : steel |
| — finish | : blued barrels, plain metal engraved action. |
| — stock | : walnut stock, with pistol-grip. |

## Bernardelli Dream Sporting, Trap and Skeet

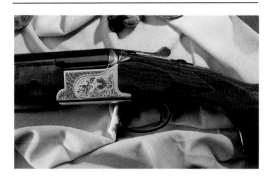

**TECHNICAL DETAILS**

| | |
|---|---|
| Gauge/calibre | : 12 |

| Chamber length | : 76mm (3in) |
| Number of barrels | : double-barrels over-and-under |
| Action | : breech-loading |
| Locking | : barrel-block locking |
| Trigger | single trigger |
| Weight | : 3–3.2kg (6lb 8oz–7lb) |
| Length | : 117 or 122cm (46 or 48in) |
| Barrel length | : 71cm (28in) Sporting/Skeet, 75cm (29½ in) Trap |
| Ejector | : automatic |
| Choke | multichoke (Sporting), ¾ and full (Trap), or Sk–Sk (Skeet) |
| Sight | 11mm (⁷⁄₁₆ in) wide ventilated rib and bead |
| Safety | : sliding catch on neck of stock |

**CHARACTERISTICS**
| — material | : steel |
| — finish | : blued barrels, plain metal action. |
| — stock | : walnut stock, with pistol-grip |

## Bernardelli Express 2000

**TECHNICAL DETAILS**
| Gauge/calibre | : .30-06 Spr., 7x65R, 8x57JRS, or 9.3x74R |
| Chamber length | : not applicable |
| Number of barrels | : double-barrels over-and-under |
| Action | : breech-loading |
| Locking | : barrel-block locking |
| Trigger | twin triggers |
| Weight | : 3.1–3.3kg (6lb 13oz–7lb 4oz) |

| Length | : 103 or 108cm (40½ or 42½ in) |
| Barrel length | : 55 or 60cm (21⅝ or 23⅝ in) |
| Ejector | : automatic |
| Choke | not applicable, rifled barrels |
| Sight | rack and bead, various mountings for telescopic sights |
| Safety | : sliding catch on neck of stock |

**CHARACTERISTICS**
| — material | : steel |
| — finish | : entirely blued or blued barrels and plain metal action. |
| — stock | : walnut stock, with pistol-grip and cheek plate |

Illustrated from top to bottom: Express 2000 with plain metal action, with blued barrel, Express VB, and Express VB Deluxe. This gun cannot be held on a shotgun certificate under United Kingdom legislation.

## Bernardelli Express VB-E

**TECHNICAL DETAILS**
| Gauge/calibre | : 7x65R, .30-06 Spr., 8x57JRS, .375 H&H Mag., or 9.3x74R |
| Chamber length | : not applicable |
| Number of barrels | : double-barrels side-by-side |
| Action | : breech-loading |
| Locking | : barrel-block locking |
| Trigger | single or twin triggers |
| Weight | : 3.1–3.6kg (6lb 13oz–7lb 14³⁄₁₆oz) |
| Length | : 103 or 108cm (40½ or 42½in) |
| Barrel length | : 55 or 60cm (21⅝ or 23⅝in) |
| Ejector | : automatic or Model VB with extractor |
| Choke | not applicable, rifled barrels |
| Sight | rack and bead, various mountings for telescopic sights |
| Safety | : sliding catch on neck of stock |

**CHARACTERISTICS**
| — material | : steel |
| — finish | : entirely blued or blued barrels and plain metal action. |
| — stock | : walnut stock, with pistol-grip and cheek plate |

Illustrated from top to bottom: Express 2000 with plain metal action, with blued barrel, Express VB, and Express VB Deluxe.

## Bernardelli Express VB De Luxe

**TECHNICAL DETAILS**
| Gauge/calibre | : 7x65R, .30-06 Spr., 8x57JRS, .375 H&H Mag., or 9.3x74R |
| Chamber length | : not applicable |
| Number of barrels | : double-barrels side-by-side |
| Action | : breech-loading |
| Locking | : barrel-block locking |
| Trigger | single or twin triggers |

| Weight | : 3.1–3.6kg (6lb 13oz–7lb 14³/₄oz) |
| Length | : 103 or 108cm (40¹/₂ or 42¹/₂ in) |
| Barrel length | : 55 or 60cm (21⁵/8 or 23⁵/8in) |
| Ejector | : automatic |
| Choke | not applicable, rifled barrels |
| Sight | rack and bead, various mountings for telescopic sights |
| Safety | : sliding catch on neck of stock |

### CHARACTERISTICS

| — material | : steel |
| — finish | : blued barrels and plain metal action and side-plates (no side-lock). |
| — stock | : walnut stock, with pistol-grip and cheek plate |

Illustrated from top to bottom: Express 2000 with plain metal action, with blued barrel, Express VB, and Express VB Deluxe.

## Bernardelli Express Minerva

### TECHNICAL DETAILS

| Gauge/calibre | : 9.3x74R |
| Chamber length | : not applicable |
| Number of barrels | : double-barrels side-by–side |
| Action | : breech-loading |
| Locking | : barrel-block locking |
| Trigger | twin triggers |
| Weight | : 3.3–3.4kg (7lb 4oz–7lb 8oz) |
| Length | : 103 or 113cm (40¹/₂ or 44¹/₂ in) |
| Barrel length | : 55 or 65cm (21⁵/8 or 25⁵/8in) |
| Ejector | : extractor |
| Choke | not applicable, rifled barrels |
| Sight | rack and bead, various mountings for telesc. sights |
| Safety | : sliding catch on neck of stock |

### CHARACTERISTICS

| — material | : steel |
| — finish | : blued barrels and plain metal action and side-plates (no side-lock); external hammers |
| — stock | : walnut stock, with pistol-grip |

Illustrated from top to bottom: Express 2000, Express VB Deluxe, and Express Minerva.

## Bernardelli Hemingway Lightweigh

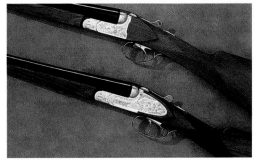

### TECHNICAL DETAILS

| Gauge/calibre | : 12, 16, or 20 |
| Chamber length | : 70mm (2³/₄in) |
| Number of barrels | : double-barrels side-by–side |
| Action | : breech-loading |
| Locking | : barrel-block locking |
| Trigger | single or twin triggers |
| Weight | : 2.8kg (6lb 4oz) |
| Length | : 109 or 114cm (43 or 45in) |
| Barrel length | : 66 or 71cm (26 or 28in) |
| Ejector | : automatic |
| Choke | to choice |
| Sight | bead |
| Safety | : sliding catch on neck of stock |

### CHARACTERISTICS

| — material | : steel |
| — finish | : blued barrels and plain metal engraved action |
| — stock | : straight English stock of walnut |

Illustrated are the Bernardelli Hemingway Lightweight (top) and Hemingway Deluxe.

## Bernardelli Hemingway Deluxe Side-lock

### TECHNICAL DETAILS

| Gauge/calibre | : 12, 16, 20, or 28 |
| Chamber length | : 70mm (2³/₄in) |
| Number of barrels | : double-barrels side-by–side |
| Action | : breech-loading |
| Locking | : barrel-block locking |
| Trigger | single or twin triggers |
| Weight | : 2.8–3.2kg (6lb 4oz–7lb) |
| Length | : 112–122cm (44–48in) |
| Barrel length | : 66–76cm (26–30in) |
| Ejector | : automatic |
| Choke | to choice |
| Sight | bead |
| Safety | : sliding catch on neck of stock |

### CHARACTERISTICS

| — material | : steel |
| — finish | : blued barrels and plain metal engraved action and side-lock plates |

— stock             : straight English stock of specially-selected walnut

Illustrated are the Bernardelli Hemingway Lightweight (top) and Hemingway Deluxe.
ᘛ

## Bernardelli Holland VB Side-lock

**TECHNICAL DETAILS**

Gauge/calibre     : 12
Chamber length   : 70mm (2³/₄in)
Number of barrels : double-barrels side-by—side
Action            : breech-loading
Locking           : barrel-block locking
Trigger             single or twin triggers
Weight            : 3.2–3.4kg (7lb–7lb 8oz)
Length            : 109–114cm (43–45in)
Barrel length     : 66–71cm (26–28in)
Ejector           : automatic
Choke               to choice
Sight               bead
Safety            : sliding catch on neck of stock

**CHARACTERISTICS**

— material         : steel
— finish            : blued barrels and plain metal engraved action and side-lock plates; Holland & Holland side-locks
— stock           : specially-selected walnut stock, with pistol-grip

Illustrated from top to bottom: Holland VB-E (English-style engraving), Holland VB-Extra (removable side-lock plates), Holland VB-E2 (with floral engraving), and the standard Holland      ᘛ

## Bernardelli Holland VB Liscio Side-lock

**TECHNICAL DETAILS**

Gauge/calibre     : 12
Chamber length   : 70mm (2³/₄in)
Number of barrels : double-barrels side-by—side
Action            : breech-loading
Locking           . barrel-block locking
Trigger             single or twin triggers
Weight            : 3.3kg (7lb 4oz)

Length            : 104–114cm (41–45in)
Barrel length     : 61–71cm (24–28in)
Ejector           : automatic
Choke               to choice
Sight               bead
Safety            : sliding catch on neck of stock

**CHARACTERISTICS**

— material         : steel
— finish            : blued barrels and plain metal engraved action and side-lock plates, inlaid with gold (Holland & Holland side-locks)
— stock           : straight English stock of specially-selected walnut
ᘛ

## Bernardelli Italia / Italia Extra external hammers

**TECHNICAL DETAILS**

Gauge/calibre     : 12, 16, or 20
Chamber length   : 70mm (2³/₄in), or 76mm (3in)
Number of barrels : double-barrels side-by—side
Action            : breech-loading
Locking           : double barrel-block locking, and Purdy locking
Trigger             twin triggers
Weight            : 3–3.2kg (6lb 9¹/₂–7lb)
Length            : 122cm (48in)
Barrel length     : 70cm (27¹/₂ in)
Ejector           : extractor
Choke               ¹/₂ and full
Sight               deep-recessed groove and bead
Safety            : half-cock of hammers

## CHARACTERISTICS

- material : steel
- finish : blued barrels and plain metal engraved action and
  side-lock plates
- stock : straight English stock of selected walnut

The lower of the two guns illustrated is the
Italia Extra, which is the deluxe version.

# Bernardelli Roma 5

## TECHNICAL DETAILS

Gauge/calibre : 12, 20, or 28
Chamber length : 70mm (2³/₄in), 76mm (3in)
Number of barrels : double-barrels side-by—side
Action : breech-loading
Locking : Purdy locking
Trigger : twin triggers
Weight : 2.7–3kg (6lb–6lb 8oz)
Length : 113–122cm (44¹/₂–48in)
Barrel length : 66–76cm (26–30in)
Ejector : automatic
Choke : ¹/₂ and full, or ³/₄ and ¹/₄
Sight : bead
Safety : automatic safety on cocking, sliding catch on neck
of stock

## CHARACTERISTICS

- material : steel
- finish : blued barrels and plain metal engraved action and
  side- plates (no side-locks)
- stock : straight English stock of walnut

Illustrated from top to bottom: Roma 5, and
Roma 6.

# Bernardelli Roma 6

## TECHNICAL DETAILS

Gauge/calibre : 12, or 20
Chamber length : 70mm (2³/₄in) or 76mm (3in) for 20 gauge
Number of barrels : double-barrels side-by—side
Action : breech-loading
Locking : Purdy locking

Trigger : twin triggers
Weight : 3–3.2kg (6lb 8oz—7lb)
Length : 112, 117, or 122cm (44, 46, or 48in)
Barrel length : 66, 71, or 76cm (26, 28, or 30in)
Ejector : automatic
Choke : to choice
Sight : bead
Safety : automatic safety on cocking, sliding catch on neck
of stock

## CHARACTERISTICS

- material : steel
- finish : blued barrels and plain metal engraved action and
  side- plates (no side-locks)
- stock : straight English stock of selected walnut

Illustrated from top to bottom: Roma 5, and
Roma 6.

# Bernardelli Roma 7, Roma 8 and Roma 9

## TECHNICAL DETAILS

Gauge/calibre : 12, 20, or 28
Chamber length : 70mm (2³/₄in) or 76mm (3in)
Number of barrels : double-barrels side-by—side
Action : breech-loading
Locking : Purdy locking
Trigger : single or twin triggers
Weight : 3–3.4kg (6lb 8oz—7lb 8oz)
Length : 117 or 122cm (46 or 48in)
Barrel length : 71 or 76cm (28 or 30in)
Ejector : automatic
Choke : to choice
Sight : bead
Safety : automatic safety on cocking, sliding catch on neck
of stock

## CHARACTERISTICS

- material : steel
- finish : blued barrels and plain metal engraved action and
  side- plates (no side-locks)
- stock : straight English stock of selected walnut

Illustrated from top to bottom: Roma 9 with gold inlay, Roma 8 with hunting engravings, and Roma 7 with decorative engravings.

## Bernardelli Saturno 200

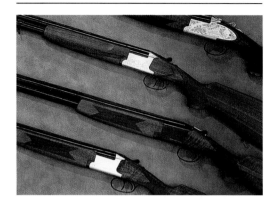

**TECHNICAL DETAILS**

Gauge/calibre : 12, or 20
Chamber length : 70mm (2³/₄in) or 76mm (3in) for 20 gauge
Number of barrels : double-barrels over-and-under
Action : breech-loading
Locking : barrel-block locking
Trigger : single or twin triggers
Weight : 2.8kg (6lb 2¹/₂ oz)
Length : 109–118cm (43–46¹/₂ in)
Barrel length : 65–75cm (25⁵/8–29¹/₂ in)
Ejector : automatic
Choke : fixed to choice or interchangeable chokes
Sight : ventilated rib and bead
Safety : sliding catch on neck of stock

**CHARACTERISTICS**

— material : steel
— finish : blued barrels and plain metal engraved action and side- plates (no side-locks)
— stock : walnut stock, with pistol-grip

Illustrated from top to bottom: Saturno 200 Saturno Luck Hunting, Saturno Luck Blue (with blued action), and Saturno Luck Argent (plain metal action).

## Bernardelli Saturno Luck

**TECHNICAL DETAILS**

Gauge/calibre : 12
Chamber length : 70mm (2³/₄in)
Number of barrels : double-barrels over-and-under
Action : breech-loading
Locking : barrel-block locking
Trigger : single or twin triggers
Weight : 3.1–3.2kg (6lb 13oz–7lb)
Length : 109–119cm (43–47in)

Barrel length : 66–76cm (26–30in)
Ejector : automatic
Choke : interchangeable chokes
Sight : ventilated rib and bead
Safety : sliding catch on neck of stock

**CHARACTERISTICS**

— material : steel
— finish : blued barrels (Luck Blue), blued barrels and plain metal action (Hunting and Argent)
— stock : walnut stock, with pistol-grip

Illustrated from top to bottom: Saturno 200 Saturno Luck Hunting, Saturno Luck Blue (with blued action), and Saturno Luck Argent (plain metal action).

## Bernardelli Sporting Clays, Skeet and Trap

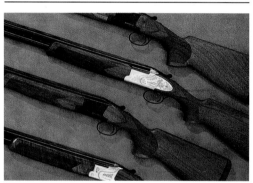

**TECHNICAL DETAILS**

Gauge/calibre : 12
Chamber length : 70mm (2³/₄in)
Number of barrels : double-barrels over-and-under
Action : breech-loading
Locking : barrel-block locking
Trigger : single trigger
Weight : 3.2–3.6kg (7lb–7lb 14³/₄oz)
Length : 114 or 119cm (45 or 47in)
Barrel length : 71 or 76cm (28 or 30in)
Ejector : automatic
Choke : interchangeable chokes
Sight : ventilated rib and bead
Safety : sliding catch on neck of stock

**CHARACTERISTICS**

— material : steel
— finish : blued or blued barrels and plain metal action with engraving
— stock : walnut stock, with pistol-grip

Illustrated from top to bottom: Pull Trap, Saturno Sporting (with decorative plates), Pull Skeet, and Model 115S.

# Bernardelli Uberto 2

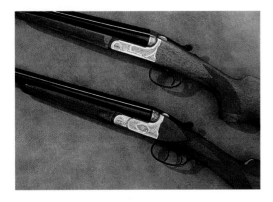

## TECHNICAL DETAILS
Gauge/calibre     : 12, 20, 28
Chamber length    : 70mm (2³/₄in), or 76mm (3in)
Number of barrels : double-barrels side-by—side
Action            : breech-loading
Locking           : Purdy locking
Trigger           single or twin triggers
Weight            : 3.2–3.4kg (7lb–7lb 8oz)
Length            : 109–127cm (43–50in)
Barrel length     : 65–75cm (25⁵/₈–29¹/₂ in)
Ejector           : automatic or extractor by choice
Choke             ¹/₂ and fill, or ³/₄ and ¹/₄
Sight             bead
Safety            : sliding catch on neck of stock

## CHARACTERISTICS
— material   : steel
— finish     : blued barrels and plain metal action with engraving
— stock      : straight English stock of walnut

Illustrated from top to bottom: Uberto 112 and Uberto 2.

# Bernardelli Uberto 112

## TECHNICAL DETAILS
Gauge/calibre     : 12
Chamber length    : 70mm (2³/₄in)
Number of barrels : double-barrels side-by—side
Action            : breech-loading
Locking           : Purdy locking
Trigger           single or twin triggers
Weight            : 3.2–3.4kg (7lb–7lb 8oz)
Length            : 109–127cm (43–50in)
Barrel length     : 65–75cm (25⁵/₈–29¹/₂ in)
Ejector           : automatic or extractor by choice
Choke             fixed to choice or interchangeable chokes
Sight             bead
Safety            : sliding catch on neck of stock

## CHARACTERISTICS
— material   : steel

---

— finish     : blued barrels and plain metal action with engraving
— stock      : walnut stock, with pistol-grip

Illustrated from top to bottom: Uberto 112 and Uberto 2.

# Bernardelli Uberto 2 Slug

## TECHNICAL DETAILS
Gauge/calibre     : 12
Chamber length    : 76mm (3in)
Number of barrels : double-barrels side-by-side
Action            : breech-loading
Locking           : barrel-block locking
Trigger           twin triggers
Weight            : 3.2kg (7lb 8oz)
Length            : 106cm (41³/₄in)
Barrel length     : 60cm (23⁵/₈in)
Ejector           : automatic
Choke             cylindrical
Sight             adjustable rack, bead, and mounting for telesc. sights
Safety            : sliding catch on neck of stock

## CHARACTERISTICS
— material   : steel
— finish     : blued barrels and plain metal action with engraving
— stock      : walnut stock, with pistol-grip

Illustrated from top to bottom: Uberto 2 Slug, and Uberto 200 Slug

# Bernardelli Uberto 200 Slug

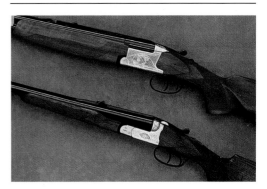

## TECHNICAL DETAILS
Gauge/calibre     : 12
Chamber length    : 76mm (3in)
Number of barrels : double-barrels over-and-under
Action            : breech-loading
Locking           : barrel-block locking
Trigger           twin triggers
Weight            : 3.2kg (7lb 8oz)
Length            : 104cm (41in)
Barrel length     : 60cm (23⁵/₈in)
Ejector           : automatic

| Choke | cylindrical |
|---|---|
| Sight | adjustable rack, bead, and mounting for telescopic sights |
| Safety | : sliding catch on neck of stock |

**CHARACTERISTICS**

| — material | : steel |
|---|---|
| — finish | : blued barrels and plain metal action with engraving |
| — stock | : walnut stock, with pistol-grip |

Illustrated from top to bottom: Uberto 2 Slug, and Uberto 200 Slug.

## Bernardelli Vincent

**TECHNICAL DETAILS**

| Gauge/calibre | : 12 |
|---|---|
| Chamber length | : 76mm (3in) |
| Number of barrels | : single-barrel |
| Magazine | : 2 or 3 cartridges |
| Action | : semi-automatic gas-operated |
| Locking | : falling-block locking |
| Trigger | single trigger |
| Weight | : 3.1–3.5kg (6lb13 oz–7lb 11oz) |
| Length | : 102–122cm (40$^1$/8–48in) |
| Barrel length | : 54.6–75cm (21$^1$/$_2$–29$^1$/$_2$ in) |
| Ejector | : extractor |
| Choke | multichoke |
| Sight | ventilated rib and bead |
| Safety | : push-button in rear of trigger guard |

**CHARACTERISTICS**

| — material | : steel |
|---|---|
| — finish | : blued (Vincent) or blued barrel and plain metal action with engraving (Vincent Deluxe) |
| — stock | : walnut stock, with pistol-grip |

Possession of shorter versions of this firearm is not permitted for hunting or other sporting purposes in a number of European countries. The law in United Kingdom requires the barrel of a shotgun to be a minimum of 24in (61cm).

# Blaser

Horst Blaser founded Blaser Jagdwaffen GmbH at Isny-im-Allgäu, Baden Würtemberg, Germany in 1977. The ancient town is close to the border with Southern Bavaria and Austria in the Allgauer Alps. The business was taken over in 1986 by Blaser's master gunsmith, Gerhard Blenk. The company specialises in high-quality hunting guns that often are embellished with exceptional engraving. Most of the models are breech-loading. The rifles are often provided with telescopic sights and Blaser only use the best sights by Zeiss, Swarovski, Schmidt & Bender, and Leupold. Blaser rifles can optionally be provided with Mag-Na-Port recoil compensators or a Kickstop recoil absorber in the stock.

## Blaser BBF-95 combination gun

**TECHNICAL DETAILS**

| Gauge/calibre | : see below |
|---|---|
| Chamber length | : see below |
| Number of barrels | : double-barrels over-and-under |
| Action | : breech-loading |

| Locking | : barrel-block locking |
| Trigger | twin triggers |
| Weight | : 2.8–3kg (6lb 2³/₄oz–6lb 10oz) |
| Length | : 102cm (40¹/₄in) |
| Barrel length | : 60cm (23⁵/₈in) |
| Ejector | : extractor |
| Choke | to choice, suitable for steel shot |
| Sight | fold-down rack and mounting for telescopic sights |
| Safety | : automatic safety, catch to enable firing mechanism |

**CHARACTERISTICS**

| — material | : steel |
| — finish | : blued barrels and plain metal action with engraving of hunting scenes to choice |
| — stock | : specially-selected walnut stock, with pistol-grip and cheek plate |

Available calibres/gauge: (smooth-bore) 12/70, 16/70, 20/70, or 20/76; (rifled barrel) choice from .22 Hornet to 9.3x74R.

🐦

## Blaser BBF 700/88 combination gun

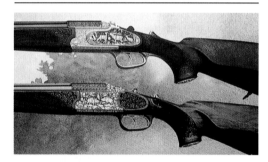

**TECHNICAL DETAILS**

| Gauge/calibre | : see below |
| Chamber length | : smooth-bore: 70mm (2³/₄in) or 76mm (3in) for gauge 20 |
| Number of barrels | : double-barrels over-and-under |
| Action | : breech-loading |
| Locking | : barrel-block locking |
| Trigger | twin triggers, adjustable trigger-pressure |
| Weight | : 2.6–3.2kg (5lb 11¹/₂oz–7lb) |
| Length | : 103cm (40⁵/₈in) |
| Barrel length | : 60cm (23⁵/₈in) |
| Ejector | : automatic or extractor |
| Choke | smooth-bore barrel full choke |
| Sight | rack and bead, mounting for telescopic sights |
| Safety | : automatic safety, firearm is cocked with cocking button on safety catch |

**CHARACTERISTICS**

| — material | : steel |
| — finish | : blued barrels, plain metal action, side-plates with engraving of hunting scenes to choice (no side-lock) |
| — stock | : specially-selected walnut stock, with pistol-grip and cheek plate |

Available calibres/gauge: (smooth-bore) 12, 16, or 20; (rifled barrel) .17 Rem., .22 Hornet, .222 Rem., .222 Rem Mag., 5.6x50R Mag., 5.6x52R, 6x62 Frères, 6x62R Frères, .243 Win., .25-06, 6.5x57R, 6.5x65R RWS, .270 Win., 7x57R, 7x65R, .308 Win., .30-06 Spr., .30R Blaser, 8x57 IRS, 8x75 RS, 9.3x74R. Illustrated from top to bottom are the BBF 700/88 Super Exclusive and the Exclusive. Double rifled and smooth-bore barrels are available for this gun. This gun cannot be held on a United Kingdom shotgun certificate.

🐦

## Blaser B 750/88 double-barrels mountain carbine (Bergstutzen)

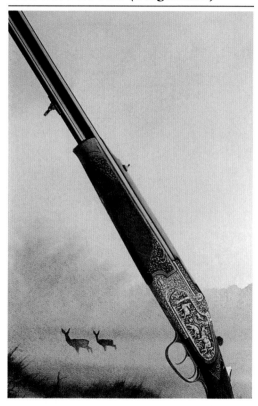

**TECHNICAL DETAILS**

| Gauge/calibre | : see below |
| Chamber length | : not applicable |
| Number of barrels | : double-barrels over-and-under |
| Action | : breech-loading |
| Locking | : barrel-block locking |
| Trigger | twin triggers, adjustable trigger-pressure |
| Weight | : 2.6–3.2kg (5lb 11¹/₂oz–7lb) |
| Length | : 103cm (40⁵/₈in) |
| Barrel length | : 60cm (23⁵/₈in) |
| Ejector | : extractor |
| Choke | rifled barrels, not applicable |

| Sight | rack and bead, mounting for telescopic sights |
|---|---|
| Safety | : automatic safety, firearm is cocked with cocking button on safety catch |

**CHARACTERISTICS**

| | |
|---|---|
| — material | : steel |
| — finish | : blued barrels and plain metal action and side-plates with engraving of hunting scenes to choice (no side-lock) |
| — stock | : specially-selected walnut stock, with pistol-grip and cheek plate |

Available calibres/gauges (upper barrel): .17 Rem., .22 Hornet, .222 Rem., .222 Rem Mag., 5.6x50R Mag., 5.6x52R; (bottom barrel) 5.6x50R Mag., 5.6x52R, 6x62R Frères, .243 Win., .25-06, 6.5x57R, 6.5x65R RWS, .270 Win., 7x57R, 7x65R, .308 Win., .30-06 Spr., .30R Blaser, 8x57 IRS, 8x75 RS, 9.3x74R. This gun cannot be held on a United Kingdom shotgun certificate.

### Blaser GB 860/88 double-barrels mountain carbine (Bergstutzen)

**TECHNICAL DETAILS**

| | |
|---|---|
| Gauge/calibre | : see below |
| Chamber length | : not applicable |
| Number of barrels | : double-barrels over-and-under |

| Action | : breech-loading |
|---|---|
| Locking | : barrel-block locking |
| Trigger | twin triggers, adjustable trigger-pressure |
| Weight | : 3.2–3.6kg (7lb–7lb 14³/₄oz) |
| Length | : 103cm (40⁵/8in) |
| Barrel length | : 60cm (23⁵/8in) |
| Ejector | : extractor |
| Choke | rifled barrels, not applicable |
| Sight | rack and bead, mounting for telescopic sights |
| Safety | : automatic safety, firearm is cocked with cocking button on safety catch |

**CHARACTERISTICS**

| | |
|---|---|
| — material | : steel |
| — finish | : blued barrels and plain metal action and side-plates with engraving of hunting scenes to choice (no side-lock) |
| — stock | : specially-selected walnut stock, with pistol-grip and cheek plate |

Available calibres (upper barrel): .222 Rem., .222 Rem Mag., 5.6x50R Mag., 5.6x52R, 6x62R Frères, .243 Win., 6.5x57R, 7x65R, 7mm Rem. Mag., .30-06 Spr., .300 Win Mag., 8x75 RS; (bottom barrel) 7x65R, 7mm Rem Mag., .30-06 Spr., .30R Blaser, .300 Win Mag., .300 Wby Mag., 8x68S, 8x75 RS, .375 H&H Mag., 9.3x62, 9.3x64, 9.3x74R. Alternative smooth-bore barrels in different gauges are also available for this gun. This gun cannot be held on a United Kingdom shotgun certificate.

### Blaser BD 880 drilling gun

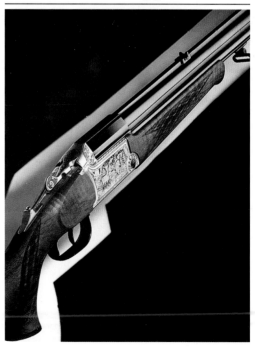

## TECHNICAL DETAILS

| | |
|---|---|
| Gauge/calibre | : see below |
| Chamber length | : see below |
| Number of barrels | : 3, 1 smooth-bore and 2 rifled barrels |
| Action | : breech-loading |
| Locking | : barrel-block locking |
| Trigger | twin triggers |
| Weight | : 3.1kg (6lb 13oz) |
| Length | : 102cm (40¹/₈in) |
| Barrel length | : 60cm (23⁵/₈in) |
| Ejector | : extractor |
| Choke | to choice |
| Sight | folding rack, clip-on mounting for telescopic sights |
| Safety | : sliding catch on neck of stock, barrel selector switch for rifled barrels, indicator for small calibre barrel on action, automatic switch when cocking for large calibre barrel |

## CHARACTERISTICS

| | |
|---|---|
| — material | : steel |
| — finish | : blued barrels and plain metal action with Arabesque engraving |
| — stock | : specially-selected walnut stock, with pistol-grip and cheek plate |

Available calibres/gauge (smooth-bore): 16/70, 20/70, or 20/76; (light calibre): .22 Hornet; (heavy calibre): .222 Rem.–9.3x74R.

# Browning

The man whose work led to today's firearms company was John Moses Browning, who lived from 1855–1926. From 1883 on he designed a large number of firearms and worked with Winchester and other companies. He was granted a patent in 1898 for a semi-automatic shotgun, the Automatic 5. Browning wanted to sell this design to Winchester but that company's management at that time turned it down. Browning was asking too much and the machine shop at Winchester was not equipped to make such a gun. He also failed to sell the design to Remington, so Browning brought the design to Europe where the Belgian Fabrique Nationale (FN) at Herstal near Liège made a number of pistols to Browning designs. The company did not hesitate to put the Browning semi-automatic shotgun into production. Browning developed his B25 shotgun in 1925, which was a revolutionary concept for its time, with barrels placed one on top of the other. This gun was introduced in 1926 and is still in production.

Browning died that same year of a heart attack while in Liège. His son, Val Browning, carried on his father's work. The present-day FN-Browning concern includes plants in the United States and Canada and is a part of the giant Winchester munitions company. The FN-Browning High Power (HP 35) pistol is extremely well-known. Beside this, there are many light and heavy calibre hand-guns. FN-Browning is also a market-leader in the field of both hunting rifles and shotguns for the field and clay-target sport.

A number of guns are produced for Browning by the Japanese firm, Miroku. The Custom department of FN-Browning can provide a wide assortment of artistic engravings for every type of Browning firearm. Since 1992, Browning shotguns have been "back-bored" or bored-out wider than the gauge.

The difference is minimal, with the normal diameter of a 12-gauge barrel being 18.4–18.45mm (approx. .725in) Browning back-bored barrels are 18.9–18.92. Browning's research has shown that the marginally wider barrels offer certain advantages over standard gauge barrels.

The resistance offered to the pellets by the barrel wall is reduced so that the shot velocity is increased.

This also causes fewer pellets to be deformed, and finally, the reduced resistance also minimises recoil.

## *Browning Anson*

## TECHNICAL DETAILS

| | |
|---|---|
| Gauge/calibre | : 12 |
| Chamber length | : 2³/₄in (70mm) |

Number of barrels : double-barrels side-by-side
Action : breech-loading
Locking : barrel-block locking
Trigger twin triggers
Weight : 6lb 10oz (3kg)
Length : 45$^1$/$_8$in (114.5cm)
Barrel length : 28$^3$/$_4$in (72cm)
Ejector : automatic
Choke fixed choke
Sight bead
Safety : sliding catch on neck of stock

**CHARACTERISTICS**
— material : steel
— finish : blued
— stock : straight English stock of walnut

The Anson 23 is illustrated. This gun is also available with side-locks.

## Browning Auto-5

**TECHNICAL DETAILS**
Gauge/calibre : 12 or 20
Chamber length : 2$^3$/$_4$in (70mm) or 3in (76mm)
Number of barrels : single
Magazine : tubular magazine for 2 or 5 cartridges
Action : semi-automatic, recoil operated
Locking : falling-block locking
Trigger single trigger
Weight : 6lb 8oz–8lb 13oz (2.9–4kg)
Length : 41$^1$/$_2$–51$^1$/$_4$in (105.5–130.2cm)
Barrel length : 22–30in (56–76cm)
Ejector : extractor
Choke Invector Plus chokes
Sight ventilated rib and bead
Safety : safety button in rear of trigger guard

**CHARACTERISTICS**
— material : steel
— finish : blued
— stock : walnut or black plastic stock (Stalker model), both with pistol-grip

## Browning B25 Hunter

**TECHNICAL DETAILS**
Gauge/calibre : 12
Chamber length : 2$^3$/$_4$in (70mm)
Number of barrels : double-barrels over-and-under
Action : breech-loading
Locking : barrel-block locking
Trigger single trigger
Weight : 7lb 8oz (3.4kg)
Length : 45$^1$/$_8$in (115cm)
Barrel length : 28in (71cm)
Ejector : automatic
Choke fixed choke to choice
Sight $^3$/$_8$in (6mm) ventilated rib and bead
Safety : sliding catch on neck of stock

**CHARACTERISTICS**
— material : steel
— finish : blued barrels with engraved action and side-plates (no side-lock)
— stock : walnut stock, with pistol-grip

## Browning B25 Sporting

**TECHNICAL DETAILS**
Gauge/calibre : 12
Chamber length : 2$^3$/$_4$in (70mm)
Number of barrels : double-barrels over-and-under
Action : breech-loading
Locking : barrel-block locking
Trigger single trigger
Weight : 7lb 9oz (3.45kg)
Length : 47$^1$/$_4$in (120cm)
Barrel length : 30in (76cm)
Ejector : automatic
Choke fixed choke to choice
Sight $^5$/$_{16}$in (8mm) ventilated rib and bead

Safety           : sliding catch on neck of stock, barrel selector

**CHARACTERISTICS**
— material       : steel
— finish         : blued barrels with plain metal engraved action
— stock          : walnut stock, with pistol-grip

Other models in the B25 Sporting range are: B25 Sporting 205 with 28in (71cm) barrel, 207 with 30in (76cm) barrel, and 208 with a 32in (81cm) barrel.

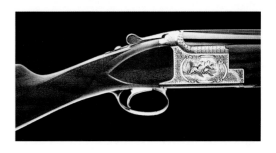

## *Browning B25 Trap Special*

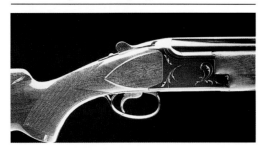

**TECHNICAL DETAILS**
Gauge/calibre     : 12
Chamber length    : 2³/₄in (70mm)
Number of barrels : double-barrels over-and-under
Action            : breech-loading
Locking           : barrel-block locking
Trigger           single trigger
Weight            : 7lb 13oz (3.54kg)
Length            : 47¹/₄in (120cm)
Barrel length     : 30in (76cm)
Ejector           : automatic
Choke             fixed choke to choice
Sight             : ⁵/₈in (16mm) ventilated rib and bead
Safety            : sliding catch on neck of stock and barrel selector

**CHARACTERISTICS**
— material        : steel
— finish          : blued barrels with plain metal engraved action
— stock           : walnut stock, with pistol-grip

## *Browning B125 Hunter*

**TECHNICAL DETAILS**
Gauge/calibre     : 12
Chamber length    : 2³/₄in (70mm)
Number of barrels : double-barrels over-and-under
Action            : breech-loading
Locking           : barrel-block locking
Trigger           single trigger
Weight            : 7lb 3oz or 7lb 4oz (3.25 or 3.3kg)
Length            : 47 or 49in (119 or 124cm)

Barrel length : 28 or 30in (71 or 76cm)
Ejector       : automatic
Choke         fixed choke
Sight         ¹/₂in (12mm) ventilated rib and bead
Safety        : sliding catch on neck of stock

**CHARACTERISTICS**
— material    : steel
— finish      : blued barrels plain metal action
— stock       : straight English stock of walnut, or with pistol-grip

There are also various models in the B125 range: Double Sporting, Special Sporting Europe, Superlight, and Trap F1.

## *Browning B127 Hunter*

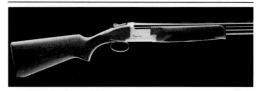

**TECHNICAL DETAILS**
Gauge/calibre     : 12
Chamber length    : 2³/₄in (70mm)
Number of barrels : double-barrels over-and-under
Action            : breech-loading
Locking           : barrel-block locking
Trigger           single trigger
Weight            : 6lb 13oz (3.1kg)
Length            : 45 or 49in (119 or 124cm)
Barrel length     : 28 or 30in (71 or 76cm)
Ejector           : automatic
Choke             ¹/₄ and ³/₄, or ¹/₂ and full
Sight             ⁹/₃₂in (7mm) ventilated rib and bead
Safety            : sliding catch on neck of stock and barrel selector

**CHARACTERISTICS**
— material        : steel
— finish          : blued barrels, light alloy action
— stock           : walnut stock

# Browning B325

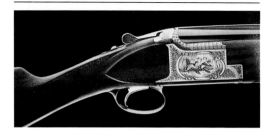

## TECHNICAL DETAILS

Gauge/calibre : 12 or 20
Chamber length : 2³/₄in (70mm)
Number of barrels : double-barrels over-and-under
Action : breech-loading
Locking : barrel-block locking
Trigger : single trigger
Weight : 6lb 2¹/₂oz–7lb 8oz (2.8–3.4kg)
Length : 43³/₄–47⁵/₈in (111–121cm)
Barrel length : 26–30in (66–76cm)
Ejector : automatic
Choke : Invector interchangeable chokes
Sight : ³/₈in (6mm) ventilated rib and bead
Safety : sliding catch on neck of stock and barrel selector

## CHARACTERISTICS

— material : steel
— finish : blued barrels, plain metal action
— stock : walnut stock, with pistol-grip

# Browning B425 Hunter

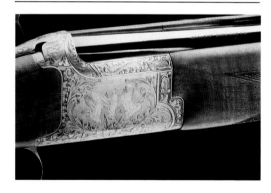

## TECHNICAL DETAILS

Gauge/calibre : 12 or 20
Chamber length : 2³/₄in (70mm) or 3in (76mm) for 20 gauge
Number of barrels : double-barrels over-and-under
Action : breech-loading
Locking : barrel-block locking
Trigger : single trigger
Weight : 6lb 3oz–6lb 13oz (2.85–3.1kg)
Length : 43³/₄–45⁵/₈in (110–116cm)
Barrel length : 26–30in (66–76cm)

Ejector : automatic
Choke : fixed or Invector interchangeable chokes
Sight : ¹/₄in (6.2mm) ventilated rib and bead
Safety : sliding catch on neck of stock

characteristics
— material : steel
— finish : blued barrels, plain metal engraved action
— stock : walnut stock, with pistol-grip

# Browning B425 Sporting Clays

## TECHNICAL DETAILS

Gauge/calibre : 12 or 20
Chamber length : 2³/₄in (70mm)
Number of barrels : double-barrels over-and-under with compensator vents
Action : breech-loading
Locking : barrel-block locking
Trigger : single trigger
Weight : 6lb 13oz–6lb 14³/₄oz (3.1–3.6kg)
Length : 45⁵/8–49⁵/8in (116–126cm)
Barrel length : 28–32in (71–81cm)
Ejector : automatic
Choke : Invector Plus interchangeable chokes
Sight : ⁷/₁₆in (10mm) ventilated rib and bead
Safety : sliding catch on neck of stock and barrel selector

## CHARACTERISTICS

— material : steel
— finish : blued barrels, plain metal action
— stock : walnut stock, with pistol-grip

A special blue-lacquered competition version for women is available of this model: the B425-WSSF (Women's Shooting Sports Foundation).

# Browning B-2000

## TECHNICAL DETAILS

Gauge/calibre : 12
Chamber length : 2³/₄in (70mm)
Number of barrels : single-barrel
Magazine : tubular magazine for 2–5 cartridges
Action : semi-automatic, gas-operated
Locking : falling-block locking
Trigger : single trigger
Weight : 6lb 13oz–7lb 11¹/₄oz (3.1–3.5kg)
Length : 48¹/₄–54³/₄in (123–130cm)
Barrel length : 26–32in (66–81cm)
Ejector : extractor

127

Chamber length : 3in (76mm) or 3³/₄in (89mm)
Number of barrels : single-barrel
Magazine : tubular magazine for 2–5 cartridges
Action : pump-action
Locking : falling-block locking
Trigger single trigger
Weight : 7lb 7oz–9lb 8oz (3.37–4.3kg)
Length : 42¹/₂–51in (108–129.6cm)
Barrel length : 22–30in (51–76cm)
Ejector : extractor
Choke Invector interchangeable chokes
Sight ⁵/₁₆in (8mm) ventilated rib and bead
Safety : safety catch on top of action

**CHARACTERISTICS**
— material : steel
— finish : blued
— stock : walnut stock, with pistol-grip

Choke fixed chokes to choice
Sight ³/₈in (6mm) ventilated rib and bead
Safety : push-button catch at rear of trigger guard

**CHARACTERISTICS**
— material : steel
— finish : blued
— stock : walnut stock, with pistol-grip

The magazine of this gun is loaded through the magazine port on the left of the system housing.

## Browning BPS Hunter
## (BPS: Browning Pump Shotgun)

**TECHNICAL DETAILS**
Gauge/calibre : 10 or 12

## Browning BPS 28 Hunting

**TECHNICAL DETAILS**
Gauge/calibre : 28
Chamber length : 2³/₄in (70mm)
Number of barrels : single-barrel
Magazine : tubular magazine for 2–4 cartridges
Action : pump-action
Locking : falling-block locking
Trigger single trigger
Weight : 7lb–7lb 1oz (3.18–3.2kg)
Length : 46³/₄–48³/₄in (119–124cm)
Barrel length : 26 or 28in (66 or 71cm)
Ejector : extractor
Choke Invector interchangeable chokes
Sight ⁵/₁₆in (8mm) ventilated rib and bead
Safety : safety catch on top of action

**CHARACTERISTICS**
— material : steel
— finish : blued
— stock : walnut stock, with pistol-grip

## Browning BPS Stalker

**TECHNICAL DETAILS**
Gauge/calibre : 12
Chamber length : 3in (76mm)
Number of barrels : single-barrel
Magazine : tubular magazine for 2–5 cartridges
Action : pump-action
Locking : falling-block locking

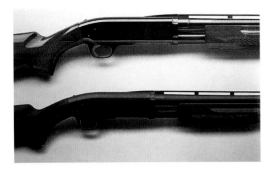

| Weight | : 7lb–7lb 4oz (3.2–3.3kg) |
| Length | : 46³/₄–48³/₄ in (119–124cm) |
| Barrel length | : 26 or 28in (66 or 71cm) |
| Ejector | : extractor |
| Choke | Invector Plus interchangeable chokes |
| Sight | ⁵/₁₆in (8mm) ventilated rib and bead |
| Safety | : safety catch on top of action |

**CHARACTERISTICS**
- material : steel
- finish : blued
- stock : walnut stock, with pistol-grip

| Trigger | single trigger |
| Weight | : 7lb 7oz–7lb 12oz (3.37–3.51kg) |
| Length | : 42¹/₂–50³/₄ in (108–129cm) |
| Barrel length | : 22–30in (51–76cm) |
| Ejector | : extractor |
| Choke | Invector interchangeable chokes |
| Sight | bead |
| Safety | : safety catch on top of action |

**CHARACTERISTICS**
- material : steel
- finish : matt black
- stock : black plastic stock, with pistol-grip

Illustrated from top to bottom: BPS Hunter and BPS Stalker.

## Browning BT-100 Trap

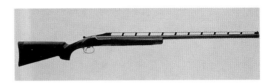

**TECHNICAL DETAILS**
| Gauge/calibre | : 12 |
| Chamber length | : 2³/₄in (70mm) |
| Number of barrels | : single-barrel (with compensator vents) |
| Action | : breech-loading |
| Locking | : barrel-block locking |
| Trigger | single trigger |
| Weight | : 8lb 6oz–8lb 10oz (3.8–3.9kg) |
| Length | : 48¹/₂–50³/₄ in (123.2–129cm) |
| Barrel length | : 32–34in (81–86cm) |
| Ejector | : automatic, can be disengaged |
| Choke | Invector Plus interchangeable chokes |
| Sight | raised ventilated rib and bead |
| Safety | : push-button safety in rear of trigger guard |

**CHARACTERISTICS**
- material : steel
- finish : blued
- stock : walnut stock, with pistol-grip and adjustable cheek plate, Monte Carlo, or thumbhole

## Browning BPS Trombone

The trigger pressure of the removable trigger mechanism can be adjusted between 3¹/₂–5¹/₂lb (1.6–2.5kg). The trigger is also equipped with a selector for disengaging the ejector. The BT 100 Trap range includes a stainless steel version and the Thumbhole with a thumbhole stock.

**TECHNICAL DETAILS**
| Gauge/calibre | : 12 |
| Chamber length | : 3in (76mm) |
| Number of barrels | : single-barrel |
| Magazine | : tubular magazine for 2–4 cartridges |
| Action | : pump-action |
| Locking | : falling-block locking |
| Trigger | single trigger |

## Browning Citori

**TECHNICAL DETAILS**
| Gauge/calibre | : 12, 20, 28, or .410 |
| Chamber length | : 2³/₄in (70mm), 3in (76mm), 3¹/₂ (89mm) |
| Number of barrels | : double-barrels, over-and-under |
| Action | : breech-loading |

**CHARACTERISTICS**
— material : steel
— finish : blued, or dull finish for Stalker models
— stock : walnut stock, with pistol-grip or black plastic for Stalker models

The Gold 10 is produced in Hunter and Stalker versions. The stalker version has a dull finish barrel and action and a black plastic stock. These guns are used by turkey hunters, and wildfowlers shooting duck and goose in the United States.

| Locking | : barrel-block locking |
|---|---|
| Trigger | single trigger |
| Weight | : 6lb–8lb 12oz (2.72–3.97kg) |
| Length | : 41–47in (104.2–119.4cm) |
| Barrel length | : 24–30in (61–76cm) |
| Ejector | : automatic |
| Choke | Invector Plus interchangeable chokes |
| Sight | ventilated rib and bead |
| Safety | : sliding catch on neck of stock |

**CHARACTERISTICS**
— material : steel
— finish : blued, or blued barrels and plain metal action
— stock : walnut stock, with pistol-grip

There are many versions of the Browning Citori, with the Lightning, High Grade, Ultra Sporting Clays, and Premiere Target series, with models such as Magnum Hunter, Sporting Hunter, Hunter, Superlight, and Upland Special.

## *Browning Gold 10 Semi-Auto*

**TECHNICAL DETAILS**
| Gauge/calibre | : 10 |
|---|---|
| Chamber length | : 3¹/₂ in (89mm) |
| Number of barrels | : single-barrel |
| Magazine | : tubular magazine for 2 or 5 cartridges |
| Action | : semi-automatic gas-operated |
| Locking | : falling-block locking |
| Trigger | single trigger |
| Weight | : 10lb 7oz–10lb 13oz (4.73–4.9kg) |
| Length | : 48, 50, or 52in (122, 127, or 132cm) |
| Barrel length | : 26, 28 or 30in (66, 71, or 76cm) |
| Ejector | : extractor |
| Choke | Invector Plus interchangeable chokes |
| Sight | ventilated rib and bead |
| Safety | : push-button safety at front of trigger guard |

## *Browning Gold 12 & 20 Hunter/ Stalker/Deer Hunter/Sporting Clays*

**TECHNICAL DETAILS**
| Gauge/calibre | : 12 or 20 |
|---|---|
| Chamber length | : 2³/₄in (70mm), 3in (76mm) or 3¹/₂ (89mm) |
| Number of barrels | : single-barrel |
| Magazine | : tubular magazine for 2 or 4 cartridges |
| Action | : semi-automatic gas-operated |
| Locking | : falling-block locking |
| Trigger | single trigger |
| Weight | : 6lb 14oz–7lb 13oz (3.11–4.9kg) |
| Length | : 42¹/₂–51in (108–129.6cm) |
| Barrel length | : 22, 26, 28 or 30in (56, 66, 71, or 76cm) |
| Ejector | : extractor |
| Choke | Invector Plus interchangeable chokes except |
| Sight | ventilated rib and bead |
| Safety | : push-button safety in rear of trigger guard |

**CHARACTERISTICS**
— material : steel barrel, light alloy action
— finish : blued, or dull finish for Stalker models
— stock : walnut stock, with pistol-grip or black plastic for Stalker models

## *Browning Light Sporting 802 ES*

**TECHNICAL DETAILS**
| Gauge/calibre | : 12 |
|---|---|
| Chamber length | : 2³/₄in (70mm) |
| Number of barrels | : double-barrels over-and-under |
| Action | : breech-loading |
| Locking | : barrel-block locking |

| Trigger | single trigger |
| Weight | : 7lb 8oz (3.4kg) |
| Length | : 45in (114cm) |
| Barrel length | : 28in (71cm) |
| Ejector | : automatic |
| Choke | Invector Plus interchangeable chokes (see remark) |
| Sight | $^1/_4$in (6.2mm) ventilated rib and bead |
| Safety | : sliding catch on neck of stock and barrel selector |

**CHARACTERISTICS**

| – materiaal | : stalen lopen, lichtmetalen bascule |
| – uitvoering | : geblauwd |
| – kolf | : walnotenhouten kolf en voorhout |

Remark: interchangeable chokes are available for this gun. This can be the Invector Plus chokes but Invector Plus 2 chokes, which are added to the barrels, are also available which increase the barrel length by 2in (5cm). The Invector Plus 4 choke set can also be attached to this gun, increasing the length of the barrel by 4in(10cm). This gives the gun its name of "Extended Swing" or ES. The gun illustrated has Invector Plus 4 chokes fitted.

## Browning Special Sporting Clays

**TECHNICAL DETAILS**

| Gauge/calibre | : 12 |
| Chamber length | : 2$^3/_4$in (70mm) |
| Number of barrels | : double-barrels over-and-under with compensator vents |
| Action | : breech-loading |
| Locking | : barrel-block locking |
| Trigger | single trigger |
| Weight | : 7lb 8oz–8lb (3.4–3.6kg) |
| Length | : 43or 45in (109.2 or 114.3cm) |
| Barrel length | : 26 or 28in (66 or 71cm) |
| Ejector | : automatic |
| Choke | Invector Plus interchangeable chokes |
| Sight | ventilated rib and bead |
| Safety | : sliding catch on neck of stock |

**CHARACTERISTICS**

| – material | : steel |
| – finish | : blued |
| – stock | : walnut stock, with pistol-grip |

## Browning Ultra Sporter Stainless

**TECHNICAL DETAILS**

| Gauge/calibre | : 12 |
| Chamber length | : 2$^3/_4$in (70mm) |
| Number of barrels | : double-barrels over-and-under with compensator vents |
| Action | : breech-loading |
| Locking | : barrel-block locking |
| Trigger | single trigger |
| Weight | : 8lb–8lb 5$^3/_4$oz (3.6–3.8kg) |
| Length | : 45–49in (114.3–124.5cm) |
| Barrel length | : 28, 30 or 32in (71, 76.2, or 81.3cm) |
| Ejector | : automatic |
| Choke | Invector Plus interchangeable chokes |
| Sight | ventilated rib and bead |
| Safety | : sliding catch on neck of stock |

**CHARACTERISTICS**

| – material | : steel barrels, stainless steel action |
| – finish | : blued barrels, plain metal action |
| – stock | : walnut stock, with pistol-grip |

This gun is also available in an entirely blued finish as Ultra Skeet, Ultra Sport, and Ultra Sporter.

# Chapuis

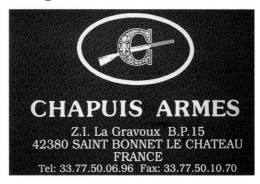

The French town of St. Etienne has long been an important centre for the arms industry. The area surrounding the town was engaged in making gun parts as a household industry during the eighteenth and nineteenth centuries. These barrels and actions were then assembled into complete firearms in the factories of St. Etienne. André Chapuis worked at home as a gunsmith in the village of St. Bonnet-le-Chateau on the river

Loire at the end of the nineteenth century. He principally made complete actions and barrels. When his son Jean also wished to join the family enterprise, Chapuis set up his own small-scale business to make complete guns. They specialized in shotguns and hunting rifles. The company had to cease production during World War II but started up once more in 1945. In the hands of the present head, René Chapuis, the firm makes an important contribution in the field of shotguns and Express game rifles of the highest quality, with much of the production still being done by hand.

## Chapuis Alfa RAlfa

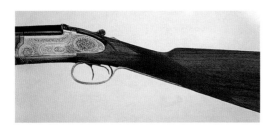

### TECHNICAL DETAILS

| | |
|---|---|
| Gauge/calibre | : 12 or 16 |
| Chamber length | : 70mm (2³/₄in) |
| Number of barrels | : double-barrels over-and-under |
| Action | : breech-loading |
| Locking | : double barrel-block locking |
| Trigger | twin triggers |
| Weight | : 2.85kg (6lb 4oz) |
| Length | : 113cm (44¹/₂ in) |
| Barrel length | : 70cm (27¹/₂ in) |
| Ejector | : automatic |
| Choke | ¹/₄ and ³/₄, or cylindrical and ¹/₂ |
| Sight | ventilated rib and bead |
| Safety | : safety catch on top of action |

### CHARACTERISTICS

| | |
|---|---|
| — material | : steel |
| — finish | : blued barrels, plain metal engraved action and side plates (no side-lock) |
| — stock | : straight English stock of walnut |

## Chapuis Alfa UGAlfa

### TECHNICAL DETAILS

| | |
|---|---|
| Gauge/calibre | : 12 or 16 |
| Chamber length | : 70mm (2³/₄in) |
| Number of barrels | : double-barrels over-and-under |
| Action | : breech-loading |
| Locking | : double barrel-block locking |
| Trigger | twin triggers |
| Weight | : 2.55–2.9kg (5lb 6oz–6lb 6oz) |

| | |
|---|---|
| Length | : 103–113cm (40¹/₂–44¹/₂in) |
| Barrel length | : 60–70cm (23⁵/₈–27¹/₂ in) |
| Ejector | : RG Alfa: automatic, UG Alfa: extractors |
| Choke | to choice |
| Sight | ventilated rib and bead |
| Safety | : safety catch on top of action |

### CHARACTERISTICS

| | |
|---|---|
| — material | : steel |
| — finish | : blued barrels, plain metal engraved action |
| — stock | : straight English stock of walnut |

Illustrated from top to bottom:
Chapuis UG Alfa and RG Alfa.

## Chapuis Prestige Double-Express

### TECHNICAL DETAILS

| | |
|---|---|
| Gauge/calibre | : 7x65R, 8x57JRS, 9.3x74R |
| Chamber length | : not applicable |
| Number of barrels | : double-barrels side-by-side |

| | |
|---|---|
| Action | : breech-loading |
| Locking | : double barrel-block locking |
| Trigger | twin triggers |
| Weight | : 3.2kg (7lb) |
| Length | : 102.5cm (40³/₈in) |
| Barrel length | : 60cm (23⁵/₈in) |
| Ejector | : automatic |
| Choke | not applicable, rifled barrels |
| Sight | adjustable rack sight and mounting for telesc. sight |
| Safety | : sliding catch on neck of stock |

**CHARACTERISTICS**

| | |
|---|---|
| — material | : steel |
| — finish | : blued barrels, plain metal action and side-lock plates engraved with hunting scenes |
| — stock | : walnut stock, with pistol-grip and cheek plate, or straight English stock of walnut |

This outstanding rifle is supplied with a Zeiss 1.5–6 x 42 telescopic sight in a leather case and with exchange smooth-bore barrels for 12 or 20 gauge.

## Chapuis Prestige Progress H&H side–lock

**TECHNICAL DETAILS**

| | |
|---|---|
| Gauge/calibre | : 12 or 20 |
| Chamber length | : 70mm (2³/₄in) |
| Number of barrels | : double-barrels side-by-side |
| Action | : breech-loading |
| Locking | : double barrel-block locking |
| Trigger | twin triggers |
| Weight | : 2.7 or 2.9kg (6lb–6lb 6oz) |
| Length | : 121cm (47⁵/₈in) |
| Barrel length | : 70cm (27¹/₂ in) |
| Ejector | : to choice |
| Choke | ¹/₄ and ³/₄, or to choice |
| Sight | bead |
| Safety | : safety catch on top of action |

**CHARACTERISTICS**

| | |
|---|---|
| — material | : steel |
| — finish | : blued barrels, plain metal engraved action and side-lock plates |
| — stock | : straight English stock of specially-selected walnut |

## Chapuis Progress Double-Express

**TECHNICAL DETAILS**

| | |
|---|---|
| Gauge/calibre | : 7x65R, 8x57JRS, 9.3x74R |
| Chamber length | : not applicable |
| Number of barrels | : double-barrels side-by-side |
| Action | : breech-loading |
| Locking | : double barrel-block locking |
| Trigger | twin triggers |
| Weight | : 3.2kg (7lb) |
| Length | : 102.5cm (40³/₈in) |
| Barrel length | : 60cm (23⁵/₈in) |
| Ejector | : extractors or ejectors |
| Choke | not applicable, rifled barrels |
| Sight | adjustable rack sight |
| Safety | : sliding catch on neck of stock, safety vents in action |

**CHARACTERISTICS**

| | |
|---|---|
| — material | : steel |
| — finish | : blued barrels, plain metal engraved action |
| — stock | : walnut stock, with pistol-grip and cheek plate |

Illustrated from top to bottom are: UG Express with extractor and RG Express with automatic ejectors.

## Chapuis Progress HG

**TECHNICAL DETAILS**

| | |
|---|---|
| Gauge/calibre | : 12, 16, or 20 |
| Chamber length | : 2³/₄in (70mm) or 76mm (3in) |

```
Number of barrels : double-barrels side-by-side
Action          : breech-loading
Locking         : double barrel-block locking
Trigger           twin triggers
Weight          : 2.8 or 2.9kg (6lb 2¹/₂oz–6lb 6oz)
Length          : 112cm (44¹/₄in)
Barrel length   : 70cm (27¹/₂ in)
Ejector         : to choice
Choke             ¹/₄ and ³/₄
Sight             bead
Safety          : safety catch on top of action
```

**CHARACTERISTICS**
```
— material      : steel
— finish        : blued barrels, plain metal engraved action
— stock         : specially-selected walnut stock
```

## *Chapuis Progress HG-Deluxe*

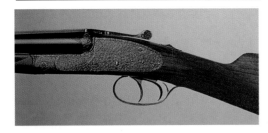

**TECHNICAL DETAILS**
```
Gauge/calibre   : 12
Chamber length  : 70mm (2³/₄in)
Number of barrels : double-barrels side-by-side
Action          : breech-loading
Locking         : double barrel-block locking
Trigger           twin triggers
Weight          : 2.55kg (5lb 9³/₄oz)
Length          : 113cm (44¹/₂ in)
Barrel length   : 60cm (23⁵/₈ in)
Ejector         : automatic
Choke             ¹/₄ and ¹/₂, 0/0 and ¹/₂
Sight             bead
Safety          : safety catch on top of action
```

**CHARACTERISTICS**
```
— material      : steel
— finish        : blued barrels, plain metal engraved action
— stock         : straight English stock of walnut
```

## *Chapuis Progress RGP Mixte*

**TECHNICAL DETAILS**
```
Gauge/calibre   : see below
Chamber length  : smooth-bore barrel: 76mm (3in)
Number of barrels : double-barrels side-by-side
Action          : breech-loading
Locking         : double barrel-block locking
Trigger           twin triggers
```

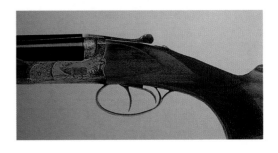

```
Weight          : 3.2kg (7lb)
Length          : 113cm (44¹/₂ in)
Barrel length   : 60cm (23⁵/₈in)
Ejector         : extractors
Choke             smooth-bore barrels: cylindrical
Sight             folding rack and bead
Safety          : safety catch on top of action
```

**CHARACTERISTICS**
```
— material      : steel
— finish        : blued barrels, plain metal engraved action
— stock         : selected walnut stock, with pistol-grip and cheek
                  plate
```

Available calibres/gauge (smooth-bore): 12 or 20 gauge; (rifled barrel): 6.5x57R, 7x65, 8X57JRS, 9.3x74R.

# Colt's Manufacturing Company Inc.

Colt Manufacturing is based in Hartford, Connecticut, on the east coast of the United States. Colt has been making firearms for more than 160 years. At first the company only made revolvers but by the beginning of the twentieth century, Colt also started to make semi-automatic pistols. Colt introduced their .45 ACP pistol that was designed by John Moses Browning, in 1911. Colt also made a range of rifles until about ten year ago, such as the Colt Colteer, Stagecoach, and small calibre carbines for .22 LR. Colt also produced their Standard Pump pump-action shotgun but all these guns have disappeared from the company's range. The company made civilian versions of its famous Colt M-16 army rifle as Colt AR-15. Colt made some 3,440,000 M-16 rifles in the various versions. The company introduced the Armsmear shotgun in 1995, their first new double-barrelled shotgun for 30 year.

## Colt Armsmear

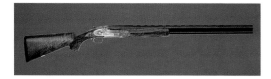

**TECHNICAL DETAILS**

| | |
|---|---|
| Gauge/calibre | : 12 |
| Chamber length | : 2³/₄in (70mm) |
| Number of barrels | : double-barrels over-and-under |
| Action | : breech-loading |
| Locking | : barrel-block locking |
| Trigger | single trigger |
| Weight | : 4lb (1.8kg) |
| Length | : 44³/₄ or 46¹/₂ in (113.7 or 118cm) |
| Barrel length | : 28 or 30in (71 or 76cm) |
| Ejector | : automatic |
| Choke | interchangeable chokes |
| Sight | ventilated rib and bead |
| Safety | : sliding catch on neck of stock |

**CHARACTERISTICS**

| | |
|---|---|
| — material | : steel |
| — finish | : blued barrels; CAS1000:plain metal action engraved with hunting scenes; CAS2000 has engravings with gold inlay on decorative side-plates |
| — stock | : European walnut |

# Cosmi Americo & Figlio

The Italian firearms company of Cosmi from Ancona makes shotguns that are of great interest from a technical standpoint. The founder of the company is Ditta Cosmi, who designed his gun in 1930.

The tubular magazine is housed in the stock of the gun and the cartridge feed is via the bottom of the action.

It is not only the action which moves back on cocking; the barrel also moves backwards on sliders in the action.

The special semi-automatic mechanism of this gun includes inertia locking. The gun is cocked with the help of a bolt.

The receiver or action body (it is a combina tion of both) has Westley-Richards type locking. Cosmi make each gun individually to requirements of their customer.

If required, the guns can also be finished with hand-crafted engravings.

## Cosmi Semi-Auto

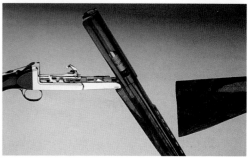

**TECHNICAL DETAILS**

| | |
|---|---|
| Gauge/calibre | : 12 or 20 |
| Chamber length | : 70mm (2³/₄in) or 76mm (3in) |
| Number of barrels | : single-barrel |
| Magazine | : tubular magazine for 2, 3, or 8 cartridges in stock |
| Action | : semi-automatic and breech-loading |
| Locking | : inertia locking with recoiling barrel |
| Trigger | single trigger |
| Weight | : approx. 3—3.5kg (6lb 10oz—7lb 11oz) |
| Length | : to choice |
| Barrel length | : to choice |
| Ejector | : extractor |
| Choke | to choice or interchangeable chokes |
| Sight | ventilated rib and bead |
| Safety | : sliding catch on neck of stock |

**CHARACTERISTICS**

| | |
|---|---|
| — material | : action of nickel-steel, barrel of Boehler-Antinit steel |
| — finish | : blued barrel, plain metal action |
| — stock | : specially-selected walnut stock, with pistol-grip, or with straight English stock |

A lightweight titanium version of this gun is also available.

# CZ

The name of CZ stands for Ceska Zbrojovka. CZ is based in Uhersky Brod, a small town in the foothills of the Carpathian mountains, in the south of Moravia, in the Czech Republic. The armaments industry grew rapidly in the new Czechoslovakia after World War I when the fledgling nation had to equip its new army from scratch. Factories such as Zbrojovka Brno, Ceska Zbrojovka Strakonice, and Zavody Skoda are the best-known names. The first of these, based in Brno, developed a light machine-gun, the 2-GB-33, which they sold the rights of under licence to the Royal Ordnance small arms factory at Enfield where it was produced as the world-famous Bren gun.

The present-day Ceska Zbrojovka or CZ, was set-up in July, 1936 as a subsidiary of CZ Strakonice, which was in turn a subsidiary of Zbrojovka Brno. During World War II the occupying German forces renamed the company Böhmische Waffenwerke (Bohemian armaments factory). The entire region came under Russian control after World War II.

The new communist rulers nationalised the company in 1947 and the production was mainly given over to army firearms such as Kalashnikov rifles.
The company name was changed in about 1956 into Ceska Zavody Motocyclove and at that time the company mainly produced motorcycles. The company moved to its present home in Uhersky Brod in 1958. The range has been expanded during the 60 years that the company has existed in its present form to include a wide assortment of pistols, rifles, and other guns.

CZ is currently the largest maker of light calibre firearms and exports its products to more than 70 countries throughout the world. The present range includes bolt-action rifles, semi-automatic pistols, shotguns, and air weapons. These products were little known during the "cold war". When the

"iron curtain" fell, the firearms of CZ quickly became extremely popular because of their excellent value for money in terms of the relatively low cost for such quality. The company is also known as Brno, and Brünner.

## CZ Model 581

**TECHNICAL DETAILS**

Gauge/calibre : 12
Chamber length : 70mm (2³/₄in)
Number of barrels : double-barrels over-and-under
Action : breech-loading
Locking : Kersten locking and barrel-block locking
Trigger single or twin triggers
Weight : 3.9kg (8lb 8oz)
Length : 115cm (45¹/₄in)
Barrel length : 71cm (28in)
Ejector : automatic
Choke interchangeable chokes
Sight bead
Safety : automatic safety; sliding catch on neck of stock, barrel selector, dropped-gun safety

**CHARACTERISTICS**

— material : steel
— finish : blued
— stock : specially-selected walnut stock, with pistol-grip

## CZ Model 584 combination gun

**TECHNICAL DETAILS**

Gauge/calibre : see below
Chamber length : smooth-bore barrel: 70mm (2³/₄in)
Number of barrels : double-barrels over-and-under
Action : breech-loading
Locking : Kersten locking and barrel-block locking
Trigger twin triggers
Weight : 3.5kg (7lb 11oz)
Length : 105.5cm (41¹/₂ in)
Barrel length : 62cm (24³/₄in)

| | |
|---|---|
| Ejector | : extractor |
| Choke | smooth-bore barrel: to choice |
| Sight | rack and bead |
| Safety | : automatic safety; sliding catch on neck of stock, barrel selector, dropped-gun safety |

**CHARACTERISTICS**
- material : steel
- finish : blued
- stock : specially-selected walnut stock, with pistol-grip

Available calibres/gauge (smooth-bore barrel): 12; (rifled barrel): .222 Rem, .223 Rem, 5.6x52 Savage, .243 Win., 7x57R, 7x65R, .308 Win., .30-06 Spr. This gun cannot be held on a shotgun certificate under United Kingdom legislation.

🖐️

# Dakota

The Dakota Arms Company Inc. is a relatively new and small-scale America arms manufacturer. The founder, Don Allen, was an airline pilot flying Boeing 727's for Northwest Airlines until 1984. He had made rifles based on the Model 70 Winchester as a hobby since 1962.

When he retired in 1984, he and his wife founded Dakota Arms, based at Sturgis in South Dakota. His first rifle was the Dakota model 76 that he introduced in 1987.
Allen went on to develop six different rifles with exceptional characteristics for hunting medium to big game and then brought out a traditional side-by-side shotgun in the autumn of 1995. This gun, the American Legend is of a quality that it is difficult to better and is comparable to the guns of Parker and Fox.

The outstanding shotgun is supplied in a leather case and with a signed copy of the book Game Gun by the American author Richard S. Grozik.
The American Legend can be bought as a pair in 20 or 12 gauge. Such a pair costs about $50,000.

## Dakota American Legend 20 Limited Edition Juxtaposé

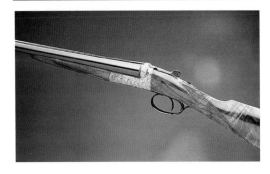

**TECHNICAL DETAILS**
| | |
|---|---|
| Gauge/calibre | : 20 (12 also available to order) |
| Chamber length | : 2³/₄in (70mm) |
| Number of barrels | : double-barrels side-by-side |
| Action | : breech-loading |
| Locking | : double barrel-block locking |
| Trigger | twin triggers |
| Weight | : 6lb 9¹/₂oz (3kg) |
| Length | : 45¹/₄in (115cm) |
| Barrel length | : 27¹/₄in (69cm) |
| Ejector | : automatic |
| Choke | to choice |
| Sight | bead |
| Safety | : sliding catch on top of action |

**CHARACTERISTICS**
- material : steel
- finish : blued barrels, plain metal action is hand engraved
- stock : straight English stock of specially-selected English walnut

This exceptional shotgun is produced to a quality that makes it a collector's item rather than a gun for everyday use. The basic price is $18,000 but extras are readily available, such as pistol-grip ($350), single trigger ($750).
Custom versions are available to order. It is anticipated the Dakota Arms will bring out more special editions in the future.

# Fabarm

Fabarm is an ultra-modern Italian firearms company based at Travagliato in the Brescia region. The company name is derived from Fabbrica Bresciana Armi. The company's range includes a wide assortment of over-and-under shotguns for field use and shoot-

ing sports, plus a fine range of side-by-side guns, both with and without side-locks. There are also semi-automatic shotguns, and pump-action guns for clay shooting. In addition to these sporting firearms, Fabarm make police firearms such as the SDASS riot guns. The steel firearms use nickel-chromium-molybdenum steel. Lightweight guns use the aluminium-based alloy Ergal 55 for the actions. All the firearms have walnut stocks and fore-arms, except those shotguns with plastic stocks. A number of the shotguns are supplied with Inner-Choke interchangeable chokes which provide cylindrical, $^1/_4$, $^1/_2$, $^3/_4$, and full choke. Choke tubes for use with steel shot are also available to order for $^1/_2$ and full choke. Fabarm shotguns can also be equipped with a Multi-Choke system.

## Fabarm Beta Europe Field

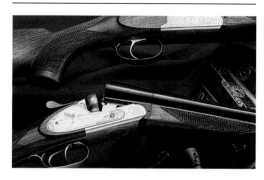

**TECHNICAL DETAILS**
Gauge/calibre   : 12
Chamber length   : 70mm (2$^3/_4$in)
Number of barrels : double-barrels side-by-side
Action       : breech-loading
Locking       : double barrel-block locking
Trigger       single or twin triggers
Weight       : 2.95kg (6lb 8oz)
Length       : 114cm (44$^7/_8$in)
Barrel length   : 71cm (28in)

Ejector     : automatic
Choke       fixed: $^3/_4$ and full
Sight       bead
Safety       : sliding catch on neck of stock

**CHARACTERISTICS**
— material     : steel
— finish     : blued barrels, plain metal action with engraved side-lock plates or standard action (without side-lock)
— stock     : straight English stock of walnut

## Fabarm Ellegi Inner-Choke

**TECHNICAL DETAILS**
Gauge/calibre   : 12
Chamber length   : 76mm (3in)
Number of barrels : single-barrel
Magazine     : tubular magazine for 2 or 3 cartridges
Action       : semi-automatic gas-operated
Locking       : falling-block locking
Trigger       single trigger
Weight       : 3.1–3.3g (6lb 13oz–7lb 4oz)
Length       : 121, 125, or 130cm (47$^5/_8$, 49$^1/_4$, or 51$^3/_{16}$in)
Barrel length   : 66, 71, or 76cm (26, 28, or 30in)
Ejector     : extractor
Choke       Inner-Choke set: $^1/_2$, $^3/_4$, or full
Sight       ventilated rib and bead
Safety       : bush-button safety in rear of trigger guard

**CHARACTERISTICS**
— material     : steel barrel, light alloy action body
— finish     : blued
— stock     : walnut stock, with pistol-grip

## Fabarm Euro 3

**TECHNICAL DETAILS**
Gauge/calibre   : 12
Chamber length   : 76mm (3in)
Number of barrels : single-barrel
Magazine     : tubular magazine for 2 cartridges
Action       : semi-automatic gas-operated
Locking       : falling-block locking
Trigger       single trigger
Weight       : 2.75g (6lb)

Length           : 117cm (46in)
Barrel length    : 62cm (24³/₈in)
Ejector          : extractor
Choke            fixed: ¹/₄
Sight            bead
Safety           : bush-button safety in rear of trigger guard

**CHARACTERISTICS**
— material       : steel barrel, light alloy action body
— finish         : blued
— stock          : walnut stock, with pistol-grip

## Fabarm Gamma Lux Competition Sporting

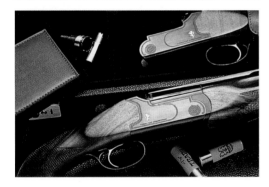

**TECHNICAL DETAILS**
Gauge/calibre      : 12 or 20
Chamber length     : 70mm (2³/₄in); 20 gauge also 76mm (3in)
Number of barrels : double-barrels over-and-under
Action             : breech-loading
Locking            : barrel-block locking
Trigger            single trigger
Weight             : 3.2–3.4kg (7lb–7lb 8oz)
Length             : 127, 130, or 132cm (50, 51³/₁₆, or 52in)
Barrel length      : 71, 74, or 76cm (28, 29, or 30in)
Ejector            : automatic
Choke              interchangeable Inner-Choke
Sight              ventilated rib and bead
Safety             : sliding catch on neck of stock

**CHARACTERISTICS**
— material       : steel

— finish         : blued
— stock          : walnut stock, with pistol-grip

## Fabarm Gamma Lux hunter

**TECHNICAL DETAILS**
Gauge/calibre      : 12
Chamber length     : 70mm (2³/₄in)
Number of barrels : double-barrels over-and-under
Action             : breech-loading
Locking            : barrel-block locking
Trigger            single trigger
Weight             : 3.15–3.25kg (6lb 14³/₄–7lb 2³/₄oz)
Length             : 115cm (45¹/₄in)
Barrel length      : 71ccm (28in)
Ejector            : automatic
Choke              interchangeable or fixed choke: ¹/₂ and full
Sight              ventilated rib and bead
Safety             : sliding catch on neck of stock

**CHARACTERISTICS**
— material       : steel
— finish         : blued barrels, plain metal action
— stock          : walnut stock, with pistol-grip

## Fabarm Gamma Lux Superlight Hunter

**TECHNICAL DETAILS**
Gauge/calibre      : 12 or 20
Chamber length     : 70mm (2³/₄in) or 76mm (3in)
Number of barrels : double-barrels over and under
Action             : breech-loading

| Locking | : barrel-block locking |
| Trigger | single trigger |
| Weight | : 2.4–2.75kg (5lb 4½ oz–6lb) |
| Length | : 109 or 114cm (42⅞ or 44⅞in) |
| Barrel length | : 66 or 71ccm (26 or 28in) |
| Ejector | : automatic |
| Choke | interchangeable or ¼ and ¾ or ½ and full |
| Sight | ventilated rib and bead |
| Safety | : sliding catch on neck of stock |

**CHARACTERISTICS**

| – material | : steel barrels, light alloy action |
| – finish | : blued barrels, plain metal action |
| – stock | : walnut stock, with pistol-grip |

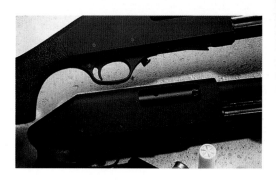

## *Fabarm Max Luxus*

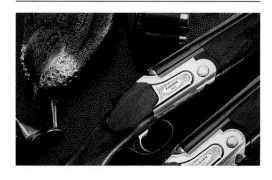

**TECHNICAL DETAILS**

| Gauge/calibre | : 12 or 20 |
| Chamber length | : 70mm (2¹/₄in); 20 gauge also 76mm (3in) |
| Number of barrels | : double-barrels over-and-under |
| Action | : breech-loading |
| Locking | : barrel-block locking |
| Trigger | single trigger |
| Weight | : 3.2–3.4kg (7lb–7lb 8oz) |
| Length | : 127, 130, or 132cm (50, 51³/₁₆, or 52in) |
| Barrel length | : 71, 74, or 76cm (28, 29, or 30in) |
| Ejector | : automatic |
| Choke | interchangeable Inner-Choke |
| Sight | ventilated rib and bead |
| Safety | : sliding catch on neck of stock |

**CHARACTERISTICS**

| – material | : steel |
| – finish | : blued |
| – stock | : walnut stock, with pistol-grip |

## *Fabarm SDASS Police Martial 20 (R2)*

**TECHNICAL DETAILS**

| Gauge/calibre | : 12 |
| Chamber length | : 76mm (3in) |
| Number of barrels | : single-barrel |
| Magazine | : tubular magazine for 7 cartridges |
| Action | : pump-action |

| Locking | : falling-block locking |
| Trigger | single trigger |
| Weight | : 2.75g (6lb) |
| Length | : 105cm (41⁵/₁₆ in) |
| Barrel length | : 50cm (19³/₄ in) |
| Ejector | : extractor |
| Choke | cylindrical |
| Sight | bead |
| Safety | : bush-button safety in rear of trigger guard, action locking catch in front of trigger guard, locking safety |

**CHARACTERISTICS**

| – material | : steel barrel, light alloy action body |
| – finish | : matt black |
| – stock | : black plastic stock, with pistol-grip |

A separate pistol-grip is also available for this firearm. Under United Kingdom firearms law, shotguns are not permitted to have a magazine capacity in excess of 2 cartridges in the magazine and 1 in the barrel. The barrel of this firearm falls below United Kingdom 24in (61cm) minimum required for a gun to be held on a shotgun certificate. Similar provisions apply in certain other European countries.

# FAIR-Techni Mec

The Italian company FAIR Techni Mec was set up in 1971 to continue the activities of

Isidoro Rizzini & Co. The company is based at Marcheno in the well-known arms-making region of Brescia. The relatively young business is able to call upon the centuries of craftsmanship in the region. The brand name of their guns is FAIR. This modern company manufactures guns using computer-controlled technology (Cad-Cam) and computer numerical control (CNC) processes for the production machines. The actions of their shotguns are silver-satin chrome finished, polished steel, or blued, depending on the model. The Italian national testing centre at Gardone tests the shotguns to a pressure of 1200 bar, which is more than adequate for steel shot. Certain models from the wide range have screw-in chokes. FAIR call this Interchoke.

## FAIR Imperial II

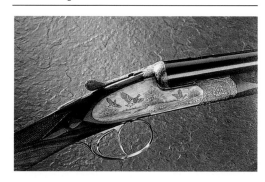

**TECHNICAL DETAILS**

| | |
|---|---|
| Gauge/calibre | : 12, 20, 28, or .410 |
| Chamber length | : 70mm (2³/₄in); 76mm (3in) for 20 gauge |
| Number of barrels | : double-barrels side-by-side |
| Action | : breech-loading |
| Locking | : barrel-block locking |
| Trigger | twin triggers |
| Weight | : 2.8–3.2kg (6lb 2¹/₂ oz–7lb) |
| Length | : 112–122cm (44–48in) |
| Barrel length | : 66–76cm (26–30in) |
| Ejector | : automatic |
| Choke | to choice |
| Sight | bead |
| Safety | : sliding catch on neck of stock |

**CHARACTERISTICS**

| | |
|---|---|
| — material | : steel |
| — finish | : blued barrels, plain metal action with engraved side-plates (no side-lock) |
| — stock | : straight English stock of selected walnut |

## FAIR LX 680

**TECHNICAL DETAILS**

| | |
|---|---|
| Gauge/calibre | : 12 |
| Chamber length | : 70mm (2³/₄in) |
| Number of barrels | : double-barrels over-and-under |
| Action | : breech-loading |
| Locking | : barrel-block locking |
| Trigger | single trigger |
| Weight | : 3.1kg (6lb 13oz) |
| Length | : 114cm (44⁷/₈ in) |
| Barrel length | : 70cm (27¹/₂ in) |
| Ejector | : automatic |
| Choke | ¹/₂ and full, or Interchoke |
| Sight | 7mm (⁹/₃₂ in) ventilated rib with bead |
| Safety | : sliding catch on neck of stock |

**CHARACTERISTICS**

| | |
|---|---|
| — material | : steel |
| — finish | : blued barrels, satin chrome action engraved with floral and hunting motifs |
| — stock | : walnut stock, with pistol-grip |

## FAIR LX 902

## TECHNICAL DETAILS

Gauge/calibre : 12 or 20
Chamber length : 70mm (2³/₄in) or 76mm (3in) for 20 gauge
Number of barrels : double-barrels over-and-under
Action : breech-loading
Locking : barrel-block locking
Trigger : single trigger
Weight : 2.75 or 3.15kg (6lb or 6lb 14³/₄oz)
Length : 114cm (44⁷/₈in)
Barrel length : 68 or 70cm (26³/₄ or 27¹/₂ in)
Ejector : automatic
Choke : ¹/₂ and full; ¹/₄ and ³/₄; or Interchoke
Sight : 7mm (⁹/₃₂ in) ventilated rib with bead
Safety : sliding catch on neck of stock

## CHARACTERISTICS

— material : steel
— finish : blued barrels, satin chrome action with engravings of hunting motifs on side-plates (no side-lock)
— stock : straight English stock of walnut

# FAIR SRC 622

## TECHNICAL DETAILS

Gauge/calibre : 20, 28, or .410
Chamber length : 70mm (2³/₄in) or 76mm (3in)
Number of barrels : double-barrels over-and-under
Action : breech-loading
Locking : barrel-block locking
Trigger : single trigger
Weight : 2.75kg (6lb)
Length : 111cm (43³/₄in)
Barrel length : 68cm (26³/₄in)
Ejector : automatic
Choke : ¹/₄ and ³/₄; Interchoke for 20 gauge
Sight : 6mm (³/₈ in) ventilated rib with bead
Safety : sliding catch on neck of stock

## CHARACTERISTICS

— material : steel
— finish : blued barrels, satin chrome action with engravings of hunting motifs on side-plates (no side-lock)
— stock : walnut stock, with pistol-grip

# FAIR SRL 702 Trap

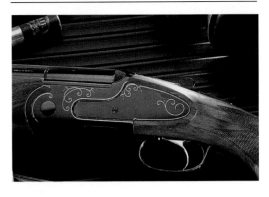

## TECHNICAL DETAILS

Gauge/calibre : 12 or 20 (SRC 702)
Chamber length : 70mm (2³/₄in)
Number of barrels : double-barrels over-and-under
Action : breech-loading
Locking : barrel-block locking
Trigger : single trigger
Weight : 3.35 or 3.7kg (7lb 6oz or 8lb 2¹/₄oz)
Length : 118 or 121cm (46 ¹/₂ or 47⁵/₈in)
Barrel length : 74 or 76cm (29¹/₈ or 30in)
Ejector : automatic
Choke : ³/₄ and full
Sight : 9 or 11mm (³/₈ or ⁷/₁₆ in) wide ventilated rib with bead
Safety : sliding catch on neck of stock

## CHARACTERISTICS

— material : steel
— finish : blued barrels, blued action with decorative gold inlay engravings
— stock : walnut stock, with pistol-grip

# FAIR SRL 802 Skeet

## TECHNICAL DETAILS

Gauge/calibre : 12 or 20 (SRC 802)
Chamber length : 70mm (2³/₄in)
Number of barrels : double-barrels over-and-under
Action : breech-loading
Locking : barrel-block locking on bottom barrel
Trigger : single trigger

| | |
|---|---|
| Weight | : 3.15 or 3.4kg (6lb 14³/₄oz or 7lb 8oz) |
| Length | : 114, 116 or 118cm (44⁷/₈, 45⁵/₈, or 46¹/₂ in) |
| Barrel length | : 66, 68, or 70cm (26, 26³/₄, or 27¹/₂ in) |
| Ejector | : automatic |
| Choke | cylindrical (both barrels) |
| Sight | 9 or 11mm (³/₈ or ⁷/₁₆ in) wide ventilated rib with bead |
| Safety | : sliding catch on neck of stock |

### CHARACTERISTICS
| | |
|---|---|
| — material | : steel |
| — finish | : blued barrels, satin-chrome action with English style engraved side-plates (no side-lock) |
| — stock | : walnut stock, with pistol-grip |

# Fanzoj

The Austrian firm of Johann Fanzoj Jagd-waffen is based in Ferlach, which has been famous for its gunsmiths since the sixteenth century. Fanzoj specialise in hunting guns.

Once military firearms were made in Ferlach but the accent has shifted in the past 200 years to small-scale production by hand of shotguns and hunting rifles of very high quality. Fanjoj has been making firearms that no-one else makes since 1760. The triple-barrelled rifle is a unique example of their craft skills. The attention to detail at every stage of the production of their guns can withstand the closest scrutiny.

### CHARACTERISTICS
| | |
|---|---|
| — material | : steel |
| — finish | : blued barrels, plain metal engraved side-plates |
| — stock | : very special walnut stock with pistol-grip and cheek plate, or straight English stock |

The close-up photograph clearly shows the three barrels one on top of another. The heavy locking lugs can be seen on either side of the barrel block. This is the Kersten or double Greener locking.

## Fanzoj Triple-Express rifle

### TECHNICAL DETAILS
| | |
|---|---|
| Gauge/calibre | : to customer's choice: all existing calibres and combinations are available |
| Chamber length | : not applicable |
| Number of barrels | : triple-barrels over-and-under |
| Action | : breech-loading |
| Locking | . double barrel block lock and Kersten locking |
| Trigger | twin triggers |
| Weight | : approx. 4.5kg (9lb 14oz) |
| Length | : 107cm (42in) |
| Barrel length | : 61cm (24in) |
| Ejector | : extractor |
| Choke | not applicable: rifled barrels |
| Sight | fixed rack sight; special clip-on mount for telescopic sight |
| Safety | : safety catch behind locking lever; barrel selector |

## Fanzoj Double-Express rifle

### TECHNICAL DETAILS
| | |
|---|---|
| Gauge/calibre | : all existing calibres |
| Chamber length | : not applicable |
| Number of barrels | : double-barrels side-by-side |
| Action | : breech-loading |
| Locking | : double barrel block lock and conical upper lug (doll's head) |
| Trigger | twin triggers |
| Weight | : approx. 4.5kg (9lb 14oz) |
| Length | : 107cm (42in) |
| Barrel length | : 61cm (24in) |
| Ejector | : extractor |
| Choke | not applicable: rifled barrels |
| Sight | Express folding sight, mounting for telescopic sight |
| Safety | : safety catch behind locking lever |

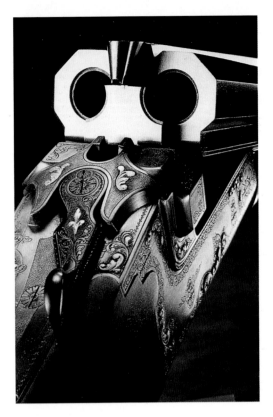

TECHNICAL DETAILS

Gauge/calibre : .470 NE (Nitro Express)
Chamber length : not applicable
Number of barrels : double-barrels side-by-side
Action : breech-loading
Locking : double barrel block lock and Kersten locking
Trigger twin triggers
Weight : approx.4.5kg (9lb 14oz)
Length : 107cm (42in)
Barrel length : 61cm (24in)
Ejector : automatic
Choke not applicable: rifled barrels
Sight Express folding sight; mounting for telescopic sight
Safety : safety catch behind locking lever


CHARACTERISTICS

— material : steel
— finish : blued octagonal barrels, blued action with decorative special engravings
— stock : specially-selected walnut stock with pistol-grip and cheek plate

☙

## *Fanzoj Double-Express Side-Lock*

TECHNICAL DETAILS

Gauge/calibre : .470 NE (Nitro Express)
Chamber length : not applicable
Number of barrels : double-barrels side-by-side
Action : breech-loading
Locking : barrel block lock and conical upper lug (doll's head)
Trigger twin triggers
Weight : approx.4.5kg (9lb 14oz)
Length : 107cm (42in)
Barrel length : 61cm (24in)
Ejector : automatic
Choke not applicable: rifled barrels
Sight fixed rack sight; mounting for telescopic sight
Safety : safety catch behind locking lever


CHARACTERISTICS

— material : steel
— finish : blued barrels, special engravings on Holland & Holland side-locks
— stock : special Caucasian walnut stock with pistol-grip and cheek plate

☙

CHARACTERISTICS

— material : steel
— finish : blued and engraved
— stock : specially-selected walnut stock with pistol-grip and cheek plate, or straight English stock

The close-up photograph clearly shows the additional upper locking. The extended ridge forms a conical locking lug also known as a "doll's head". Machining of this feature requires considerable precision and is therefore a costly process. This gun cannot be held on a shotgun certificate under United Kingdom legislation.

☙

## *Fanzoj Double-Express .470 NE*

## Fanzoj Triple-Express Super

### TECHNICAL DETAILS

| | |
|---|---|
| Gauge/calibre | : see below |
| Chamber length | : not applicable |
| Number of barrels | : triple-barrels over-and-under |
| Action | : breech-loading |
| Locking | : double barrel block lock and Kersten locking |
| Trigger | twin triggers |
| Weight | : approx.4.5kg (9lb 14oz) |
| Length | : 104cm (41in) |
| Barrel length | : 61cm (24in) |
| Ejector | : extractor |
| Choke | not applicable: rifled barrels |
| Sight | fixed rack sight; mounting for telescopic sight |
| Safety | : safety catch behind locking lever |

### CHARACTERISTICS

| | |
|---|---|
| — material | : steel |
| — finish | : blued barrels, plain metal side-plates (no side-lock) engraved with hunting motifs |
| — stock | : special Caucasian walnut stock with pistol-grip or straight English stock |

Available calibres/gauges (upper barrel): .22 Hornet; (middle barrel): 6.5 x 57R; (bottom barrel): 9.3 x 74R. This rifle is supplied with a Zeiss-Diavari 2.5–10 x 48 telescopic sight, calibrated to 100m (328ft).

# Fausti cav. Stefano & Figlie

FABBRICA D'ARMI
FAUSTI CAV. STEFANO
& Figlie s.n.c.

Stefano Fausti established his gunsmith's workshop in Marcheno in the Italian firearm's region of Valle Trompia. Fausti exported guns from the outset to both North and South America but more recently he has also sold throughout Europe. The high quality of his guns are achieved by using computer numerical control (CNC) to operate the machines. Fausti also uses Cad-Cam systems to design and develop his new models. The entire production is a mere 1,000 guns per month. All his guns are available with interchangeable stocks. Alternative barrels are also available for certain models for 10, 12, and 20 gauge in both normal and lightweight versions. Some notion of the extent of the Fausti service can be grasped from the knowledge that clients can have their guns serviced in the factory.

A subsidiary company known as V.I.T. makes gun parts for Fausti and others. The three daughters of Fausti, Giovanna, Elena, and Barbara, work for the company. The Elgioba shotgun introduced in 1966 bears a little of each of their names.

## Fausti Classic

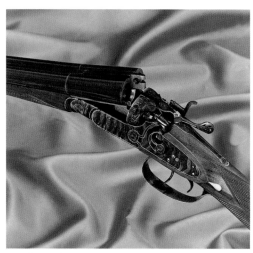

### TECHNICAL DETAILS

| | |
|---|---|
| Gauge/calibre | : 12, 16, 20, 24, 28, 32, or .410 |
| Chamber length | : 70 (2³/₄in) or 76mm (3in) |
| Number of barrels | : double-barrels side-by-side |
| Action | : breech-loading |
| Locking | : barrel-block locking |
| Trigger | twin triggers |
| Weight | : 3.2 or 3.4kg (7lb or 7lb 8oz) |
| Length | : 109 or 114cm (43 or 45in) |
| Barrel length | : 66 or 71cm (26 or 28in) |

| Ejector | : extractor |
| --- | --- |
| Choke | $^1/_4$ and $^1/_2$, or $^1/_2$ and full |
| Sight | recessed 10mm ($^7/_{16}$in) wide rib and bead |
| Safety | : sliding catch on neck of stock |

**CHARACTERISTICS**

| — material | : steel |
| --- | --- |
| — finish | : blued barrels, plain metal engraved action and Holland & Holland side-lock plates; external hammers |
| — stock | : specially-selected walnut stock with pistol-grip or straight English stock |

## Fausti Dallas

**TECHNICAL DETAILS**

| Gauge/calibre | : 10 |
| --- | --- |
| Chamber length | : 89mm ($3^3/_4$in) |
| Number of barrels | : double-barrels over-and-under |
| Action | : breech-loading |
| Locking | : barrel-block locking |
| Trigger | single or twin triggers |
| Weight | : 3.4 or 3.6kg (7lb 8oz or 7lb $14^3/_{40}$oz) |
| Length | : 112 or 126cm ($44^1/_8$ or $45^5/_8$in) |
| Barrel length | : 66 or 81cm (26 or 32in) |
| Ejector | : extractor |
| Choke | multichoke |
| Sight | 12mm ($^1/_2$in) wide ventilated rib and bead |
| Safety | : sliding catch on neck of stock, barrel selector with single trigger at front of trigger |

**CHARACTERISTICS**

| — material | : steel |
| --- | --- |
| — finish | : blued |
| — stock | : walnut stock, with pistol-grip |

This type of gun is widely used in USA for hunting wild turkey. Certain European countries other than the United Kingdom do not permit the use of 10 gauge shot.

## Fausti Elegant EL

**TECHNICAL DETAILS**

| Gauge/calibre | : 12, 16, 20, 24, 28, 32, or .410 |
| --- | --- |
| Chamber length | : 70mm ($2^3/_4$in) or 76mm (3in) |

| Number of barrels | : double-barrels over-and-under |
| --- | --- |
| Action | : breech-loading locking |
| Locking | : barrel-block locking |
| Trigger | single or twin triggers |
| Weight | : 3–3.2kg (6lb 8oz–7lb) |
| Length | : 112, 117, or 122cm (44, 46 or 48in) |
| Barrel length | : 66, 71 or 76cm (26, 28 or 30in) |
| Ejector | : extractor or automatic ejector |
| Choke | $^1/_4$ and $^1/_2$, $^1/_2$ and full, or $^3/_4$ and full |
| Sight | 7mm ($^9/_{32}$in) wide ventilated rib with bead |
| Safety | : sliding catch on neck of stock, barrel selector with single trigger in front of trigger guard |

**CHARACTERISTICS**

| — material | : steel |
| --- | --- |
| — finish | : blued, or blued barrels and plain metal action |
| — stock | : walnut stock, with pistol-grip |

## Fausti Elegant ST (Standard)

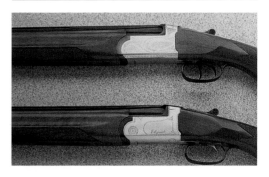

**TECHNICAL DETAILS**

| Gauge/calibre | : 12, 16, 20, 24, 28, 32, or .410 |
| --- | --- |
| Chamber length | : 70mm ($2^3/_4$in) or 76mm (3in) |
| Number of barrels | : double-barrels over-and-under |
| Action | : breech-loading |
| Locking | : barrel-block locking |
| Trigger | single or twin triggers |
| Weight | : 3–3.2kg (6lb 8oz–7lb) |
| Length | : 112, 117, or 122cm (44, 46 or 48in) |
| Barrel length | : 66, 71 or 76cm (26, 28 or 30in) |
| Ejector | : extractor or automatic ejector |
| Choke | $^1/_4$ and $^1/_2$, $^1/_2$ and full, or $^3/_4$ and full |
| Sight | 7mm ($^9/_{32}$in) wide ventilated rib with bead |
| Safety | : sliding catch on neck of stock, barrel selector with single trigger in front of trigger guard |

## CHARACTERISTICS

- material : steel
- finish : blued, or blued barrels and plain metal action
- stock : walnut stock, with pistol-grip

This gun is also available in Trap, Skeet, or Sporting Clays versions.

## Fausti Elgioba

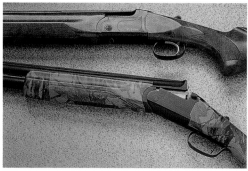

**TECHNICAL DETAILS**

| | |
|---|---|
| Gauge/calibre | : 12, 16, 20, 24, 28, 32, or 36 |
| Chamber length | : 70mm (2³/₄in) or 76mm (3in) |
| Number of barrels | : double-barrels over-and-under |
| Action | : breech-loading |
| Locking | : barrel-block locking |
| Trigger | single trigger |
| Weight | : 3–3.2kg (6lb 8oz–7lb) |
| Length | : 112, 117, or 122cm (44, 46 or 48in) |
| Barrel length | : 66, 71 or 76cm (26, 28 or 30in) |
| Ejector | : automatic |
| Choke | ¹/₄ and ¹/₂, ¹/₂ and full, or ³/₄ and full or inter-changeable chokes |
| Sight | 7mm (⁹/₃₂in) wide ventilated rib with bead |
| Safety | : sliding catch on neck of stock |

**CHARACTERISTICS**

- material : steel
- finish : blued
- stock : walnut stock, with pistol-grip, also available in camouflage colourings

## Fausti Leader Sporting

**TECHNICAL DETAILS**

| | |
|---|---|
| Gauge/calibre | : 12 or 20 |
| Chamber length | : 70mm (2³/₄in) or 76mm (3in) |
| Number of barrels | : double-barrels over-and-under |
| Action | : breech-loading |
| Locking | : barrel-block locking |
| Trigger | single or twin triggers |
| Weight | : 3.2–3.6kg (7lb–7lb 14³/₄oz) |
| Length | : 109–119cm (42³/₄–46³/₄in) |
| Barrel length | : 66, 71 or 76cm (26, 28 or 30in) |

| | |
|---|---|
| Ejector | : automatic |
| Choke | interchangeable chokes or fixed chokes to choice |
| Sight | 7 or 10mm (⁹/₃₂ or ⁷/₁₆in) wide ventilated rib with bead |
| Safety | : sliding catch on neck of stock, barrel selector for single trigger in front of trigger guard |

**CHARACTERISTICS**

- material : steel
- finish : blued barrels, plain metal action; SP & FP models have decorative side-plates (not side-locks)
- stock : walnut stock, with pistol-grip

## Fausti Leader ST Hunting

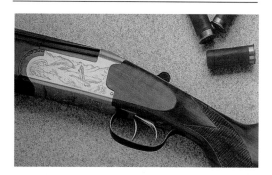

**TECHNICAL DETAILS**

| | |
|---|---|
| Gauge/calibre | : 12, 16, or 20 |
| Chamber length | : 70mm (2³/₄in) or 76mm (3in) |
| Number of barrels | : double-barrels over-and-under |
| Action | : breech-loading locking |
| Locking | : barrel-block locking |
| Trigger | single or twin triggers |
| Weight | : 3–3.2kg (6lb 8oz–7lb) |
| Length | : 112, 117, or 122cm (44, 46 or 48in) |
| Barrel length | : 66, 71 or 76cm (26, 28 or 30in) |
| Ejector | : automatic |
| Choke | ¹/₄ and ¹/₂, ¹/₂ and full, or ³/₄ and full |
| Sight | 7mm (⁹/₃₂in) wide ventilated rib with bead |
| Safety | : sliding catch on neck of stock, barrel selector with single trigger in front of trigger guard |

**CHARACTERISTICS**

- material : steel

- finish : blued barrels and plain metal action with hunting engravings
- stock : walnut stock, with pistol-grip

This gun is also available for slugs with 58.4cm (23 in) rifled barrels with cylindrical chokes.

## Fausti Leader Trap EL /Skeet EL

### TECHNICAL DETAILS
Gauge/calibre : 12 or 20
Chamber length : 70mm (2³/₄in)
Number of barrels : double-barrels over-and-under
Action : breech-loading
Locking : barrel-block locking
Trigger single trigger
Weight : 3.2–3.6kg (7lb–7lb 14³/₄oz)
Length : 109–119cm (42⁷/₈–46⁷/₈in)
Barrel length : Trap: 76cm (30in); Skeet: 66 or 71cm (26 or 28in)
Ejector : automatic
Choke Trap: ³/₄ and full; Skeet: cylindrical and skeet
Sight 10mm (⁷/₁₆in) wide ventilated rib with bead
Safety : sliding catch on neck of stock, barrel selector in front of trigger guard

### CHARACTERISTICS
- material : steel
- finish : blued with gold lining of the action for Gold Series or plain metal action
- stock : walnut stock, with pistol-grip

## Fausti Progress

### TECHNICAL DETAILS
Gauge/calibre : 12
Chamber length : 76mm (3in)
Number of barrels : single-barrel
Magazine : 2 or 4 cartridges
Action : semi-automatic gas-operated
Locking : falling-block locking
Trigger single trigger
Weight : 3.1kg (6lb 13oz)
Length : 114cm (44⁷/₈ in)
Barrel length : 71cm (28in)

Ejector : extractor
Choke multichoke
Sight 7mm (⁹/₃₂ in) wide ventilated rib with bead
Safety : push-button safety in rear of trigger guard

### CHARACTERISTICS
- material : steel barrels, with light alloy (Ergal 55) action body
- finish : blued barrel and plain metal action body with engravings
- stock : walnut stock, with pistol-grip

## Fausti Projet

### TECHNICAL DETAILS
Gauge/calibre : 12, 16, 20, 24, 28, 32, or .410
Chamber length : 70mm (2³/₄in) or 76mm (3in)
Number of barrels : double-barrels over-and-under
Action : breech-loading
Locking : barrel-block locking
Trigger single or twin triggers
Weight : 3–3.2kg (6lb 8oz–7lb)
Length : 112, 117, or 122cm (44, 46 or 48in)
Barrel length : 66, 71 or 76cm (26, 28 or 30in)
Ejector : extractor
Choke ¹/₄ and ¹/₂, ¹/₂ and full, or ³/₄ and full
Sight 7mm (⁹/₃₂in) wide ventilated rib with bead
Safety : sliding catch on neck of stock

### CHARACTERISTICS
- material : steel
- finish : blued, or blued barrels and plain metal action
- stock : walnut stock, with pistol-grip

## Fausti Senator Holland & Holland

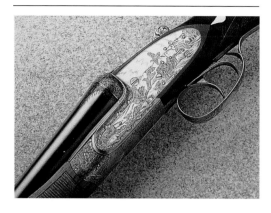

### TECHNICAL DETAILS

Gauge/calibre : 12, 16, or 20
Chamber length : 70mm (2³/₄in) or 76mm (3in)
Number of barrels : double-barrels side-by-side
Action : breech-loading
Locking : barrel-block locking
Trigger single or twin triggers
Weight : 3.2–3.4kg (7lb–7lb 8oz)
Length : 109 or 114cm (43 or 45in)
Barrel length : 66 or 71cm (26 or 28in)
Ejector : extractor or automatic ejector
Choke ¼ and ½, or ½ and full
Sight 10mm (⁷/₁₆in) wide ventilated rib with bead
Safety : sliding catch on neck of stock, barrel selector with single trigger in front of trigger guard

### CHARACTERISTICS

— material : steel
— finish : blued barrels and plain metal engraved action and side-lock plates (Holland & Holland side-lock)
— stock : specially-selected walnut stock, with pistol-grip or straight English stock

## Fausti Style EL

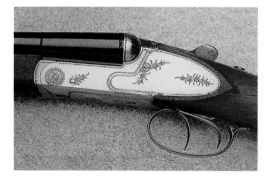

### TECHNICAL DETAILS

Gauge/calibre : 12, 16, 20, 24, 28, 32, or .410
Chamber length : 70mm (2³/₄in) or 76mm (3in)

---

Number of barrels : double-barrels side-by-side
Action : breech-loading
Locking : barrel-block locking
Trigger twin triggers
Weight : 3.2–3.4kg (7lb–7lb 8oz)
Length : 109–119cm (43–46⁷/₈ in)
Barrel length : 66, 71, or 76cm (26, 28, or 30in)
Ejector : extractor or automatic ejector
Choke ¼ and ½, ½ and full, or ³/₄ and full
Sight 10mm (⁷/₁₆in) wide recessed rib with bead
Safety : sliding catch on neck of stock

### CHARACTERISTICS

— material : steel
— finish : blued barrels and plain metal engraved action and side-plates (no side-lock)
— stock : straight English stock of selected walnut

## Fausti Style ST

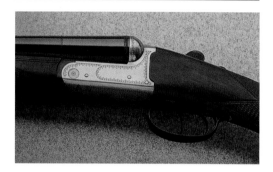

### TECHNICAL DETAILS

Gauge/calibre : 12, 16, 20, 24, 28, 32, or .410
Chamber length : 70mm (2³/₄in) or 76mm (3in)
Number of barrels : double-barrels side-by-side
Action : breech-loading
Locking : barrel-block locking
Trigger twin triggers
Weight : 3.2–3.4kg (7lb–7lb 8oz)
Length : 109–119cm (43–46⁷/₈in)
Barrel length : 66, 71, or 76cm (26, 28, or 30in) Canard model 81cm (32in)
Ejector : extractor or automatic ejector
Choke ¼ and ½, ½ and full, ³/₄ and full, or Canard model full/full
Sight 10mm (⁷/₁₆in) wide recessed rib with bead
Safety : sliding catch on neck of stock

### CHARACTERISTICS

— material : steel
— finish : blued barrels and plain metal action; both barrels can be discharged simultaneously with Canard model
— stock : walnut stock, with pistol-grip, or straight English stock

# Ferlach

**TECHNICAL DETAILS**

| | |
|---|---|
| Gauge/calibre | : 12 |
| Chamber length | : 70mm (2³/₄in) |
| Number of barrels | : double-barrels side-by-side |
| Action | : breech-loading |
| Locking | : double barrel-block locking |
| Trigger | twin triggers |
| Weight | : 3.1kg (6lb 13oz) |
| Length | : 114cm (44³/₄in) |
| Barrel length | : 72cm (28³/₄in) |
| Ejector | : automatic |
| Choke | fixed choke to choice |
| Sight | bead |
| Safety | : sliding catch on neck of stock |

**CHARACTERISTICS**

| | |
|---|---|
| — material | : steel |
| — finish | : blued, plain metal action and side-lock plates with floral engraving, removable side-locks |
| — stock | : straight English stock of selected Austrian walnut |

The area surrounding Ferlach in Austria has been renowned for making firearms since the sixteenth century. Until 1900, this was mainly the production of military weapons, not just for the Austrian army but also for export. A gunsmith's guild was formed in Ferlach in about 1850 and this also founded a school for training armourers. For the past 100 years, the emphasis has been on small-scale production of exclusive and had-crafted shotguns, hunting rifles, and combination guns of the highest quality. More recently, the gunsmiths in Ferlach have united to win a wider share of the market. The great strength of these companies is that they make guns that no other gun companies produce. The triple- and quadruple-barrelled guns are unique examples of their exceptional craft skills. The greatest attention is given to every detail, so that these guns can withstand the closest and most critical of scrutiny.

## Ferlach side-by-side side-lock 17E

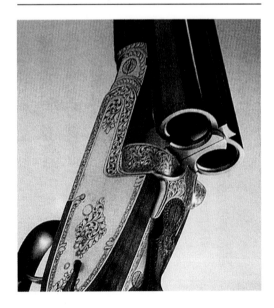

## Ferlach over-and-under 20E

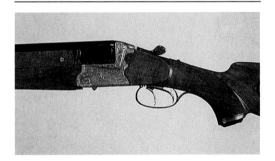

**TECHNICAL DETAILS**

| | |
|---|---|
| Gauge/calibre | : 12 |
| Chamber length | : 70mm (2³/₄in) |
| Number of barrels | : double-barrels over-and-under |
| Action | : breech-loading |
| Locking | : double barrel-block locking and Kersten locking |
| Trigger | twin triggers |
| Weight | : 3.42kg (7lb 8 oz) |
| Length | : 115cm (45¹/₄in) |
| Barrel length | : 71cm (28in) |
| Ejector | : automatic |
| Choke | fixed choke to choice |
| Sight | bead |
| Safety | : sliding catch on neck of stock |

**CHARACTERISTICS**

| | |
|---|---|
| — material | : steel |
| — finish | : blued barrels, plain metal action with decorative engraving |
| — stock | : selected walnut stock, with pistol-grip and cheek plate |

## Ferlach over-and-under side-lock 24E

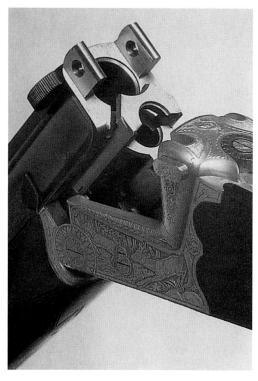

### TECHNICAL DETAILS

Gauge/calibre : 12
Chamber length : 70mm (2³/₄in)
Number of barrels : double-barrels over-and-under
Action : breech-loading
Locking : double barrel-block locking and Kersten locking
Trigger single trigger
Weight : 3.42kg (7lb 8oz)
Length : 115cm (45¹/₄in)
Barrel length : 71cm (28in)
Ejector : automatic
Choke fixed choke to choice
Sight ventilated rib and bead
Safety : sliding catch on neck of stock and barrel selector

### CHARACTERISTICS

— material : steel
— finish : blued barrels, plain metal action with decorative engraving on side-lock plates
— stock : straight English stock of selected walnut

— stock : selected walnut stock, with pistol-grip and cheek plate

## Ferlach over-and-under combination gun 33H (external hammers)

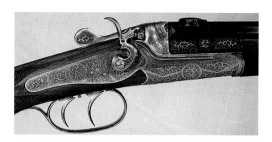

### TECHNICAL DETAILS

Gauge/calibre : upper barrel: 12 gauge; bottom barrel: choice of calibre
Chamber length : 70mm (2³/₄in)
Number of barrels : double-barrels over-and-under
Action : breech-loading
Locking : double barrel-block locking and Kersten locking
Trigger twin triggers
Weight : 3.3kg (7lb 4oz)
Length : 108cm (41in)
Barrel length : 64cm (25¹/₄in)
Ejector : extractor
Choke smooth-bore barrel: fixed choke to choice
Sight rack and bead sight

## Ferlach over-and-under combination gun 33

### TECHNICAL DETAILS

Gauge/calibre : upper barrel: 12 gauge; bottom barrel: choice of calibre
Chamber length : 70mm (2³/₄in)
Number of barrels : double-barrels over-and-under
Action : breech-loading
Locking : double barrel-block locking and Kersten locking
Trigger twin triggers
Weight : 3.5kg (7lb 11oz)
Length : 110cm (43¹/₄in)
Barrel length : 66cm (26in)
Ejector : automatic
Choke smooth-bore barrel: fixed choke to choice
Sight rack and bead sight, special mount for telescopic sight
Safety : sliding catch on neck of stock, barrel selector

### CHARACTERISTICS

— material : steel
finish : blued barrels, plain metal action with decorative engraving on side-lock plates

Safety          : sliding catch on neck of stock, barrel selector

### CHARACTERISTICS
— material       : steel
— finish         : blued barrels, plain metal action with engravings of
                   hunting scenes on side-lock plates
— stock          : selected walnut stock, with pistol-grip and cheek
                   plate

## *Ferlach triple-barrel model 41*

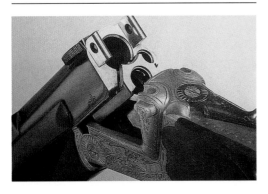

Number of barrels : triple-barrelled
Action          : breech-loading
Locking         : double barrel-block locking and double Greener locking
Trigger         twin triggers
Weight          : 3.4kg (7lb 8oz)
Length          : 107cm (42¹/₈in)
Barrel length   : 65cm (25⁵/₈in)
Ejector         : extractor
Choke           smooth-bore barrel: to choice
Sight           special mount for telescopic sight
Safety          : sliding catch on neck of stock, barrel selector for
                  rifled barrels

### CHARACTERISTICS
— material       : steel
— finish         : blued barrels, plain metal action with engravings of
                   hunting scenes
— stock          : selected walnut stock, with pistol-grip and cheek
                   plate

Available calibres/gauges (both upper barrels): 12/70; (bottom rifled barrel): to choice.

### TECHNICAL DETAILS
Gauge/calibre    : see below
Chamber length   : smooth-bore: 70mm (2³/₄in)
Number of barrels : triple-barrelled
Action          : breech-loading
Locking         : barrel-block locking and Kersten locking
Trigger         twin triggers
Weight          : 3.5kg (7lb 11oz)
Length          : 103cm (40¹/₂ in)
Barrel length   : 61cm (24in)
Ejector         : extractor
Choke           smooth-bore barrel: to choice
Sight           rack and bead sight, special mount for telesc. sight
Safety          : sliding catch on neck of stock, barrel selector for
                  rifle barrels

## *Ferlach triple–barrel Model 55*

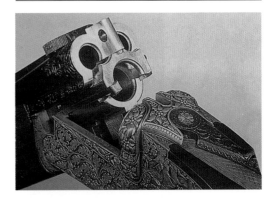

### CHARACTERISTICS
— material       : steel
— finish         : blued barrels, plain metal action with engravings of
                   hunting scenes
— stock          : selected walnut stock, with pistol-grip and cheek
                   plate

Available calibres/gauges (smooth-bore barrel): 12/70; (full-bore): to choice; (3rd barrel): .22 LR or .22 WMR.

## *Ferlach triple–barrel Model 50*

### TECHNICAL DETAILS
Gauge/calibre    : see below
Chamber length   : smooth-bore: 70mm (2³/₄in)

### TECHNICAL DETAILS
Gauge/calibre    : see below
Chamber length   : smooth-bore: 70mm (2³/₄in)
Number of barrels : triple-barrelled

| | |
|---|---|
| Action | : breech-loading |
| Locking | : double barrel-block locking and double Greener locking |
| Trigger | twin triggers |
| Weight | : 3.5kg (7lb 11oz) |
| Length | : 104cm (41in) |
| Barrel length | : 61cm (24in) |
| Ejector | : extractor |
| Choke | smooth-bore barrel: to choice |
| Sight | rack and bead; special mount for telescopic sight |
| Safety | : sliding catch on neck of stock, barrel selector on left of stock, behind side-lock plates |

### CHARACTERISTICS
| | |
|---|---|
| — material | : steel |
| — finish | : blued barrels, plain metal action with engravings of hunting scenes on side-lock plates |
| — stock | : selected walnut stock, with pistol-grip and cheek plate |

Available calibres/gauges (both upper barrels): choice of rifle calibre; (bottom barrel): 12/70.

ᴗ

## Ferlach 63E Express side-lock rifle

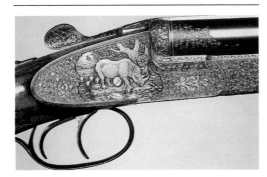

### TECHNICAL DETAILS
| | |
|---|---|
| Gauge/calibre | : to choice from 7x65R up to .458 Win. Mag. |
| Chamber length | : not applicable |
| Number of barrels | : double-barrels side-by-side |
| Action | : breech-loading |
| Locking | : Greener transverse locking and barrel-block locking |
| Trigger | twin triggers |
| Weight | : 3.5–4.5kg (7lb 11oz–9lb 14oz) |
| Length | : 104–114cm (41–44⁷/₈in) |
| Barrel length | : 61, 63.5, or 66cm (24, 25, or 26in) |
| Ejector | : automatic |
| Choke | not applicable, rifled barrels |
| Sight | express folding sight and mount for telescopic sight |
| Safety | : automatic on cocking, sliding catch on neck of stock |

### CHARACTERISTICS
| | |
|---|---|
| — material | : steel |
| — finish | : blued barrels, plain metal action and side-lock plates with engravings of game motifs |

| | |
|---|---|
| — stock | : specially-selected walnut stock, with pistol-grip and cheek plate |

ᴗ

## Ferlach 66E Express over-and-under side-lock rifle

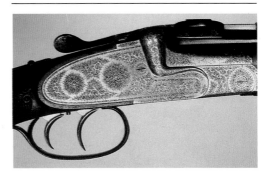

### TECHNICAL DETAILS
| | |
|---|---|
| Gauge/calibre | : to choice from all appropriate calibres |
| Chamber length | : not applicable |
| Number of barrels | : double-barrels over-and-under |
| Action | : breech-loading |
| Locking | : Kersten locking and barrel-block locking |
| Trigger | twin triggers |
| Weight | : 3.5–4.5kg (7lb 11oz–9lb 14oz) |
| Length | : 104–114cm (41–44⁷/₈in) |
| Barrel length | : 61 or 66cm (24 or 26in) |
| Ejector | : automatic |
| Choke | not applicable, rifled barrels |
| Sight | express folding sight and mount for telescopic sight |
| Safety | : automatic on cocking, sliding catch on neck of stock |

### CHARACTERISTICS
| | |
|---|---|
| — material | : steel |
| — finish | : blued barrels, plain metal action and side-lock plates with engravings of game motifs |
| — stock | : specially-selected walnut stock, with pistol-grip and cheek plate |

ᴗ

## Ferlach 68 over-and-under mountain carbine (Bergstutzen)

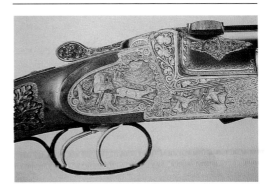

## TECHNICAL DETAILS

Gauge/calibre : upper barrel: .22 LR/.22 WMR; bottom barrel: choice up to 5.6x50R
Chamber length : not applicable
Number of barrels : double-barrels over-and-under
Action : breech-loading
Locking : Kersten locking and barrel-block locking
Trigger : twin triggers
Weight : 3.3–3.6kg (7lb 4oz–7lb 14³/₄oz)
Length : 104 or 108cm (41 or 42¹/₂in)
Barrel length : 61 or 63.5cm (24 or 25in)
Ejector : extractor
Choke : not applicable, rifled barrels
Sight : express folding sight and mount for telescopic sight
Safety : automatic on cocking, sliding catch on neck of stock

## CHARACTERISTICS

— material : steel
— finish : blued barrels, plain metal action and side-plates with engravings of game motifs (no side-lock)
— stock : specially-selected walnut stock, with pistol-grip and cheek plate

🥄

## Ferlach quad-barrel 90

## TECHNICAL DETAILS

Gauge/calibre : see below
Chamber length : smooth-bore: 70mm (2³/₄in)
Number of barrels : quadruple-barrels
Action : breech-loading
Locking : barrel-block locking and double Greener locking
Trigger : twin triggers
Weight : 3.9kg (8lb 9¹/₂oz)
Length : 103cm (40¹/₂in)
Barrel length : 60cm (23⁵/₈in)
Ejector : extractor
Choke : smooth-bore barrel: to choice
Sight : rack and bead plus mount for telescopic sight
Safety : sliding catch on neck of stock and barrel selector for rifled barrels

## CHARACTERISTICS

— material : steel
— finish : blued barrels, plain metal action with engravings of hunting scenes
— stock : selected walnut stock, with pistol-grip and cheek plate

Available calibres/gauges – both middle barrels (smooth-bore): 12/70; top barrel: .22 LR or .22 WMR; bottom barrel: rifle calibre to choice. 🥄

## Ferlach quad-barrel 91

## TECHNICAL DETAILS

Gauge/calibre : see below
Chamber length : smooth-bore: 70mm (2³/₄in)
Number of barrels : quadruple-barrels
Action : breech-loading
Locking : barrel-block locking and Kersten locking
Trigger : twin triggers
Weight : 3.9kg (8lb 9¹/₂oz)
Length : 103cm (40¹/₂in)
Barrel length : 60cm (23⁵/₈in)
Ejector : extractor
Choke : smooth-bore barrel: to choice
Sight : rack and bead
Safety : sliding catch on neck of stock and barrel selector for rifled barrels

## CHARACTERISTICS

— material : steel
— finish : blued barrels, plain metal action with engravings of hunting scenes
— stock : select. walnut stock, with pistol-grip and cheek plate

Available calibres/gauges – bottom and top barrels (smooth-bore): 12/70; left-hand barrel: .22 LR or .22 WMR; right-hand barrel: rifle calibre to choice. 🥄

# Ferlib

The area surrounding the Italian town of Gardone Valle Trompia in the province of Brescia has been associated with gun-making for many centuries. The relatively small firm of Ferlib di Tanfoglio Ivano is based in the town. Ferlib has become legendary, above all for the standard of its engraving work. The company became renowned for its Picasso gun, the "Omaggio a Picasso" (homage to Picasso). This side-by-side gun has Holland & Holland side-locks with engravings that were inspired by the artist Pablo Picasso. Another superb example of their skill and artistry is the "Tra Gli Uliveti" side-by-side side-lock gun with truly fine engravings of hunting motifs. Most Ferlib guns are made to special order. Customers make their choice from samples of engraving or supply their own personal designs. The specifications given below are merely guidelines since a Ferlib gun has no standard specification because they are custom made to the client's requirements. This is equally true of the stock with a choice from straight English stock or one with a pistol-grip. Those who appreciate a traditional hand-made side-by-side shotgun will be pleased with a Ferlib gun.

## Ferlib Fantasy

**TECHNICAL DETAILS**

Gauge/calibre    : 12, 16, 20, or 28
Chamber length   : 70mm (2³/₄in)
Number of barrels : double-barrels side-by-side
Action           : breech loading
Locking          : barrel-block locking with side-locks

| | |
|---|---|
| Trigger | single trigger |
| Weight | : 3.4–3.6kg (7lb 8oz–7lb 14³/₄oz) |
| Length | : 111–124cm (43³/₄–49¹/₄in) |
| Barrel length | : 63–76cm (24³/₄–29⁷/₈in) |
| Ejector | : to choice |
| Choke | to choice |
| Sight | bead |
| Safety | : sliding catch on neck of stock |

**CHARACTERISTICS**

| | |
|---|---|
| – material | : steel |
| – finish | : blued barrels, plain metal action and side-lock plates with engravings |
| – stock | : specially-selected walnut stock, with pistol-grip |

## Ferlib Premier

**TECHNICAL DETAILS**

Gauge/calibre    : 12, 16, 20, or 28
Chamber length   : 70mm (2³/₄in)
Number of barrels : double-barrels side-by-side
Action           : breech-loading
Locking          : barrel-block locking with side-locks
Trigger          single trigger
Weight           : 3.4–3.6kg (7lb 8oz–7lb 14³/₄oz)
Length           : 111–124cm (43³/₄–49¹/₄in)
Barrel length    : 63–76cm (24³/₄–29⁷/₈in)
Ejector          : to choice
Choke            to choice

| Sight | bead |
|---|---|
| Safety | : sliding catch on neck of stock |

**CHARACTERISTICS**
| — material | : steel |
|---|---|
| — finish | : blued, with engraved action and side-lock plates |
| — stock | : specially-selected walnut stock |
| 🐦 | |

## *Ferlib Rex*

**TECHNICAL DETAILS**
| Gauge/calibre | : 12, 16, 20, or 28 |
|---|---|
| Chamber length | : 70mm (2³/₄in) |
| Number of barrels | : double-barrels side-by-side |
| Action | : breech-loading |
| Locking | : barrel-block locking with side-locks |
| Trigger | twin triggers |
| Weight | : 3.4–3.6kg (7lb 8oz–7lb 14³/₄oz) |
| Length | : 111–124cm (43³/₄–49¹/₄in) |
| Barrel length | : 63–76cm (24³/₄–29⁷/₈in) |
| Ejector | : to choice |
| Choke | to choice |
| Sight | bead |
| Safety | : sliding catch on neck of stock |

**CHARACTERISTICS**
| — material | : steel |
|---|---|
| — finish | : blued, with engraved action and side-lock plates |
| — stock | : specially-selected walnut stock |
| 🐦 | |

## *Ferlib Tra Gli Uliveti*

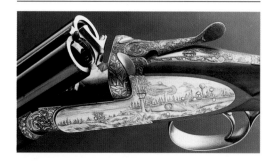

**TECHNICAL DETAILS**
| Gauge/calibre | : 12, 16, 20, or 28 |
|---|---|
| Chamber length | : 70mm (2³/₄in) |

| Number of barrels | : double-barrels side-by-side |
|---|---|
| Action | : breech-loading |
| Locking | : barrel-block locking with side-locks |
| Trigger | single trigger |
| Weight | : 3.4–3.6kg (7lb 8oz–7lb 14³/₄oz) |
| Length | : 111–124cm (43³/₄–49¹/₄in) |
| Barrel length | : 63–76cm (24³/₄–29⁷/₈in) |
| Ejector | : to choice |
| Choke | to choice |
| Sight | bead |
| Safety | : sliding catch on neck of stock |

**CHARACTERISTICS**
| — material | : steel |
|---|---|
| — finish | : blued, with engraved plain metal action and side-lock plates |
| — stock | : specially-selected walnut stock |
| 🐦 | |

# A.H. Fox

The original hand-crafted shotguns by A. H. Fox were made in Philadelphia in the American state of Pennsylvania between 1905 and 1931. The US President Theodore Roosevelt was given an FE grade Fox shotgun in 1909 for a hunting trip to Africa.

Only 3,500 of this model were originally made in both 12 and 20 gauge.

The US firm Connecticut Shotgun Manufacturing Company has been making them again by traditional means since 1994.

Every Fox shotgun is bespoke made to the customer's requirements. The wood for the stocks is specially selected from Turkish walnut. Fox shotguns are traditional side-by-side guns and the quality of their build and finish can pass muster with the sternest critic. These guns are considered to be as good an investment in the United States as gold and diamonds.

The basic price for such a gun, excluding the engraving costs, vary from $9,500–$26,000.

## Fox CE Grade

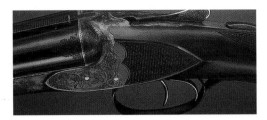

**TECHNICAL DETAILS**

Gauge/calibre     : 16, 20, 28, or .410
Chamber length    : 76mm (3in)
Number of barrels : double-barrels side-by-side
Action            : breech-loading
Locking           : double barrel-block locking
Trigger             twin triggers
Weight            : 2.7–3.2kg (6lb–7lb)
Length            : to choice
Barrel length     : to choice
Ejector           : to choice
Choke               to choice
Sight               golden bead
Safety            : sliding catch on neck of stock

**CHARACTERISTICS**

— material        : steel
— finish          : blued barrels, tempered action with engravings to
                    choice
— stock           : straight English stock of specially-selected Turkish
                    walnut

## Fox DE-20 Grade

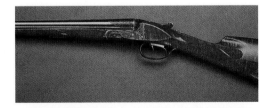

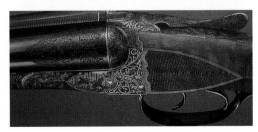

**TECHNICAL DETAILS**

Gauge/calibre     : 20
Chamber length    : 76mm (3in)
Number of barrels : double-barrels side-by-side
Action            : breech-loading

Locking           : double barrel-block locking
Trigger             twin triggers
Weight            : 2.7–3.2kg (6lb–7lb)
Length            : to choice
Barrel length     : to choice
Ejector           : to choice
Choke               to choice
Sight               golden bead
Safety            : sliding catch on neck of stock

**CHARACTERISTICS**

— material        : steel
— finish          : blued barrels, tempered action with engravings to
                    choice
— stock           : straight English stock of specially-selected Turkish
                    walnut

## Fox FE Grade

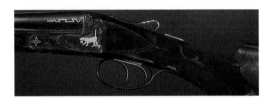

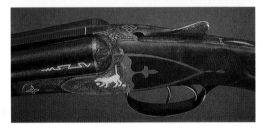

**TECHNICAL DETAILS**

Gauge/calibre     : 12, 16, 20, or 28
Chamber length    : 76mm (3in)
Number of barrels : double-barrels side-by-side
Action            : breech-loading
Locking           : double barrel-block locking
Trigger             twin triggers
Weight            : 2.7–3.2kg (6lb–7lb)
Length            : to choice
Barrel length     : to choice
Ejector           : to choice
Choke               to choice
Sight               golden bead
Safety            : sliding catch on neck of stock

**CHARACTERISTICS**

— material        : steel
— finish          : blued barrels, tempered action with gold inlaid
                    engravings to choice
— stock           : straight English stock of specially-selected Turkish
                    walnut

## Fox Special Grade

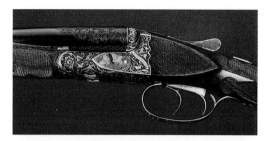

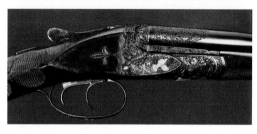

**TECHNICAL DETAILS**

| | |
|---|---|
| Gauge/calibre | : 12, 16, or 20 |
| Chamber length | : 76mm (3in) |
| Number of barrels | : double-barrels side-by-side |
| Action | : breech-loading |
| Locking | : double barrel-block locking |
| Trigger | twin triggers |
| Weight | : 2.7–3.2kg (6lb–7lb) |
| Length | : to choice |
| Barrel length | : to choice |
| Ejector | : to choice |
| Choke | to choice |
| Sight | golden bead |
| Safety | : sliding catch on neck of stock |

**CHARACTERISTICS**

| | |
|---|---|
| — material | : steel |
| — finish | : blued barrels, tempered action with customised gold inlaid engravings to choice |
| — stock | : straight English stock of specially-selected Turkish walnut |

## Fox XE Grade

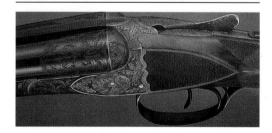

**TECHNICAL DETAILS**

| | |
|---|---|
| Gauge/calibre | : 16, 20, 28, or .410 |

---

| | |
|---|---|
| Chamber length | : 76mm (3in) |
| Number of barrels | : double-barrels side-by-side |
| Action | : breech-loading |
| Locking | : double barrel-block locking |
| Trigger | twin triggers |
| Weight | : 2.7–3.2kg (6lb–7lb) |
| Length | : to choice |
| Barrel length | : to choice |
| Ejector | : to choice |
| Choke | to choice |
| Sight | golden bead |
| Safety | : sliding catch on neck of stock |

**CHARACTERISTICS**

| | |
|---|---|
| — material | : steel |
| — finish | : blued barrels, tempered action with engravings to choice |
| — stock | : straight English stock of specially-selected Turkish walnut |

# Franchi

The Italian gun-maker Luigi Franchi is established at Fornaci in the Brescia region in the north of Italy. This modern business draws on a centuries-old gun-making tradition. The Franchi company make a number of excellent over-and-under shotguns plus a couple of semi-automatic models. Until 1985, the company still produced a few traditional side-by-side shotguns such as their Imperiale Montecarlo Extra with side-locks, the Astore, Albatros, and Franchi 300. Unfortunately these superb guns are no longer made.

The best known products from the company are their riot-guns, such as the SPAS-12 (introduced in 1983) and the SPAS-15. Both these guns are both semi-automatic and pump-action because they can be changed over by means of a push-button switch.

## Franchi Alcione 97.12

**TECHNICAL DETAILS**

| | |
|---|---|
| Gauge/calibre | : 12 |

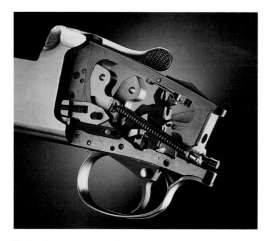

Chamber length : 70mm (2³/₄in) or 76mm (3in)
Number of barrels : double-barrels over-and-under
Action : breech-loading
Locking : barrel-block locking
Trigger single trigger with barrel selector or twin triggers
Weight : 3–3.2kg (6lb 9¹/₂oz–7lb)
Length : 115–124cm (45¹/₄–48³/₄in)
Barrel length : 62–71cm (24–28in)
Ejector : automatic
Choke fixed chokes to choice or Franchok interchangeable chokes
Sight ventilated barrel rib and bead
Safety : sliding catch on neck of stock

### CHARACTERISTICS
— material : steel
— finish : blued barrels, plain metal action
— stock : walnut stock, with pistol-grip

A number of interchangeable barrels in various lengths are available for this gun.

## Franchi Alcione SL.12

### TECHNICAL DETAILS
Gauge/calibre : 12
Chamber length : 70mm (2³/₄in) or 76mm (3in)
Number of barrels : double-barrels over-and-under
Action : breech-loading
Locking : barrel-block locking
Trigger single trigger with barrel selector or twin triggers
Weight : 3–3.2kg (6lb 9¹/₂oz–7lb)
Length : 115–124cm (45¹/₄–48³/₄in)
Barrel length : 62–71cm (24–28in)

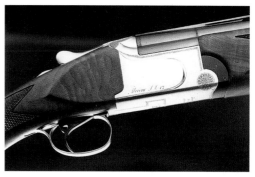

Ejector : automatic
Choke fixed chokes to choice or Franchok interchangeable chokes
Sight ventilated barrel rib and bead
Safety : sliding catch on neck of stock

### CHARACTERISTICS
— material : steel
— finish : blued barrels, plain metal action
— stock : walnut stock, with pistol-grip

A number of interchangeable barrels in various lengths are available for this gun.

## Franchi Alcione 2000SX

### TECHNICAL DETAILS
Gauge/calibre : 12
Chamber length : 70mm (2³/₄in)
Number of barrels : double-barrels over-and-under
Action : breech-loading
Locking : barrel-block locking
Trigger single trigger with barrel selector or twin triggers
Weight : 3.1–3.2kg (6lb 13oz–7lb)
Length : 115–124cm (45¹/₄–48³/₄in)
Barrel length : 62–71cm (24–28in)
Ejector : automatic
Choke fixed chokes to choice or Franchok interchangeable chokes
Sight ventilated barrel rib and bead
Safety : sliding catch on neck of stock

## CHARACTERISTICS

- material    : steel
- finish      : blued barrels, plain metal action with engravings
- stock      : walnut stock, with pistol-grip

## Franchi Dominator

### TECHNICAL DETAILS

| | |
|---|---|
| Gauge/calibre | : 12 |
| Chamber length | : 70mm (2³/₄in) |
| Number of barrels | : double-barrels over-and-under |
| Action | : breech-loading |
| Locking | : barrel-block locking |
| Trigger | single trigger with barrel selector or twin triggers |
| Weight | : 3–3.1kg (6lb 9¹/₂oz–6lb 13oz) |
| Length | : 115–122cm (45¹/₄–48in) |
| Barrel length | : 71, 74, or 76cm (28, 29¹/₈ or 30in) |
| Ejector | : automatic |
| Choke | fixed chokes to choice or Franchok interchangeable chokes |
| Sight | ventilated barrel rib and bead |
| Safety | : sliding catch on neck of stock |

### CHARACTERISTICS

- material    : steel
- finish      : blued
- stock      : walnut stock, with pistol-grip

## Franchi Falconet 97.12

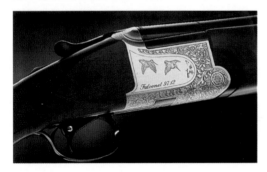

### TECHNICAL DETAILS

| | |
|---|---|
| Gauge/calibre | : 12 |
| Chamber length | : 70mm (2³/₄in) |
| Number of barrels | : double-barrels over-and-under |
| Action | : breech-loading |
| Locking | : barrel-block locking |
| Trigger | single trigger with barrel selector or twin triggers |
| Weight | : 2.8kg (6lb 2¹/₂oz) |

---

| | |
|---|---|
| Length | : 115–120cm (45¹/₄–47¹/₄in) |
| Barrel length | : 66–71cm (26–28in) |
| Ejector | : automatic |
| Choke | fixed chokes to choice or Franchok interchangeable chokes |
| Sight | ventilated barrel rib and bead |
| Safety | : sliding catch on neck of stock |

### CHARACTERISTICS

- material    : steel barrels, light-alloy action
- finish      : blued barrels, plain metal action with various engravings
- stock      : walnut stock, with pistol-grip

A number of interchangeable barrels in various lengths are available for this gun.

## Franchi Falconet 2000 SL

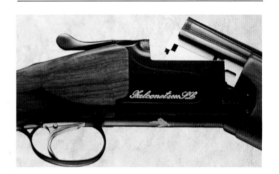

### TECHNICAL DETAILS

| | |
|---|---|
| Gauge/calibre | : 12 |
| Chamber length | : 70mm (2³/₄in) |
| Number of barrels | : double-barrels over-and-under |
| Action | : breech-loading |
| Locking | : barrel-block locking |
| Trigger | single trigger with barrel selector or twin triggers |
| Weight | : 2.7–2.8kg (6lb–6lb 2¹/₂oz) |
| Length | : 112–120cm (44¹/₄in–47¹/₄in) |
| Barrel length | : 62–71cm (24–28in) |
| Ejector | : automatic |
| Choke | fixed chokes to choice or Franchok interchangeable chokes |
| Sight | ventilated barrel rib and bead |
| Safety | : sliding catch on neck of stock |

### CHARACTERISTICS

- material    : steel barrel, light alloy action
- finish      : blued
- stock      : walnut stock, with pistol-grip

## Franchi Sous Bois

### TECHNICAL DETAILS

| | |
|---|---|
| Gauge/calibre | : 12 |
| Chamber length | : 70mm (2³/₄in) |

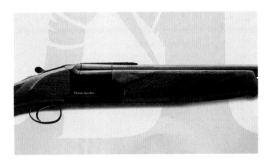

Number of barrels : double-barrels over-and-under
Action            : breech-loading
Locking           : barrel-block locking
Trigger             single trigger with barrel selector
Weight            : 2.6kg (5lb 11¹/₂oz)
Length            : 112cm (44¹/₄in)
Barrel length     : 62cm (24in)
Ejector           : automatic
Choke               top barrel with ¹/₂ choke, bottom barrel rifled for
                    slugs
Sight               short barrel rib above chamber and bead
Safety            : sliding catch on neck of stock

**CHARACTERISTICS**
— material        : steel barrel, light alloy action
— finish          : blued
— stock           : walnut stock, with pistol-grip

## Franchi Grand Prix 90 VL

**TECHNICAL DETAILS**
Gauge/calibre     : 12
Chamber length    : 70mm (2³/₄in)
Number of barrels : double-barrels over-and-under
Action            : breech-loading
Locking           : barrel-block locking
Trigger             single trigger with adjustment
Weight            : 3–3.2kg (6lb 9¹/₂oz–7lb)
Length            : 115–122cm (45¹/₄–48in)
Barrel length     : 71, 74, or 76cm (28, 29¹/₈, or 30in)
Ejector           : automatic
Choke               fixed chokes to choice or Franchok interchangeable
                    chokes
Sight               ventilated barrel rib and bead
Safety            : sliding catch on neck of stock

**CHARACTERISTICS**
— material        : steel

— finish          : blued barrels, plain metal action and side-plates
                    (no side-lock)
— stock           : walnut stock, with pistol-grip

## Franchi Pump PA-8L

**TECHNICAL DETAILS**
Gauge/calibre     : 12
Chamber length    : 76mm (3in)
Number of barrels : single-barrel
Magazine          : tubular magazine for 3–7 cartridges
Action            : pump-action
Locking           : falling-block locking
Trigger             single trigger
Weight            : 3kg (6lb 9¹/₂oz)
Length            : 107cm (42¹/₈in)
Barrel length     : 47.5 or 61cm (18³/₄ or 23⁵/₈in) with Variomix
                    add-on choke
Ejector           : extractor
Choke               Variomix add-on chokes
Sight               bead
Safety            : push-button safety in front of trigger guard

**CHARACTERISTICS**
— material        : steel
— finish          : matt black
— stock           : folding metal stock, with plastic pistol-grip

This gun is also available as model PA-7 with a black painted wooden stock with pistol grip, or PA-8E with a plastic stock.

A gun held on a United Kingdom shotgun certificate must be restricted to a magazine capacity to 2 cartridges in a magazine and 1 in the barrel.

The minimum length of barrel is 24in (61cm). Similar restrictions apply elsewhere in Europe.

## Franchi SPAS-12

**TECHNICAL DETAILS**

| | |
|---|---|
| Gauge/calibre | : 12 |
| Chamber length | : 70mm (2³/₄in) |
| Number of barrels | : single-barrel |
| Magazine | : tubular magazine for 3–7 cartridges |
| Action | : semi-automatic (gas-operated) and pump-action by selector switch |
| Locking | : falling-block locking |
| Trigger | single trigger |
| Weight | : 4kg (8lb 12³/₄oz) |
| Length | : 107cm (42¹/₈in) |
| Barrel length | : 55cm (21⁵/₈in) |
| Ejector | : extractor |
| Choke | Variomix add-on chokes |
| Sight | rack and bead |
| Safety | : push-button safety in front of trigger guard |

**CHARACTERISTICS**

| | |
|---|---|
| – material | : steel |
| – finish | : matt black |
| – stock | : folding metal stock or with plastic stock with pistol-grip |

There is a selector switch in the bottom of the fore-arm to select either semi-automatic or pump-action. A gun held on a United Kingdom shotgun certificate must be restricted to a magazine capacity to 2 cartridges in a magazine and 1 in the barrel. The minimum length of barrel is 24in (61cm). Similar restrictions apply elsewhere in Europe.

## Franchi SPAS-15

**TECHNICAL DETAILS**

| | |
|---|---|
| Gauge/calibre | : 12 |
| Chamber length | : 70mm (2³/₄in) |
| Number of barrels | : single-barrel |

| | |
|---|---|
| Magazine | : cartridge holder for 2 or 6 cartridges |
| Action | : semi-automatic (gas-operated) and pump-action by selector switch |
| Locking | : falling-block locking |
| Trigger | single trigger |
| Weight | : 3.9 or 4.1kg (8lb 9¹/₄oz or 9lb) |
| Length | : 98 or 100cm (38⁵/₈ or 39³/₈in) |
| Barrel length | : 45cm (17³/₄in) |
| Ejector | : extractor |
| Choke | Variomix add-on chokes |
| Sight | rack and bead |
| Safety | : push-button safety left front of trigger guard and grip safety in the front of the pistol-grip |

**CHARACTERISTICS**

| | |
|---|---|
| – material | : steel barrel, light alloy action body |
| – finish | : matt black |
| – stock | : folding metal stock or black painted hardwood stock with pistol-grip |

There is a selector switch in the bottom of the fore-arm to select either semi-automatic or pump-action. A gun held on a United Kingdom shotgun certificate must be restricted to a magazine capacity to 2 cartridges in a magazine and 1 in the barrel. The minimum length of barrel is 24in (61cm). Similar restrictions apply elsewhere in Europe.

## Franchi Sporting 2000

**TECHNICAL DETAILS**

| | |
|---|---|
| Gauge/calibre | : 12 |
| Chamber length | : 70mm (2³/₄in) |
| Number of barrels | : double-barrels over-and-under |
| Action | : breech-loading |
| Locking | : barrel-block locking |
| Trigger | single trigger |
| Weight | : 3.45kg (7lb 9oz) |
| Length | : 115 or 120cm (45¹/₄in or 47¹/₄in) |
| Barrel length | : 71 or 76cm (28 or 30in) |
| Ejector | : automatic |
| Choke | fixed choke: ¹/₂ and full or Franchok interchangeable |
| Sight | ventilated barrel rib and bead |
| Safety | : sliding catch on neck of stock |

**CHARACTERISTICS**

| | |
|---|---|
| – material | : steel |

– finish          : blued
– stock          : walnut stock, with pistol-grip

## Franchi 48 AL

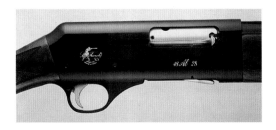

### TECHNICAL DETAILS

Gauge/calibre     : 12, 20, or 28
Chamber length    : 70mm (2³/₄in)
Number of barrels : single-barrel
Magazine          : tubular magazine for 2 cartridges
Action            : semi-automatic recoil-action
Locking           : rotating bolt locking
Trigger           single trigger
Weight            : 2.6–2.9kg (6lb 11¹/₂oz–6lb 6oz)
Length            : 104–120cm (41–47¹/₄in)
Barrel length     : 60–76cm (23⁵/₈–30in)
Ejector           : extractor
Choke             fixed choke: ¹/₂, ³/₄,or full, or Franchok inter-
                  changeable chokes
Sight             ventilated barrel rib and bead
Safety            : push-button safety in rear of trigger guard

### CHARACTERISTICS

– material        : steel barrel, light alloy action body
– finish          : blued
– stock           : walnut stock, with pistol-grip

## Franchi 48 AL Black Magic

### TECHNICAL DETAILS

Gauge/calibre     : 12, 20, or 28
Chamber length    : 70mm (2³/₄in)
Number of barrels : single-barrel
Magazine          : tubular magazine for 2 cartridges
Action            : semi-automatic recoil-action
Locking           : rotating bolt locking
Trigger           single trigger
Weight            : 2.6–2.9kg (6lb 11¹/₂oz–6lb 6oz)
Length            : 104–120cm (41–47¹/₄in)
Barrel length     : 60–76cm (23⁵/₈–30in)

Ejector           : extractor
Choke             fixed choke or Franchok interchangeable chokes
Sight             ventilated barrel rib and bead
Safety            : push-button safety in rear of trigger guard

### CHARACTERISTICS

– material        : steel barrel, light alloy action body
– finish          : blued barrel, matt black action body with decora-
                  tive lining
– stock           : walnut stock, with pistol-grip

## Franchi 610 VSL Variopress

### TECHNICAL DETAILS

Gauge/calibre     : 12
Chamber length    : 76mm (3in)
Number of barrels : single-barrel
Magazine          : tubular magazine for 2 cartridges
Action            : semi-automatic gas-operated
Locking           : rotating bolt locking
Trigger           single trigger
Weight            : 3.2–3.3kg (7lb–7lb 4oz)
Length            : 104–120cm (41–47¹/₄in)
Barrel length     : 60–76cm (23⁵/₈–30in)
Ejector           : extractor
Choke             fixed choke or choice of Franchok or Variomix
                  interchangeable chokes
Sight             ventilated barrel rib and bead
Safety            : push-button safety in front of trigger guard

### CHARACTERISTICS

– material        : steel barrel, light alloy action body
– finish          : blued barrel, matt black action body with decora-
                  tive lining
– stock           : walnut stock, with pistol-grip

The gas piston is surrounded by a spiral spring which absorbs the recoil. This enables all types of shotgun cartridges to be used.

## Franchi 612/620 VS Variopress

### TECHNICAL DETAILS

Gauge/calibre     : 12 or 20
Chamber length    : 76mm (3in)

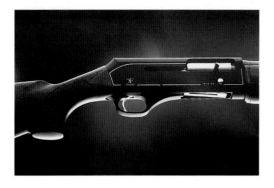

| | |
|---|---|
| Number of barrels | : single-barrel |
| Magazine | : tubular magazine for 2 cartridges |
| Action | : semi-automatic gas-operated |
| Locking | : rotating bolt locking |
| Trigger | single trigger |
| Weight | : 2.65–3.2kg (5lb 13¹/₄oz–7lb) |
| Length | : 104–120cm (41–47¹/₄in) |
| Barrel length | : 60–76cm (23⁵/₈–30in) |
| Ejector | : extractor |
| Choke | fixed choke or Franchok interchangeable chokes |
| Sight | ventilated barrel rib and bead |
| Safety | : push-button safety in front of trigger guard |

**CHARACTERISTICS**

| | |
|---|---|
| — material | : steel barrel, light alloy action body |
| — finish | : blued barrel, matt black action body with decorative lining |
| — stock | : walnut stock, with pistol-grip |

The gas piston is surrounded by a spiral spring which absorbs the recoil. This enables all types of shotgun cartridges to be used. The shortest barrel of this gun falls just under the minimum barrel length required by United Kingdom shotgun legislation of 24in (61cm).

🐦 🦃

### *Franchi 612 VSL/VSGL Variopress*

**TECHNICAL DETAILS**

| | |
|---|---|
| Gauge/calibre | : 12 or 20 |
| Chamber length | : 76mm (3in) |
| Number of barrels | : single-barrel |
| Magazine | : tubular magazine for 2 cartridges |
| Action | : semi-automatic gas-operated |

| | |
|---|---|
| Locking | : rotating bolt locking |
| Trigger | single trigger |
| Weight | : 2.65–3.2kg (5lb 13¹/₄oz–7lb) |
| Length | : 104–120cm (41–47¹/₄in) |
| Barrel length | : 60–76cm (23⁵/₈–30in) |
| Ejector | : extractor |
| Choke | fixed choke or Franchok interchangeable chokes |
| Sight | ventilated barrel rib and bead |
| Safety | : push-button safety in front of trigger guard |

**CHARACTERISTICS**

| | |
|---|---|
| — material | : steel barrel, light alloy action body |
| — finish | : blued barrel, blued action body with gold inlay hunting scenes (612 VSL) or plain metal action body with gold inlay hunting scenes (612 VSGL) |
| — stock | : walnut stock, with pistol-grip |

The gas piston is surrounded by a spiral spring which absorbs the recoil. This enables all types of shotgun cartridges to be used. The shortest barrel of this gun falls just under the minimum barrel length required by United Kingdom shotgun legislation of 24in (61cm).

🐦 🦃

## Frankonia Jagd

The firm of Waffen Frankonia was established in 1907 by Nikolaus Hoffmann in Würzburg, Bavaria, in Germany. Frankonia grew over the years from a small gunsmith to become a major firearms concern. The company's factories were devastated by Allied bombing in 1945.

Hoffman started his business up again in 1956 with some 80 employees.

Today Frankonia has a chain of gun shops throughout Germany. The company name changed in the mid 1970's to Frankonia Jagd (hunting). Most of their shops have a gunsmith's workshop for repairs and minor adaptations. During the past decade, subsidiaries have been established in France, Denmark, Belgium, and the Czech Republic. Frankonia also sells by mail order from its head office in Würzburg, where guns can be customised to the client's requirements.

The company also runs its own training courses for gunsmiths. Frankonia also makes a superb range of rifles based on the famous Mauser 98 system, which the sell under the name Frankonia Favorit.

The company also have a number of shotguns and combination guns made by Italian and Eastern European makers.

## Frankonia/Baikal single-barrel

**TECHNICAL DETAILS**
Gauge/calibre    : 12
Chamber length    : 70mm (2³/₄in) or 76mm (3in)
Number of barrels : single-barrel
Action    : breech-loading
Locking    : barrel-block locking with locking lever behind trigger guard
Trigger    single trigger
Weight    : 2.6kg (5lb 3oz)
Length    : 115cm (45¹/₄in)
Barrel length    : 73cm (29¹/₂in)
Ejector    : automatic or solely with extractor
Choke    fixed full
Sight    bead
Safety    : push-button safety catch in trigger guard

**CHARACTERISTICS**
— material    : steel
— finish    : blued
— stock    : hardwood stock, with pistol-grip

## Frankonia Astore side–by–side

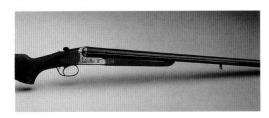

**TECHNICAL DETAILS**
Gauge/calibre    : 12
Chamber length    : 70mm (2³/₄in)
Number of barrels : double-barrels side-by-side
Action    : breech-loading
Locking    : barrel-block locking
Trigger    single trigger
Weight    : 3.2kg (7lb)
Length    : 115cm (45¹/₄in)
Barrel length    : 70cm (27¹/₂in)
Ejector    : automatic or solely with extractor
Choke    fixed ¹/₂ and full
Sight    recessed rib with bead
Safety    : sliding catch on neck of stock, no barrel selector

**CHARACTERISTICS**
— material    : steel
— finish    : blued barrels, plain metal action with hunting motifs
— stock    : walnut stock, with pistol-grip

## Frankonia/Baikal Taiga side–by–side

**TECHNICAL DETAILS**
Gauge/calibre    : 12
Chamber length    : 70mm (2³/₄in)
Number of barrels : double-barrels side-by-side
Action    : breech-loading
Locking    : double barrel-block locking
Trigger    twin triggers
Weight    : 3.2kg (7lb)
Length    : 112cm (44¹/₈in)
Barrel length    : 72cm (28³/₈in)
Ejector    : automatic or solely with extractor
Choke    fixed ¹/₂ and full
Sight    bead
Safety    : sliding catch on neck of stock

— material : steel
— finish : blued
— stock : hardwood stock, with pistol-grip

## *Frankonia/Baikal Tundra Super*

**TECHNICAL DETAILS**

Gauge/calibre : 12
Chamber length : 70mm (2³/₄in)
Number of barrels : double-barrels over-and-under
Action : breech-loading
Locking : barrel-block locking
Trigger single trigger
Weight : 3.1–3.3kg (6lb 13oz–7l 4oz)
Length : 112cm (44¹/₈in)
Barrel length : 73cm (28¹/₄in)
Ejector : automatic or solely with extractor
Choke fixed ¹/₂ and full
Sight ventilated rib and bead
Safety : sliding catch on neck of stock, barrel selector

**CHARACTERISTICS**

— material : steel
— finish : blued
— stock : walnut stock, with pistol-grip

Interchangeable barrels are available for this gun from 67cm (26³/₈in), which are ideal for use as Skeet barrels.

## *Frankonia BBF combination gun*

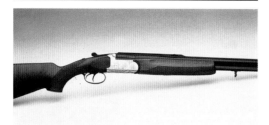

**TECHNICAL DETAILS**

Gauge/calibre : see below
Chamber length : smooth-bore: 70mm (2³/₄in)
Number of barrels : double-barrels over-and-under

Action : breech-loading
Locking : barrel-block locking
Trigger twin triggers
Weight : 3.2kg (7lb)
Length : 114cm (44⁷/₈in)
Barrel length : 65cm (28⁵/₈in)
Ejector : automatic
Choke to choice
Sight folding rack and bead; rail for telescopic sight
Safety : sliding catch on neck of stock

**CHARACTERISTICS**

— material : steel
— finish : blued barrels, plain metal action with hunting motif
— stock : walnut stock, with pistol-grip

Available calibres/gauges (smooth-bore): 12/70; (rifled barrel): .222 Rem., 6.5x57R, 7x65R, .30-06 Spr.

## *Frankonia BBF deluxe combination gun Luxus*

**TECHNICAL DETAILS**

Gauge/calibre : see below
Chamber length : smooth-bore: 70mm (2³/₄in)
Number of barrels : double-barrels over-and-under
Action : breech-loading
Locking : barrel-block locking
Trigger twin triggers
Weight : 3.3kg (7lb 4oz)
Length : 114cm (44⁷/₈in)
Barrel length : 65cm (28⁵/₈in)
Ejector : automatic
Choke to choice
Sight folding rack and bead; rail for telescopic sight
Safety : sliding catch on neck of stock

**CHARACTERISTICS**

— material : steel
— finish : blued barrels, plain metal action with hunting motif
— stock : walnut stock, with pistol-grip and cheek plate

Available calibres/gauges (smooth-bore): 12/70; (rifled barrel): .222 Rem., 6.5x57R, 7x65R, .30-06 Spr.

## Frankonia/Brünner 500 BBF combination gun

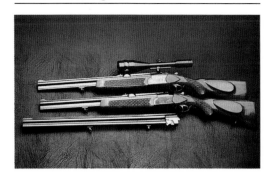

**TECHNICAL DETAILS**

Gauge/calibre : see below
Chamber length : smooth-bore: 70mm (2³/₄in)
Number of barrels : double-barrels over-and-under
Action : breech-loading
Locking : Purdy locking
Trigger twin triggers
Weight : 3.3kg (7lb 4oz)
Length : 100cm (39³/₈in)
Barrel length : 60cm (23⁵/₈in)
Ejector : automatic
Choke smooth-bore: fixed full choke
Sight folding rack and bead; rail for telescopic sight
Safety : sliding catch on neck of stock

**CHARACTERISTICS**

— material : steel
— finish : blued
— stock : walnut stock, with pistol-grip and cheek plate

Available calibres/gauges (smooth-bore): 12/70; (rifled barrel): .222 Rem., 5.6x50R Mag., 5.6x52R, 7x57R, 7x65R, .243 Win., .30-06 Spr., .308 Win. Interchangeable barrels are available for 12 gauge shot cartridges and various rifle calibres, and also double 12 gauge barrels with ³/₄ and full chokes.

## Frankonia/Ayora hammer

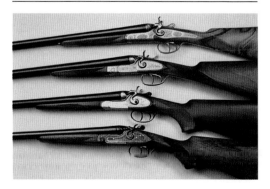

**TECHNICAL DETAILS**

Gauge/calibre : 12, 16, or 20
Chamber length : 70mm (2³/₄in)
Number of barrels : double-barrels side-by-side
Action : breech-loading
Locking : double barrel-block locking
Trigger twin triggers
Weight : 3.2kg (7lb)
Length : 125cm (49¹/₄in)
Barrel length : 71cm (28in)
Ejector : automatic
Choke ¹/₂ and full choke
Sight recessed rib and bead
Safety : half-cock of external hammers

**CHARACTERISTICS**

— material : steel
— finish : blued barrels, tempered metal action with side-lock plates
— stock : walnut stock, with pistol-grip

Illustrated from top to bottom are: Frankonia/Ayora, Frankonia/Italia, Frankonia/Bernardelli, and Frankonia/Siace Deluxe 370 B.

## Frankonia/Italia hammer

**TECHNICAL DETAILS**

Gauge/calibre : 12
Chamber length : 70mm (2³/₄in)
Number of barrels : double-barrels side-by-side
Action : breech-loading
Locking : double barrel-block locking
Trigger twin triggers
Weight : 3.1kg (6lb 13oz)
Length : 120cm (47¹/₄in)
Barrel length : 70cm (27¹/₂in)
Ejector : automatic
Choke fixed ¹/₂ and full choke
Sight recessed rib and bead
Safety : half-cock of external hammers

**CHARACTERISTICS**

— material : steel
— finish : blued barrels, plain metal action with hunting scenes on side-lock plates
— stock : walnut stock, with pistol-grip

Illustrated from top to bottom are: Frankonia/Ayora, Frankonia/Italia, Frankonia/Bernardelli, and Frankonia/Siace Deluxe 370 B.

## Frankonia/Bernardelli hammer

**TECHNICAL DETAILS**

Gauge/calibre : 12
Chamber length : 70mm (2³/₄in)
Number of barrels : double-barrels side-by-side
Action : breech-loading

| Locking | : double barrel-block and Purdy locking |
|---|---|
| Trigger | twin triggers |
| Weight | : 3.2kg (7lb) |
| Length | : 122cm (48in) |
| Barrel length | : 70cm (27$^1$/$_2$in) |
| Ejector | : extractor only |
| Choke | fixed $^3$/$_4$ and full choke |
| Sight | recessed rib and bead |
| Safety | : half-cock of external hammers |

**CHARACTERISTICS**

| — material | : steel |
|---|---|
| — finish | : blued barrels, plain metal action with hunting scenes on side-lock plates |
| — stock | : straight English stock of walnut |

Illustrated from top to bottom are: Franko-nia/Ayora, Frankonia/Italia, Frankonia/Ber-nardelli, and Frankonia/Siace Deluxe 370 B. ✍

## Frankonia/Siace Deluxe 370 B hammer

**TECHNICAL DETAILS**

| Gauge/calibre | : 12 |
|---|---|
| Chamber length | : 70mm (2$^3$/$_4$in) |
| Number of barrels | : double-barrels side-by-side |
| Action | : breech-loading |
| Locking | : double barrel-block locking |
| Trigger | twin triggers |
| Weight | : 3.1kg (6lb 13oz) |
| Length | : 123cm (48$^1$/$_4$in) |
| Barrel length | : 71cm (28in) |
| Ejector | : automatic |
| Choke | fixed: $^1$/$_2$ and full choke |
| Sight | recessed rib and bead |
| Safety | : half-cock of external hammers |

**CHARACTERISTICS**

| — material | : steel |
|---|---|
| — finish | : blued barrels, plain metal action and side-lock plates: hand-engraved with floral motifs |
| — stock | : straight English stock of walnut |

Illustrated from top to bottom are: Franko-nia/Ayora, Frankonia/Italia, Frankonia/Ber-nardelli, and Frankonia/Siace Deluxe 370 B. ✍

## Frankonia/Fias Mercury Jaguar

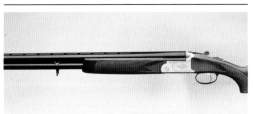

| Gauge/calibre | : 12 |
|---|---|
| Chamber length | : 70mm (2$^3$/$_4$in) |
| Number of barrels | : double-barrels over-and-under |
| Action | : breech-loading |
| Locking | : double barrel-block locking |
| Trigger | single trigger |
| Weight | : 3.2kg (7lb) |
| Length | : 110cm (43$^1$/$_4$in) |
| Barrel length | : 70cm (27$^1$/$_2$in) |
| Ejector | : automatic or solely with extractor |
| Choke | $^1$/$_2$ and full choke |
| Sight | ventilated rib and bead |
| Safety | : sliding catch on neck of stock which also acts as barrel selector |

**CHARACTERISTICS**

| — material | : steel |
|---|---|
| — finish | : blued barrels, plain metal action |
| — stock | : walnut stock, with pistol-grip |

This gun is also available with a twin triggers and with 68cm (26$^3$/$_4$in) barrel with $^1$/$_4$ and $^3$/$_4$ chokes.

## Frankonia Scirocco

**TECHNICAL DETAILS**

| Gauge/calibre | : 12 |
|---|---|
| Chamber length | : 70mm (2$^3$/$_4$in) |
| Number of barrels | : double-barrels over-and-under |
| Action | : breech-loading |
| Locking | : double barrel-block locking |
| Trigger | single trigger |
| Weight | : 3.3kg (7lb 4oz) |
| Length | : 112cm (44$^1$/$_8$in) |
| Barrel length | : 70cm (27$^1$/$_2$in) |
| Ejector | : automatic or solely with extractor |
| Choke | fixed $^1$/$_2$ and full choke |
| Sight | ventilated rib and bead |
| Safety | : sliding catch on neck of stock |

**CHARACTERISTICS**

| — material | : steel |
|---|---|
| — finish | : blued barrels, plain metal action with hunting motif |
| — stock | : walnut stock, with pistol-grip |

This gun is available in several versions: with ejector or solely with extractor, twin triggers, or a lightweight version of 2.9kg (6lb 6oz). ✍

## Frankonia deluxe side-lock

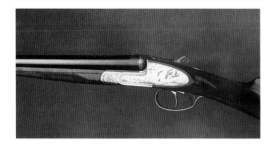

**TECHNICAL DETAILS**

Gauge/calibre : 12
Chamber length : 70mm (2³/₄in)
Number of barrels : double-barrels side-by-side
Action : breech-loading
Locking : double barrel-block locking
Trigger : twin triggers
Weight : 3.2kg (7lb)
Length : 123cm (48¹/₄in)
Barrel length : 71cm (28in)
Ejector : automatic
Choke : fixed ¹/₂ and full choke
Sight : recessed rib and bead
Safety : sliding catch on neck of stock

**CHARACTERISTICS**

— material : steel
— finish : blued barrels, plain metal action with hunting motif on side-lock plates
— stock : straight English stock of selected walnut

# Gaucher Armes

The French firearms company of Gaucher Armes was established in 1834 by Antoine Gaucher in the outstanding French munitions town of St. Etienne. Until World War I, Gaucher chiefly made heavy calibre double-barrelled express big game rifles. After World War II, the company started to make lighter calibre guns. The present range consists of double-barrelled express rifles, shotguns, small calibre rifles, silenced rifles, and single-shot pistols for silhouette target shooting. Gaucher guns represent good value for money and are ideal for every day use. The shotguns have barrel-block locking

and transverse locking of the Webley & Scott type.

## Gaucher Bivouac Double-Express

**TECHNICAL DETAILS**

Gauge/calibre : 9.3x74R, 8x57JRS, or 7x65R
Chamber length : not applicable
Number of barrels : double-barrels side-by-side
Action : breech-loading
Locking : Webley & Scott transverse locking and double barrel-block locking
Trigger : twin triggers
Weight : 3.1–3.4kg (6lb 13–7lb 8oz)
Length : 105cm (41³/₄in)
Barrel length : 60cm (23⁵/₈in)
Ejector : extractor
Choke : not applicable, rifled barrels
Sight : Express folding sight and bead, special mount for telescopic sight
Safety : sliding catch behind locking lever

**CHARACTERISTICS**

— material : steel
— finish : blued, plain metal side-plates with engravings of hunting motifs (no side-locks)
— stock : walnut stock, with pistol-grip and cheek plate or straight English stock

## Gaucher 801 Sport

**TECHNICAL DETAILS**

Gauge/calibre : 12 or 16
Chamber length : 70mm (2³/₄in)
Number of barrels : double-barrels side by side
Action : breech-loading
Locking : double barrel-block and transverse locking

169

(Webley & Scott system)
Trigger         twin triggers
Weight        : 3kg (6lb 9$^1$/$_2$oz)
Length        : 116cm (47$^3$/$_4$in)
Barrel length   : 70cm (27$^1$/$_2$in)
Ejector      : automatic
Choke        fixed $^1$/$_2$ and full choke
Sight         bead
Safety        : sliding catch on neck of stock

**CHARACTERISTICS**
— material     : steel
— finish       : blued
— stock       : walnut stock, with pistol-grip

## Gaucher 802 deluxe

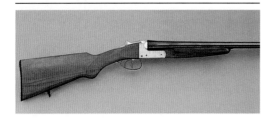

**TECHNICAL DETAILS**
Gauge/calibre   : 12, 16, or 20
Chamber length  : 70mm (2$^3$/$_4$in)
Number of barrels : double-barrels side-by-side
Action        : breech-loading
Locking      : barrel-block and transverse locking (Webley & Scott system)
Trigger      twin triggers
Weight      : 3kg (6lb 9$^1$/$_2$oz)
Length      : 116cm (47$^3$/$_4$in)
Barrel length : 70cm (27$^1$/$_2$in)
Ejector     : automatic
Choke      fixed $^1$/$_2$ and full choke
Sight       bead
Safety     : sliding catch on neck of stock

**CHARACTERISTICS**
— material   : steel
— finish     : blued barrels, matt-chromed action
— stock     : walnut stock, with pistol-grip

## Gaucher 804 Magnum

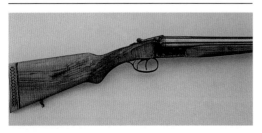

**TECHNICAL DETAILS**
Gauge/calibre   : 12
Chamber length  : 76mm (3in)
Number of barrels : double-barrels side-by-side
Action        : breech-loading
Locking      : barrel-block and transverse locking (Webley & Scott system)
Trigger      twin triggers
Weight      : 3.2kg (7lb)
Length      : 126cm (49$^5$/$_8$in)
Barrel length : 80cm (31$^1$/$_2$in)
Ejector     : automatic
Choke      fixed $^1$/$_2$ and full choke
Sight       bead
Safety     : sliding catch on neck of stock

**CHARACTERISTICS**
— material   : steel
— finish     : blued
— stock     : walnut stock, with pistol-grip

## Gaucher 809 Excellence

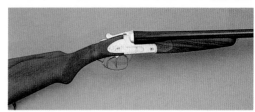

**TECHNICAL DETAILS**
Gauge/calibre   : 12, 16, or 20
Chamber length  : 70mm (2$^3$/$_4$in)
Number of barrels : double-barrels side-by-side
Action        : breech-loading
Locking      : barrel-block and transverse locking (Webley & Scott system)
Trigger      twin triggers
Weight      : 3.1kg (6lb 13oz)
Length      : 116cm (47$^3$/$_4$in)
Barrel length : 70cm (27$^3$/$_4$in)
Ejector     : automatic
Choke      fixed $^3$/$_4$ and full choke
Sight       bead
Safety     : sliding catch on neck of stock

**CHARACTERISTICS**
— material   : steel
— finish     : blued barrels, matt-chromed action with side-lock plates
— stock     : walnut stock, with pistol-grip

## Gaucher 813 Excellence

**TECHNICAL DETAILS**
Gauge/calibre   : 20

The right-hand barrel of this gun is rifled for use with slugs. Replacement 70cm (27 1/2in) barrels are also available. This gun cannot be held on a United Kingdom shotgun certificate.

☜

| | |
|---|---|
| Chamber length | : 70mm (2³/₄in) |
| Number of barrels | : double-barrels side-by-side |
| Action | : breech-loading |
| Locking | : barrel-block and transverse locking (Webley & Scott system) |
| Trigger | twin triggers |
| Weight | : 2.5kg (5lb 8oz) |
| Length | : 116cm (47³/₄in) |
| Barrel length | : 70cm (27¹/₂in) |
| Ejector | : automatic |
| Choke | fixed ¹/₂ and full choke |
| Sight | bead |
| Safety | : sliding catch on neck of stock |

**CHARACTERISTICS**

| | |
|---|---|
| — material | : steel |
| — finish | : blued barrels, tempered action |
| — stock | : straight English walnut stock |

☜

## Gaucher 830 Special

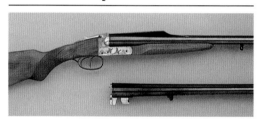

**TECHNICAL DETAILS**

| | |
|---|---|
| Gauge/calibre | : 12 |
| Chamber length | : 70mm (2³/₄in) |
| Number of barrels | : double-barrels side-by-side |
| Action | : breech-loading |
| Locking | : barrel-block and transverse locking (Webley & Scott system) |
| Trigger | twin triggers |
| Weight | : 3.1kg (6lb 13oz) |
| Length | : 105cm (41¹/₄in) |
| Barrel length | : 56cm (22in) |
| Ejector | : automatic |
| Choke | fixed chokes: cylindrical and full choke |
| Sight | bead |
| Safety | : sliding catch on neck of stock |

**CHARACTERISTICS**

| | |
|---|---|
| — material | : steel |
| — finish | : blued barrels, plain metal action with hunting scenes |
| — stock | : walnut stock, with pistol-grip |

## Gaucher 831 Becassier

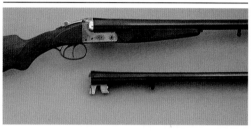

**TECHNICAL DETAILS**

| | |
|---|---|
| Gauge/calibre | : 12 |
| Chamber length | : 76mm (3in) |
| Number of barrels | : double-barrels side-by-side |
| Action | : breech-loading |
| Locking | : double barrel-block locking and transverse locking (Webley & Scott system) |
| Trigger | twin triggers |
| Weight | : 2.6kg (5lb 11¹/₂oz) |
| Length | : 115cm (45¹/₂in) |
| Barrel length | : 60cm (23⁵/₈in) |
| Ejector | : automatic |
| Choke | fixed chokes: cylindrical and ¹/₂ |
| Sight | bead |
| Safety | : sliding catch on neck of stock |

**CHARACTERISTICS**

| | |
|---|---|
| — material | : steel |
| — finish | : blued barrels, plain metal action with hunting motifs |
| — stock | : walnut stock, with pistol-grip |

The right-hand barrel of this gun is rifled for use with slugs. Replacement 70cm (27¹/₂in) barrels are also available. This gun cannot be held on a United Kingdom shotgun certificate.

☜

## Gaucher Simplarm

**TECHNICAL DETAILS**

| | |
|---|---|
| Gauge/calibre | : 12 |
| Chamber length | : 70mm (2³/₄in) |
| Number of barrels | : single-barrel |
| Action | : breech-loading |

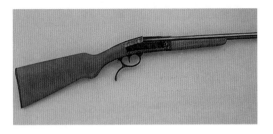

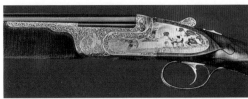

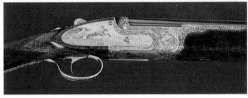

| Locking | : barrel-block locking by means of trigger guard hook |
|---|---|
| Trigger | single trigger |
| Weight | : 2.7kg (6lb) |
| Length | : 122cm (48in) |
| Barrel length | : 80cm (31¹/₂in) |
| Ejector | : automatic |
| Choke | fixed full choke |
| Sight | bead |
| Safety | : closing safety |

**CHARACTERISTICS**

| — material | : steel |
|---|---|
| — finish | : blued barrel, tempered action |
| — stock | : hardwood stock, with pistol-grip |

🖐

| Locking | : double barrel-block locking |
|---|---|
| Trigger | single trigger |
| Weight | : 2.7–3.5kg (6lb–7lb 11oz) |
| Length | : to choice |
| Barrel length | : to choice |
| Ejector | : to choice |
| Choke | to choice |
| Sight | to choice |
| Safety | : sliding catch on neck of stock |

**CHARACTERISTICS**

| — material | : steel |
|---|---|
| — finish | : blued barrels, plain metal action and side-lock plates with engraving to choice |
| — stock | : straight English stock of specially-selected walnut |

🖐

# Gazalan

Gazalan is a brand name of the Connecticut Shotgun Manufacturing Company of New Britain, in Connecticut, USA. CSM produces an exceptional range of guns under this name that are made by hand in America. Gazalan guns were introduced in 1994 and they are above all renowned for the quality of their engraving. The artistry is performed on one of a pair of guns by the Italian brothers Stefano and Giancarlo Pedretti. The other gun of the pair is engraved by Staduto Giovanni of Creative Arts. The guns are solely made and engraved to order. Consequently there is virtually no standard technical data because the overall length, barrel length, and choice of chokes is determined by the customer. The specially-selected walnut used for the stocks comes from Turkey. The basic price for one of these guns, excluding the engraving is in the region of $38,000.

## *Gazalan Setter side-lock*

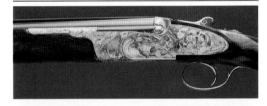

**TECHNICAL DETAILS**

| Gauge/calibre | : 12, 16, 20, 28, or .410 |
|---|---|
| Chamber length | : to choice |
| Number of barrels | : double-barrels over-and-under |
| Action | : breech-loading |
| Locking | : double barrel-block locking |
| Trigger | single trigger |
| Weight | : 2.7–3.5kg (6lb–7lb 11oz) |

## *Gazalan Pointer side-lock*

**TECHNICAL DETAILS**

| Gauge/calibre | : 12, 16, 20, 28, or .410 |
|---|---|
| Chamber length | : to choice |
| Number of barrels | : double-barrels over-and-under |
| Action | : breech-loading |

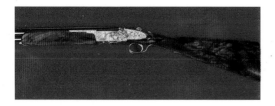

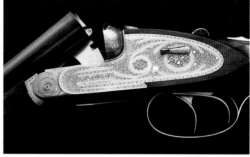

Length : to choice
Barrel length : to choice
Ejector : to choice
Choke to choice
Sight to choice
Safety : sliding catch on neck of stock

### CHARACTERISTICS
— material : steel
— finish : blued barrels, plain metal action and side-lock plates with engraving to choice
— stock : straight English stock of specially-selected walnut

Note the way the engravings run through from the action towards the fore-arm.

# Granger

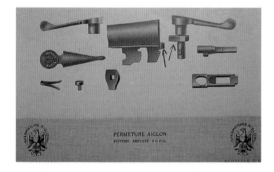

Granger Fusil Aiglon was founded in 1902 in St. Etienne, France by George Granger and Aimé Coeur Tyrode.

Tyrode lodged a patent application in 1913 on the special Aiglon locking. He was succeeded in 1934 by Henri Guichard. The company won a number of prizes at international exhibitions, including a gold medal at the 1937 World Exhibition in Paris. The partner Georges Granger has also been the recipient of numerous business distinctions and awards such as "Best French Craftsman" in 1968 and "Master Craftsman" in 1978. The guns made by the Granger company are largely bespoke guns hand-made to the individual wishes of the customer.

The shooter or "gun" is measured for his or her gun as a tailor measures for a suit. Consequently, such guns are not available from stock. The measuring is carried out using a measurement gun the dimensions of which can be adapted to the body measurements of the customer. For this reason, many of the technical characteristics below are "to choice" since virtually no standard measurements exist. For this reason also, Granger does not have a "range of models".

The guns shown are representative of the special guns which Granger have made. The Aiglon locking consists of a double barrel block lock together with a turnable lock, linked to a locking lever which engages with an extended lug on the underside of the side-by-side barrels. This unusual type of triple locking can be seen from various illustrations.

## *Granger Anglaise side-lock*

### TECHNICAL DETAILS
Gauge/calibre : 12, 16, or 20
Chamber length : to choice
Number of barrels : double-barrels side-by-side
Action : breech-loading
Locking : double barrel block and Aiglon locking
Trigger twin triggers
Weight : to choice
Length : to choice
Barrel length : to choice
Ejector : automatic
Choke to choice

Sight            barrel rib and bead
Safety           : automatic after breeching gun, sliding catch on
                 neck of stock

**CHARACTERISTICS**
— material       : steel
— finish         : blued barrels, plain metal action and side-lock
                 plates with engraving to choice; side-lock plates
                 can be removed
— stock          : straight English stock of very specially-selected walnut
🖤

## *Granger Ciselure side-lock*

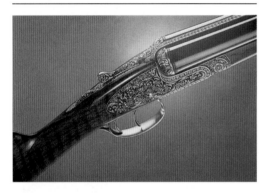

Trigger          twin triggers
Weight           : to choice
Length           : to choice
Barrel length    : to choice
Ejector          : automatic
Choke            to choice
Sight            barrel rib and bead
Safety           : automatic after breeching gun, sliding catch on
                 neck of stock

**CHARACTERISTICS**
— material       : steel
— finish         : blued barrels with gold inlay on the rims, plain
                 metal and engraved action and side-lock plates
— stock          : straight English stock of very specially-selected and
                 carved walnut
🖤

**TECHNICAL DETAILS**
Gauge/calibre      : 12, 16, or 20
Chamber length     : to choice
Number of barrels  : double-barrels side-by-side
Action             : breech-loading
Locking            : double barrel block and Aiglon locking
Trigger            twin triggers
Weight             : to choice
Length             : to choice
Barrel length      : to choice
Ejector            : automatic
Choke              to choice
Sight              barrel rib and bead
Safety             : automatic after breeching gun, sliding catch on
                   neck of stock

**CHARACTERISTICS**
— material         : steel
— finish           : blued barrels, plain metal action and side-lock
                   plates with engraving to choice; side-lock plates
                   can be removed
— stock            : straight English stock of specially-selected walnut
🖤

## *Granger Fine Anglaise à Bouquets side-lock*

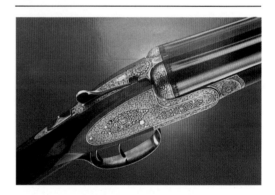

## *Granger Ciselure side-lock*

**TECHNICAL DETAILS**
Gauge/calibre      : 12, 16, or 20
Chamber length     : to choice
Number of barrels : double-barrels side-by-side
Action             : breech-loading
Locking            : double barrel block and Aiglon locking

**TECHNICAL DETAILS**
Gauge/calibre      : 12, 16, or 20
Chamber length     : to choice
Number of barrels : double-barrels side-by-side
Action             : breech-loading
Locking            : double barrel block and Aiglon locking
Trigger            twin triggers
Weight             : to choice
Length             : to choice
Barrel length      : to choice
Ejector            : automatic
Choke              to choice

| Sight | barrel rib and bead |
| Safety | : automatic after breeching gun, sliding catch on neck of stock |

**CHARACTERISTICS**

| — material | : steel |
| — finish | : blued barrels, plain metal action and side-lock plates with engraving to choice; side-lock plates can be removed |
| — stock | : straight English stock of specially-selected walnut |

## Granger Incrustation side-lock

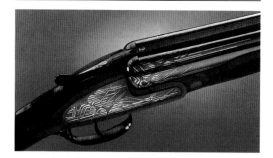

**TECHNICAL DETAILS**

| Gauge/calibre | : 12, 16, or 20 |
| Chamber length | : to choice |
| Number of barrels | : double-barrels side-by-side |
| Action | : breech-loading |
| Locking | : double barrel block and Aiglon locking |
| Trigger | twin triggers |
| Weight | : to choice |
| Length | : to choice |
| Barrel length | : to choice |
| Ejector | : automatic |
| Choke | to choice |
| Sight | barrel rib and bead |
| Safety | : automatic after breeching gun, sliding catch on neck of stock |

**CHARACTERISTICS**

| — material | : steel |
| — finish | : blued; barrels, action, and side-lock plates are inlaid with gold and platinum; side-lock plates can be removed |
| — stock | : straight English stock of very specially-selected walnut |

## Granger Meilleur Ouvrier de France side-lock

**TECHNICAL DETAILS**

| Gauge/calibre | : 12, 16, or 20 |
| Chamber length | : to choice |
| Number of barrels | : double-barrels side-by-side |
| Action | : breech-loading |

| Locking | : double barrel block and Aiglon locking |
| Trigger | twin triggers |
| Weight | : to choice |
| Length | : to choice |
| Barrel length | : to choice |
| Ejector | : automatic |
| Choke | to choice |
| Sight | barrel rib and bead |
| Safety | : automatic after breeching gun, sliding catch on neck of stock |

**CHARACTERISTICS**

| — material | : steel |
| — finish | : blued barrels with gold and platinum inlay in modern-style engraving, plain metal action and side-lock plates with engraving |
| — stock | : straight English stock of very specially-selected walnut |

The first example of this type of gun was made for an exhibition in 1978, leading to the company's engraver being awarded a citation for the best engraving work.

## Granger Scène de Chasse side-lock

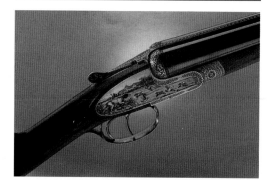

**TECHNICAL DETAILS**

| Gauge/calibre | : 12, 16, or 20 |
| Chamber length | : to choice |

Number of barrels : double-barrels side-by-side
Action       : breech-loading
Locking     : double barrel block and Aiglon locking
Trigger      twin triggers
Weight      : to choice
Length      : to choice
Barrel length  : to choice
Ejector     : automatic
Choke       to choice
Sight       barrel rib and bead
Safety      : automatic after breeching gun, sliding catch on neck of stock

**CHARACTERISTICS**
— material   : steel
— finish     : blued barrels, plain metal action and side-lock plates with engraving to choice; side-lock plates can be removed
— stock     : straight English stock of specially-selected walnut

## *Granger Scène de Chasse II side-lock*

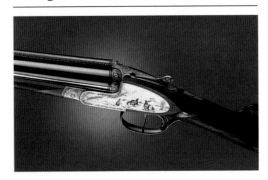

**TECHNICAL DETAILS**
Gauge/calibre  : 12, 16, or 20
Chamber length : to choice
Number of barrels : double-barrels side-by-side
Action       : breech-loading
Locking     : double barrel block and Aiglon locking
Trigger      twin triggers
Weight      : to choice
Length      : to choice
Barrel length  : to choice
Ejector     : automatic
Choke       to choice
Sight       barrel rib and bead
Safety      : automatic after breeching gun, sliding catch on neck of stock

**CHARACTERISTICS**
— material   : steel
— finish     : blued barrels, plain metal engraved action and side-lock plates; side-lock plates can be removed
— stock:    straight English stock of specially-selected walnut

# Harrington & Richardson (H&R) / New England Firearms (NEF)

Harrington & Richardson were founded in 1871 by the Americans Gilbert Henderson Harrington and Franklin Wesson. Previously, Harrington had worked for the Ballard & Fairbanks company producing revolvers on a small scale at Worcester, Massachusetts. Franklin Wesson previously had a small gun-making workshop. In view of the large demand for double-barrelled shotguns, the companies decided to start making them.

Both firms entered into licensing with the English firm of Anson & Deely but with the steep rise in demand for H&R revolvers they ceased production of shotguns in 1886.

The company was reorganised in 1888 and the name changed to Harrington & Richardson Arms Company. Both directors died in 1897 within a short time of each other.

A triumvirate was formed, consisting of a Mr Brooks, the former chief clerk and finance manager, Edwin C. Harrington, the 20-year old son of the founder, and daughter Mary A. Richardson, which carried the business forward.

The company moved to Garner, Massachusetts after a considerable time in Worcester. Today's H&R range consists of single-barrel shotguns, rifles, and revolvers. Under the name of its New England Firearms subsidiary, the company also produce simple, reliable and modestly priced guns.

## *H&R/NEF Pardner Youth*

**TECHNICAL DETAILS**
Gauge/calibre  : 20, 28, or .410
Chamber length  : 3in (76mm)

Number of barrels : single-barrel
Action         : breech-loading
Locking        : locking lugs
Trigger          single trigger
Weight         : 5–6lb (2.3–2.7kg)
Length         : 36in (91cm)
Barrel length  : 22in (55.9cm)
Ejector        : automatic
Choke            fixed ½ choke
Sight            bead
Safety         : transfer bar safety system

### CHARACTERISTICS
— material     : steel
— finish       : blued barrel, tempered action
— stock        : straight English hardwood stock

The short barrel length of this gun falls below the minimum required in the United Kingdom for a shotgun certificate of 24in (61cm). Similar restrictions apply elsewhere in Europe.

## H&R/NEF Special Purpose Magnum-10

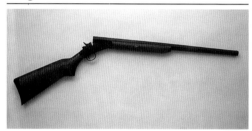

### TECHNICAL DETAILS
Gauge/calibre    : 10
Chamber length   : 3½ in (89mm)
Number of barrels : single-barrel
Action           : breech-loading
Locking          : locking lugs
Trigger            single trigger
Weight           : 9lb 4oz (4.2kg)
Length           : 40in (91cm)
Barrel length    : 24in (61cm)
Ejector          : automatic
Choke              fixed ½ choke
Sight              bead
Safety           : transfer bar safety system

### CHARACTERISTICS
— material     : steel
— finish       : blued
— stock        : English hardwood stock, with pistol-grip

Some European countries, although not the U.K., ban the use of 10 gauge firearms

## H&R/NEF Survivor

### TECHNICAL DETAILS
Gauge/calibre    : 12, 20, or .410
Chamber length   : 3in (76mm)
Number of barrels : single-barrel
Action           : breech-loading
Locking          : locking lugs
Trigger            single trigger
Weight           : 6lb (2.7kg)
Length           : 36in (91.4cm)
Barrel length    : 22in (55.9cm)
Ejector          : automatic
Choke              fixed ½ choke
Sight              bead
Safety           : transfer bar safety system

### CHARACTERISTICS
— material     : steel
— finish       : matt blued
— stock        : black plastic stock, with pistol-grip and storage space for extra cartridges

The short barrel length of this gun falls below the minimum required in the United Kingdom for a shotgun certificate of 24in (61cm). Similar restrictions apply elsewhere in Europe.

## H&R/NEF Topper Deluxe

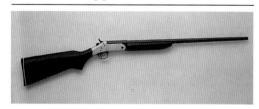

### TECHNICAL DETAILS
Gauge/calibre    : 12
Chamber length   : 3½ in (89mm)
Number of barrels : single-barrel
Action           : breech-loading
Locking          : locking lugs
Trigger            single trigger
Weight           : 6lb 8oz (3kg)
Length           : 43in (109.2cm)
Barrel length    : 28in (71cm)
Ejector          : automatic
Choke              interchangeable chokes

| Sight | bead |
|---|---|
| Safety | : transfer bar safety system |

**CHARACTERISTICS**
- material : steel
- finish : blued barrel, nickel-plated action
- stock : black-painted hardwood stock, with pistol-grip

☞

## H&R/NEF Tracker Slug

**TECHNICAL DETAILS**
| Gauge/calibre | : 12 or 20 |
|---|---|
| Chamber length | : 3in (76mm) |
| Number of barrels | : single-barrel |
| Action | : breech-loading |
| Locking | : locking lugs |
| Trigger | single trigger |
| Weight | : 6lb (2.7kg) |
| Length | : 40in (101.6cm) |
| Barrel length | : 24in (61cm) |
| Ejector | : automatic |
| Choke | cylindrical |
| Sight | adjustable rack and bead |
| Safety | : transfer bar safety system |

**CHARACTERISTICS**
- material : steel
- finish : blued barrel, tempered action
- stock : hardwood stock, with pistol-grip

☞

## H&R/NEF Ultra Slug Gun Hunter

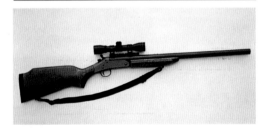

**TECHNICAL DETAILS**
| Gauge/calibre | : 12 or 20 |
|---|---|
| Chamber length | : 3in (76mm) |
| Number of barrels | : single-barrel |
| Action | : breech-loading |
| Locking | : locking lugs |
| Trigger | single trigger |
| Weight | : 8–9lb (3.63–4.09kg) |

| Length | : 38in (96.5cm) |
|---|---|
| Barrel length | : 24in (61cm) |
| Ejector | : extractor only |
| Choke | rifled barrel |
| Sight | none, mounting for telescopic sight |
| Safety | : transfer bar safety system |

**CHARACTERISTICS**
- material : steel
- finish : blued barrel, matt blue action
- stock : hardwood stock, with pistol-grip

This gun is also available as model 928 with
a laminated stock in camouflage colours.

☞

# Heym

The German firearms
company of Friedrich Wilhelm Heym was founded
in 1865 in Münnerstadt in
Bavaria. The company was
taken over in 1912 by the
son of the founder, Adolf
Heym and in turn by his
son, August, in 1920. During that time the
Heym company principally made Anson &
Deely triple-barrelled guns.

During World War II, the company switched
to production of arms for the German war
effort. After the war, when the occupying
Allies banned production of firearms, Heym
was forced to switch to making air guns. This
continued until 1952, when Heym were
granted permission to produce firearms.
Since then the company has become
renowned for its high quality rifles and shotguns. Only the finest quality Krupp steel is
used and the company's engraving is considered by many to be unequalled. Most of the
guns are breech-loading rifles and shotguns.
The triple-barrel guns with one or two
smooth-bore barrels supplemented with one
or two rifled barrels are closely associated
with the company. Heym guns are relatively
expensive because of the high standards of
their gunsmiths' art and their fine engraving.

## Heym 22 S2 Bock combination gun

**TECHNICAL DETAILS**
| Gauge/calibre | : see below |
|---|---|
| Chamber length | : smooth-bore: 70mm (2³/₄in) or 76mm (3in) |

Number of barrels : double-barrels over-and-under
Action : breech-loading
Locking : barrel-block locking
Trigger : twin triggers
Weight : 2.6kg (5lb 11¹/₂ oz)
Length : 102cm (40¹/₈ in)
Barrel length : 61cm (24in)
Ejector : automatic, can be disengaged
Choke : to choice
Sight : folding sight and bead; suitable for mounting telescopic sight
Safety : sliding catch on neck of stock, automatic prevention against accidental discharge

CHARACTERISTICS
— material : steel barrels, light alloy action
— finish : blued barrel, plain metal action
— stock : walnut stock, with pistol-grip

Available calibres/gauges (top smooth-bore barrel): 12, 16, or 20; (bottom rifled barrel): .22 Hornet, .222 Rem., .222 Rem. Mag., .22-250 Rem., 5.6x50R, 5.6x52R, .243 Win., 6.5x55 SM, 6.5x57R, 6.5x64 Brenneke, 6.5x65R, 7X57R, 7x65R, .308 Win., .30-06 Spr., .30R Blaser, 8x57 IRS.

## Heym 25 Bock combination gun

TECHNICAL DETAILS
Gauge/calibre : see below
Chamber length : smooth-bore: 70mm (2³/₄in) or 76mm (3in)
Number of barrels : double-barrels over-and-under
Action : breech-loading
Locking : barrel-block locking
Trigger : twin triggers
Weight : 2.6kg (5lb 11¹/₂ oz)
Length : 101cm (39³/₄in)

Barrel length : 60cm (23⁵/₈in)
Ejector : extractor only
Choke : to choice
Sight : folding sight and bead; for mounting telescopic sight
Safety : sliding catch on neck of stock, automatic prevention against accidental discharge

CHARACTERISTICS
— material : steel barrels, light alloy action
— finish : blued barrels, plain metal action with hunting engravings
— stock : walnut stock, with pistol-grip

Available calibres/gauges (top smooth-bore barrel): 12, 16, or 20; (bottom rifled barrel): .22 Hornet, .222 Rem., .222 Rem. Mag., .22-250 Rem., 5.6x50R, 5.6x52R, 6x62 Frères, 6.5x55 SM, 6.5x57R, 6.5x65R, .243 Win., 7X57R, 7x65R, .308 Win., .30-06 Spr., .30R Blaser, 8x57 Mauser.

## Heym 33 deluxe triple-barrel combination gun

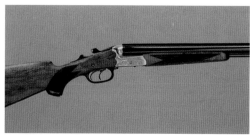

TECHNICAL DETAILS
Gauge/calibre : see below
Chamber length : smooth-bore: 70mm (2³/₄in) or 76mm (3in)
Number of barrels : triple-barrel: 2 smooth-bore barrels, 1 rifle barrel
Action : breech-loading
Locking : Blitz, Greener, and double barrel-block locking
Trigger : twin triggers
Weight : 3.5–3.7kg (7lb 11oz–8lb 2¹/₄oz)
Length : 106cm (41³/₄in)
Barrel length : 63.5cm (25in)
Ejector : extractor only
Choke : to choice
Sight : bead; suitable for mounting telescopic sight

Safety : sliding catch on neck of stock, load indicator beside locking lever, separate cocking for rifle barrel

## CHARACTERISTICS
— material : steel barrels, stainless-steel action
— finish : blued barrels, plain metal action with engravings
— stock : walnut stock, with pistol-grip

Available calibres/gauges (smooth-bore): 16, or 20; (rifled): .22 Hornet, .222 Rem., .222 Rem. Mag., .243 Win., .270 Win., 5.6x50R Mag., 5.6x52R, 5.6x57R, 6.5x55 SM, 6.5x57R, 6.5x65 RWS, 7X57R, 7x65R, .308 Win., .30-06 Spr., .30 Blaser, 8x57 IRS, 8x75 RWS, 9.3x74R.

☙

## Heym 35 triple-barrel combination gun

### TECHNICAL DETAILS
Gauge/calibre : see below
Chamber length : smooth-bore: 70mm (2³/₄in) or 76mm (3in)
Number of barrels : triple-barrel: 1 smooth-bore barrel, 2 rifle barrels
Action : breech-loading
Locking : side-lock, double Greener, and barrel-block locking
Trigger twin triggers
Weight : 3.5–3.7kg (7lb 11oz–8lb 2¹/₄oz)
Length : 106cm (41³/₄in)
Barrel length : 63.5cm (25in)
Ejector : extractor only
Choke to choice
Sight folding sight; suitable for mounting telescopic sight
Safety : sliding catch on neck of stock, selector for rifle barrels, load indicator beside locking lever

### CHARACTERISTICS
— material : steel
— finish : blued barrels, plain metal side-plates with hunting engravings
— stock : walnut stock, with pistol-grip

Available calibres/gauges (top smooth-bore barrel): 16, or 20; (centre and bottom rifled barrels choice from small calibre): .22 WMR, .22 Hornet, .222 Rem., .222 Rem. Mag.,.223 Rem., 5.6x50R Mag., 5.6x52R; (for bottom rifled barrel): 6.5x57R, 6.5x65 RWS, 7X57R, 7x65R, .308 Win., .30-06 Spr., .30R Blaser, 8x57 JRS, 8x75 RWS, 9.3x74R.

☙

## Heym 37 triple-barrel combination gun

### TECHNICAL DETAILS
Gauge/calibre : see below
Chamber length : smooth-bore: 70mm (2³/₄in) or 76mm (3in)
Number of barrels : triple-barrel: 2 smooth-bore barrels, 1 rifle barrel
Action : breech-loading
Locking : Greener, and double barrel-block locking
Trigger twin triggers
Weight : 3.5–3.7kg (7lb 11oz–8lb 2¹/₄oz)
Length : 106cm (41³/₄in)
Barrel length : 63.5cm (25in)
Ejector : extractor only
Choke to choice
Sight bead; suitable for mounting telescopic sight
Safety : sliding catch on neck of stock, load indicator beside locking lever, separate cocking for rifle barrel

### CHARACTERISTICS
— material : steel barrels, stainless-steel action
— finish : blued barrels, plain metal action with engravings
— stock : walnut stock, with pistol-grip

Available calibres/gauges (smooth-bore): 12, 16, or 20; (rifled): .22 Hornet, .222 Rem., .222 Rem. Mag., .243 Win., 5.6x50R Mag., 5.6x52R, 5.6x57R, 6.5x55 SM, 6.5x57R, 6.5x65 RWS, .270 Win., 7X57R, 7x65R, .308 Win., .30-06 Spr., .30 Blaser, 8x57 IRS, 8x75 RWS, 9.3x74R.

☙

## Heym 37B triple-barrel combination gun

### TECHNICAL DETAILS
Gauge/calibre : see below
Chamber length : smooth-bore: 70mm (2³/₄in) or 76mm (3in)
Number of barrels : triple-barrel: 2 rifled barrels, 1 smooth-bore barrel
Action : breech-loading
Locking : Greener, and double barrel-block locking

| Trigger | twin triggers |
| --- | --- |
| Weight | : 3.5–3.7kg (7lb 11oz–8lb 2¹/₄oz) |
| Length | : 106cm (41³/₄in) |
| Barrel length | : 63.5cm (25in) |
| Ejector | : extractor only |
| Choke | to choice |
| Sight | fixed rack and bead; suitable for mounting telescopic sight |
| Safety | : sliding catch on neck of stock, load indicator beside locking lever, separate cocking for each barrel |

**CHARACTERISTICS**

| — material | : steel |
| --- | --- |
| — finish | : blued barrels, plain metal action with engravings |
| — stock | : walnut stock, with pistol-grip |

 Available calibres/gauges (smooth-bore): 12; (rifled): 7x65R,.30-06 Spr., .30R Blaser, 8x57 IRS, 8x75 RWS, 9.3x74R.

## Heym 55 BF or F Bock combination gun

**TECHNICAL DETAILS**

| Gauge/calibre | : see below |
| --- | --- |
| Chamber length | : smooth-bore: 70mm (2³/₄in) or 76mm (3in) |
| Number of barrels | : double-barrels over-and-under |
| Action | : breech-loading |
| Locking | : double Greener, and barrel-block locking |
| Trigger | twin triggers |
| Weight | : 3.1–3.2kg (6lb 13oz–7lb) |
| Length | : 106–114.5cm (41³/₄–45in) |
| Barrel length | : 63.5–72cm (25–28³/₈in) |
| Ejector | : extractor only |
| Choke | smooth-bore barrel to choice |
| Sight | model 55BF: folding sight, suitable for mounting telescopic sight; model 55F: bead |
| Safety | : sliding catch on neck of stock, load indicator |

**CHARACTERISTICS**

| — material | : steel barrels, stainless-steel action |
| --- | --- |
| — finish | : blued barrel, plain metal side-lock plates with engravings |
| — stock | : engraved walnut stock, with pistol-grip |

Available calibres/gauges (top smooth-bore barrel): 12, 16, or 20; (bottom rifled barrel): .22 Hornet, .222 Rem., .222 Rem. Mag., 5.6x50R Mag., 5.6x52R, 5.6x57R, .243 Win., 6.5x55 SM, 6.5x57R, 6.5x65 RWS, .270 Win., 7x65R, .308 Win., .30-06 Spr., .30 R Blaser, 8x57 Mauser, 8x75 RS, 9.3x74R. This gun is typically for big game and has one pre-set trigger per barrel.

## Heym 55 BS

**TECHNICAL DETAILS**

| Gauge/calibre | : see below |
| --- | --- |
| Chamber length | : not applicable |
| Number of barrels | : double-barrels over-and-under |
| Action | : breech-loading |
| Locking | : barrel-block and Kersten locking |
| Trigger | twin triggers, front with pre-set |
| Weight | : 3.1–3.6kg (6lb 13oz–7lb 14³/₁₆oz) |
| Length | : 106 or 114.5cm (41³/₄ or 45in) |
| Barrel length | : 63.5 or 72cm (25 or 28³/₈in) |
| Ejector | : extractor only |
| Choke | not applicable, rifled barrels |
| Sight | fixed rack sight, mounting telescopic sight |
| Safety | : sliding catch on neck of stock, load indicator by locking lever |

**CHARACTERISTICS**

| — material | : steel |
| --- | --- |
| — finish | : blued barrels, silver-plated action with engravings |

– stock : specially-selected walnut stock, with pistol-grip and cheek plate

Available calibres (top barrel): .22 Hornet, .222 Rem., .222 Rem. Mag., 5.6x50R Mag., 5.6x52R: (bottom barrel): 7x65R, .30-06 Spr., .308 Win., 8x57 IRS, 8x75 RS, 9.3x74R. Special large-calibre version – (top barrel): .243 Win., 6.5x55 SM, 5.6x57R, 6.5x65R-RWS, 7x65R, .30-06 Spr., .308 Win., .30 R Blaser; (bottom barrel): .300 Win. Mag., .375 H&H Mag., .416 Rigby, .458 Win. Mag., .470 NE (Nitro Express).

## Heym 80 B

### TECHNICAL DETAILS
Gauge/calibre : see below
Chamber length : not applicable
Number of barrels : double-barrels side-by-side
Action : breech-loading
Locking : double barrel-block locking
Trigger single or twin triggers
Weight : 3.2kg (7lb)
Length : 103cm (40¹/₂in)
Barrel length : 60cm (23⁵/₈in)
Ejector : extractor
Choke not applicable, rifled barrels
Sight fixed rack sight with mounting for telescopic sight
Safety : sliding catch on neck of stock, load indicator by locking lever

### CHARACTERISTICS
– material : steel
– finish : blued barrels, silver-plated side-plates with engravings (no side-lock)
– stock : very exclusive stock of root walnut, with pistol-grip and cheek plate

Available calibres: 7x65R, .30-06 Spr., .30R Blaser, 8x57 IRS, 8x75 RS, 9.3x74R. Model 80B is available in two versions: model B with twin triggers with the front one acting as a pre-set, and 80 B-H (illustrated) with a single trigger and manual cocking. The firing mechanism remains inert after breaking the breech until the button is pushed on the safety catch.

## Heym 88 B Safari

### TECHNICAL DETAILS
Gauge/calibre : see below
Chamber length : not applicable
Number of barrels : double-barrels side-by-side
Action : breech-loading
Locking : Greener, and double barrel-block locking, modified Anson lock with double lever safety
Trigger twin triggers
Weight : 4.5kg (9lb 14oz)
Length : 104.5cm (41¹/₄in)
Barrel length : 61cm (24in)
Ejector : extractor
Choke not applicable, rifled barrels
Sight Express folding sight and mounting for telescopic sight
Safety : sliding catch on neck of stock, load indicator by locking lever

### CHARACTERISTICS
– material : steel
– finish : blued barrels, silver-plated side-plates with engravings (no side-lock)
– stock : specially-selected walnut stock, with pistol-grip and cheek plate

Available calibres: .375 H&H Mag., .458 Win. Mag., .470 NE (Nitro Express), .500 NE, .600 NE.

## Heym 88 B/SS

### TECHNICAL DETAILS
Gauge/calibre : see below
Chamber length : not applicable
Number of barrels : double-barrels over-and-under
Action : breech-loading
Locking : Greener, and double barrel-block locking
Trigger twin triggers
Weight : 3.6kg (7lb 14³/₄oz)
Length : 107cm (42¹/₄in)

| | |
|---|---|
| Barrel length | : 63.5cm (25in) |
| Ejector | : automatic |
| Choke | not applicable, rifled barrels |
| Sight | fixed rack sight and mounting for telescopic sight |
| Safety | : sliding catch on neck of stock, load indicator by locking lever |

**CHARACTERISTICS**

| | |
|---|---|
| — material | : steel |
| — finish | : blued barrels, silver-plated side-plates with engravings (no side-lock) |
| — stock | : specially-selected walnut stock, with pistol-grip and cheek plate |

Available calibres: 7x65R, .30-06 Spr., .30 R Blaser, 8x57 IRS, 8x75RS, .375 H&H Mag., 9.3x74R.

# Iga

Iga shotguns are made by Amantino & Cia at Veranopolis in Brazil. Both side-by-side and over-and-under guns have barrel-block locking. The over-and-under guns have two pins on either side of the upper barrel.

Iga guns are imported into USA and elsewhere in South America by Stoeger Inc., who are also known for shooting catalogues such as The *Shooter's Bible*.

## Iga Coach Gun

**TECHNICAL DETAILS**

| | |
|---|---|
| Gauge/calibre | : 12, 20, or .410 |
| Chamber length | : 76mm (3in) |
| Number of barrels | : double-barrels side-by-side |
| Action | : breech-loading |
| Locking | : barrel-block locking |
| Trigger | twin triggers |

| | |
|---|---|
| Weight | : 3.1kg (6lb 13oz) |
| Length | : 93cm (36½in) |
| Barrel length | : 51cm (20in) |
| Ejector | : automatic |
| Choke | ½ and ¼ |
| Sight | bead |
| Safety | : automatic safety, sliding catch on neck of stock |

**CHARACTERISTICS**

| | |
|---|---|
| — material | : steel |
| — finish | : blued or nickel-plated |
| — stock | : hardwood stock with engraving or black painted (Coach Gun Nickel) |

The barrel length of this gun falls under the legal minimum of 24in (61cm) for a United Kingdom shotgun certificate. Similar restrictions apply in other European countries.

## Iga Condor I

**TECHNICAL DETAILS**

| | |
|---|---|
| Gauge/calibre | : 12 or 20 |
| Chamber length | : 76mm (3in) |
| Number of barrels | : double-barrels over-and-under |
| Action | : breech-loading |
| Locking | : conical lugs on either side of upper barrel |
| Trigger | single trigger |
| Weight | : 3.6kg (7lb 14³/₄oz) |
| Length | : 111–116cm (43³¹/₂–45¹/₂in) |
| Barrel length | : 66–71cm (26–28in) |
| Ejector | : automatic |
| Choke | ¼ and ½ or ½ and full, or interchangeable chokes |
| Sight | bead |
| Safety | : automatic safety, sliding catch on neck of stock |

## CHARACTERISTICS
— material         : steel
— finish           : blued
— stock            : hardwood stock with pistol-grip

Illustrated (from top to bottom) are: IGA Condor I and the Uplander.

🕊️

## Iga Condor II

### TECHNICAL DETAILS
Gauge/calibre     : 12
Chamber length    : 76mm (3in)
Number of barrels : double-barrels over-and-under
Action            : breech-loading
Locking           : conical lugs on either side of upper barrel
Trigger             single trigger
Weight            : 3.6kg (7lb 14³/₄oz)
Length            : 111–116cm (43¹/₂–45¹/₂in)
Barrel length     : 66–71cm (26–28in)
Ejector           : extractor
Choke               ¹/₄ and ¹/₂ or ¹/₂ and full
Sight               ventilated rib and bead
Safety            : sliding catch on neck of stock

### CHARACTERISTICS
— material         : steel
— finish           : blued
— stock            : hardwood stock with pistol-grip

Illustrated (from top to bottom) are: IGA Condor I and the Uplander.

🕊️

## Iga Condor Supreme

### TECHNICAL DETAILS
Gauge/calibre     : 12 or 20
Chamber length    : 76mm (3in)
Number of barrels : double-barrels over-and-under
Action            : breech-loading
Locking           : conical lugs on either side of upper barrel
Trigger             single trigger
Weight            : 3.6kg (7lb 14³/₄oz)
Length            : 111–116cm (43¹/₂ –45¹/₂ in)

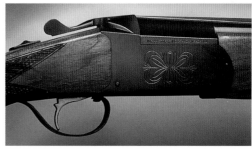

Barrel length     : 66–71cm (26–28in)
Ejector           : automatic
Choke               interchangeable chokes
Sight               ventilated rib and bead
Safety            : sliding catch on neck of stock plus barrel elector

### CHARACTERISTICS
— material         : steel
— finish           : blued
— stock            : hardwood stock with pistol-grip

🕊️ 🐓

## Iga Era-2000

### TECHNICAL DETAILS
Gauge/calibre     : 12
Chamber length    : 76mm (3in)

| | |
|---|---|
| Number of barrels | : double-barrels over-and-under |
| Action | : breech-loading |
| Locking | : barrel-block locking |
| Trigger | single trigger |
| Weight | : 3.6kg (7lb 14³/₄oz) |
| Length | : 111–116cm (43¹/₂–45¹/₂in) |
| Barrel length | : 66–71cm (26–28in) |
| Ejector | : extractor |
| Choke | interchangeable chokes |
| Sight | ventilated rib and bead |
| Safety | : sliding catch on neck of stock |

**CHARACTERISTICS**
- material : steel
- finish : blued
- stock : hardwood stock with pistol-grip

Illustrated (from left to right) are: IGA Era 2000 and the Uplander.

## Iga Ladies/Youth

**TECHNICAL DETAILS**

| | |
|---|---|
| Gauge/calibre | : 20 or .410 |
| Chamber length | : 76mm (3in) |
| Number of barrels | : double-barrels side-by-side |
| Action | : breech-loading |
| Locking | : barrel-block locking |
| Trigger | twin triggers |
| Weight | : 3kg (6lb 8oz) |
| Length | : 101.6cm (40in) |
| Barrel length | : 61cm (24in) |
| Ejector | : extractor |
| Choke | ¹/₂ and ¹/₄; full and ¹/₂ (Youth) |
| Sight | bead |
| Safety | : automatic safety, sliding catch on neck of stock |

**CHARACTERISTICS**
- material : steel
- finish : blued
- stock : hardwood stock with pistol-grip

Illustrated (from top to bottom) are: IGA Ladies model and Youth model.

## Iga Uplander

**TECHNICAL DETAILS**

| | |
|---|---|
| Gauge/calibre | : 12, 20, 28, or .410 |
| Chamber length | : 76mm (3in) |
| Number of barrels | : double-barrels side-by-side |
| Action | : breech-loading |
| Locking | : barrel-block locking |
| Trigger | twin triggers |
| Weight | : 3–3.4kg (6lb 8oz–7lb 8oz)) |
| Length | : 106–112cm (42–44in) |
| Barrel length | : 66–71cm (26–28in) |
| Ejector | : automatic |
| Choke | ¹/₄ and ¹/₂, ¹/₂ and full, full and full, or interchangeable chokes |
| Sight | bead |
| Safety | : automatic safety, sliding catch on neck of stock |

**CHARACTERISTICS**
- material : steel
- finish : blued
- stock : hardwood stock with pistol-grip

Illustrated (from top to bottom) are: IGA Condor I and the Uplander.

# Imperator

The German company Wischo Jagd & Sportwaffen GmbH is a trading firm which represents a number of gunmakers in Europe and Germany. In addition to the general models, Wischo also frequently has special models produced by a number of makers for them to sell exclusively. Imperator shotguns are made in Italy by Fabarm and others. These are not standard Fabarm guns but guns made to Wischo specifications.

## Imperator Extra Light II/IV

**TECHNICAL DETAILS**

| | |
|---|---|
| Gauge/calibre | : 20 |

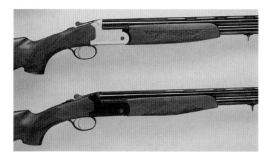

Chamber length   : 70mm (2³/₄in) or 76mm (3in)
Number of barrels : double-barrels over-and-under
Action           : breech-loading
Locking          : barrel-block locking
Trigger          single trigger
Weight           : 2-4 or 2.8kg (5lb 4oz or 6lb 2¹/₂oz)
Length           : 116cm (45⁵/₈in)
Barrel length    : 71cm (28in)
Ejector          : automatic
Choke            ¹/₂ and full
Sight            ventilated rib and bead
Safety           : sliding catch on neck of stock

### CHARACTERISTICS
— material   : steel barrels, light alloy action
— finish     : blued (II) or blued barrels and plain metal engraved action (IV)
— stock      : walnut stock, with pistol-grip

Illustrated are: Extra Light ELL IV (top) and
Extra Light II.

## Imperator III side–by–side

### TECHNICAL DETAILS
Gauge/calibre    : 12
Chamber length   : 70mm (2³/₄in)
Number of barrels : double-barrels side-by-side
Action           : breech-loading
Locking          : double barrel-block locking
Trigger          single trigger
Weight           : 3kg (6lb 9¹/₂oz)
Length           : 114cm (44⁷/₈in)
Barrel length    : 71cm (28in)
Ejector          : automatic
Choke            ¹/₂ and full
Sight            recessed rib with bead
Safety           : sliding catch on neck of stock and barrel selector

### CHARACTERISTICS
— material   : steel
— finish     : blued barrels, silvered action with Arabesque decoration
— stock      : walnut stock, with pistol-grip

## Imperator 93/93E Hunter

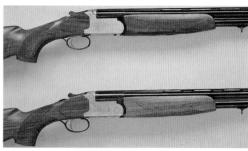

### TECHNICAL DETAILS
Gauge/calibre    : 12
Chamber length   : 70mm (2³/₄in)
Number of barrels : double-barrels over-and-under
Action           : breech-loading
Locking          : barrel-block locking
Trigger          single trigger
Weight           : 3.1kg (6lb 13oz)
Length           : 116cm (45⁵/₈in)
Barrel length    : 71cm (28in)
Ejector          : automatic (93E) or with extractor (93)
Choke            ¹/₂ and full
Sight            7mm (⁹/₃₂in) ventilated rib with bead
Safety           : sliding catch on neck of stock and barrel selector

### CHARACTERISTICS
— material   : steel
— finish     : blued barrels, silvered action with edge decoration
— stock      : walnut stock, with pistol-grip

## Imperator 93 Skeet/Trap

### TECHNICAL DETAILS
Gauge/calibre    : 12

| Chamber length | : 70mm (2³/₄in) |
| Number of barrels | : double-barrels over-and-under |
| Action | : breech-loading |
| Locking | : barrel-block locking |
| Trigger | single trigger |
| Weight | : Skeet: 3.2kg (7lb); Trap 3.85kg (8lb 8oz) |
| Length | : Skeet 116cm (45⁵/₈in); Trap 121cm (47⁵/₁₆in) |
| Barrel length | : Skeet: 71cm (28in); Trap 76cm (30in) |
| Ejector | : automatic |
| Choke | Skeet: skeet/skeet chokes; Trap: ³/₄ and full |
| Sight | 10mm ( ⁷/₁₆in) ventilated rib with red plastic bead |
| Safety | : sliding catch on neck of stock |

**CHARACTERISTICS**
- material : steel
- finish : blued
- stock : walnut stock, with pistol-grip

Illustrated from top to bottom are: 93 Trap and 93 Skeet.

## Imperator 1000-SLF Super Goose

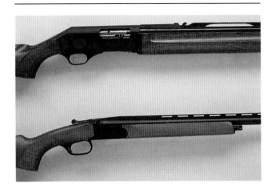

**TECHNICAL DETAILS**
| Gauge/calibre | : 12 |
| Chamber length | : 76mm (3in) |
| Number of barrels | : single-barrel |
| Magazine | : tubular magazine for 2 cartridges |
| Action | : semi-automatic (gas-operated) |
| Locking | : rotating locking |
| Trigger | single trigger |
| Weight | : 3.4kg (7lb 8oz) |
| Length | : 145cm (57¹/₈in) |
| Barrel length | : 90cm (35¹/₂ in) |
| Ejector | : extractor |
| Choke | interchangeable chokes |
| Sight | 12mm (¹/₂in) ventilated rib with folding rack and bead |
| Safety | : push-button catch at rear of trigger guard |

**CHARACTERISTICS**
- material : steel
- finish : blued
- stock : walnut stock, with pistol-grip

Illustrated from top to bottom are: 1000 SLF Super Goose and Imperator Omega.

## Imperator Omega

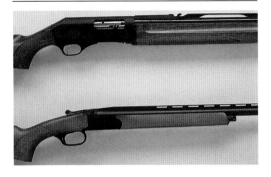

**TECHNICAL DETAILS**
| Gauge/calibre | : 12 |
| Chamber length | : 76mm (3in) |
| Number of barrels | : single-barrel |
| Action | : breech-loading |
| Locking | : barrel-block locking |
| Trigger | single trigger |
| Weight | : 2.7kg (6lb) |
| Length | : 116cm (45⁵/₈in) |
| Barrel length | : 71cm (28in) |
| Ejector | : automatic |
| Choke | full choke |
| Sight | ventilated rib and bead |
| Safety | : push-button in trigger guard |

**CHARACTERISTICS**
- material : steel
- finish : blued
- stock : hardwood stock, with pistol-grip

Illustrated from top to bottom are: 1000 SLF Super Goose and Imperator Omega.

## Imperator SDASS Hunter pump-action repeater

**TECHNICAL DETAILS**
| Gauge/calibre | : 12 |

| | |
|---|---|
| Chamber length | : 76mm (3in) |
| Number of barrels | : single-barrel |
| Magazine | : tubular magazine for 2, 7, or 8 cartridges |
| Action | : pump-action |
| Locking | : rotating locking |
| Trigger | single trigger |
| Weight | : 3.1kg (6lb 13oz) |
| Length | : 127cm (50in) |
| Barrel length | : 71cm (28in) |
| Ejector | : extractor |
| Choke | interchangeable chokes |
| Sight | 7mm ($^9/_{32}$in) barrel rib with bead |
| Safety | : push-button catch in front of trigger guard |

**CHARACTERISTICS**

| | |
|---|---|
| — material | : steel |
| — finish | : matt black |
| — stock | : hardwood stock, with pistol-grip |

Firearms legislation in the United Kingdom limits magazine capacity to 2 cartridges in the magazine and 1 in the chamber for a shotgun. To comply, the magazine must not be capable of accepting more. Similar restrictions apply in other European countries. Illustrated from top to bottom are: SDASS Super Goose and SDASS Hunter.

## Imperator SDASS Magnum

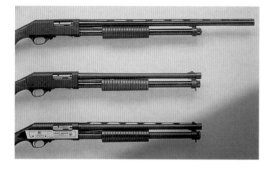

**TECHNICAL DETAILS**

| | |
|---|---|
| Gauge/calibre | : 12 |
| Chamber length | : 76mm (3in) |
| Number of barrels | : single-barrel |
| Magazine | : tubular magazine for 2, 7, or 8 cartridges |
| Action | : pump-action |
| Locking | : rotating locking |
| Trigger | single trigger |
| Weight | : 3.1kg (6lb 13oz) |
| Length | : 105cm (41$^3/_8$in) |
| Barrel length | : 50cm (19$^3/_4$in) |
| Ejector | : extractor |
| Choke | interchangeable chokes |
| Sight | ventilated rib with bead |
| Safety | : push-button catch in front of trigger guard |

**CHARACTERISTICS**

| | |
|---|---|
| — material | : steel |
| — finish | : matt black |
| — stock | : hardwood stock, with pistol-grip |

This gun cannot be held on a shotgun certificate in the United Kingdom because its barrel length is less than the minimum of 24in (61cm) required.

Similar restrictions apply in certain other European countries. Illustrated from top to bottom are: SDASS Magnum, SDASS Police Magnum, and SDASS Police Combat-Special.

## Imperator SDASS Police Combat-Special

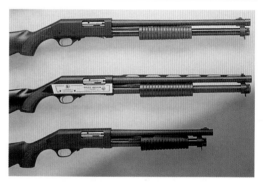

**TECHNICAL DETAILS**

| | |
|---|---|
| Gauge/calibre | : 12 |
| Chamber length | : 76mm (3in) |
| Number of barrels | : single-barrel |
| Magazine | : tubular magazine for 5 or 6 cartridges |
| Action | : pump-action |
| Locking | : rotating locking |
| Trigger | single trigger |
| Weight | : 2.7kg (6lb) |
| Length | : 90.8cm (35$^3/_4$in) |
| Barrel length | : 36cm (14$^1/_8$in) |
| Ejector | : extractor |
| Choke | cylindrical |
| Sight | bead |
| Safety | : push-button catch in front of trigger guard |

**CHARACTERISTICS**

| | |
|---|---|
| — material | : steel |
| — finish | : matt black |
| — stock | : black plastic stock, with pistol-grip |

This gun cannot be held on a shotgun certificate in the United Kingdom because its barrel length is less than the minimum of 24in

(61cm) required. Similar restrictions apply in certain other European countries.

Illustrated from top to bottom are: SDASS Magnum, SDASS Police Magnum, and SDASS Police Combat-Special.

## *Imperator SDASS Police Magnum*

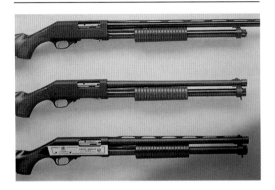

### TECHNICAL DETAILS
| | |
|---|---|
| Gauge/calibre | : 12 |
| Chamber length | : 76mm (3in) |
| Number of barrels | : single-barrel |
| Magazine | : tubular magazine for 7 or 8 cartridges |
| Action | : pump-action |
| Locking | : rotating locking |
| Trigger | single trigger |
| Weight | : 3.1kg (6lb 13oz) |
| Length | : 105cm (41³/₈in) |
| Barrel length | : 50cm (19³/₄in) |
| Ejector | : extractor |
| Choke | interchangeable chokes |
| Sight | ventilated rib and bead |
| Safety | : push-button catch in front of trigger guard |

### CHARACTERISTICS
| | |
|---|---|
| — material | : steel |
| — finish | : matt black |
| — stock | : black plastic stock, with pistol-grip |

This gun cannot be held on a shotgun certificate in the United Kingdom because its barrel length is less than the minimum of 24in (61cm) required.
Similar restrictions apply in certain other European countries.

Illustrated from top to bottom are: SDASS Magnum, SDASS Police Magnum, and SDASS Police Combat-Special.

## *Imperator SDASS Super Goose*

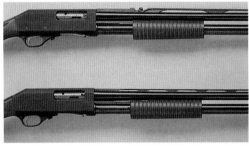

### TECHNICAL DETAILS
| | |
|---|---|
| Gauge/calibre | : 12 |
| Chamber length | : 76mm (3in) |
| Number of barrels | : single-barrel |
| Magazine | : tubular magazine for 2, 7, or 8 cartridges |
| Action | : pump-action |
| Locking | : rotating locking |
| Trigger | single trigger |
| Weight | : 3.1kg (6lb 13oz) |
| Length | : 145cm (57¹/₄in) |
| Barrel length | : 90cm (35¹/₂ in) |
| Ejector | : extractor |
| Choke | interchangeable chokes |
| Sight | 12mm (¹/₂in) ventilated rib with folding rack and bead |
| Safety | : push-button catch at rear of trigger guard |

### CHARACTERISTICS
| | |
|---|---|
| — material | : steel |
| — finish | : matt black |
| — stock | : hardwood stock, with pistol-grip |

Firearms legislation in the United Kingdom limits magazine capacity to 2 cartridges in the magazine and 1 in the chamber for a shotgun. To comply, the magazine must not be capable of accepting more. Similar restrictions apply in other European countries. Illustrated from top to bottom are: SDASS Super Goose and SDASS Hunter.

# Kettner

The German trading company of Eduard Kettner expanded during the space of ten years into a major company with many branches. The original firm was located in Cologne but now has twenty branches in Germany and some major shops in France, Austria, Switzerland, Spain, Hungary, and Belgium. Most of the branches have a gunsmith's workshop. A mail order business is also operated from the head office in Cologne. Kettner's catalogue gets thicker year by year. The company financially support a number of nature conservation projects in Germany by means of the Heinz Sielmann Foundation and lobbies politicians through a group designed to promote hunting interests (Förderkreis Jagdpolitiek). The company is of similar size to Frankonia Jagd. Kettner has long since sold a number of guns under its own name. These are of good quality and competitively priced.

## Kettner Campione

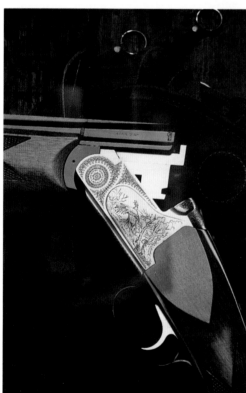

**TECHNICAL DETAILS**

| | |
|---|---|
| Gauge/calibre | : 12 |
| Chamber length | : 70mm (2³/₄in) |
| Number of barrels | : double-barrels over-and-under |
| Action | : breech-loading |
| Locking | : barrel-block locking |
| Trigger | single or twin triggers |

| | |
|---|---|
| Weight | : 3.1kg (6lb 13oz) |
| Length | : 114cm (44⁷/₈in) |
| Barrel length | : 70cm (27¹/₂ in) |
| Ejector | : ejector or extractor by choice |
| Choke | fixed ¹/₄ and ³/₄ chokes or 5-part interchangeable chokes |
| Sight | 6mm (³/₈in) ventilated rib with bead |
| Safety | : sliding catch on neck of stock, also barrel selector |

**CHARACTERISTICS**

| | |
|---|---|
| — material | : steel |
| — finish | : blued barrels, plain metal action with hunting engravings |
| — stock | : walnut stock, with pistol-grip |

## Kettner Condor Ejector

**TECHNICAL DETAILS**

| | |
|---|---|
| Gauge/calibre | : 12 |
| Chamber length | : 70mm (2³/₄in) |
| Number of barrels | : double-barrels over-and-under |
| Action | : breech-loading |
| Locking | : barrel-block locking |
| Trigger | single trigger |
| Weight | : 3kg (6lb 9¹/₂oz) |
| Length | : 114cm (44⁷/₈in) |
| Barrel length | : 71cm (28in) |
| Ejector | : automatic |
| Choke | fixed chokes: ³/₄ and ¹/₄ |
| Sight | 7mm (⁹/₃₂in) ventilated rib with bead |
| Safety | : sliding catch on neck of stock, also barrel selector |

**CHARACTERISTICS**

| | |
|---|---|
| — material | : steel |
| — finish | : blued barrels, plain metal action with decorative engravings |
| — stock | : walnut stock, with pistol-grip |

## Kettner Condor Extra-Light

## TECHNICAL DETAILS

Gauge/calibre : 12
Chamber length : 70mm (2³/₄in)
Number of barrels : double-barrels over-and-under
Action : breech-loading
Locking : barrel-block locking
Trigger single trigger
Weight : 2.8kg (6lb 3oz)
Length : 110cm (43¹/₄in)
Barrel length : 67cm (26³/₄in)
Ejector : automatic
Choke fixed chokes: ³/₄ and ¹/₄
Sight 7mm (⁹/₃₂in) ventilated rib with bead
Safety : sliding catch on neck of stock

## CHARACTERISTICS

— material : steel barrels, light alloy action
— finish : blued
— stock : walnut stock, with pistol-grip

Locking : barrel-block locking
Trigger single trigger
Weight : 3kg (6lb 9¹/₂oz)
Length : 114cm (44⁷/₈in)
Barrel length : 71cm (28in)
Ejector : extractor
Choke fixed chokes: ³/₄ and ¹/₄
Sight 7mm (⁹/₃₂in) ventilated rib with bead
Safety : sliding catch on neck of stock, also barrel selector

## CHARACTERISTICS

— material : steel
— finish : blued barrels, plain metal action with floral engravings
— stock : walnut stock, with pistol-grip

# Kettner Condor Parcours de Chasse (Sporting Clays)

## TECHNICAL DETAILS

Gauge/calibre : 12
Chamber length : 70mm (2³/₄in)
Number of barrels : double-barrels over-and-under
Action : breech-loading
Locking : barrel-block locking
Trigger single trigger
Weight : 3kg (6lb 9¹/₂oz)
Length : 114cm (44⁷/₈in)
Barrel length : 71cm (28in)
Ejector : automatic
Choke 5 part interchangeable chokes
Sight 7mm (⁹/₃₂in) ventilated rib with bead
Safety : sliding catch on neck of stock

## CHARACTERISTICS

— material : steel
— finish : blued barrels, plain metal action with Arabesque engravings
— stock : walnut stock, with pistol-grip

# Kettner Condor Standard

## TECHNICAL DETAILS

Gauge/calibre : 12
Chamber length : 70mm (2³/₄in)
Number of barrels : double-barrels over-and-under
Action : breech-loading

# Kettner hunter

## TECHNICAL DETAILS

Gauge/calibre : 12
Chamber length : 70mm (2³/₄in)
Number of barrels : double-barrels side-by-side
Action : breech-loading
Locking : double barrel-block locking
Trigger twin triggers
Weight : 3kg (6lb 9¹/₂oz)
Length : 114cm (44⁷/₈in)
Barrel length : 71cm (28in)
Ejector : extractor
Choke fixed ¹/₂ and full chokes
Sight 7mm (⁹/₃₂in) ventilated rib with bead
Safety : sliding catch on neck of stock

## CHARACTERISTICS

— material : steel
— finish : blued barrels, tempered action
— stock : straight English walnut stock

# Kettner Hunter Elegance side-lock

## TECHNICAL DETAILS

Gauge/calibre : 12

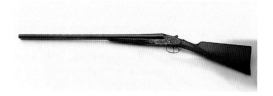

Chamber length    : 70mm (2³/₄in)
Number of barrels : double-barrels side-by-side
Action            : breech-loading
Locking           : double barrel-block locking
Trigger             twin triggers
Weight            : 3.2kg (7lb)
Length            : 114cm (44⁷/₈in)
Barrel length     : 71cm (28in)
Ejector           : extractor
Choke               fixed ¹/₂ and full chokes
Sight               bead
Safety            : sliding catch on neck of stock

### CHARACTERISTICS

— material        : steel
— finish          : blued barrels, tempered action and side-lock plates
— stock           : straight English walnut stock
🖐

## Kettner Pointer

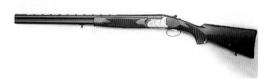

### TECHNICAL DETAILS

Gauge/calibre     : 12
Chamber length    : 70mm (2³/₄in)
Number of barrels : double-barrels over-and-under
Action            : breech-loading
Locking           : barrel-block locking
Trigger             single or twin triggers
Weight            : 3.15kg (6lb 14³/₄oz)
Length            : 114cm (44⁷/₈in)
Barrel length     : 79cm (27¹/₂in)
Ejector           : automatic
Choke               fixed ¹/₂ and full chokes or 5 part interchangeable chokes
Sight               7mm (⁹/₃₂in) ventilated rib with bead
Safety            : sliding catch on neck of stock, also barrel selector

### CHARACTERISTICS

— material        : steel
— finish          : blued barrels, plain metal action with hunting engravings
— stock           : walnut stock, with pistol-grip
🖐

## Kettner Pointer Light

### TECHNICAL DETAILS

Gauge/calibre     : 12
Chamber length    : 70mm (2³/₄in)
Number of barrels : double-barrels over-and-under
Action            : breech-loading
Locking           : barrel-block locking
Trigger             single or twin triggers
Weight            : 2.7kg (6lb)
Length            : 114cm (44⁷/₈in)
Barrel length     : 70cm (27¹/₂in)
Ejector           : automatic
Choke               fixed ¹/₄ and ³/₄ chokes or 5 part interchangeable chokes
Sight               7mm (⁹/₃₂in) ventilated rib with bead
Safety            : sliding catch on neck of stock

### CHARACTERISTICS

— material        : steel barrel, light alloy action (Ergal 55)
— finish          : blued barrels, plain metal action with engravings of hunting motifs or gun dog's head
— stock           : walnut stock, with pistol-grip
🖐

## Kettner S 2000 deluxe combination gun

### TECHNICAL DETAILS

Gauge/calibre     : 12; see below for rifle calibres
Chamber length    : smooth-bore barrel: 70mm (2³/₄in)
Number of barrels : double-barrels over-and-under
Action            : breech-loading
Locking           : barrel-block locking
Trigger             twin triggers, front one with pre-set
Weight            : 3.4kg (7lb 8oz)
Length            : 109cm (42⁷/₈in)
Barrel length     : 65cm (25¹/₂in)
Ejector           : extractor only
Choke               smooth-bore barrels: fixed ³/₄
Sight               folding rack sight with special Kettner swivel mount for telescopic sight
Safety            : sliding catch on neck of stock

### CHARACTERISTICS

— material        : steel (rifled barrel is special Delcour barrel)

– finish : blued barrels, plain metal action with hunting engravings on side-plates (no side-lock)
– stock : selected walnut stock, with pistol-grip and cheek plate

Available calibres/gauge (rifled): 5.6x50R Mag., 6.5x57R, 7x65R, .30-06 Spr., 9.3x74R. Double over-and-under smooth-bore barrels are also available for this gun with a ventilated rib – barrel length:71cm (28in), overall length: 114cm (44⁷/₈in) with fixed ¾ and full chokes.

## Kettner S 2000 standard combination gun

**TECHNICAL DETAILS**

| | |
|---|---|
| Gauge/calibre | : 12; see below for rifle calibres |
| Chamber length | : smooth-bore barrel: 70mm (2³/₄in) |
| Number of barrels | : double-barrels over-and-under |
| Action | : breech-loading |
| Locking | : barrel-block locking |
| Trigger | twin triggers, front one with pre-set |
| Weight | : 3.4kg (7lb 8oz) |
| Length | : 109cm (42⁷/₈in) |
| Barrel length | : 65cm (25¹/₂in) |
| Ejector | : extractor only |
| Choke | smooth-bore barrels: fixed ³/₄ |
| Sight | folding rack sight with special Kettner swivel mount for telescopic sight |
| Safety | : sliding catch on neck of stock |

**CHARACTERISTICS**

| | |
|---|---|
| – material | : steel (rifled barrel is special Delcour barrel) |
| – finish | : blued barrels, plain metal action with hunting engravings |
| – stock | : selected walnut stock, with pistol-grip and cheek plate |

Available rifle calibres: 5.6x50R Mag., 6.5x57R, 7x65R, .30-06 Spr., 9.3x74R.

## Kettner S 2020 Extra Light combination gun

**TECHNICAL DETAILS**

| | |
|---|---|
| Gauge/calibre | : 20; see below for rifle calibres |
| Chamber length | : smooth-bore barrel: 76mm (3in) |
| Number of barrels | : double-barrels over-and-under |
| Action | : breech-loading |
| Locking | : barrel-block locking |
| Trigger | twin triggers, front one with pre-set |

| | |
|---|---|
| Weight | : 3kg (6lb 9¹/₂oz) |
| Length | : 109cm (42⁷/₈in) |
| Barrel length | : 65cm (25¹/₂in) |
| Ejector | : extractor only |
| Choke | smooth-bore barrels: fixed ³/₄ |
| Sight | folding rack sight with special Kettner swivel mount for telescopic sight |
| Safety | : sliding catch on neck of stock |

**CHARACTERISTICS**

| | |
|---|---|
| – material | : steel barrel, light alloy action (Ergal 55) |
| – finish | : blued barrels, plain metal action with hunting engravings |
| – stock | : walnut stock, with pistol-grip and cheek plate |

Available rifle calibres: .22 Hornet, .222 Rem., .223 Rem., 5.6x50R Mag.

## Kettner S 2020 Light combination gun

**TECHNICAL DETAILS**

| | |
|---|---|
| Gauge/calibre | : 20; see below for rifle calibres |
| Chamber length | : smooth-bore barrel: 76mm (3in) |
| Number of barrels | : double-barrels over-and-under |
| Action | : breech-loading |
| Locking | : barrel-block locking |
| Trigger | twin triggers, front one with pre-set |
| Weight | : 3.3kg (7lb 4oz) |
| Length | : 109cm (42⁷/₈in) |
| Barrel length | : 65cm (25¹/₂in) |
| Ejector | : extractor only |
| Choke | smooth-bore barrels: fixed ³/₄ |
| Sight | folding rack sight with special Kettner swivel mount for telescopic sight |
| Safety | : sliding catch on neck of stock |

**CHARACTERISTICS**

| | |
|---|---|
| – material | : steel |
| – finish | : blued barrels, plain metal action with hunting engravings |
| – stock | : walnut stock, with pistol-grip and cheek plate |

Available rifle calibres: .22 Hornet, .222 Rem., .223 Rem., 5.6x50R Mag.

## Kettner San Remo side-lock

**TECHNICAL DETAILS**
Gauge/calibre : 12, 16, and 20
Chamber length : 70mm (2³/₄in)
Number of barrels : double-barrels side-by-side
Action : breech-loading
Locking : double barrel-block locking
Trigger twin triggers
Weight : 2.8 or 2.9kg (6lb 2¹/₂oz or 6lb 6oz)
Length : 112cm (44¹/₄in)
Barrel length : 70cm (27¹/₂in)
Ejector : automatic, Holland & Holland system
Choke fixed ¹/₂ and full
Sight bead
Safety : sliding catch on neck of stock, cocking indicator on
top of action

**CHARACTERISTICS**
— material : steel
— finish : blued barrels, light metal action and side-lock
plates with floral engravings; side-locks are removable by hand
— stock : straight English walnut stock

Illustrated from top to bottom:
San Remo and San Remo deluxe side-lock.

## Kettner San Remo Classic side-lock

**TECHNICAL DETAILS**
Gauge/calibre : 12 or 20
Chamber length : 70mm (2³/₄in)
Number of barrels : double-barrels side-by-side
Action : breech-loading
Locking ; double barrel-block locking
Trigger twin triggers
Weight : 2.9kg (6lb 6oz)

Length : 112cm (44¹/₈in)
Barrel length : 70cm (27¹/₂in)
Ejector : automatic, Holland & Holland system
Choke fixed ¹/₄ and ³/₄
Sight low barrel rib and bead
Safety : sliding catch on neck of stock, cocking indicator on
top of action

**CHARACTERISTICS**
— material : steel
— finish : blued barrels, light metal action and side-lock
plates with Arabesque engravings
— stock : straight English walnut stock

## Kettner San Remo deluxe side-lock

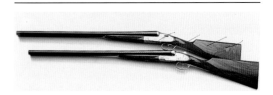

**TECHNICAL DETAILS**
Gauge/calibre : 12, 16, and 20
Chamber length : 70mm (2³/₄in)
Number of barrels : double-barrels side-by-side
Action : breech-loading
Locking : double barrel-block locking
Trigger twin triggers
Weight : 2.8 or 2.9kg (6lb 2³/₄oz or 6lb 6oz)
Length : 112cm (44¹/₈in)
Barrel length : 70cm (27¹/₂in)
Ejector : automatic, Holland & Holland system
Choke fixed ¹/₄ and ³/₄
Sight low barrel rib and bead
Safety : sliding catch on neck of stock, cocking indicator on
top of action

**CHARACTERISTICS**
— material : steel
— finish : blued barrels, light metal action and side-lock
plates with floral engravings
— stock : straight English stock of walnut root

Illustrated from top to bottom: San Remo
and San Remo deluxe side-lock.

## Kettner Duck Special

**TECHNICAL DETAILS**
Gauge/calibre : 12
Chamber length : 70mm (2³/₄in)
Number of barrels : double-barrels over-and-under
Action : breech-loading
Locking : barrel-block locking
Trigger single trigger

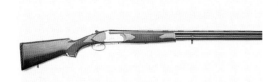

| Weight | : 3.15kg (6lb 14³/₄oz) |
|---|---|
| Length | : 114cm (44⁷/₈in) |
| Barrel length | : 70cm (27¹/₂in) |
| Ejector | : automatic |
| Choke | fixed ¹/₂ and full or 5 part interchangeable chokes |
| Sight | 7mm (⁹/₃₂in) ventilated rib with bead |
| Safety | : sliding catch on neck of stock, also barrel selector |

**CHARACTERISTICS**
— material     : steel
— finish       : blued barrels, plain metal action with duck engravings
— stock        : walnut stock, with pistol-grip

## *Kettner Spread-shot Special Superlight*

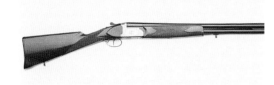

**TECHNICAL DETAILS**
Gauge/calibre     : 12
Chamber length    : 70mm (2³/₄in)
Number of barrels : double-barrels over-and-under
Action            : breech-loading
Locking           : barrel-block locking
Trigger           twin triggers
Weight            : 2.65kg (5lb 13¹/₄oz)
Length            : 104cm (41in)
Barrel length     : 60cm (23⁵/₈in)
Ejector           : automatic
Choke             interchangeable chokes; bottom barrel has special rifling for wider spread of shot
Sight             6mm (¹/₄in) rib with bead
Safety            : sliding catch on neck of stock

**CHARACTERISTICS**
— material     : steel barrels, light alloy action (Ergal 55)
— finish       : blued barrels, plain metal action with engravings of gun dog's head
— stock        : straight English walnut stock

## *Kettner Wild Boar Special*

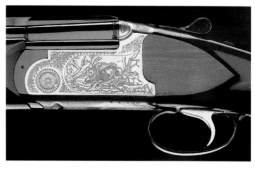

**TECHNICAL DETAILS**
Gauge/calibre     : 12
Chamber length    : 70mm (2³/₄in)
Number of barrels : double-barrels over-and-under; bottom barrel rifled for slugs
Action            : breech-loading
Locking           : barrel-block locking
Trigger           single trigger
Weight            : 3.1kg (6lb 13oz)
Length            : 110cm (43¹/₄in)
Barrel length     : 68cm (26³/₄in)
Ejector           : automatic
Choke             bottom barrel ¹/₂ or interchangeable chokes
Sight             10mm (⁷/₁₆in) high rib with folding rack sight and bead
Safety            : sliding catch on neck of stock, also barrel selector

**CHARACTERISTICS**
— material     : steel
— finish       : blued barrels, plain metal action with engravings of wild boar
— stock        : walnut stock, with pistol grip

Certain European countries do not permit hunting of wild boar with 12 gauge lead projectiles (slugs). This gun cannot be held on a shotgun certificate in the United Kingdom because of the rifling to its barrels.

## *Kettner Snipe Special*

**TECHNICAL DETAILS**
Gauge/calibre     : 12

| | |
|---|---|
| Chamber length | : 70mm (2³/₄in) |
| Number of barrels | : double-barrels over-and-under |
| Action | : breech-loading |
| Locking | : barrel-block locking |
| Trigger | single trigger |
| Weight | : 3kg (6lb 9¹/₂oz) |
| Length | : 108cm (42¹/₂in) |
| Barrel length | : 66cm (26in) |
| Ejector | : automatic |
| Choke | fixed ¹/₂ and cylindrical chokes |
| Sight | 6mm (³/₈in) wide rib with bead |
| Safety | : sliding catch on neck of stock, also barrel selector |

### CHARACTERISTICS

| | |
|---|---|
| — material | : steel |
| — finish | : blued barrels, plain metal action with hunting engravings |
| — stock | : walnut stock, with pistol grip |

## Kettner Turin

### TECHNICAL DETAILS

| | |
|---|---|
| Gauge/calibre | : 12 |
| Chamber length | : 70mm (2³/₄in) |
| Number of barrels | : double-barrels over-and-under |
| Action | : breech-loading |
| Locking | : barrel-block locking |
| Trigger | single trigger |
| Weight | : 3.15kg (6lb 14³/₄oz) |
| Length | : 114cm (44⁷/₈in) |
| Barrel length | : 70cm (27¹/₂in) |
| Ejector | : automatic |
| Choke | fixed ¹/₂ and full chokes |
| Sight | 7mm (⁹/₃₂in) ventilated rib with bead |
| Safety | : sliding catch on neck of stock, also barrel selector |

### CHARACTERISTICS

| | |
|---|---|
| — material | : steel |
| — finish | : blued barrels, plain metal action with hunting engravings on side-plates (no side-lock) |
| — stock | : walnut stock, with pistol grip and cheek plate |

## Kettner Turin Classic

### TECHNICAL DETAILS

| | |
|---|---|
| Gauge/calibre | : 12 |
| Chamber length | : 70mm (2³/₄in) |
| Number of barrels | : double-barrels over-and-under |
| Action | : breech-loading |
| Locking | : barrel-block locking |
| Trigger | single trigger |
| Weight | : 3.15kg (6lb 14³/₄oz) |

| | |
|---|---|
| Length | : 114cm (44⁷/₈in) |
| Barrel length | : 70cm (27¹/₂in) |
| Ejector | : automatic |
| Choke | fixed ¹/₂ and full chokes |
| Sight | 7mm (⁹/₃₂in) ventilated rib with bead |
| Safety | : sliding catch on neck of stock, also barrel selector |

### CHARACTERISTICS

| | |
|---|---|
| — material | : steel |
| — finish | : blued barrels, plain metal action with hunting engravings on side-plates (no side-lock) |
| — stock | : straight English walnut stock |

# Krieghoff

Ludwig Krieghoff established a gunsmith's workshop in Suhl in Germany in 1886.

The business was originally known as Sempert & Krieghoff. The co-founder Sempert soon departed to the USA. The firm specialised in making hunting guns but this changed as a result of World War I when the production was switched to producing weapons for the war.

Meanwhile Heinrich, the son of Ludwig, entered the business and underwent several years training at Suhl, and also at the FN factory in Belgium, and at Sheffield in Britain. Turnover slumped enormously after World War I and many gunmakers went bust. Krieghoff managed to win a huge order from the Netherlands which enabled them to survive. In the early 1930's, the company employed 150 workers and made hunting guns and drilling rifles.

Once the Nazi regime came to power, Krieghoff was compelled to switch over to supporting the weapons build up. The number of workers rapidly shot up from 2,000 in 1940 to 6,000 by 1944. At the end of the war, Suhl was occupied by the Americans but the sector was soon handed over to the Russians who dismantled the factory in 1947 and blew it up.

The Krieghoff family fled to the Western allied zone in 1945 and in 1950, Krieghoff started up again at Heidenheim near Ulm making shotguns and drilling rifles. The problems were enormous. There was a shortage of skilled craftsmen and investment capital was scarce.

The company moved to Ulm in 1960 and up to the present day the factory has been constantly renewed and improved, with substantial investment by Krieghoff in computer-controlled (CNC) machinery. The introduction of a new type of shotgun (the K-80) in 1980 was a tremendous success. This gun has unusual locking by which the upper part of the action slides forwards on runners to engage with two lugs on either side of the upper barrel.

The company introduced the KS-5, a new type of Trap shotgun, in 1985. The rather modern-looking competition gun sells particularly well in the United States. When Germany was reunited, Krieghoff once again established a factory in Suhl to supply the main factory at Ulm. An American subsidiary, Krieghoff International Inc. was also established in Ottsville, Pennsylvania. The

present day Krieghoff company is led by Heinz Ulrich Krieghoff and his son Dieter.

## Krieghoff Classic 'Big Five' Express

**TECHNICAL DETAILS**

| | |
|---|---|
| Gauge/calibre | : see below |
| Chamber length | : not applicable |
| Number of barrels | : double-barrels side-by-side |
| Action | : breech-loading |
| Locking | : double barrel-block locking and central lug between barrels |
| Trigger | twin triggers |
| Weight | : 4.2–4.8kg (9lb 4oz–10lb 8oz) |
| Length | : 104cm (41in) |
| Barrel length | : 56cm (22in) |
| Ejector | : extractor only |
| Choke | not applicable, rifled barrels |
| Sight | folding Express rack sight and bead, suitable for mounting telescopic sight |
| Safety | : sliding catch on neck of stock, also serves as double locking hand cocking lever |

**CHARACTERISTICS**

| | |
|---|---|
| — material | : steel |
| — finish | : blued barrels, plain metal action with choice of African big game engravings |
| — stock | : selected walnut stock, with pistol-grip and cheek plate. The stock has a Krieghoff recoil damper system incorporated |

Available calibres/gauges (both barrels are the same calibre): .375 Mag. NE (Nitro Express), .375 H&H Mag., .416 Rigby, .458 Win. Mag., .500/.416 NE, .500 NE.

This rifle is supplied with a superb gun case. Illustrated from top to bottom are: Classic 'Big Five' and Classic 'S'.

## Krieghoff Classic 'S' Express

**TECHNICAL DETAILS**

Gauge/calibre    : see below
Chamber length   : not applicable
Number of barrels : double-barrels side-by-side
Action           : breech-loading
Locking          : double barrel-block locking and central lug between barrels
Trigger          single or twin triggers
Weight           : 3.3–3.6kg (7lb 4oz–7lb 14 ³/₄oz)
Length           : 104cm (41in)
Barrel length    : 56cm (22in)
Ejector          : extractor only
Choke            not applicable, rifled barrels
Sight            folding Express rack sight and bead, suitable for mounting telescopic sight
Safety           : sliding catch on neck of stock, also serves as double locking hand cocking lever

**CHARACTERISTICS**

— material       : steel
— finish         : blued barrels, plain metal action with choice of engravings
— stock          : selected walnut stock, with pistol-grip and cheek plate. The stock has a Krieghoff recoil damper system incorporated

Available calibres (both barrels are the same calibre): 7x65R, .308 Win., .30-06 Spr., .30 R Blaser, 8x57 IRS, 8x75RS, 9.3x74R. Illustrated from top to bottom are: Classic 'Big Five' and Classic 'S'.

## Krieghoff K-80 Skeet

**TECHNICAL DETAILS**

Gauge/calibre    : 12, 20, 28, or .410
Chamber length   : 76mm (3in)
Number of barrels : double-barrels over-and-under

---

Action           : breech-loading
Locking          : Krieghoff K-80 patent locking
Trigger          single trigger with switch on/off barrel selector in front of trigger
Weight           : 3.6kg (7lb 14³/₄oz)
Length           : 116–121cm (47³/₄–47¹/₂ in)
Barrel length    : 71 or 76cm (28 or 30in)
Ejector          : automatic
Choke            Skeet choke (both barrels) or interchangeable chokes
Sight            8 or 12mm (⁵/₁₆ or ¹/₂ in) ventilated rib and bead
Safety           : sliding catch can be disconnected

**CHARACTERISTICS**

— material       : steel
— finish         : blued barrels, plain metal action with gold inlay
— stock          : European walnut stock

## Krieghoff K-80 Sporting

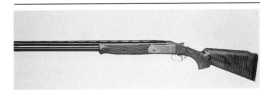

**TECHNICAL DETAILS**

Gauge/calibre    : 12
Chamber length   : 76mm (3in)
Number of barrels : double-barrels over-and-under (see below)
Action           : breech-loading
Locking          : Krieghoff K-80 patent locking
Trigger          single trigger with switch on/off barrel selector in front of trigger
Weight           : 3.6–3.97kg (7lb 14³/₄oz–8lb 12oz)
Length           : 120, 125, or 130cm (47¹/₄, 49¹/₄, or 51¹/₄in)
Barrel length    : 71, 76, or 81cm (28, 30, or 32in)
Ejector          : automatic
Choke            interchangeable chokes
Sight            8mm (⁵/₁₆in) ventilated rib and bead
Safety           : sliding catch can be disconnected

**CHARACTERISTICS**

— material       : steel
— finish         : blued barrels, plain metal engraved action
— stock          : European walnut stock

## Krieghoff K-80 Trap

**TECHNICAL DETAILS**

Gauge/calibre    : 12
Chamber length   : 70mm (2³/₄in)
Number of barrels : double-barrels over-and-under (see below)
Action           : breech-loading
Locking          : Krieghoff K-80 patent locking
Trigger          single trigger with switch on/off barrel selector in front of trigger

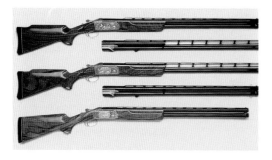

| Weight | : 3.97kg (8lb 12oz) |
|---|---|
| Length | : 120–130cm (47$\frac{1}{4}$–51$\frac{1}{4}$in) |
| Barrel length | : 76, 81, or 86cm (30, 32, or 34in) |
| Ejector | : automatic |
| Choke | interchangeable chokes |
| Sight | 12mm ($\frac{1}{2}$in) ventilated rib and bead |
| Safety | : sliding catch can be disconnected |

**CHARACTERISTICS**
- material : steel
- finish : blued barrels, plain metal engraved action with gold inlay
- stock : European walnut stock

This gun has exchangeable under-single barrels.

🐓

## Krieghoff K-80 Under-Single-Trap

**TECHNICAL DETAILS**

| Gauge/calibre | : 12 |
|---|---|
| Chamber length | : 70mm (2$\frac{3}{4}$in) |
| Number of barrels | : single-barrel |
| Action | : breech-loading |
| Locking | : Krieghoff K-80 patent locking |
| Trigger | single trigger with switch on/off barrel selector in front of trigger |
| Weight | : 3.97kg (8lb 12oz) |
| Length | : 125–130cm (49$\frac{1}{4}$–51$\frac{1}{4}$in) |
| Barrel length | : 81 or 86cm (32 or 34in) |
| Ejector | : automatic |
| Choke | interchangeable chokes |
| Sight | 12mm ($\frac{1}{2}$in) ventilated high rib and bead |
| Safety | : sliding catch can be disconnected |

**CHARACTERISTICS**
- material : steel
- finish : blued barrels, plain metal engraved action, gold inlaid to choice
- stock : European walnut stock

🐓

## Krieghoff KS-5 Special Trap

**TECHNICAL DETAILS**

| Gauge/calibre | : 12 |
|---|---|
| Chamber length | : 70mm (2$\frac{3}{4}$in) |
| Number of barrels | : single-barrel (under single) |
| Action | : breech-loading |
| Locking | : double barrel-block locking |
| Trigger | single trigger |
| Weight | : 3.86–4kg (8lb 7$\frac{3}{4}$oz–8lb 12$\frac{3}{4}$oz) |
| Length | : 127 or 132cm (50 or 52in) |
| Barrel length | : 81 or 86cm (32 or 34in) |
| Ejector | : automatic |
| Choke | fixed full choke or interchangeable chokes |
| Sight | specially adjustable sighting rib to vary the sighting line |
| Safety | : none |

**CHARACTERISTICS**
- material : steel
- finish : blued barrels, nickel-steel action
- stock : European walnut stock with adjustable cheek plate

This futuristic Trap gun is supplied with an aluminium gun case.

🐓

## Krieghoff Neptun/10 Primus Triple-barrel (Drilling)

**TECHNICAL DETAILS**

| Gauge/calibre | : see below |
|---|---|
| Chamber length | : see below |
| Number of barrels | : triple-barrels |
| Action | : breech-loading |
| Locking | : double barrel-block locking |
| Trigger | twin triggers |
| Weight | : 3–3.6kg (6lb 9$\frac{1}{2}$oz–7lb 14$\frac{3}{4}$oz) |
| Length | : to choice |
| Barrel length | : to choice |
| Ejector | : extractor only |

| Choke | to choice |
| Sight | to choice, special mount for telescopic sight |
| Safety | : sliding catch on neck of stock can be switched to automatic cocking on breaking breech or manual cocking |

**CHARACTERISTICS**

| — material | : steel |
| — finish | : blued barrels, nickel-steel action with side-lock plates engraved to choice; side-locks can be removed by hand |
| — stock | : specially-selected European walnut stock |

Available calibres/gauges (double smooth-bore barrels and single rifled barrel or double rifled barrels and single smooth-bore): smooth-bore– 12/70, 12/76, 16/70, 20/70, 20/76; rifled: all suitable calibres from .22 Hornet to 9.3x74R. This special Krieghoff gun with side-locks is only made to order.

## *Krieghoff Neptun/15 Primus 'M' Triple-barrel (Drilling)*

**TECHNICAL DETAILS**

| Gauge/calibre | : see below |
| Chamber length | : see below |
| Number of barrels | : triple-barrels |
| Action | : breech-loading |
| Locking | : double barrel-block locking and Greener locking |
| Trigger | twin triggers |
| Weight | : 3–3.6kg (6lb 9¹/₂oz–7lb 14³/₄oz) |
| Length | : to choice |
| Barrel length | : to choice |
| Ejector | : extractor only |
| Choke | to choice |
| Sight | to choice, special mount for telescopic sight |

| Safety | : sliding catch on neck of stock can be switched to automatic cocking on breaking breech or manual cocking |

**CHARACTERISTICS**

| — material | : steel |
| — finish | : blued barrels, nickel-steel action with side-lock plates with exceptional high-relief engravings; side-locks can be removed by hand |
| — stock | : specially-selected European walnut stock |

Available calibres/gauges (double smooth-bore barrels and single rifled barrel or double rifled barrels and single smooth-bore): smooth-bore– 12/70, 12/76, 16/70, 20/70, 20/76; rifled: all suitable calibres from .22 Hornet to 9.3x74R. This special Krieghoff gun with side-locks is only made to order.

## *Krieghoff Plus/1 Triple-barrel (Drilling) combination*

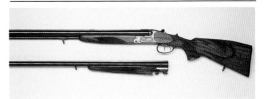

**TECHNICAL DETAILS**

| Gauge/calibre | : see below |
| Chamber length | : see below |
| Number of barrels | : triple-barrels, two smooth-bore, 1 rifle barrel |
| Action | : breech-loading |
| Locking | : double barrel-block locking |
| Trigger | twin triggers |
| Weight | : 2.9–3.4kg (6lb–7lb 8oz) |
| Length | : to choice |
| Barrel length | : to choice |
| Ejector | : extractor only |
| Choke | to choice |
| Sight | folding rack and bead |
| Safety | : sliding catch on neck of stock, manual cocking, closing safety |

**CHARACTERISTICS**

| — material | : steel barrels, light ally action |
| — finish | : blued barrels, plain metal action with choice of engravings |
| — stock | : European walnut stock |

Available calibres/gauges (double smooth-bore barrels and single rifled barrel): smooth-bore– 12/70, 12/76, 16/70, 20/70, 20/76; rifled: all suitable calibres from .22 Hornet to 9.3x74R. Exchangeable smooth-bore barrels are available for this gun.

## Krieghoff Teck/3 Combi

**TECHNICAL DETAILS**

| | |
|---|---|
| Gauge/calibre | : see below |
| Chamber length | : see below |
| Number of barrels | : double-barrels over-and-under |
| Action | : breech-loading |
| Locking | : double barrel-block and Kersten locking |
| Trigger | twin triggers |
| Weight | : 2.7–3.6kg (6lb–7lb 14³/₄oz) |
| Length | : 108cm (42¹/₂in) |
| Barrel length | : 63.5cm (25in) |
| Ejector | : extractor only |
| Choke | smooth-bore: fixed ³/₄ |
| Sight | folding rack and bead |
| Safety | : sliding safety-catch on neck of stock, manual cocking as optional extra |

**CHARACTERISTICS**

| | |
|---|---|
| — material | : steel |
| — finish | : blued barrels, bare metal action with choice of reliefs |
| — stock | : European walnut stock |

Available calibres/gauges (smooth-bore): 12/70, 12/76, 16/70, 20/70, 20/76; (rifled barrel): 7x65R, .308 Win., .30-06 Spr., .30R Blaser, 8x57 IRS, 8x75 RS, 9.3x74R.

## Krieghoff Trumpf/5 Drilling

**TECHNICAL DETAILS**

| | |
|---|---|
| Gauge/calibre | : see below |
| Chamber length | : see below |
| Number of barrels | : triple-barrels (see below) |
| Action | : breech-loading |
| Locking | : double barrel block locking and Greener locking |
| Trigger | twin triggers |
| Weight | : 2.9–3.4kg (6lb 6oz–7lb 8oz) |

Length : 108cm (42¹/₂ in)
Barrel length : 63.5cm (25in)
Ejector : extractor only
Choke to choice
Sight folding rack; special mount for telescopic sight
Safety : sliding safety-catch on neck of stock , automatic or manual cocking

**CHARACTERISTICS**

| | |
|---|---|
| — material | : steel |
| — finish | : blued barrels, polished bare metal action with choice of engravings |
| — stock | : stock material to choice |

Available calibres/gauges (2 smooth-bore barrels and 1 rifled barrel or 2 rifled-barrels and 1 smooth-bore barrel) smooth-bore: 12/70, 12/76, 16/70, 20/70, 20/76; rifled: all suitable calibres from .22 Hornet to 9.3x74R.

## Krieghoff Ulm/8 Combi

**TECHNICAL DETAILS**

| | |
|---|---|
| Gauge/calibre | : see below |
| Chamber length | : see below |
| Number of barrels | : double-barrels over-and-under |
| Action | : breech-loading |
| Locking | : double barrel-block and Kersten locking |
| Trigger | twin triggers |
| Weight | : 2.8–3.8kg (6lb 2¹/₂ oz–8lb 6oz) |
| Length | : 108cm (42¹/₂in) |
| Barrel length | : 63.5cm (25in) |
| Ejector | : extractor only |
| Choke | to choice |
| Sight | folding rack and bead |
| Safety | : sliding safety-catch on neck of stock , automatic or manual cocking |

**CHARACTERISTICS**

| | |
|---|---|
| — material | : steel |
| — finish | : blued barrels, nickel-steel action with choice of engravings for side-lock plates |
| — stock | : European walnut stock |

Available calibres/gauges (smooth-bore): 12/70, 12/76, 16/70, 20/70, 20/76; (rifled): 7x65R, .308 Win., .30-06 Spr., .30R Blaser, 8x57 IRS, 8x75 RS, 9.3x74R. Replacement double smooth-bore barrels are also available for this gun.

## Krieghoff Ultra 12/1 Combi

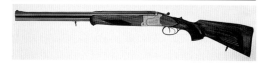

### TECHNICAL DETAILS

Gauge/calibre : see below
Chamber length : see below
Number of barrels : double-barrels over-and-under
Action : breech-loading
Locking : double barrel-block locking
Trigger single or twin triggers
Weight : 2.6–3kg (5lb 11½ oz–6lb 9½ oz)
Length : 108cm (42½ in)
Barrel length : 63.5cm (25in)
Ejector : extractor only
Choke to choice
Sight folding rack and bead
Safety : sliding safety-catch on neck of stock is also dou-ble-barrel manual cocking system

### CHARACTERISTICS

— material : steel barrels, light alloy action
— finish : blued barrels, bare metal action with choice of engravings
— stock : stock material to choice

Available calibres/gauges (smooth-bore): 12/70, 12/76; (rifled): all suitable calibres from .22 Hornet to 9.3x74R.

## Krieghoff Ultra 20/5 Combi

### TECHNICAL DETAILS

Gauge/calibre : see below
Chamber length : see below
Number of barrels : double-barrels over-and-under
Action : breech-loading
Locking : double barrel-block locking
Trigger single or twin triggers
Weight : 2.5–3.2kg (5lb 8oz–7lb)

Length : 108cm (42½ in)
Barrel length : 63.5cm (25in)
Ejector : extractor only
Choke to choice
Sight folding rack and bead
Safety : sliding safety-catch on neck of stock is also double-barrel manual cocking system

### CHARACTERISTICS

— material : steel barrels, light alloy action
— finish : blued barrels, bare metal action with choice of engravings
— stock : stock material to choice

Available calibres/gauges (smooth-bore): 20/70, 20/76; (rifled): all suitable calibres from .22 Hornet to 9.3x74R. Illustrated from top to bottom: Ultra 20 double-barrel rifle same calibre, Ultra 20 Bergstutzen (mountain carbine) double-barrel rifle different calibres, Ultra 20 combi, 1 rifle/1smooth-bore barrel.

## Krieghoff Ultra 20/5 Express

### TECHNICAL DETAILS

Gauge/calibre : see below
Chamber length : not applicable
Number of barrels : double-barrels over-and-under
Action : breech-loading
Locking : double barrel-block locking
Trigger single or twin triggers
Weight : 2.9–3.6kg (6lb 6oz–7lb 14¾oz)
Length : 104cm (41in)
Barrel length : 56cm (22in)
Ejector : extractor only
Choke not applicable, rifled barrels
Sight folding rack and bead, suitable for telesc. sight
Safety : sliding safety-catch on neck of stock is also double-barrel manual cocking system

### CHARACTERISTICS

— material : steel, or steel barrels and light alloy action (350g/12¼oz lighter)
— finish : blued barrels, bare metal action with choice of engravings
— stock : selected walnut stock, with pistol-grip and cheek plate

Available calibres/gauges (both of same calibre): 7x65R, .308 Win., .30-06 Spr., .30R Blaser, 8x57 IRS, 8x75 RS, 9.3x74R. This gun cannot be held on a shotgun certificate under United Kingdom legislation.

# Lanber

Lanber is the brand name of Comlanber, short for Commercial Lanber, a gunmaking company based at Zaldibar in the Spanish Basque territory. The company makes a fine range of side-by-side shotguns and a small range of semi-automatic shotguns with recoil-actions. The tubular magazines can accommodate 5 cartridges but can be blocked with a wooden plug to limit capacity to 2 cartridges to comply with the legal requirements in a number of European countries. For the United Kingdom, a permanent block is required. A lever on the right-hand side of the action body of the semi-automatics enables the slider to be locked in the rear position to facilitate loading via the port on the bottom of the housing. A catch on the right front of the trigger guard releases the slider catch.

## Lanber Aventura

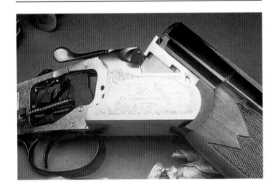

**TECHNICAL DETAILS**
Gauge/calibre : 12
Chamber length : 70mm (2³/₄in)
Number of barrels : double-barrels over-and-under
Action : breech-loading
Locking : barrel-block locking
Trigger : twin triggers
Weight : 2.8–3.2kg (6lb 2¹/₂ oz–7lb)
Length : 111 or 114cm (43³/₄ or 44⁷/₈in)
Barrel length : 66 or 70cm (26 or 27¹/₂in)
Ejector : automatic or extractor
Choke : ¹/₄ and ³/₄ or ¹/₂ and full, or interchang. choke set
Sight : ventilated rib and bead
Safety : sliding safety-catch on neck of stock

**CHARACTERISTICS**
— material : steel

— finish : blued, or blued barrels and bare metal action with engravings
— stock : walnut stock, with pistol-grip

## Lanber Plus

**TECHNICAL DETAILS**
Gauge/calibre : 12
Chamber length : 70mm (2³/₄in)
Number of barrels : double-barrels over-and-under
Action : breech-loading
Locking : barrel-block locking
Trigger : single trigger
Weight : 3.3–3.6kg (7lb 4oz–7lb 14³/₁₀oz)
Length : 115 or 120cm (45¹/₄ or 47¹/₄in)
Barrel length : 70 or 75cm (27¹/₂ or 29¹/₂ in)
Ejector : automatic
Choke : interchangeable choke set
Sight : ventilated rib and bead
Safety : sliding safety-catch on neck of stock

**CHARACTERISTICS**
— material : steel
— finish : blued barrels and bare metal action with Arabesque engravings
— stock : walnut stock, with pistol grip

## Lanber Sporting

**TECHNICAL DETAILS**

| | |
|---|---|
| Gauge/calibre | : 12 |
| Chamber length | : 70mm (2³/₄in) |
| Number of barrels | : double-barrels over-and-under |
| Action | : breech-loading |
| Locking | : barrel-block locking |
| Trigger | single trigger |
| Weight | : 3.3kg (7lb 4 oz) |
| Length | : 115cm (45¹/₄in) |
| Barrel length | : 70cm (27¹/₂in) |
| Ejector | : automatic |
| Choke | interchangeable choke set |
| Sight | ventilated rib and bead |
| Safety | : sliding safety-catch on neck of stock |

**CHARACTERISTICS**

| | |
|---|---|
| — material | : steel |
| — finish | : blued barrels and bare metal action |
| — stock | : walnut stock, with pistol-grip |

### Lanber Victoria

**TECHNICAL DETAILS**

| | |
|---|---|
| Gauge/calibre | : 12 |
| Chamber length | : 70mm (2³/₄in) |
| Number of barrels | : single-barrels |
| Magazine | : tubular magazine for 2 cartridges |
| Action | : semi-automatic |
| Locking | : falling block locking |
| Trigger | single trigger |
| Weight | : 2.95–3.15kg (6lb 7oz–6lb 14³/₄oz) |
| Length | : 122 or 126cm (48 or 49⁵/₈in) |
| Barrel length | : 67 or 71cm (26⁵/₈ or 28in) |
| Ejector | : automatic |
| Choke | interchangeable choke set with 3 or 5 chokes |
| Sight | ventilated rib and bead |
| Safety | : push-button in rear of trigger guard, slider lock on right of action body |

**CHARACTERISTICS**

| | |
|---|---|
| — material | : steel or with light alloy casing (Victoria Light) |
| — finish | : blued |

— stock : walnut stock, with pistol-grip

## Laurona

The Laurona company of Eibar in Spain was founded by four gunsmiths in 1941. The word "laurona" in the Basque language means "of the four." In those days the company produced just one side-by-side shotgun each day but the company moved to larger premises in 1964 and introduced its first over-and-under gun at the same time.

The company developed an unusual trigger mechanism with a double function. Both triggers can be used as normal to each fire an individual barrel but both triggers can also separately fire either barrel. The system was awarded a Product Award of Merit in 1983

204

by the American Firearms Industry organization. The company moved to even bigger premises in 1971, when the machinery was also total modernised.

The company introduced an entirely new metal treatment in 1972 for the non-corrosive black-chrome coating of metal and switched over to interchangeable chokes sets in the 1980's. These were improved in 1990 by introduction of parabolic curves so that the chokes could be used with steel shot. New production techniques were developed in 1991 for production of double-barrelled rifles and combined guns.

The company was extensively reorganized in 1994 and the name changed to Armas Eibar S.A.L. Laurona (in which "SAL" stands for "sociedad anonima limitada" or private limited company.

## Laurona Express 2000 XE

**TECHNICAL DETAILS**
Gauge/calibre      : see below
Chamber length     : not applicable
Number of barrels : double-barrels over-and-under
Action             : breech-loading
Locking            : barrel-block locking
Trigger            single trigger or twin triggers with double function
Weight             : 3.7–4.2kg (8lb 2$^1$/$_4$oz–9lb 4oz)
Length             : 104 or 107cm (41 or 42$^1$/$_8$in)
Barrel length      : 61 or 64cm (24 or 25$^1$/$_4$in)
Ejector            : extractor
Choke              not applicable, rifled barrels
Sight              rack and bead; 13mm ($^1$/$_2$in) wide shoe for telescopic sight
Safety             : sliding safety-catch on neck of stock

**CHARACTERISTICS**
— material         : steel
— finish           : black-chrome protective coating and bare metal action with hunting engravings
— stock            : walnut stock, with pistol-grip and cheek plate

Available calibres: 7x65R, 30-06 Spr., 8x57 JRS, .375 H&H Mag., 9.3x74R. Exchange

barrels in various shotgun gauges are available for this gun. Rifled barrels can be aligned by an adjustment screw at the muzzle.

## Laurona Express 3000 E

**TECHNICAL DETAILS**
Gauge/calibre      : 9.3x74R
Chamber length     : not applicable
Number of barrels : double-barrels side-by-side
Action             : breech-loading
Locking            : barrel-block locking
Trigger            twin triggers with double function
Weight             : 3.7kg (8lb 2$^1$/$_4$oz)
Length             : 104cm (41in)
Barrel length      : 61cm (24in)
Ejector            : extractor
Choke              not applicable, rifled barrels
Sight              rack and bead; 13mm ($^1$/$_2$in) wide shoe for telescopic sight
Safety             : sliding safety-catch on neck of stock

**CHARACTERISTICS**
— material         : steel
— finish           : black-chrome protective coating and bare metal action with hunting engravings
— stock            : walnut stock, with pistol-grip and cheek plate

## Laurona Express Savannah

**TECHNICAL DETAILS**
Gauge/calibre      : 9.3x74R
Chamber length     : not applicable
Number of barrels : double-barrels side-by-side
Action             : breech-loading
Locking            : barrel-block locking
Trigger            twin triggers with double function
Weight             : 3.7kg (8lb 2$^1$/$_4$oz)
Length             : 104cm (41in)

| Barrel length | : 61cm (24in) |
|---|---|
| Ejector | : extractor |
| Choke | not applicable, rifled barrel |
| Sight | rack and bead; 13mm ($^1/_2$in) wide shoe for telescopic sight |
| Safety | : sliding safety-catch on neck of stock |

### CHARACTERISTICS

| — material | : steel |
|---|---|
| — finish | : black-chrome protective coating and bare metal action and side plates with decorative engravings (no side lock) |
| — stock | : walnut stock, with pistol-grip and cheek plate |

## Laurona Express Savannah Luxe

### TECHNICAL DETAILS

| Gauge/calibre | : 9.3x74R |
|---|---|
| Chamber length | : not applicable |
| Number of barrels | : double-barrels side-by-side |
| Action | : breech-loading |
| Locking | : barrel-block locking |
| Trigger | twin triggers with double function |
| Weight | : 3.7kg (8lb 2$^1/_4$oz) |
| Length | : 104cm (41in) |
| Barrel length | : 61cm (24in) |
| Ejector | : extractor |
| Choke | not applicable, rifled barrel |
| Sight | rack and bead; 13mm ($^1/_2$in) wide shoe for telescopic sight |
| Safety | : sliding safety-catch on neck of stock |

### CHARACTERISTICS

| — material | : steel |
|---|---|
| — finish | : black-chrome protective coating and bare metal action and side plates with hunting engravings (no side lock) |
| — stock | : stock of specially-selected walnut, with pistol-grip and cheek plate |

## Laurona Hunting 85

### TECHNICAL DETAILS

| Gauge/calibre | : 12 |
|---|---|
| Chamber length | : 70mm (2$^3/_4$in) or 76mm (3in) |
| Number of barrels | : double-barrels over-and-under |
| Action | : breech-loading |
| Locking | : barrel-block locking |
| Trigger | single trigger or twin triggers with double function |
| Weight | : 3.1kg (6lb 13oz) |

| Length | : 114cm (44$^7/_8$ in) |
|---|---|
| Barrel length | : 71cm (28in) |
| Ejector | : automatic |
| Choke | interchangeable set |
| Sight | 7mm ($^9/_{32}$in) wide ventilated rib and bead |
| Safety | : sliding safety-catch on neck of stock |

### CHARACTERISTICS

| — material | : steel |
|---|---|
| — finish | : black-chrome protective coating and bare metal action with decorative engravings |
| — stock | : walnut stock, with pistol-grip |

## Laurona Hunting Derby

### TECHNICAL DETAILS

| Gauge/calibre | : 12 |
|---|---|
| Chamber length | : 70mm (2$^3/_4$in) or 76mm (3in) |

Number of barrels : double-barrels over-and-under
Action : breech-loading
Locking : barrel-block locking
Trigger single trigger or twin triggers with double function
Weight : 3.1kg (6lb 13oz)
Length : 114cm (44$^7$/$_8$in)
Barrel length : 71cm (28in)
Ejector : automatic
Choke interchangeable set
Sight 7mm ($^9$/$_{32}$in) wide ventilated rib and bead
Safety : sliding safety-catch on neck of stock

**CHARACTERISTICS**
— material : steel
— finish : black-chrome protective coating and bare metal action engraved with various hunting motifs
— stock : walnut stock, with pistol-grip

## *Laurona Hunting Laurona*

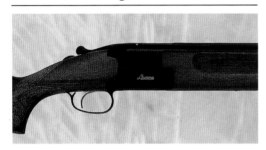

**TECHNICAL DETAILS**
Gauge/calibre : 12
Chamber length : 70mm (2$^3$/$_4$in) or 76mm (3in)
Number of barrels : double-barrels over-and-under
Action : breech-loading
Locking : barrel-block locking
Trigger single trigger or twin triggers with double function
Weight : 3.1kg (6lb 13oz)
Length : 114cm (44$^7$/$_8$in)
Barrel length : 71cm (28in)
Ejector : automatic
Choke interchangeable set
Sight 7mm ($^9$/$_{32}$in) wide ventilated rib and bead
Safety : sliding safety-catch on neck of stock

**CHARACTERISTICS**
— material : steel
— finish : black-chrome protective coating
— stock : walnut stock, with pistol-grip

## *Laurona Olympic*

**TECHNICAL DETAILS**
Gauge/calibre . 12
Chamber length : 70mm (2$^3$/$_4$in) or 76mm (3in)

Number of barrels : double-barrels over-and-under
Action : breech-loading
Locking : barrel-block locking
Trigger single trigger or twin triggers with double function
Weight : 3.1kg (6lb 13oz)
Length : 114cm (44$^7$/$_8$in)
Barrel length : 71cm (28in)
Ejector : automatic
Choke interchangeable set
Sight 7mm ($^9$/$_{32}$in) wide ventilated rib and bead
Safety : sliding safety-catch on neck of stock

**CHARACTERISTICS**
— material : steel
— finish : black-chrome protective coating
— stock : walnut stock, with pistol-grip

## *Laurona Compak*

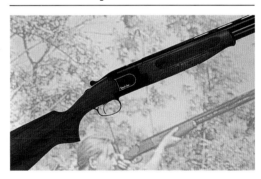

**TECHNICAL DETAILS**
Gauge/calibre : 12
Chamber length : 70mm (2$^3$/$_4$in) or 76mm (3in)
Number of barrels : double-barrels over-and-under
Action : breech-loading
Locking : barrel-block locking
Trigger single or twin triggers
Weight : 3.1–3.55kg (6lb 13oz–7lb 13oz)
Length : 114–119cm (44$^7$/$_8$–46$^7$/$_8$in)
Barrel length : 71, 74, or 76cm (28, 29$^1$/$_8$, or 30in)
Ejector : automatic
Choke interchangeable set
Sight 11mm ($^7$/$_{16}$in) wide ventilated rib and bead
Safety : sliding safety-catch on neck of stock

## CHARACTERISTICS
— material : steel
— finish : black-chrome protective coating
— stock : walnut stock, with pistol-grip

# Laurona Sporting Gold

## TECHNICAL DETAILS
Gauge/calibre : 12
Chamber length : 70mm (2³/₄in)
Number of barrels : double-barrels over-and-under
Action : breech-loading
Locking : barrel-block locking
Trigger single trigger
Weight : 3.55kg (7lb 13oz)
Length : 114–119cm (44⁷/₈–46⁷/₈in)
Barrel length : 71, 74, or 76cm (28, 29¹/₈, or 30in)
Ejector : automatic
Choke interchangeable set
Sight 11mm (⁷/₁₆in) wide ventilated rib and bead
Safety : sliding safety-catch on neck of stock

## CHARACTERISTICS
— material : steel
— finish : black-chrome protective coating, gold lining on action
— stock : walnut stock, with pistol-grip

# Laurona Trap Criterium

## TECHNICAL DETAILS
Gauge/calibre : 12

Chamber length : 70mm (2³/₄in)
Number of barrels : double-barrels over-and-under
Action : breech-loading
Locking : barrel-block locking
Trigger single trigger
Weight : 3.55kg (7lb 13oz)
Length : 117 or 119cm (46 or 46⁷/₈in)
Barrel length : 74 or 76cm (29¹/₈ or 30in)
Ejector : automatic
Choke interchangeable set
Sight 11mm (⁷/₁₆in) wide ventilated rib and bead
Safety : sliding safety-catch on neck of stock

## CHARACTERISTICS
— material : steel
— finish : black-chrome protective coating, bare metal action with engravings of clay pigeon shooting
— stock : walnut stock, with pistol-grip

# Laurona Trap Gold XMS

## TECHNICAL DETAILS
Gauge/calibre : 12
Chamber length : 70mm (2³/₄in)
Number of barrels : double-barrels over-and-under
Action : breech-loading
Locking : barrel-block locking
Trigger single trigger
Weight : 3.55kg (7lb 13oz)
Length : 117 or 119cm (46 or 46⁷/₈in)
Barrel length : 74 or 76cm (29¹/₈ or 30in)
Ejector : automatic
Choke interchangeable set
Sight 11mm (⁷/₁₆in) wide ventilated rib and bead
Safety : sliding safety-catch on neck of stock

## CHARACTERISTICS
— material : steel
— finish : black-chrome protective coating, gold-lined action
— stock : walnut stock, with pistol-grip

# Laurona Trap Gold XS

## TECHNICAL DETAILS
Gauge/calibre : 12
Chamber length : 70mm (2³/₄in)

Number of barrels : double-barrels over-and-under
Action : breech-loading
Locking : barrel-block locking
Trigger single trigger
Weight : 3.5kg (7lb 13oz)
Length : 117 or 119cm (46 or 46$^7$/$_8$in)
Barrel length : 74 or 76cm (29$^1$/$_8$ or 30in)
Ejector : automatic
Choke fixed choke
Sight 11mm ($^7$/$_{16}$in) wide ventilated rib and bead
Safety : sliding safety-catch on neck of stock

**CHARACTERISTICS**
— material : steel
— finish : black-chrome protective coating, gold-lined action
— stock : walnut stock, with pistol-grip
🐓

## *Laurona Trap London*

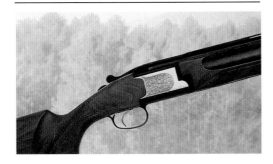

**TECHNICAL DETAILS**
Gauge/calibre : 12
Chamber length : 70mm (2$^3$/$_4$in)
Number of barrels : double-barrels over-and-under
Action : breech-loading
Locking : barrel-block locking
Trigger single trigger
Weight : 3.55kg (7lb 13oz)
Length : 117 or 119cm (46 or 46$^7$/$_8$in)
Barrel length : 74 or 76cm (29$^1$/$_8$ or 30in)
Ejector : automatic
Choke interchangeable set
Sight 11mm ($^7$/$_{16}$in) wide ventilated rib and bead
Safety : sliding safety-catch on neck of stock

**CHARACTERISTICS**
— material : steel
— finish : black-chrome protective coating, bare metal action
with decorative engraving
— stock : walnut stock, with pistol-grip
🐓

## *Laurona Woodcock Derby*

**TECHNICAL DETAILS**
Gauge/calibre : 12
Chamber length : 70mm (2$^3$/$_4$in) or 76mm (3in)

Number of barrels : double-barrels over-and-under
Action : breech-loading
Locking : barrel-block locking
Trigger single trigger
Weight : 2.9–3kg (6lb–6lb 9$^1$/$_2$oz)
Length : 104 or 109cm (41 or 42$^7$/$_8$in)
Barrel length : 55 or 60cm (21$^5$/8 or 23$^5$/8in)
Ejector : automatic
Choke top barrel with interchangeable chokes, bottom
barrel is rifled for slugs
Sight 7mm ($^9$/$_{32}$in) wide ventilated rib and bead
Safety : sliding safety-catch on neck of stock

**CHARACTERISTICS**
— material : steel
— finish : blued with special corrosion-resistant coating
— stock : walnut stock, with pistol-grip
🥄

# Lebeau-Courally

The Belgian city of Liège has been known
for making armaments since the Middle
Ages. By the end of the eighteenth century,
the accent had switched to producing
firearms. The industry worked with countless gunsmiths who made parts at home for
the manufacturers who finally assembled the
guns and then sold them under their own
name. The Industrial Revolution did not
reform industry in Liège until the late nineteenth century when guns started to be mass
produced in factories.

Today the city is one of the most important
firearms centres in the world with an annual
production of 1.6 million firearms.
The gunsmiths of Liège are above all famous
for their high-quality engraving work
together with the excellent standard of their
gunmaking. The gunsmith Auguste Lebeau

started his own business in 1865 which went on to win many top prizes at various World exhibitions and became famous as suppliers to the courts of Italy, Russia, and Spain. The business was continued by Ferdinand Courally in 1896 and was bought by the Liège gunmaker Joseph Verees in 1952.
He headed the business until 1982. The present owner, Anne-Marie Moermans continues the business in the traditional way. Guns are made to the customer's individual requirements. This applies not only to the overall length, chokes, and engravings, but also to the choice of timber for the stock and fore-end. The Boss Verees model is a memorial to the former owner. Lebeau-Courally specialise in making Express rifles. The guns that emanate from this house are not just exceptional weapons, they are valuable investment objects.

## *Lebeau-Courally Ambassadeur*

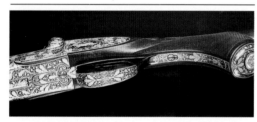

### TECHNICAL DETAILS
Gauge/calibre : 20
Chamber length : 76mm (3in)
Number of barrels : double-barrels over-and-under
Action : breech-loading
Locking : Greener and barrel-block locking
Trigger twin triggers
Weight : approx. 3.2kg (7lb)
Length : to choice
Barrel length : to choice
Ejector : to choice
Choke to choice
Sight bead
Safety : sliding safety-catch on neck of stock

### CHARACTERISTICS
— material : steel
— finish : blued with special engraving of hunting motifs on side-plates, inlaid with gold
— stock : stock of specially-selected walnut

An interchangeable barrel is also available for this gun with Express calibre 9.3x74R.

## *Lebeau-Courally Ardennes*

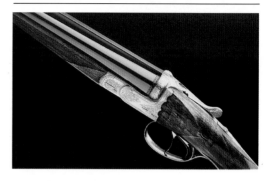

### TECHNICAL DETAILS
Gauge/calibre : 9.3x74R
Chamber length : not applicable
Number of barrels : double-barrels side-by-side
Action : breech-loading
Locking : double barrel-block locking
Trigger twin triggers
Weight : approx. 3.7kg (8lb 3oz)
Length : to choice
Barrel length : to choice
Ejector : to choice
Choke to choice
Sight Express folding sight and bead
Safety : sliding safety-catch on neck of stock

### CHARACTERISTICS
— material : steel
— finish : blued barrels. bare metal action with decorative engraving
— stock : stock of specially-selected walnut, with pistol-grip and cheek plate

## *Lebeau-Courally Battue (driven game)*

### TECHNICAL DETAILS
Gauge/calibre : 9.3x74R
Chamber length : not applicable
Number of barrels : double-barrels over-and-under
Action : breech-loading
Locking : double barrel-block locking
Trigger twin triggers

| Weight | : approx. 3.8kg (8lb 5³/₄oz) |
|---|---|
| Length | : to choice |
| Barrel length | : to choice |
| Ejector | : to choice |
| Choke | not applicable, rifled barrels |
| Sight | Express folding sight and bead |
| Safety | : sliding safety-catch on neck of stock |

**CHARACTERISTICS**

| — material | : steel |
|---|---|
| — finish | : blued barrels. action and side-lock plates with special engraving |
| — stock | : stock of specially-selected walnut |

🥄

## Lebeau-Courally Big Five Express

**TECHNICAL DETAILS**

| Gauge/calibre | : .458 Win. Mag. |
|---|---|
| Chamber length | : not applicable |
| Number of barrels | : double-barrels side-by-side |
| Action | : breech-loading |
| Locking | : double barrel-block locking |
| Trigger | twin triggers |
| Weight | : approx. 4.2kg (9lb 4oz) |
| Length | : to choice |
| Barrel length | : to choice |
| Ejector | : to choice |
| Choke | not applicable, rifled barrels |
| Sight | Express folding sight and bead, special mounting for telescopic sight |
| Safety | : sliding safety-catch on neck of stock |

**CHARACTERISTICS**

| — material | : steel |
|---|---|
| — finish | : blued barrels. action and side-lock plates with special engraving of African big game |
| — stock | : stock of specially-selected walnut |

Interchangeable barrels are supplied with this gun for the .375 H&H Express calibre. This double-barrel Express rifle was made as a result of the film In the blood which depicts a hunting safari by the US President Theodore Roosevelt in 1909.

🥄

## Lebeau-Courally Boss Verrees

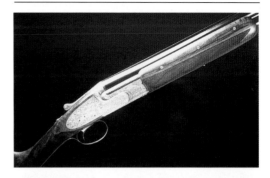

**TECHNICAL DETAILS**

| Gauge/calibre | : 12 |
|---|---|
| Chamber length | : 70mm (2³/₄in) |
| Number of barrels | : double-barrels over-and-under |
| Action | : breech-loading |
| Locking | : double barrel-block locking |
| Trigger | single trigger |
| Weight | : approx. 3.25kg (7lb 2oz) |
| Length | : to choice |
| Barrel length | : to choice |
| Ejector | : automatic |
| Choke | to choice |
| Sight | barrel rib and bead |
| Safety | : sliding safety-catch on neck of stock |

**CHARACTERISTICS**

| — material | : steel |
|---|---|
| — finish | : blued barrels, engraved bare metal action and side-lock plates |
| — stock | : stock and fore-end of specially-selected walnut |

🥄

## Lebeau-Courally Boss Verrees Pair

**TECHNICAL DETAILS**

| Gauge/calibre | : 20 |
|---|---|
| Chamber length | : 76mm (3in) |
| Number of barrels | : double-barrels side-by-side |
| Action | : breech-loading |
| Locking | : double barrel-block locking |
| Trigger | twin triggers |
| Weight | : approx. 3.25kg (7lb 2oz) |

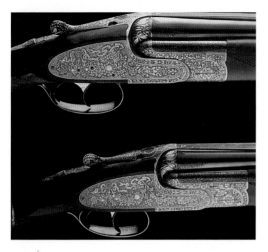

Gauge/calibre      : 20
Chamber length     : 76mm (3in)
Number of barrels : double-barrels side-by-side
Action             : breech-loading
Locking            : Greener and barrel-block locking
Trigger            twin triggers
Weight             : approx. 3.2kg (7lb)
Length             : to choice
Barrel length      : to choice
Ejector            : to choice
Choke              to choice
Sight              bead
Safety             : sliding safety-catch on neck of stock

**CHARACTERISTICS**
— material      : steel
— finish        : blued barrels, bare metal action and removable
                  side-lock plates with gold inlaid engraving
— stock         : straight English stock of specially-selected walnut

Length             : to choice
Barrel length      : to choice
Ejector            : automatic
Choke              to choice
Sight              barrel rib and bead
Safety             : sliding safety-catch on neck of stock

**CHARACTERISTICS**
— material      : steel
— finish        : blued barrels, engraved bare metal action and side-
                  lock plates
— stock         : stock and fore-end of specially-selected walnut

These special guns can be ordered as a pair
and are supplied in a leather-covered gun
case.

# *Lebeau-Courally Chambord*

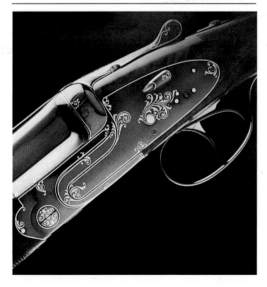

# *Lebeau-Courally Comte de Paris*

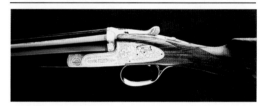

**TECHNICAL DETAILS**
Gauge/calibre      : 20
Chamber length     : 76mm (3in)
Number of barrels : double-barrels side-by-side
Action             : breech-loading
Locking            : double barrel-block locking
Trigger            single trigger
Weight             : approx. 3.1kg (6lb 13oz)
Length             : to choice
Barrel length      : to choice
Ejector            : to choice
Choke              to choice
Sight              bead
Safety             : sliding safety-catch on neck of stock

**CHARACTERISTICS**
— material      : steel
— finish        : blued, engraved bare metal action and removable
                  side-lock plates
— stock         : straight English stock of specially-selected walnut

# *Lebeau-Courally Edimbourg Pair*

**TECHNICAL DETAILS**
Gauge/calibre      : 20

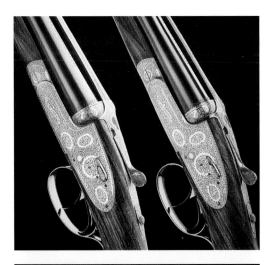

Chamber length   : 76mm (3in)
Number of barrels : double-barrels side-by-side
Action          : breech-loading
Locking        : double barrel-block locking
Trigger        twin triggers
Weight         : approx. 3.1kg (6lb 13oz)
Length         : to choice
Barrel length  : to choice
Ejector        : to choice
Choke         to choice
Sight          bead
Safety         : sliding safety-catch on neck of stock

**CHARACTERISTICS**
— material     : steel
— finish       : blued, engraved bare metal action and removable side-lock plates
— stock      : straight English stock of specially-selected walnut

The pair of guns have gold inlaid numbers "1" and "2" and are supplied in a leather-covered gun case

## Lebeau-Courally Nimrod

**TECHNICAL DETAILS**
Gauge/calibre   : 12
Chamber length   : 70mm (2³/₄in)
Number of barrels : double-barrels side-by-side
Action           : breech-loading
Locking         : double barrel-block locking
Trigger         twin triggers
Weight          : approx. 3.2kg (7lb)
Length          : to choice
Barrel length   : to choice
Ejector         : to choice
Choke          to choice
Sight           bead
Safety          : sliding safety-catch on neck of stock

**CHARACTERISTICS**
— material     : steel
— finish       : blued barrels, engraved bare metal action and removable side-lock plates
— stock      : straight English stock of specially-selected walnut

## Lebeau-Courally Safari 470NE

**TECHNICAL DETAILS**
Gauge/calibre   : .470 NE (Nitro Express)
Chamber length   : not applicable
Number of barrels : double-barrels side-by-side
Action          : breech-loading
Locking        : double barrel-block locking

| Trigger | twin triggers |
|---|---|
| Weight | : approx.4kg (8lb 13oz) |
| Length | : to choice |
| Barrel length | : to choice |
| Ejector | : to choice |
| Choke | not applicable, rifled barrels |
| Sight | Express folding sight and bead |
| Safety | : sliding safety-catch on neck of stock |

**CHARACTERISTICS**

| | |
|---|---|
| — material | : steel |
| — finish | : blued barrels, bare metal action and removable side-lock plates are engraved with hunting scenes of African big game |
| — stock | : stock of specially-selected walnut, with pistol-grip and cheek plate |

## *Lebeau-Courally Traditional Side by Side*

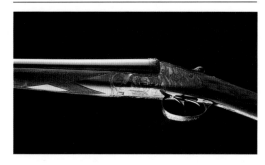

**TECHNICAL DETAILS**

| | |
|---|---|
| Gauge/calibre | : 20 |
| Chamber length | : 76mm (3in) |
| Number of barrels | : double-barrels side-by-side |
| Action | : breech-loading |
| Locking | : double barrel-block locking |
| Trigger | twin triggers |
| Weight | : approx. 3.1kg (6lb 13oz) |
| Length | : to choice |
| Barrel length | : to choice |
| Ejector | : to choice |
| Choke | to choice |
| Sight | bead |
| Safety | : sliding safety-catch on neck of stock |

**CHARACTERISTICS**

| | |
|---|---|
| — material | : steel |
| — finish | : blued barrels, tempered action and side-lock plates |
| — stock | : straight English stock of specially-selected walnut |

## *Lebeau-Courally Side by Side Prince Koudacheff*

**TECHNICAL DETAILS**

| | |
|---|---|
| Gauge/calibre | : 12 |

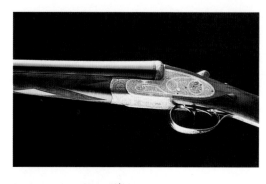

| | |
|---|---|
| Chamber length | : 70mm (2³/₄in) |
| Number of barrels | : double-barrels side-by-side |
| Action | : breech-loading |
| Locking | : double barrel-block locking |
| Trigger | twin triggers |
| Weight | : approx. 3.25kg (7lb 2oz) |
| Length | : to choice |
| Barrel length | : to choice |
| Ejector | : automatic |
| Choke | to choice |
| Sight | barrel rib and bead |
| Safety | : sliding safety-catch on neck of stock |

**CHARACTERISTICS**

| | |
|---|---|
| — material | : steel |
| — finish | : blued barrels, engraved bare metal action and side-lock plates |
| — stock | : straight English stock of specially-selected walnut |

## *Lebeau-Courally over–and–under 28*

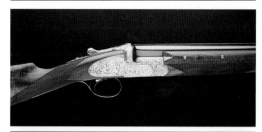

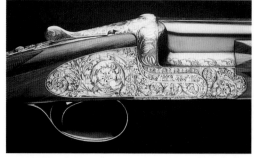

**TECHNICAL DETAILS**

| | |
|---|---|
| Gauge/calibre | : 28 |

| | |
|---|---|
| Chamber length | : 70mm (2³/₄in) |
| Number of barrels | : double-barrels over-and-under |
| Action | : breech-loading |
| Locking | : double barrel-block locking |
| Trigger | single trigger |
| Weight | : approx. 3kg (6lb 9¹/₂oz) |
| Length | : to choice |
| Barrel length | : to choice |
| Ejector | : to choice |
| Choke | to choice |
| Sight | barrel rib and bead |
| Safety | : sliding safety-catch on neck of stock |

**CHARACTERISTICS**

| | |
|---|---|
| — material | : steel |
| — finish | : blued barrels, engraved bare metal action and side-lock plates |
| — stock | : straight English stock of specially-selected walnut |

🖑

## *Lebeau-Courally Versailles Trio*

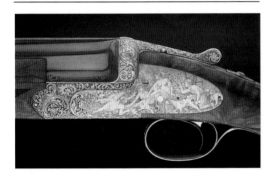

**TECHNICAL DETAILS**

| | |
|---|---|
| Gauge/calibre | : 20 |
| Chamber length | : 70mm (2³/₄in) |
| Number of barrels | : double-barrels over-and-under |
| Action | : breech-loading |
| Locking | : Greener and barrel-block locking |
| Trigger | single trigger |
| Weight | : approx. 3kg (6lb 9¹/₂ oz) |
| Length | : to choice |
| Barrel length | : to choice |
| Ejector | : automatic |
| Choke | to choice |
| Sight | barrel rib and bead |
| Safety | : sliding safety-catch on neck of stock |

**CHARACTERISTICS**

| | |
|---|---|
| — material | : steel |
| — finish | : blued barrels, bare metal action and side-lock plates are engraved in Louis XV mythological style |
| — stock | : straight English stock of specially-selected walnut |

The Lebeau-Courally Versailles Trio is a matched set of three guns with consecutive numbers.

🖑

# Ljutic

Al Ljutic was born in Tonapah, Nevada, in 1917, as the son of a Serbian immigrant. He founded a small gunsmith's workshop in Reno, Nevada in 1952.

Because he spent his days repairing the faults in his customer's guns, he decided to build a gun without any of the weak points that were found in the guns he repaired. This resulted in highly specialized guns which caused not a little amusement in their early days until scores of shooters walked off with the prizes at clay pigeon shooting matches.

Nadine Ljutic, wife and Managing Director of the company, has won many prizes in the

Lady Trap discipline with her number 2 Ljutic gun. This gun has fired more than 1,5 million cartridges and still functions as new. Joe Ljutic, son of Al and Nadine, won his first national championship at the age of 15 with a gun made for him by his father.

The family won 36 matches between them in the period 1966–1990. Joe Ljutic has worked now for some years for the company. Al Ljutic's slogan is: "Custom crafted to last a lifetime." Ljutic guns with low serial numbers, which have often shot more than 1 million cartridges, now fetch exceptional prices from collectors. Ljutic guns have a style which you either like or hate.

The technical aspect of the guns is beyond reproach. One unusual aspect of Ljutic guns is the apparent lack of a locking lever. The locking lever is incorporated in the front of the trigger guard and is pressed in to breach the gun.

The single-barrel Mono Guns have been described in gun magazines as the "ultimate shotgun." The company has been based at Yakima, Washington where, for a long time, guns have been made to customer's specifications.

The range includes shotguns for Trap, Skeet, Sporting Clays, and for field shooting. The parts are machined from solid metal because Al Ljutic is opposed to moulded and stamped parts.

The quality of their guns is borne out by the fact that it is not unusual for them to fire 500,000 to 1 million cartridges before any parts need replacing. The prototype of the Mono Gun has meanwhile fired 1.5 million cartridges and still works superbly.

All the Ljutic guns are designed by Al Ljutic. He is also the designer and patentee for the gas repeating mechanism used in firearms such as the Springfield M-14 and Colt M-16. Ljutic guns have remarkable appearances: this is because of their high ventilated barrel rib. In addition to the Mono Guns, the company also make double-barrel over-and-under shotguns – the LM6 range.

Ljutic is also the developer and manufacturer of the recoilless Space shotgun which has an ingenious damper which reduces recoil by more than 20 per cent.

The basic prices vary from $5,000 for a standard Mono Gun to $18,000 for a double-barrel LM6.

## Ljutic Classic Mono Gun Hunter I

**TECHNICAL DETAILS**

| | |
|---|---|
| Gauge/calibre | : 12 |
| Chamber length | : 2³/₄in (70mm) or 3in (76mm) |
| Number of barrels | : single-barrel |
| Action | : breech-loading |
| Locking | : barrel-block locking with locking lever in front of trigger guard |
| Trigger | single trigger |
| Weight | : 7lb 4oz–8lb 13oz (3.3–4kg) |
| Length | : to choice |
| Barrel length | : 30–34in (76–86cm) |
| Ejector | : automatic |
| Choke | Slim-line interchangeable chokes |
| Sight | ventilated barrel rib and bead |
| Safety | : none |

**CHARACTERISTICS**

| | |
|---|---|
| – material | : steel |
| – finish | : blued |
| – stock | : walnut stock, with pistol-grip and raised comb |

## Ljutic Classic Mono Gun Hunter II

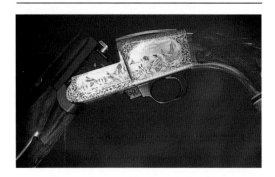

**TECHNICAL DETAILS**

Gauge/calibre : 12
Chamber length : 2³/₄in (70mm) or 3in (76mm)
Number of barrels : single-barrel
Action : breech-loading
Locking : barrel-block locking with locking lever in front of trigger guard
Trigger : single trigger
Weight : 7lb 4oz–8lb 13oz (3.3–4kg)
Length : to choice
Barrel length : 30–34in (76–86cm)
Ejector : automatic
Choke : Slim-line interchangeable chokes
Sight : ventilated barrel rib and bead
Safety : none

characteristics

— material : steel
— finish : blued
— stock : walnut stock, with pistol-grip and raised comb

## Ljutic Classic Mono Gun Standard

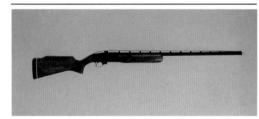

**TECHNICAL DETAILS**

Gauge/calibre : 12
Chamber length : 2³/₄in (70mm) or 3in (76mm)
Number of barrels : single-barrel
Action : breech-loading
Locking : barrel-block locking with locking lever in front of trigger guard
Trigger : single trigger
Weight : 7lb 4oz–8lb 13oz (3.3–4kg)
Length : to choice
Barrel length : 30–34in (76–86cm)
Ejector : automatic
Choke : Slim-line interchangeable chokes
Sight : ventilated barrel rib and bead
Safety : none

**CHARACTERISTICS**

— material : steel
— finish : blued
— stock : walnut stock, with pistol-grip and raised comb

This gun is available with a ventilated barrel rib of various heights. The gun can also be produced in stainless steel.

## Ljutic LM6 Over-and-Under

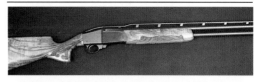

**TECHNICAL DETAILS**

Gauge/calibre : 12
Chamber length : 2³/₄in (70mm) or 3in (76mm)
Number of barrels : double-barrel over-and-under
Action : breech-loading
Locking : barrel-block locking with locking lever in front of trigger guard
Trigger : single trigger
Weight : 7lb–8lb 8oz (3.2–3.9kg)
Length : to choice
Barrel length : 28–32in (71–81cm)
Ejector : automatic
Choke : Slim-line interchangeable chokes
Sight : raised ventilated barrel rib and bead
Safety : none

**CHARACTERISTICS**

— material : steel
— finish : blued
— stock : stock of selected walnut, with pistol-grip and raised comb

This gun is available in different versions: Trap, Skeet, Sporting Clays, and International Trap & Skeet. Alternative barrels are also available in various lengths, forms, and gauges.

## Ljutic LTX Mono Gun High Grade

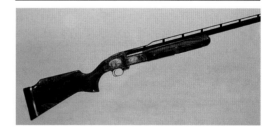

**TECHNICAL DETAILS**

Gauge/calibre : 12
Chamber length : 2³/₄in (70mm) or 3in (76mm)
Number of barrels : single-barrel
Action : breech-loading
Locking : barrel-block locking with locking lever in front of trigger guard

| Trigger | single trigger |
| Weight | : 8lb 4oz–8lb 12oz (3.7–4kg) |
| Length | : to choice |
| Barrel length | : 28–34in (71–86cm) |
| Ejector | : automatic |
| Choke | Slim-line interchangeable chokes |
| Sight | raised ventilated barrel rib and bead |
| Safety | : none |

**CHARACTERISTICS**

| — material | : steel |
| — finish | : blued barrels, bare metal action with engraving |
| — stock | : stock of specially-selected walnut, with pistol-grip and raised comb |

This gun is also available in stainless steel.

## Ljutic LTX Mono Gun Standard

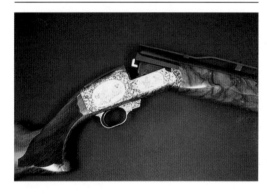

**TECHNICAL DETAILS**

| Gauge/calibre | : 12 |
| Chamber length | : $2^3/_4$in (70mm) or 3in (76mm) |
| Number of barrels | : single-barrel |
| Action | : breech-loading |
| Locking | : barrel-block locking with locking lever in front of trigger guard |
| Trigger | single trigger |
| Weight | : 8lb 4oz–8lb 12oz (3.7–4kg) |
| Length | : to choice |
| Barrel length | : 28–34in (71–86cm) |
| Ejector | : automatic |
| Choke | Slim-line interchangeable chokes |
| Sight | raised ventilated barrel rib and bead |
| Safety | : none |

**CHARACTERISTICS**

| — material | : steel |
| — finish | : blued |
| — stock | : stock of specially-selected walnut, with pistol-grip and raised comb |

This gun is also available in stainless steel.

## Ljutic LTX Mono Gun Trap

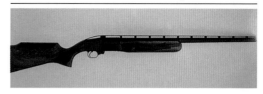

**TECHNICAL DETAILS**

| Gauge/calibre | : 12 |
| Chamber length | : $2^3/_4$in (70mm) |
| Number of barrels | : single-barrel |
| Action | : breech-loading |
| Locking | : barrel-block locking with locking lever in front of trigger guard |
| Trigger | single trigger |
| Weight | : 8lb 4oz–8lb 12oz (3.7–4kg) |
| Length | : to choice |
| Barrel length | : 32 or 34in (80 or 86cm) |
| Ejector | : automatic |
| Choke | Slim-line interchangeable chokes |
| Sight | ventilated barrel rib and bead |
| Safety | : none |

**CHARACTERISTICS**

| — material | : steel |
| — finish | : blued |
| — stock | : walnut stock, with pistol-grip and raised comb |

This gun is also available with a standard barrel rib (see photo) or with medium or Olympic (high) ribs. The gun is also available in stainless steel.

## Ljutic Recoiless Space Shotgun

**TECHNICAL DETAILS**

| Gauge/calibre | : 12 |
| Chamber length | : $2^3/_4$in (70mm) |
| Number of barrels | : single-barrel |
| Action | : bolt-action |
| Locking | : locking lugs |
| Trigger | single press-button trigger in front of pistol-grip |
| Weight | : 8lb 8oz (3.9kg) |

| Length | : to choice |
|---|---|
| Barrel length | : 30in (76cm): other lengths to choice |
| Ejector | : automatic |
| Choke | Slim-line interchangeable chokes |
| Sight | bead, mount for telescopic sight |
| Safety | : none |

**CHARACTERISTICS**

| — material | : steel or stainless steel |
|---|---|
| — finish | : blued |
| — stock | : walnut stock, with specially-shaped pistol-grip |

This gun is also available with rifled barrel for.308 Win.

## *Ljutic Recoiless Space Gun*

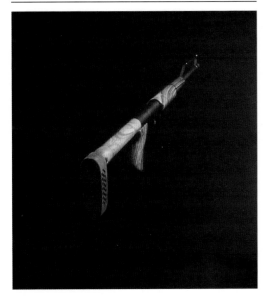

**TECHNICAL DETAILS**

| Gauge/calibre | : 12 |
|---|---|
| Chamber length | : 2³/₄in (70mm) |
| Number of barrels | : single-barrel |
| Action | : bolt-action |
| Locking | : locking lugs |
| Trigger | single press-button trigger in front of pistol-grip |
| Weight | : 8lb 8oz (3.9kg) |
| Length | : to choice |
| Barrel length | : 30in (76cm); other lengths to choice |
| Ejector | : automatic |
| Choke | Slim-line interchangeable chokes |
| Sight | special raised barrel rib with notch and bead |
| Safety | : none |

**CHARACTERISTICS**

| — material | : steel or stainless steel |
|---|---|
| — finish | . blued |
| — stock | : walnut stock, with specially-shaped pistol-grip |

## *Ljutic Selka Double Space Gun Limited Production*

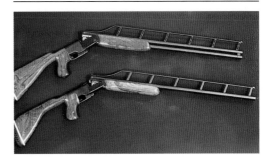

**TECHNICAL DETAILS**

| Gauge/calibre | : 12 |
|---|---|
| Chamber length | : 2³/₄in (70mm) |
| Number of barrels | : double-barrels over-and-under |
| Action | : breech-loading |
| Locking | : barrel locking with locking lever in the front of the trigger guard |
| Trigger | single press-button trigger |
| Weight | : approx. 8lb 8oz (3.9kg) |
| Length | : to choice |
| Barrel length | : 30in (76cm); other lengths to choice |
| Ejector | : automatic |
| Choke | Slim-line interchangeable chokes |
| Sight | raised barrel rib with notch and bead |
| Safety | : none |

**CHARACTERISTICS**

| — material | : steel or stainless steel |
|---|---|
| — finish | : blued, or blued barrels and bare metal action with engraving of choice |
| — stock | : stock of selected walnut, with specially-shaped pistol-grip (see photo). |

This model is also available in stainless steel. Illustrated from top to bottom: double-barrelled and single barrelled.

## *Ljutic Selka Mono Space Gun Limited Production*

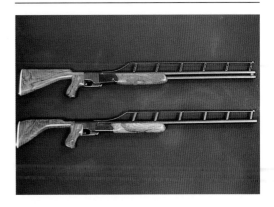

## TECHNICAL DETAILS

Gauge/calibre : 12
Chamber length : 2³/₄in (70mm)
Number of barrels : single-barrel
Action : breech-loading
Locking : barrel locking with locking lever in the front of the trigger guard
Trigger : single press-button trigger
Weight : approx. 8lb 2¹/₄oz (3.7kg)
Length : to choice
Barrel length : 28 or 30in (71 or 76cm); other lengths to choice
Ejector : automatic
Choke : Slim-line interchangeable chokes
Sight : raised barrel rib with notch and bead
Safety : none

## CHARACTERISTICS

— material : steel or stainless steel
— finish : blued, or blued barrels and bare metal action with engraving of choice
— stock : stock of selected walnut, with specially-shaped pistol-grip (see photo).

This model is also available in stainless steel. Illustrated from top to bottom: double-barrelled and single barrelled.

# Magtech

Magtech is the brand name of the Brazilian weapons and munitions manufacturer Companhia Brasileira de Cartuchos (CBC) based in São Paulo. They make a range of shotguns and small calibres rifles under the brand name Magtech.

The company was set up in 1926 by a family of Italian immigrants called Matarazzo, under the name Companhia Brasileira Cartucheria. In those days the company mainly made shotgun cartridges for the domestic market but it developed in a few decades into a major company with exports of munitions to many countries.

From 1936 to 1979, the company was jointly owned by the American Remington Arms Company and ICI (Imperial Chemical Industries) of Britain. The company was taken over in 1979 by the Arbi and Imbel groups, two major Brazilian corporations involved in tourism, the steel industry, and manufacture

of munitions. This is when the name was changed to Companhia Brasileira de Cartuchos (CBC). The brass cartridge cases for ammunition are produced by a subsidiary company S.A. Marvin of Nova Iguaçu near Rio de Janeiro. The company underwent major reorganization in 1991 and 1992. Under the management of the well-known munitions specialist Charles von Helle and with help from several German technological institutes, the production of munitions was totally modernized. The company does a lot of its own product development and has a number of 400m (437yds) testing ranges. About 80 percent of the company's output is exported to countries throughout the world.

## Magtech MT 586.2

### TECHNICAL DETAILS

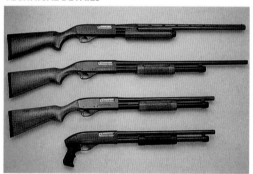

Gauge/calibre : 12
Chamber length : 76mm (3in)
Number of barrels : single-barrel
Magazine : tubular magazine for 2 or 4 cartridges
Action : pump-action
Locking : falling block locking
Trigger : single trigger
Weight : 3.2–3.35kg (7lb–7lb 6oz)
Length : 113–128cm (44 ¹/₄–50 ¹/₄in)
Barrel length : 61–76cm (24–30in)
Ejector : automatic
Choke : interchangeable chokes
Sight : bead
Safety : push-button in rear of trigger guard

### CHARACTERISTICS

— material : steel, chrome-molybdenum barrels
— finish : blued
— stock : stock of Brazilian hardwood, with pistol-grip

Illustrated from top to bottom: 586.2VR, 586.2, 586.2P, and 586.2PG.

## Magtech MT 586.2P

**TECHNICAL DETAILS**
Gauge/calibre : 12
Chamber length : 76mm (3in)
Number of barrels : single-barrel
Magazine : tubular magazine for 2 or 8 cartridges
Action : pump-action
Locking : falling block locking
Trigger : single trigger
Weight : 3.3kg (7lb 4oz)
Length : 99.7cm (39¼in)
Barrel length : 48.3cm (19in)
Ejector : extractor
Choke : cylindrical
Sight : bead
Safety : push-button in rear of trigger guard

**CHARACTERISTICS**
— material : steel, chrome-molybdenum barrels
— finish : blued
— stock : stock of Brazilian hardwood, with pistol-grip

Illustrated from top to bottom: 586.2VR, 586.2, 586.2P, and 586.2PG. This gun cannot be held on a United Kingdom shotgun certificate because it barrel is shorter than the minimum 24in (61cm) required. Shotguns are also not permitted to have magazines with a capacity of more than 1 cartridge in the barrel and 2 in the magazine. Similar restrictions apply in a number of European countries.

## Magtech MT 586.2PG

**TECHNICAL DETAILS**
Gauge/calibre : 12
Chamber length : 76mm (3in)
Number of barrels : single-barrel
Magazine : tubular magazine for 2 or 8 cartridges
Action : pump-action
Locking : falling block locking
Trigger : single trigger
Weight : 3kg (6lb 9½oz)
Length : 74.3cm (29¼in)
Barrel length : 48.3cm (19in)
Ejector : extractor
Choke : cylindrical
Sight : bead
Safety : push-button in rear of trigger guard

**CHARACTERISTICS**
— material : steel, chrome-molybdenum barrel
— finish : blued
— stock : plastic stock, with pistol-grip

Illustrated from top to bottom: 586.2VR, 586.2, 586.2P, and 586.2PG. This gun can-

not be held on a United Kingdom shotgun certificate because it barrel is shorter than the minimum 24in (61cm) required. Shotguns are also not permitted to have magazines with a capacity of more than 1 cartridge in the barrel and 2 in the magazine. Similar restrictions apply in a number of European countries.

## Magtech MT 586.2VR

**TECHNICAL DETAILS**
Gauge/calibre : 12
Chamber length : 76mm (3in)
Number of barrels : single-barrel
Magazine : tubular magazine for 2 or 4 cartridges
Action : pump-action
Locking : falling block locking
Trigger : single trigger
Weight : 3.4 or 3.5kg (7lb 8oz–7lb 11oz)
Length : 118 or 123cm (46¼ or 48¼in)
Barrel length : 66 or 71cm (26 or 28in)
Ejector : extractor
Choke : interchangeable choke set
Sight : ventilated rib and bead
Safety : push-button in rear of trigger guard

**CHARACTERISTICS**
— material : steel, chrome-molybdenum barrels
— finish : blued
— stock : Brazilian hardwood stock, with pistol-grip

Illustrated from top to bottom: 586.2VR, 586.2, 586.2P, and 586.2PG.

# Marlin

John Mahlon Marlin set-up his own business in New Haven, Connecticut in 1870, and his early successes were with his 1891 and 1893 model rifles that today are Marlin's models 39 and 336. His company also made a range of revolvers, pistols, and derringers between 1870 and 1899. When a new smokeless cartridge, the .30-30 Winchester, was introduced, he immediately brought out an appropriate range of rifles for it. Famous models from those times are his 1891 and 1897 rifles that were used by Annie Oakley and "Buffalo Bill" Cody in their Wild West shows. John Marlin died in 1901 and the business was carried on by his two sons. In that same year, they took over the Ideal Manufacturing Company that they sold again in 1925 to Lyman. During that time they also made other products, such as shoe-horns and handcuffs. Early in World War I, in 1915, Marlin was purchased by a New York trading company which changed the company name to the Marlin Rockwell Corporation. Production of sporting and hunting rifles dwindled significantly and the main activity was the manufacture of the Colt-Browning M1895 machine-gun for the US Army. After the war, Rockwell had no interest in sporting and hunting rifles so Marlin-Rockwell continued as an independent concern until 1923. In 1953, the company introduced its Micro-Groove system. The machining of rifling in barrels had been a long-winded and costly process but Marlin's engineers developed a process in which a large number of small and shallow grooves could be cut in one procedure.

The business moved to an entirely new factory in North Haven, Connecticut, in 1969. The Marlin Company has a small range of shotguns, consisting of two smooth-bore guns with long barrels for geese and a number of slug guns for use with solid projectiles in shotgun-type cartridges in 12 gauge. The barrels of these guns are rifled and the guns are used for hunting medium-sized game.

## Marlin 50 DL Goose Gun

### TECHNICAL DETAILS
| | |
|---|---|
| Gauge/calibre | : 12 |
| Chamber length | : 3in (76mm) |
| Number of barrels | : single-barrel |
| Magazine | : holder for 2 cartridges |
| Action | : bolt-action |
| Locking | : double locking lugs on bolt |
| Trigger | single trigger |
| Weight | : 7lb (3.2kg) |
| Length | : 48¹/₄in (122.6cm) |
| Barrel length | : 28in (71cm) |
| Ejector | : extractor |

| | |
|---|---|
| Choke | ¹/₂ |
| Sight | fixed U-shape notch |
| Safety | : push-button on right behind bolt, load indicator at rear of bolt, closing safety |

### CHARACTERISTICS
| | |
|---|---|
| — material | : steel |
| — finish | : matt black |
| — stock | : black plastic stock, with pistol-grip |

## Marlin 55 GDL Goose Gun

### TECHNICAL DETAILS
| | |
|---|---|
| Gauge/calibre | : 12 |
| Chamber length | : 3in (76mm) |
| Number of barrels | : single-barrel |
| Magazine | : holder for 2 cartridges |
| Action | : bolt-action |
| Locking | : double locking lugs on bolt |
| Trigger | single trigger |
| Weight | : 6lb 14³/₄oz (3.6kg) |
| Length | : 56³/₄in (144.2cm) |
| Barrel length | : 36in (91cm) |
| Ejector | : extractor |
| Choke | special full choke for steel shot |
| Sight | fixed U-shape notch |
| Safety | : push-button on right behind bolt, load indicator at rear of bolt, closing safety |

### CHARACTERISTICS
| | |
|---|---|
| — material | : steel |
| — finish | : matt black |
| — stock | : black plastic stock, with pistol-grip |

## Marlin 512 Slugmaster

### TECHNICAL DETAILS
| | |
|---|---|
| Gauge/calibre | : 12 |
| Chamber length | : 3in (76mm) |
| Number of barrels | : single-barrel |
| Magazine | : holder for 2 cartridges |
| Action | : bolt-action |
| Locking | : double locking lugs on bolt |
| Trigger | single trigger |
| Weight | : 8lb (3.6kg) |
| Length | : 44³/₄in (114cm) rifled barrel |

| Barrel length | : 21in (53cm) |
|---|---|
| Ejector | : extractor |
| Choke | none |
| Sight | notch and bead, mounting rail for telescopic sight |
| Safety | : push-button on right behind bolt, load indicator at rear of bolt, closing safety |

**CHARACTERISTICS**

| — material | : steel |
|---|---|
| — finish | : matt black |
| — stock | : black plastic stock, with pistol-grip |

This gun cannot be held on a shotgun certificate under United Kingdom legislation.

## Marlin 512 DL Slugmaster

**TECHNICAL DETAILS**

| Gauge/calibre | : 12 |
|---|---|
| Chamber length | : 3in (76mm) |
| Number of barrels | : single-barrel |
| Magazine | : holder for 2 cartridges |
| Action | : bolt-action |
| Locking | : double locking lugs on bolt |
| Trigger | single trigger |
| Weight | : 7lb 8oz (3.4kg) |
| Length | : 44³/₄in (114cm) rifled barrel |
| Barrel length | : 21in (53cm) |
| Ejector | : extractor |
| Choke | none |
| Sight | adjustable height notch and bead, mounting rail for telescopic sight |
| Safety | : push-button on right behind bolt, load indicator at rear of bolt, closing safety |

**CHARACTERISTICS**

| — material | : steel |
|---|---|
| — finish | : matt black |
| — stock | : black plastic stock, with pistol-grip |

The 12 gauge gun has a rifled barrel.

# Marocchi

The Italian company Armi Marocchi has been making sporting guns since 1922.
The company uses professional hunters and clay pigeon shooters in the process of development of a gun.
In 1957, Marocchi won the main prize at the International Inventors Exhibition with a

gun powered by high-pressure $CO_2$. This was a technical innovation at the time but has become more widely used since.
Marocchi has subsequently stopped making air weapons. Since setting up their factory, Marocchi have made 250,000 guns which are simple in concept, well made, and reasonably priced.

## Marocchi America

**TECHNICAL DETAILS**

| Gauge/calibre | : 12 |
|---|---|
| Chamber length | : 70mm (2³/₄in) |
| Number of barrels | : double-barrels over-and-under |
| Action | : breech-loading |
| Locking | : barrel-block locking |
| Trigger | single trigger |
| Weight | : 3.5–3.6kg (7lb 11oz–7lb 14³/₄oz) |
| Length | : 112–116cm (441/8–45¹/₄in) |
| Barrel length | : 72.5–76cm (28¹/₂–30in) |
| Ejector | : automatic |
| Choke | ³/₄ and ¹/₄, or ¹/₂ and full |
| Sight | 10mm (⁷/₁₆in) wide ventilated rib with bead |
| Safety | : sliding safety catch on neck of stock |

**CHARACTERISTICS**

| — material | : steel |
|---|---|
| — finish | : blued, or with blued barrels and bare metal engraved action |
| — stock | : walnut stock, with pistol-grip |

## Marocchi Contrast Cup

**TECHNICAL DETAILS**

| Gauge/calibre | : 12 |
|---|---|
| Chamber length | : 70mm (2³/₄in) |
| Number of barrels | : double-barrels over-and-under |
| Action | : breech-loading |

Locking          : barrel-block locking
Trigger            single trigger
Weight           : 3.5–3.65kg (7lb 11oz–8lb)
Length           : 112–116cm (44¹/₈–45³/₄in)
Barrel length    : 72.5–76cm (28¹/₂–30in)
Ejector          : automatic
Choke              ³/₄ and ¹/₄, or ¹/₂ and full
Sight              10mm (⁷/₁₆in) wide ventilated rib with bead
Safety           : sliding safety catch on neck of stock

### CHARACTERISTICS
— material       : steel
— finish         : blued, or with blued barrels and bare metal action
— stock          : walnut stock, with pistol-grip

## Marocchi Contrast Skeet

### TECHNICAL DETAILS
Gauge/calibre    : 12
Chamber length   : 70mm (2³/₄in)
Number of barrels : double-barrels over-and-under
Action           : breech-loading
Locking          : barrel-block locking
Trigger            single trigger
Weight           : 3.5kg (7lb 11oz)
Length           : 117–121cm (46–47⁵/₈in)
Barrel length    : 67 or 71cm (26³/₈ or 28in)
Ejector          : automatic
Choke              skeet/skeet
Sight              10mm (⁷/₁₆in) wide ventilated rib with bead
Safety           : sliding safety catch on neck of stock

### CHARACTERISTICS
— material       : steel

— finish         : blued barrels and bare metal action
— stock          : walnut stock, with pistol-grip

## Marocchi Prestige Black Gold

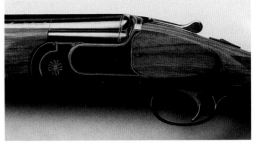

### TECHNICAL DETAILS
Gauge/calibre    : 12
Chamber length   : 70mm (2³/₄in)
Number of barrels : double-barrels over-and-under
Action           : breech-loading
Locking          : barrel-block locking
Trigger            single trigger
Weight           : 3.5–3.65kg (7lb 11oz–8lb)
Length           : 112–116cm (44¹/₈–45³/₄in)
Barrel length    : 72.5–76cm (28¹/₂–30in)
Ejector          : automatic
Choke              ³/₄ and ¹/₄, or ¹/₂ and full
Sight              10mm (⁷/₁₆in) wide ventilated rib with bead
Safety           : sliding safety catch on neck of stock

### CHARACTERISTICS
— material       : steel
— finish         : blued, with gold-lined action
— stock          : stock of selected walnut, with pistol-grip

## Marocchi SM 28L Side-lock

### TECHNICAL DETAILS
Gauge/calibre    : to choice
Chamber length   : to choice
Number of barrels : double-barrels side-by-side

| Action | : breech-loading |
|---|---|
| Locking | : double barrel-block locking |
| Trigger | single or twin triggers |
| Weight | : 3.1–3.3kg (6lb 13oz–7lb 4oz) |
| Length | : 111–126cm (43³/₄–49⁵/₈in) |
| Barrel length | : 61–76cm (24–30in) |
| Ejector | : automatic or extractor to choice |
| Choke | to choice |
| Sight | bead |
| Safety | : sliding safety catch on neck of stock |

## CHARACTERISTICS

| — material | : steel |
|---|---|
| — finish | : blued, with gold-lined action and side-lock plates |
| — stock | : straight English stock of selected walnut |

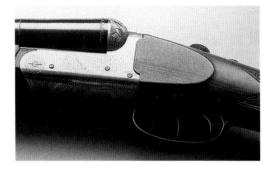

## *Marocchi SM 28L/M Extra Side-lock*

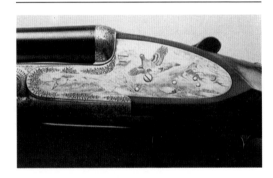

## TECHNICAL DETAILS

| Gauge/calibre | : to choice |
|---|---|
| Chamber length | : to choice |
| Number of barrels | : double-barrels side-by-side |
| Action | : breech-loading |
| Locking | : double barrel-block locking |
| Trigger | single or twin triggers |
| Weight | : 3.1–3.3kg (6lb 13oz–7lb 4oz) |
| Length | : 111–126cm (43³/₄–49⁵/₈in) |
| Barrel length | : 61–76cm (24–30in) |
| Ejector | : automatic or extractor to choice |
| Choke | to choice |
| Sight | bead |
| Safety | : sliding safety catch on neck of stock |

## CHARACTERISTICS

| Gauge/calibre | : 12, 16, 20, or 24 |
|---|---|
| Chamber length | : to choice |
| Number of barrels | : double-barrels side-by-side |

## *Marocchi SM 53*

## TECHNICAL DETAILS

| Gauge/calibre | : 12, 16, 20, or 24 |
|---|---|
| Chamber length | : to choice |

| Number of barrels | : double-barrels side-by-side |
|---|---|
| Action | : breech-loading |
| Locking | : barrel-block locking |
| Trigger | single or twin triggers |
| Weight | : 3.1–3.2kg (6lb 13oz–7lb) |
| Length | : 111–126cm (43³/₄–49⁵/₈in) |
| Barrel length | : 61–76cm (24–30in) |
| Ejector | : automatic or extractor to choice |
| Choke | to choice |
| Sight | bead |
| Safety | : sliding safety catch on neck of stock |

## CHARACTERISTICS

| — material | : steel |
|---|---|
| — finish | : blued barrels, engraved bare metal action |
| — stock | : walnut stock, with pistol-grip |

## *Marocchi SM 53 L/M Extra*

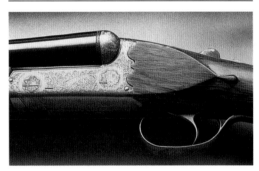

## TECHNICAL DETAILS

| Gauge/calibre | : 12, 16, 20, or 24 |
|---|---|
| Chamber length | : to choice |
| Number of barrels | : double-barrels side-by-side |
| Action | : breech-loading |
| Locking | : barrel-block locking |
| Trigger | single or twin triggers |
| Weight | : 3–3.1kg (6lb 9¹/₂ oz–6lb 13oz) |
| Length | : 111–126cm (43³/₄–49⁵/₈ in) |
| Barrel length | : 61–76cm (24–30in) |
| Ejector | : automatic or extractor to choice |
| Choke | to choice |
| Sight | bead |

Safety                : sliding safety catch on neck of stock

## CHARACTERISTICS
— material             : steel
— finish               : blued barrels, engraved bare metal action
— stock                : straight English stock of selected walnut
🖾

## *Marocchi SM 57 SS*

## TECHNICAL DETAILS
Gauge/calibre      : 12, 16, or 20
Chamber length     : 70mm (2³/₄in) or 76mm (3in) for 20 gauge
Number of barrels : double-barrels over-and-under
Action             : breech-loading
Locking            : Kersten locking
Trigger              twin triggers
Weight             : 3.1kg (6lb 13oz)
Length             : 121cm (47⁵/₈in)
Barrel length      : 71cm (28in)
Ejector            : automatic
Choke                interchangeable chokes
Sight                7mm (⁹/₃₂in) wide ventilated rib and bead
Safety             : sliding safety catch on neck of stock

## CHARACTERISTICS
— material             : steel
— finish               : blued barrels, engraved bare metal action
— stock                : walnut stock, with pistol-grip
🖾  🐦

## *Marocchi SM 76 Combination gun*

## TECHNICAL DETAILS
Gauge/calibre      : smooth-bore: 12; rifled barrel see below
Chamber length     : smooth-bore barrel: 70mm (2³/₄in)
Number of barrels : double-barrels over-and-under
Action             : breech-loading
Locking            : Kersten locking
Trigger              twin triggers
Weight             : 3.4–3.5kg (7lb 8oz–7lb 9¹/₂oz)
Length             : 110–115cm (43¹/₄–45¹/₄in)
Barrel length      : 61–66cm (24–26in)
Ejector            : extractor
Choke                smooth-bore barrel: to choice
Sight                folding sight with bead; mount for telescopic sight
Safety             : sliding safety catch on neck of stock

## CHARACTERISTICS
— material             : steel
— finish               : blued, or blued barrels and engraved bare metal action
— stock                : walnut stock, with pistol-grip

Available rifle calibres: 5.6x52R, 6.5x57R, 7x57R, and 7x65R.
🖾

## *Marocchi Snipe*

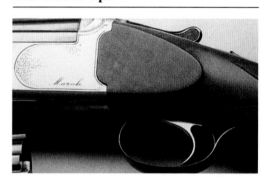

## TECHNICAL DETAILS
Gauge/calibre      : 12
Chamber length     : 70mm (2³/₄in)
Number of barrels : double-barrels over-and-under
Action             : breech-loading
Locking            : double barrel-block locking
Trigger              single or twin triggers
Weight             : 3kg (6lb 9¹/₂ oz)
Length             : 111cm (43³/₄in)
Barrel length      : 70cm (27¹/₂ in)
Ejector            : automatic
Choke                to choice
Sight                10mm (⁷/₁₆in) ventilated rib with bead
Safety             : sliding safety catch on neck of stock

## CHARACTERISTICS
— material             : steel
— finish               : blued barrels, bare metal action
— stock                : walnut stock, with pistol-grip

## Marocchi Trap / Skeet 73

### TECHNICAL DETAILS

| | |
|---|---|
| Gauge/calibre | : 12 |
| Chamber length | : 70mm (2³/₄in) |
| Number of barrels | : double-barrels over-and-under |
| Action | : breech-loading |
| Locking | : barrel-block locking |
| Trigger | single trigger |
| Weight | : 3.4–3.5kg (7lb 8oz–7lb 9¹/₂oz ) |
| Length | : 111–115cm (43³/₄–45¹/₄in) |
| Barrel length | : 71cm (28in) Skeet, 74cm (29¹/₂ in) Trap |
| Ejector | : automatic |
| Choke | Trap or Skeet to choice |
| Sight | 12mm (¹/₁₆in) wide ventilated rib with bead |
| Safety | : sliding safety catch on neck of stock |

### CHARACTERISTICS

| | |
|---|---|
| — material | : steel |
| — finish | : blued barrels, engraved bare metal action |
| — stock | : walnut stock, with pistol-grip |

## Marocchi Trapper

### TECHNICAL DETAILS

| | |
|---|---|
| Gauge/calibre | : 12 or 20 |
| Chamber length | : 70mm (2³/₄in) or 76mm (3in) for 20 gauge |
| Number of barrels | : double-barrels over-and-under |
| Action | : breech-loading |
| Locking | : barrel-block locking |
| Trigger | single trigger |
| Weight | : 2.7–3kg (6lb–6lb 9¹/₂ oz ) |
| Length | : 110 or 113cm (43¹/₄ or 44¹/₂ in) |

| | |
|---|---|
| Barrel length | : 68 or 71cm (26³/₄ or 28in) |
| Ejector | : automatic |
| Choke | to choice |
| Sight | 7mm (⁹/₃₂in) wide ventilated rib and bead |
| Safety | : sliding safety catch on neck of stock |

### CHARACTERISTICS

| | |
|---|---|
| — material | : steel |
| — finish | : blued, or blued barrels and engraved bare metal action |
| — stock | : walnut stock, with pistol-grip |

# Merkel

The German town of Suhl in Thuringia has been renowned for its armourers for more than five hundred years. The finest weapons from the area bear names such as Merkel, Simson, and Haenel. Suhl is mainly known for its hand-made guns and outstandingly fine engraving. Merkel is the best-known of the names. The company mainly produces breech-loading shotguns, combined guns, and double- and triple-barrelled guns, that have at least one rifled barrel.

After World War II, Thuringia fell within the Russian zone and formed part of East Germany as it then was or the DDR and some western countries were not permitted to import such weapons from "behind the Iron Curtain." When the two German republics were reunified after the fall of the Berlin wall, the factories in Suhl once again gained access to a world market.

In terms of their quality and superlative finish, Merkel rifles are among the best there are in the world.

## Merkel 40E

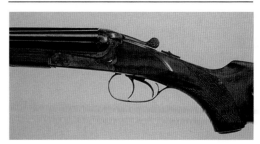

## TECHNICAL DETAILS

| | |
|---|---|
| Gauge/calibre | : 12, 16, 20, or 28 |
| Chamber length | : 70mm (2³/₄in) or 76mm (3in) |
| Number of barrels | : double-barrels side-by-side |
| Action | : breech-loading |
| Locking | : Greener and double barrel-block locking |
| Trigger | twin triggers (Anson & Deeley lock) |
| Weight | : 3—3.2kg (6lb 9¹/₂ oz—7lb) |
| Length | : 112 or 115cm (44¹/₈ or 45¹/₄in) |
| Barrel length | : 68 or 71cm (26¹/₈ or 28in) |
| Ejector | : automatic |
| Choke | : ¹/₂ and full, ¹/₄ and ³/₄, or cylindrical and ¹/₂ |
| Sight | bead |
| Safety | : automatic safety after breaking gun, safety lever in lock, load indicator per barrel |

## CHARACTERISTICS

| | |
|---|---|
| — material | : steel |
| — finish | : tempered or grey lacquered, lightly engraved action |
| — stock | : specially-selected walnut, with pistol-grip and cheek plate |

## *Merkel 50E*

## TECHNICAL DETAILS

| | |
|---|---|
| Gauge/calibre | : 12, 16, 20, or 28 |
| Chamber length | : 70mm (2³/₄in) or 76mm (3in) |
| Number of barrels | : double-barrels side-by-side |
| Action | : breech-loading |
| Locking | : Greener and double barrel-block locking |
| Trigger | twin triggers (Anson & Deeley side-lock) |
| Weight | : 3—3.2kg (6lb 9¹/₂oz—7lb) |
| Length | : 112 or 115cm (44¹/₈ or 45¹/₄in) |
| Barrel length | : 68 or 71cm (26¹/₈ or 28in) |
| Ejector | : automatic |
| Choke | : ¹/₂ and full, ¹/₄ and ³/₄, or cylindrical and ¹/₂ |
| Sight | bead |
| Safety | : automatic safety after breaking gun, safety lever in lock, load indicator per barrel |

## CHARACTERISTICS

| | |
|---|---|
| — material | : steel |
| — finish | : grey lacquered, action and side-lock plates engraved with hunting motif |
| — stock | : specially-selected walnut, with pistol-grip and cheek plate |

## *Merkel 60E Side-lock*

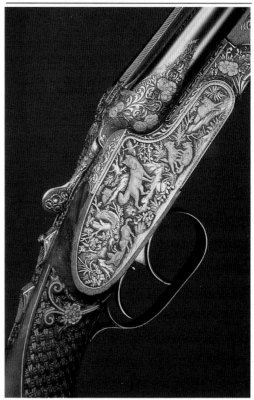

## TECHNICAL DETAILS

| | |
|---|---|
| Gauge/calibre | : 12, 16, 20, or 28 |
| Chamber length | : 70mm (2³/₄in) or 76mm (3in) |
| Number of barrels | : double-barrels side-by-side |
| Action | : breech-loading |
| Locking | : Greener and double barrel-block locking |
| Trigger | twin triggers (Holland & Holland side-lock) |
| Weight | : 3—3.2kg (6lb 9¹/₂ oz—7lb) |
| Length | : 112 or 115cm (44¹/₈ or 45¹/₄in) |
| Barrel length | : 68 or 71cm (26¹/₈ or 28in) |
| Ejector | : automatic |
| Choke | : ¹/₂ and full, ¹/₄ and ³/₄, or cylindrical and ¹/₂ |
| Sight | bead |
| Safety | : autom. safety after breaking gun, safety lever in lock |

## CHARACTERISTICS

| | |
|---|---|
| — material | : steel |
| — finish | : grey lacquered, engraved action and side-lock plates |
| — stock | : specially-selected walnut, with pistol-grip and cheek plate |

## *Merkel 90S Drilling*

### TECHNICAL DETAILS

| | |
|---|---|
| Gauge/calibre | : see below |
| Chamber length | : 70mm (2³/₄in) or 76mm (3in) for 20 gauge |
| Number of barrels | : triple-barrels |

| Action | : breech-loading |
| Locking | : Greener and double barrel-block locking |
| Trigger | twin triggers |
| Weight | : 3.3–3.5kg (7lb 4oz–7lb 11oz) |
| Length | : 107cm (42¹/₈in) |
| Barrel length | : 63cm (24³/₄in) |
| Ejector | : combined extractor for 3 barrels |
| Choke | to choice for smooth-bore barrels |
| Sight | solid rib, folding sight for rifle barrel, bead |
| Safety | : automatic safety after breaking gun, separate cocking for rifle barrel, load indicator per barrel on top of action |

### CHARACTERISTICS

| — material | : steel |
| — finish | : tempered, light engraving of action, barrel, and/or stock |
| — stock | : specially-selected walnut, with pistol-grip and cheek plate |

Available calibres/gauges (smooth-bore): 12, 16, or 20; (rifle) – for 90S: 6.5x57R, 7x65R; for 90K: 8x75RS, .30R Blaser.

## Merkel 95K Drilling (triple-barrel)

### TECHNICAL DETAILS

| Gauge/calibre | : see below |
| Chamber length | : 70mm (2³/₄in) or 76mm (3in) for 20 gauge |
| Number of barrels | : triple-barrels |
| Action | : breech-loading |
| Locking | : Greener and double barrel-block locking |

| Trigger | twin triggers |
| Weight | : 3.3–3.5kg (7lb 4oz–7lb 11oz) |
| Length | : 107cm (42¹/₈in) |
| Barrel length | : 63cm (24³/₄in) |
| Ejector | : combined extractor for 3 barrels |
| Choke | to choice for smooth-bore barrels |
| Sight | solid rib, folding sight for rifle barrel, bead |
| Safety | : automatic safety after breaking gun, separate cocking for rifle barrel by pressing back safety catch, load indicator per barrel on top of action |

### CHARACTERISTICS

| — material | : steel |
| — finish | : tempered or grey lacquered, engraving of action, barrel, and/or stock |
| — stock | : specially-selected walnut, with pistol-grip |

Available calibres/gauges (smooth-bore): 12, 16, or 20; (rifle): 9.3x74R, .30-06 Spr., .308 Win.

## Merkel 95S Drilling (triple-barrel)

### TECHNICAL DETAILS

| Gauge/calibre | : see below |
| Chamber length | : 70mm (2³/₄in) or 76mm (3in) for 20 gauge |
| Number of barrels | : triple-barrels |
| Action | : breech-loading |
| Locking | : Greener and double barrel-block locking |
| Trigger | twin triggers |
| Weight | : 3.3–3.5kg (7lb 4oz–7lb 11oz) |
| Length | : 107cm (42¹/₈in) |
| Barrel length | : 63cm (24³/₄in) |
| Ejector | : combined extractor for 3 barrels |
| Choke | to choice for smooth-bore barrels |
| Sight | solid rib, folding sight for rifle barrel, bead |
| Safety | : automatic safety after breaking gun, separate cocking for rifle barrel by pressing back safety catch, load indicator per barrel on top of action |

### CHARACTERISTICS

| — material | : steel |
| — finish | : tempered or grey lacquered, engravings of hunting motifs on action |
| — stock | : specially-selected walnut, with pistol-grip |

Available calibres/gauges (smooth-bore): 12,
16, or 20; (rifle): 7x57R, 8x57 IRS.
🝐

## *Merkel 150*

| | |
|---|---|
| Sight | fixed notch and bead |
| Safety | : automatic safety after breaking gun, sliding safety catch on neck of stock |

**CHARACTERISTICS**

| | |
|---|---|
| — material | : steel |
| — finish | : blued barrels, bare metal action and side-lock plates with hunting engravings (Holland & Holland side-lock) |
| — stock | : selected walnut, with pistol-grip and cheek plate or straight English stock |

Available calibres: 7x57R, 7x65R, .30-06
Spr., .308 Win., .30 R Blaser, 8x57 IRS,
8x75RS, 9.3x74R. This gun cannot be held
on a shotgun certificate under United Kingdom legislation.
🝐

**TECHNICAL DETAILS**

| | |
|---|---|
| Gauge/calibre | : see below |
| Chamber length | : not applicable |
| Number of barrels | : double-barrels side-by-side |
| Action | : breech-loading |
| Locking | : transverse Greener and double barrel-block locking |
| Trigger | twin triggers |
| Weight | : 3.4–3.6kg (7lb 8oz–7lb 14³/₄oz) |
| Length | : 103cm (40¹/₂in) |
| Barrel length | : 60cm (23⁵/₈in) |
| Ejector | : automatic or extractor |
| Choke | not applicable, rifled barrels |
| Sight | fixed notch and bead |
| Safety | : automatic safety after breaking gun, sliding safety catch on neck of stock |

**CHARACTERISTICS**

| | |
|---|---|
| — material | : steel |
| — finish | : blued barrels, bare metal action and side-plates with hunting engravings (no side-lock) |
| — stock | : selected walnut, with pistol-grip and cheek plate or straight English stock |

Available calibres: 7x57R, 7x65R, .30-06
Spr., .308 Win., .30 R Blaser, 8x57 IRS,
8x75RS, 9.3x74R.
🝐

## *Merkel 160 deluxe*

**TECHNICAL DETAILS**

| | |
|---|---|
| Gauge/calibre | : see below |
| Chamber length | : not applicable |
| Number of barrels | : double-barrels side-by-side |
| Action | : breech-loading |
| Locking | : transverse Greener and double barrel-block locking |
| Trigger | twin triggers |
| Weight | : 3.4–3.6kg (7lb 8oz–7lb 14³/₄oz) |
| Length | : 103cm (40¹/₂ in) |
| Barrel length | : 60cm (23⁵/₈in) |
| Ejector | : automatic or extractor |
| Choke | not applicable, rifled barrels |

## *Merkel 201E*

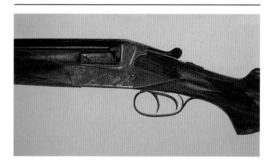

**TECHNICAL DETAILS**

| | |
|---|---|
| Gauge/calibre | : 12, 16, 20, and 28 |
| Chamber length | : 70mm (2³/₄in) or 76mm (3in) |
| Number of barrels | : double-barrels over-and-under |
| Action | : breech-loading |
| Locking | : barrel-block and Kersten locking |
| Trigger | twin triggers |
| Weight | : 3.2–3.4kg (7lb–7lb 8oz) |
| Length | : 112 or 115cm (44¹/₈ or 45¹/₄in) |
| Barrel length | : 68 or 71cm (26³/₄ or 28in) |
| Ejector | : automatic |
| Choke | ¹/₂ and full, ¹/₄ and ³/₄, or cylindrical and ¹/₂ |
| Sight | bead |
| Safety | : automatic safety after breaking gun, sliding safety catch on neck of stock |

## CHARACTERISTICS

- material : steel
- finish : blued barrels, bare metal action with hunting engravings
- stock : walnut stock, with pistol-grip

## Merkel 203E

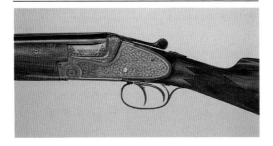

### TECHNICAL DETAILS

| | |
|---|---|
| Gauge/calibre | : 12, 16, 20, and 28 |
| Chamber length | : 70mm (2³/₄in) or 76mm (3in) |
| Number of barrels | : double-barrels over-and-under |
| Action | : breech-loading |
| Locking | : barrel-block and Kersten locking |
| Trigger | twin triggers |
| Weight | : 3–3.2kg (6lb 9¹/₂ oz–7lb) |
| Length | : 112 or 115cm (44¹/₈ or 45¹/₄in) |
| Barrel length | : 68 or 71cm (26³/₄ or 28in) |
| Ejector | : automatic |
| Choke | ¹/₂ and full, ¹/₄ and ³/₄, or cylindrical and ¹/₂ |
| Sight | bead |
| Safety | : automatic safety after breaking gun, sliding safety catch on neck of stock |

### CHARACTERISTICS

- material : steel
- finish : blued barrels, bare metal action and Holland & Holland side-lock with decorative engravings
- stock : straight English stock of walnut

## Merkel 211 Combination gun

### TECHNICAL DETAILS

| | |
|---|---|
| Gauge/calibre | : see below |
| Chamber length | : smooth-bore: 70mm (2³/₄in) or 76mm (3in) |
| Number of barrels | : double-barrels over-and-under |
| Action | : breech-loading |
| Locking | : barrel-block locking combined with Kersten locking |
| Trigger | twin triggers |

---

| | |
|---|---|
| Weight | : 3.2kg (7lb) |
| Length | : 105–108cm (41³/₈–42¹/₂in) |
| Barrel length | : 68–71cm (26³/₄–28in) |
| Ejector | : extractor |
| Choke | full |
| Sight | solid barrel rib and bead |
| Safety | : sliding safety catch on neck of stock, automatic safety after breaking gun, load indicator on top of action |

### CHARACTERISTICS

- material : steel
- finish : blued barrels, bare metal action with hunting engravings
- stock : selected walnut, with pistol-grip and cheek plate

Available calibres/gauges (upper smooth-bore barrel): 12, 16, 20, and 28; (bottom rifle barrel): 5.6x52R, 7x57R, 7x65R, 8x57 IRS, 8x75RS, 9.3x74R, .30 R Blaser, .308 Win., .30-06 Spr.

## Merkel 303E

### TECHNICAL DETAILS

| | |
|---|---|
| Gauge/calibre | : 12, 16, 20, and 28 |
| Chamber length | : 70mm (2³/₄in) or 76mm (3in) |
| Number of barrels | : double-barrels over-and-under |
| Action | : breech-loading |
| Locking | : barrel-block locking and Kersten locking |
| Trigger | twin triggers |
| Weight | : 3.2–3.4kg (7lb–7lb 8oz) |
| Length | : 112 or 115cm (44¹/₈ or 45¹/₄in) |
| Barrel length | : 68 or 71cm (26³/₄ or 28in) |
| Ejector | : automatic |
| Choke | ¹/₂ and full, ¹/₄ and ³/₄, or cylindrical and ¹/₂ |
| Sight | bead |
| Safety | : automatic safety after breaking gun, sliding safety catch on neck of stock |

### CHARACTERISTICS

- material : steel
- finish : blued barrels, bare metal action and Holland & Holland side-lock with decorative engravings
- stock : stock of specially-selected walnut, with pistol-grip and cheek plate

## Merkel 313E Luxury Combination gun

**TECHNICAL DETAILS**

| | |
|---|---|
| Gauge/calibre | : see below |
| Chamber length | : smooth-bore: 70mm (2³/₄in) or 76mm (3in) |
| Number of barrels | : double-barrels over-and-under |
| Action | : breech-loading |
| Locking | : barrel-block locking combined with Kersten locking |
| Trigger | twin triggers |
| Weight | : 3.2kg (7lb) |
| Length | : 108cm (42¹/₂in) |
| Barrel length | : 71cm (28in) |
| Ejector | : automatic |
| Choke | full |
| Sight | solid barrel rib and bead, special mount for telescopic sight |
| Safety | : sliding safety catch on neck of stock, automatic safety after breaking gun, load indicator on top of action |

**CHARACTERISTICS**

| | |
|---|---|
| — material | : steel |
| — finish | : blued barrels, bare metal action with gold inlaid hunting engravings on side-lock plates |
| — stock | : selected walnut, with pistol-grip and cheek plate |

Available calibres/gauges (upper smooth-bore barrel): 12, 16, 20, and 28; (bottom rifle barrel): 5.6x52R, 7x57R, 7x65R, 8x57 IRS, 8x75RS, 9.3x74R, .30 R Blaser, .308 Win., .30-06 Spr.

# Mitchell Arms Inc.

The American firm of Mitchell Arms was started in 1984 by John Mitchell after the bankruptcy in 1984 of the High Standard Arms concern, of which he had been a director. Mitchell Arms is based in Santa Ana, California. At first the new company directed its efforts towards making military-style weapons in .22 LR calibre, such as the Colt M16, Kalashnikov AK-47, and French MAS assault rifle. Mitchell Arms also made replicas of the Colt Single Action Army (Peacemaker) in .44 Magnum and .45 Long Colt calibres and traded in a range of replicas of large calibre black-powder revolvers originally made by Colt and Remington. These were produced by the famous Uberti arms factory in Italy.

Mitchell produces a number of models of carbines that externally resemble submachine guns which used to be manufactured by the American firm, Feather, as AT-22 and AT-9. The company has also made single-barrel smooth-bores since 1994. The range includes pump-action shotguns for hunting but also riot guns for police and military use. Most of the Mitchell pump-action guns have a barrel length of 18³/4in (51cm) or 20in (51cm) but model 9108 is available with a 24in (61cm) barrel.

## Mitchell High Standard 9108

MITCHELL ARMS MODEL 9108 12-GAUGE PUMP-ACTION

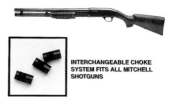

INTERCHANGEABLE CHOKE SYSTEM FITS ALL MITCHELL SHOTGUNS

**TECHNICAL DETAILS**

| | |
|---|---|
| Gauge/calibre | : 12 |
| Chamber length | : 3in (76mm) |
| Number of barrels | : single-barrel |
| Magazine | : tubular magazine for 7 cartridges |
| Action | : pump-action |
| Locking | : falling block locking |
| Trigger | single trigger |
| Weight | : 7lb 8oz (3.4kg) |
| Length | : 43³/4in (110cm) |
| Barrel length | : 24in (61cm) |
| Ejector | : extractor |
| Choke | interchangeable chokes |
| Sight | bead |
| Safety | : push-button safety catch at rear of trigger guard, closing safety |

**CHARACTERISTICS**

| | |
|---|---|
| — material | : steel |
| — finish | : blued |
| — stock | : hardwood stock, with pistol-grip |

The magazine capacity of this shotgun exceeds the maximum of 2 for a United

Kingdom shotgun certificate. Similar restrictions apply in other European countries.

# Mossberg

The American firm of Mossberg of North Haven, Connecticut, celebrated its 75th anniversary in 1997. The company has produced a great deal of technical innovation in its time which other manufacturers have copied.

Many of the improvements have been designed in such a way that they can also be used in older Mossberg shotguns.

The company has a basic range with models suitable for various purposes. For instance the 835 Ulti-Mag is available in a deluxe version but also as slug gun, combination gun, and various field and hunting versions including camouflage finish, and as an outstanding hunting gun – the Viking.

The company also make riot guns for military use by the US Army and others.

Only Mossberg guns are able to meet the stringent military specifications.

Mossberg took over the Advanced Ordnance Corporation in 1966, which makes parts and special tools for the armaments, automobile, and aerospace industries.

The company also set-up a joint venture in Israel in 1996 with Israel Military Industries. This new company, Uzi America supplies the Jericho pistol (known as Eagle in North America), Uzi machine pistol, and Galil rifle.

The customers are principally governments.

## Mossberg 500 American Field

**TECHNICAL DETAILS**

| | |
|---|---|
| Gauge/calibre | : 12 |
| Chamber length | : 3in (76mm) |
| Number of barrels | : single-barrel with compensator vents |
| Magazine | : 2 cartridges |
| Action | : pump-action |
| Locking | : falling block locking |
| Trigger | single trigger |

| | |
|---|---|
| Weight | : 7lb 4oz (3.3kg) |
| Length | : 48in (122cm) |
| Barrel length | : 28in (71cm) |
| Ejector | : extractor |
| Choke | Accu-choke interchangeable chokes |
| Sight | ventilated rib and bead |
| Safety | : sliding safety catch on top of action body |

**CHARACTERISTICS**

| | |
|---|---|
| – material | : steel |
| – finish | : blued |
| – stock | : hardwood stock, with pistol-grip |

## Mossberg 500 Bantam Camo

**TECHNICAL DETAILS**

| | |
|---|---|
| Gauge/calibre | : 20 |
| Chamber length | : 3in (76mm) |
| Number of barrels | : single-barrel with compensator vents |
| Magazine | : 2 cartridges |
| Action | : pump-action |
| Locking | : falling block locking |
| Trigger | single trigger |
| Weight | : 6lb 4oz (2.8kg) |
| Length | : 44in (112cm) |
| Barrel length | : 22in (56cm) |
| Ejector | : extractor |
| Choke | Accu-choke interchangeable chokes |
| Sight | ventilated rib and bead |
| Safety | : sliding safety catch on top of action body |

**CHARACTERISTICS**

| | |
|---|---|
| – material | : steel |
| – finish | : plastic coating in camouflage colours |
| – stock | : hardwood stock in camouflage colours, with pistol-grip |

The barrel of this shotgun is too short for a United Kingdom shotgun certificate (minimum length 24in (61cm).

## Mossberg 500 Crown Grade

### TECHNICAL DETAILS
Gauge/calibre : 12 or .410
Chamber length : 3in (76mm)
Number of barrels : single-barrel with compensator vents
Magazine : 2 cartridges
Action : pump-action
Locking : falling block locking
Trigger single trigger
Weight : 7lb 4oz (3.3kg)
Length : 48in (122cm)
Barrel length : 28in (71cm)
Ejector : extractor
Choke Accu-choke interchangeable chokes
Sight ventilated rib and bead
Safety : sliding safety catch on top of action body

### CHARACTERISTICS
— material : steel
— finish : blued, with decorative engraving of action body
— stock : walnut stock, with pistol-grip

## Mossberg 500 Home Security

### TECHNICAL DETAILS
Gauge/calibre : 20
Chamber length : 3in (76mm)
Number of barrels : single-barrel with compensator vents
Magazine : 8 cartridges
Action : pump-action
Locking : falling block locking
Trigger single trigger
Weight : 7lb (3.2kg)
Length : 46½ in (118cm)
Barrel length : 21in (53cm)
Ejector : extractor
Choke cylindrical
Sight bead
Safety : sliding safety catch on top of action body

### CHARACTERISTICS
— material : steel

— finish : matt black coating
— stock : black plastic stock, with pistol-grip

The barrel of this shotgun is too short for a United Kingdom shotgun certificate (minimum length 24in/61cm). The magazine too has to be permanently limited to 2 cartridges to comply for UK requirements.

## Mossberg 500 Hunter

### TECHNICAL DETAILS
Gauge/calibre : 12
Chamber length : 3in (76mm)
Number of barrels : single-barrel with compensator vents
Magazine : 2 cartridges
Action : pump-action
Locking : falling block locking
Trigger single trigger
Weight : 7lb 14oz (3.6kg)
Length : 54in (137cm)
Barrel length : 36in (91cm)
Ejector : extractor
Choke Accu-choke interchangeable chokes
Sight bead
Safety : sliding safety catch on top of action body

### CHARACTERISTICS
— material : steel
— finish : blued, with decorative engraving on action body
— stock : hardwood stock, with pistol-grip

## Mossberg 500 Mariner

### TECHNICAL DETAILS
Gauge/calibre : 12
Chamber length : 3in (76mm)
Number of barrels : single-barrel with compensator vents
Magazine : 6 cartridges
Action : pump-action
Locking : falling block locking
Trigger single trigger
Weight : 7lb (3.2kg)
Length : 44in (112cm)

| | |
|---|---|
| Barrel length | : 18¹/₂ in (47cm) |
| Ejector | : extractor |
| Choke | cylindrical |
| Sight | bead or adjustable ghost ring notched sight with bead |
| Safety | : sliding safety catch on top of action body |

**CHARACTERISTICS**

| | |
|---|---|
| — material | : steel |
| — finish | : matt-finish nickel plating |
| — stock | : black plastic stock, with pistol-grip |

The barrel of this shotgun is too short and the magazine exceeds the maximum of 2 cartridges for a United Kingdom shotgun certificate (minimum length 24in/61cm).

## Mossberg 500 Persuader

**TECHNICAL DETAILS**

| | |
|---|---|
| Gauge/calibre | : 12 |
| Chamber length | : 3in (76mm) |
| Number of barrels | : single-barrel with compensator vents |
| Magazine | : 6 cartridges |
| Action | : pump-action |
| Locking | : falling block locking |
| Trigger | single trigger |
| Weight | : 7lb (3.2kg) |
| Length | : 44in (112cm) |
| Barrel length | : 18¹/₂in (47cm) |
| Ejector | : extractor |
| Choke | cylindrical |
| Sight | adjustable ghost ring notched sight with bead |
| Safety | : sliding safety catch on top of action body |

**CHARACTERISTICS**

| | |
|---|---|
| — material | : steel |
| — finish | : matt-black |
| — stock | : black plastic stock, with pistol-grip |

The barrel of this shotgun is too short and the magazine exceeds the maximum of 2 cartridges for a United Kingdom shotgun certificate (minimum length 24in/61cm).

## Mossberg 500 Trophy Combo

**TECHNICAL DETAILS**

| | |
|---|---|
| Gauge/calibre | : 12 |

| | |
|---|---|
| Chamber length | : 3in (76mm) |
| Number of barrels | : single-barrel with compensator vents |
| Magazine | : 2 cartridges |
| Action | : pump-action |
| Locking | : falling block locking |
| Trigger | single trigger |
| Weight | : 7lb 4oz (3.3kg) |
| Length | : 44¹/₈ or 48in (112 or 122cm) |
| Barrel length | : 28in (71cm) and 24in (61cm) rifled barrel for slugs |
| Ejector | : extractor |
| Choke | smooth-bore barrel: Accu-choke interchangeable chokes |
| Sight | ventilated rib and bead |
| Safety | : sliding safety catch on top of action body |

**CHARACTERISTICS**

| | |
|---|---|
| — material | : steel |
| — finish | : blued, with decorative engraving on action body |
| — stock | : hardwood stock, with pistol-grip |

## Mossberg 500 USA Mil-Specification

**TECHNICAL DETAILS**

| | |
|---|---|
| Gauge/calibre | : 12 |
| Chamber length | : 3in (76mm) |
| Number of barrels | : single-barrel with compensator vents |
| Magazine | : 6 cartridges |
| Action | : pump-action |
| Locking | : falling block locking |
| Trigger | single trigger |
| Weight | : 7lb 4oz (3.3kg) |
| Length | : 42in (107cm) |
| Barrel length | : 20in (51cm) |
| Ejector | : extractor |
| Choke | cylindrical |
| Sight | bead |
| Safety | : sliding safety catch on top of action body |

**CHARACTERISTICS**

| | |
|---|---|
| — material | : steel |
| — finish | : matt-green |
| — stock | : green plastic stock, with pistol-grip |

The barrel of this shotgun is too short and the magazine exceeds the maximum of 2 cartridges for a United Kingdom shotgun certificate (minimum length 24in/61cm). Similar restrictions apply in certain other European countries.

## Mossberg 500 Viking

**TECHNICAL DETAILS**
Gauge/calibre : 12
Chamber length : 3in (76mm)
Number of barrels : single-barrel with compensator vents
Magazine : 2 cartridges
Action : pump-action
Locking : falling block locking
Trigger single trigger
Weight : 7lb (3.2kg)
Length : 48in (122cm)
Barrel length : 28in (71cm)
Ejector : extractor
Choke Accu-choke interchangeable chokes
Sight ventilated rib and bead
Safety : sliding safety catch on top of action body

**CHARACTERISTICS**
— material : steel
— finish : matt blued
— stock : green plastic stock, with pistol-grip

## Mossberg 500 Viking Hunter

**TECHNICAL DETAILS**
Gauge/calibre : 12
Chamber length : 3in (76mm)
Number of barrels : single-barrel with compensator vents
Magazine : 2 cartridges
Action : pump-action
Locking : falling block locking
Trigger single trigger

Weight : 7lb (3.2kg)
Length : 48in (122cm)
Barrel length : 24in (61cm)
Ejector : extractor
Choke not applicable, rifled barrel
Sight 1.5–4.5 Tasco telescopic sight included
Safety : sliding safety catch on top of action body

**CHARACTERISTICS**
— material : steel
— finish : matt blued
— stock : green plastic stock, with pistol-grip

The gun is provided with a plastic gun case.

## Mossberg 590 Mariner

**TECHNICAL DETAILS**
Gauge/calibre : 12
Chamber length : 3in (76mm)
Number of barrels : single-barrel with compensator
Magazine : 9 cartridges
Action : pump-action
Locking : falling block locking
Trigger single trigger
Weight : 7lb (3.2kg)
Length : 44in (112cm)
Barrel length : 20in (51cm)
Ejector : extractor
Choke cylindrical
Sight bead or adjustable ghost ring notched sight with bead
Safety : sliding safety catch on top of action body

**CHARACTERISTICS**
— material : steel
— finish : matt-finish nickel plating
— stock : black plastic stock, with pistol-grip

The barrel of this shotgun is too short and the magazine exceeds the maximum of 2 cartridges for a United Kingdom shotgun certificate (minimum length 24in/61cm).

## Mossberg 590 Persuader

**TECHNICAL DETAILS**
Gauge/calibre : 12
Chamber length : 3in (76mm)

Number of barrels : single-barrel with compensator vents
Magazine : 9 cartridges
Action : pump-action
Locking : falling block locking
Trigger single trigger
Weight : 7lb 4oz (3.3kg)
Length : 45in (114cm)
Barrel length : 20in (45cm)
Ejector : extractor
Choke cylindrical
Sight adjustable ghost ring notched sight with bead
Safety : sliding safety catch on top of action body

CHARACTERISTICS
— material : steel
— finish : matt-black
— stock : black plastic stock, with pistol-grip

The barrel of this shotgun is too short and the magazine exceeds the maximum of 2 cartridges for a United Kingdom shotgun certificate (minimum length 24in/61cm).

## Mossberg 695 Hunter

TECHNICAL DETAILS
Gauge/calibre : 12
Chamber length : 3in (76mm)
Number of barrels : single-barrel with compensator vents
Magazine : 2 cartridges
Action : bolt-action
Locking : locking lugs
Trigger single trigger
Weight : 7lb (3.2kg)
Length : 54in (137cm)
Barrel length : 36in (91cm)
Ejector : double extractor
Choke Accu-choke interchangeable chokes
Sight notched sight and bead
Safety : turnable safety ring at rear of bolt

CHARACTERISTICS
material : steel
— finish : blued

— stock : black plastic

## Mossberg 695 Hunter Slug Gun

TECHNICAL DETAILS
Gauge/calibre : 12
Chamber length : 3in (76mm)
Number of barrels : single-barrel with compensator vents
Magazine : 2 cartridges
Action : bolt-action
Locking : locking lugs
Trigger single trigger
Weight : 6lb 13oz (3.1kg)
Length : 44in (112cm)
Barrel length : 22in (56cm)
Ejector : double extractor
Choke Accu-choke interchangeable chokes
Sight notched sight and bead, includes 1.5–4.5 Bushnell telescopic sight
Safety : turnable safety ring at rear of bolt

CHARACTERISTICS
— material : steel
— finish : matt black
— stock : matt black plastic, with pistol-grip

## Mossberg 695 Woodland Turkey

TECHNICAL DETAILS
Gauge/calibre : 12
Chamber length : 3in (76mm)
Number of barrels : single-barrel with compensator vents
Magazine : 2 cartridges
Action : bolt-action
Locking : locking lugs
Trigger single trigger
Weight : 6lb 13oz (3.1kg)
Length : 44in (112cm)
Barrel length : 22in (56cm)

| Ejector | : double extractor |
|---|---|
| Choke | Accu-choke interchangeable chokes |
| Sight | notch sight and bead |
| Safety | : turnable safety ring at rear of bolt |

**CHARACTERISTICS**

| – material | : steel |
|---|---|
| – finish | : special coating in camouflage colours |
| – stock | : plastic stock in camouflage colours, with pistol-grip |

## Mossberg 835 Ulti-Mag American Field

**TECHNICAL DETAILS**

| Gauge/calibre | : 12 |
|---|---|
| Chamber length | : 3³/₄in (89mm) can also be used for 2³/₄in (70mm) and 3in (76mm) cartridges |
| Number of barrels | : single-barrel with compensator vents |
| Magazine | : 2 cartridges |
| Action | : pump-action |
| Locking | : falling block locking |
| Trigger | single trigger |
| Weight | : 7lb 11oz (3.5kg) |
| Length | : 48¹/₂ in (123cm) |
| Barrel length | : 28in (71cm) |
| Ejector | : extractor |
| Choke | Accu-choke interchangeable chokes |
| Sight | ventilated rib and bead |
| Safety | : sliding safety catch on top of action body |

**CHARACTERISTICS**

| – material | : steel |
|---|---|
| – finish | : blued |
| – stock | : hardwood stock, with pistol-grip |

## Mossberg 835 Ulti-Mag Crown Grade

**TECHNICAL DETAILS**

| Gauge/calibre | : 12 |
|---|---|
| Chamber length | : 3¹/₂ in (89mm) can also be used for 2³/₄in (70mm) and 3in (76mm) cartridges |
| Number of barrels | : single-barrel with compensator vents |
| Magazine | : 2 cartridges |

| Action | : pump-action |
|---|---|
| Locking | : falling block locking |
| Trigger | single trigger |
| Weight | : 7lb 11oz (3.5kg) |
| Length | : 48¹/₂ in (123cm) |
| Barrel length | : 28in (71cm) |
| Ejector | : extractor |
| Choke | Accu-choke interchangeable chokes |
| Sight | ventilated rib and bead |
| Safety | : sliding safety catch on top of action body |

**CHARACTERISTICS**

| – material | : steel |
|---|---|
| – finish | : blued, with decorative engraving on action body |
| – stock | : walnut stock, with pistol-grip |

## Mossberg 9200 Crown Grade Bantam

**TECHNICAL DETAILS**

| Gauge/calibre | : 12 |
|---|---|
| Chamber length | : 3in (76mm) |
| Number of barrels | : single-barrel |
| Magazine | : 2 cartridges |
| Action | : pump-action |
| Locking | : falling block locking |
| Trigger | single trigger |
| Weight | : 6lb 8oz (3kg) |
| Length | : 41in (104cm) |
| Barrel length | : 22in (56cm) |
| Ejector | : extractor |
| Choke | Accu-choke interchangeable chokes |
| Sight | ventilated rib and bead |
| Safety | : sliding safety catch on top of action body |

**CHARACTERISTICS**

| – material | : steel |
|---|---|
| – finish | : blued |
| – stock | : walnut stock, with pistol-grip |

The barrel of this shotgun is too short for a United Kingdom shotgun certificate (minimum length 24in/61cm). Similar restrictions apply in certain other European countries.

## Mossberg 9200 Crown Grade Hunter

**TECHNICAL DETAILS**

| Gauge/calibre | : 12 |
|---|---|

Chamber length   : 3in (76mm)
Number of barrels : single-barrel
Magazine        : 2 cartridges
Action          : semi-automatic (gas-pressure operated)
Locking         : falling block locking
Trigger          single trigger
Weight          : 7lb 8oz (3.4kg)
Length          : 48in (122cm)
Barrel length    : 28in (71cm)
Ejector         : extractor
Choke            Accu-choke interchangeable chokes
Sight            ventilated rib and bead
Safety          : sliding safety catch on top of action body

### CHARACTERISTICS
— material       : steel
— finish         : blued
— stock          : walnut stock, with pistol-grip

## Mossberg 9200 Hunter Mossy Oak

### TECHNICAL DETAILS
Gauge/calibre    : 12
Chamber length   : 3in (76mm)
Number of barrels : single-barrel
Magazine        : 2 cartridges
Action          : semi-automatic (gas-pressure operated)
Locking         : falling block locking
Trigger          single trigger
Weight          : 7lb 8oz (3.4kg)
Length          : 44in (112cm)
Barrel length    : 24in (61cm)
Ejector         : extractor
Choke            Accu-choke interchangeable chokes
Sight            ventilated rib and bead
Safety          : sliding safety catch on top of action body

### CHARACTERISTICS
— material       : steel
— finish         : coating in camouflage colours
— stock          : plastic stock in camouflage colours, with pistol-grip

## Mossberg 9200 Hunter Realtree

### TECHNICAL DETAILS
Gauge/calibre    : 12
Chamber length   : 3in (76mm)
Number of barrels : single-barrel
Magazine        : 2 cartridges
Action          : semi-automatic (gas-pressure operated)
Locking         : falling block locking
Trigger          single trigger
Weight          : 7lb 8oz (3.4kg)
Length          : 44in (112cm)
Barrel length    : 24in (61cm)
Ejector         : extractor
Choke            Accu-choke interchangeable chokes
Sight            ventilated rib and bead
Safety          : sliding safety catch on top of action body

### CHARACTERISTICS
— material       : steel
— finish         : coating with leaf motif
— stock          : plastic stock with leaf motif and pistol-grip

## Mossberg 9200 Pursuader

### TECHNICAL DETAILS
Gauge/calibre    : 12
Chamber length   : 3in (76mm)
Number of barrels : single-barrel
Magazine        : 5 cartridges
Action          : semi-automatic (gas-pressure operated)
Locking         : falling block locking
Trigger          single trigger
Weight          : 7lb (3.2kg)
Length          : 44in (112cm)
Barrel length    : 18¹/₂ in (47cm)
Ejector         : extractor
Choke            cylindrical
Sight            bead
Safety          : sliding safety catch on top of action body

### CHARACTERISTICS
— material       : steel

| | |
|---|---|
| – finish | : matt black |
| – stock | : black plastic stock, with pistol-grip |

The barrel of this shotgun is too short and the magazine exceeds the maximum of 2 cartridges for a United Kingdom shotgun certificate (minimum length 24in/61cm).

## Mossberg 9200 Trophy Combo

**TECHNICAL DETAILS**

| | |
|---|---|
| Gauge/calibre | : 12 |
| Chamber length | : 3in (76mm) |
| Number of barrels | : single-barrel |
| Magazine | : 2 cartridges |
| Action | : semi-automatic (gas-pressure operated) |
| Locking | : falling block locking |
| Trigger | single trigger |
| Weight | : 7lb 4oz (3.3kg) |
| Length | : 44¹/₈ or 48in (112 or 122cm) |
| Barrel length | : 28in (71cm) and 24in (61cm) rifled barrel for slugs |
| Ejector | : extractor |
| Choke | smooth-bore barrel: Accu-choke interchangeable chokes |
| Sight | ventilated rib and bead |
| Safety | : sliding safety catch on top of action body |

**CHARACTERISTICS**

| | |
|---|---|
| – material | : steel |
| – finish | : blued, with decorative engraving on action body |
| – stock | : hardwood stock, with pistol-grip and adjustable plastic cheek plate |

## Mossberg 9200 Viking Hunter

**TECHNICAL DETAILS**

| | |
|---|---|
| Gauge/calibre | : 12 |
| Chamber length | : 3in (76mm) |
| Number of barrels | : single-barrel |
| Magazine | : 2 cartridges |
| Action | : semi-automatic (gas-pressure operated) |
| Locking | : falling block locking |

| | |
|---|---|
| Trigger | single trigger |
| Weight | : 7lb 8oz (3.4kg) |
| Length | : 48in (122cm) |
| Barrel length | : 28in (71cm) |
| Ejector | : extractor |
| Choke | Accu-choke interchangeable chokes |
| Sight | ventilated rib and bead |
| Safety | : sliding safety catch on top of action body |

**CHARACTERISTICS**

| | |
|---|---|
| – material | : steel |
| – finish | : matt black |
| – stock | : green plastic stock, with pistol-grip |

# Norinco/Norconia

Norinco is the state export company for the Chinese weapons industry. Norinco trades the products of several state enterprises such as the small-bore weapons of Golden Arrow, that are made in the Zhongzhou Machinery Plant in He Nan. The military rifles come from Plant 66 in Beijing. Norinco keeps a sharp eye on the success of particular weapons and where there is demand for a specific type, it produces and sells them for very low prices. For instance they make a Chinese version of the Dragunov sniper's rifle under the type name NDM-86 that is available not only in the original 7.62 x 54R calibre, but also in .308 Winchester. The same is true of "replicas" of the well-known Kalashnikov SKS rifle that are available from them in the original 7.62 x 39mm and .223 Remington calibres. The Chinese also make the renowned AK-47 in both calibres, known as type 84S-AK in five different versions. In 1992, Norinco even brought out their own version of the Mauser (K98) KKW Wehrsport .22 LR rifle. Norinco have two models of shotgun: a double-barrels over-and-under and a pump-action shotgun. Norinco is represented in Europe by Norconia in Rottendorf, Germany, and in North America, by Interarms and Century International Arms.

## Norinco HL12-102 pump-action shotgun

**TECHNICAL DETAILS**

| | |
|---|---|
| Gauge/calibre | : 12 |
| Chamber length | : 70mm (2³/₄in) |
| Number of barrels | : single-barrel |

| Magazine | : tubular magazine for 2–5 cartridges |
| Action | : pump-action |
| Locking | : falling block locking |
| Trigger | single trigger |
| Weight | : 3.3kg (7lb 4oz) |
| Length | : 121cm (47⁵/₈in) |
| Barrel length | : 71cm (28in) |
| Ejector | : extractor |
| Choke | interchangeable chokes |
| Sight | bead |
| Safety | : push-button safety catch in rear of trigger guard |

**CHARACTERISTICS**
| — material | : steel |
| — finish | : blued |
| — stock | : hardwood stock, with pistol-grip |

## *Norinco HL12-203 over-and-under*

**TECHNICAL DETAILS**
| Gauge/calibre | : 12 |
| Chamber length | : 70mm (2³/₄in) |
| Number of barrels | : double-barrels over-and-under |
| Action | : breech-loading |
| Locking | : barrel-block locking |
| Trigger | single trigger |
| Weight | : 3.7kg (8lb 2¹/₁₀oz) |
| Length | : 120cm (47¹/₄in) |
| Barrel length | : 75cm (29¹/₂in) |
| Ejector | : extractor |
| Choke | interchangeable chokes |
| Sight | ventilated rib and bead |
| Safety | : sliding safety catch on neck of stock |

**CHARACTERISTICS**
| — material | : steel |
| — finish | : blued |
| — stock | : hardwood stock, with pistol-grip |

# Perazzi

The Italian family business of Perazzi was established in 1952 by the present owner, Daniele Perazzi. Both his son Mauro and daughter Roberta now work for the firm. Armi Perazzi is based at Botticino Mattina in Brescia. Because Armi Perazzi is a relatively modern business, it was able to start out using modern technology and today uses computer controlled (CNC) production machinery.

The company also puts a big emphasis on providing service. Armi Perazzi employs about 100 people. The main range of the company is divided into trap, skeet, sporting, and hunting guns.

Within these ranges guns are made with and without removable trigger mechanisms. Perazzi guns for the hunter can, if desired, be engraved with all manner of fine designs such as gun dogs, game, or landscapes, lakes, and woodland views.

Those who are on the Internet should look at the Perazzi home page.

Perazzi's principal activity is making sporting guns for shooters.

The first gold medal achieved with a Perazzi gun was in the Tokyo Olympiad in 1964 and since then countless international trophies have fallen to Perazzi guns, including the 1996 US Olympic Games at Atlanta when the gold, silver and bronze medals for Olympic Trap went to competitors with Perazzi guns: gold– Michael Diamond, Australia (MX8), silver – Josh Lakatos, USA (MX10, and bronze – Lance Bade, USA (Mirage).

The women's double trap gold medal was won by Ms. K. Rhode of USA with an MX12 model.

## *Perazzi DB81 Special American Single Trap Combo*

**TECHNICAL DETAILS**
| Gauge/calibre | : 12 |
| Chamber length | : 76mm (3in) |
| Number of barrels | : single-barrel |
| Action | : breech-loading |
| Locking | : barrel-block locking |
| Trigger | single trigger, removable trigger |
| Weight | : 3.7–3.9kg (8lb 2¹/₁₀oz–8lb 9¹/₁₀oz) |

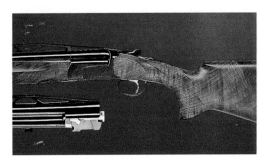

Length : 118–129cm (46¹/₂–50³/₄in)
Barrel length : 75–86cm (29¹/₂–33⁷/₈in)
Ejector : automatic
Choke interchangeable chokes
Sight 11mm (⁷/₁₆ in) wide raised ventilated rib and bead
Safety : sliding safety catch on neck of stock

CHARACTERISTICS
— material : steel
— finish : blued
— stock : walnut stock, with pistol-grip and adjustable comb

This gun is supplied with an interchangeable over-and-under double-barrels set.

## *Perazzi Extra*

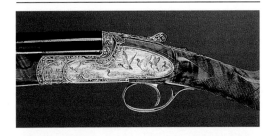

**TECHNICAL DETAILS**
Gauge/calibre : 12, 20, 28, or .410
Chamber length : 70mm (2³/₄in) or 76mm (3in)
Number of barrels : double-barrels over-and-under
Action : breech-loading
Locking : barrel-block locking
Trigger single trigger
Weight : 3.1–3.2kg (6lb 13oz–7lb)
Length : 110–114cm (43¹/₄–44⁷/₈in)
Barrel length : 66, 68, or 70cm (26, 26³/₄, or 27¹/₂in)
Ejector : automatic or extractor
Choke ¹/₄ and ³/₄, ¹/₄ and full, or interchangeable chokes
Sight 7mm (⁹/₃₂in) wide ventilated rib and bead
Safety : sliding safety catch on neck of stock, also barrel selector

**CHARACTERISTICS**
— material : steel
— finish : blued barrels, bare metal action and side-plates with hunting engravings (no side-lock)
— stock : straight English stock of selected walnut

## *Perazzi Extra Gold*

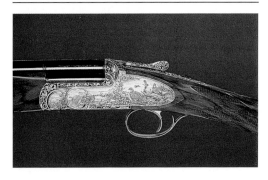

**TECHNICAL DETAILS**
Gauge/calibre : 12, 20, 28, or .410
Chamber length : 70mm (2³/₄in) or 76mm (3in)
Number of barrels : double-barrels over-and-under
Action : breech-loading
Locking : barrel-block locking
Trigger single trigger
Weight : 3.1–3.2kg (6lb 13oz–7lb)
Length : 110–114cm (43¹/₄–44⁷/₈in)
Barrel length : 66, 68, or 70cm (26, 26³/₄, or 27¹/₂in)
Ejector : automatic or extractor
Choke fixed chokes to choice, or interchangeable chokes
Sight 7mm (⁹/₃₂in) wide ventilated rib and bead
Safety : sliding safety catch on neck of stock, also barrel selector

**CHARACTERISTICS**
— material : steel
— finish : blued barrels, bare metal action and side-plates with gold inlaid hunting engravings (no side-lock)
— stock : straight English stock of specially-selected walnut

## *Perazzi Mirage*

**TECHNICAL DETAILS**
Gauge/calibre : 12

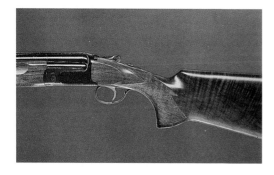

Chamber length : 70mm (2³/₄in) or 76mm (3in)
Number of barrels : double-barrels over-and-under
Action : breech-loading
Locking : barrel-block locking
Trigger single trigger, removable trigger
Weight : 3.1–3.5kg (6lb 13oz–7lb 11oz)
Length : 104–124cm (41–48³/₄in)
Barrel length : 68–80cm (26³/₄–31¹/₂in)
Ejector : automatic
Choke ³/₄ and full, ¹/₂ and full, full and full, cylindrical, or interchangeable chokes
Sight 11mm (⁹/₃₂in) wide ventilated rib and bead
Safety : sliding safety catch on neck of stock

### CHARACTERISTICS
— material : steel
— finish : blued
— stock : walnut stock, with pistol-grip

This gun is available in Olympic Trap, Double Trap, Skeet, Sporting, and Pigeon versions.

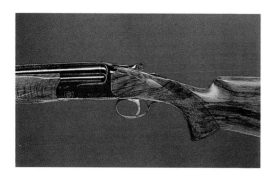

## Perazzi MX1B Pigeon

### TECHNICAL DETAILS
Gauge/calibre : 12
Chamber length : 70mm (2³/₄in) or 76mm (3in)
Number of barrels : double-barrels over-and-under
Action : breech-loading
Locking : barrel-block locking
Trigger single trigger, removable trigger

Weight : 3.1kg (6lb 13oz)
Length : 104cm (41in)
Barrel length : 70cm (27¹/₂ in)
Ejector : automatic
Choke ¹/₂ and full, full and full, or interchangeable chokes
Sight 11mm (⁹/₃₂in) wide raised ventilated rib and bead
Safety : sliding safety catch on neck of stock

### CHARACTERISTICS
— material : steel
— finish : blued
— stock : walnut stock, with pistol-grip

## Perazzi MX8 Game

### TECHNICAL DETAILS
Gauge/calibre : 12 or 20
Chamber length : 70mm (2³/₄in) or 76mm (3in)
Number of barrels : double-barrels over-and-under
Action : breech-loading
Locking : barrel-block locking
Trigger single trigger, removable trigger
Weight : 3.2–3.3kg (7lb–7lb 4oz)
Length : 112–114cm (44¹/₈–44⁷/ in)
Barrel length : 68 or 70cm (26³/₄–27¹/₂in)
Ejector : automatic
Choke interchangeable chokes
Sight 7mm (⁹/₃₂in) ventilated rib and bead
Safety : sliding safety catch on neck of stock, also barrel selector

### CHARACTERISTICS
— material : steel
— finish : blued barrel and action or bare metal action
— stock : walnut stock: straight English or with pistol-grip

## Perazzi MX8 Olympic

### TECHNICAL DETAILS
Gauge/calibre : 12 or 20
Chamber length : 70mm (2³/₄in) or 76mm (3in)
Number of barrels : double-barrels over-and-under
Action : breech-loading
Locking : barrel-block locking

| Trigger | single trigger, removable trigger |
|---|---|
| Weight | : 3.1–3.5kg (6lb 13oz–7lb 11oz) |
| Length | : 104–130cm (41–51³/₁₆in) |
| Barrel length | : 68–86cm (26³/₄–33⁷/₈in) |
| Ejector | : automatic |
| Choke | ³/₄ and full, ¹/₂ and full, full and full, cylindrical, or interchangeable chokes |
| Sight | 11mm (⁹/₃₂in) wide ventilated rib and bead |
| Safety | : sliding safety catch on neck of stock |

**CHARACTERISTICS**

| — material | : steel |
|---|---|
| — finish | : blued |
| — stock | : walnut stock, with pistol-grip |

This gun is available in Olympic Trap, Double Trap, Skeet, Sporting, and American (Single) Trap Combo versions. The last of these models has interchangeable single and over-and-under double-barrels.

## *Perazzi MX10 Olympic*

**TECHNICAL DETAILS**

| Gauge/calibre | : 12 or 20 |
|---|---|
| Chamber length | : 70mm (2³/₄in) or 76mm (3in) |
| Number of barrels | : double-barrels over-and-under |
| Action | : breech-loading |
| Locking | : barrel-block locking |
| Trigger | single trigger, removable trigger |
| Weight | : 3.1–3.5kg (6lb 13oz–7lb 11oz) |
| Length | : 104–130cm (41–51³/₁₆in) |
| Barrel length | : 70–86cm (27¹/₂–33⁷/₈in) |
| Ejector | : automatic |
| Choke | interchangeable chokes |

| Sight | 11mm (⁹/₃₂in) wide raised ventilated rib and bead |
|---|---|
| Safety | : sliding safety catch on neck of stock |

**CHARACTERISTICS**

| — material | : steel |
|---|---|
| — finish | : blued |
| — stock | : walnut stock, with pistol-grip and adjustable comb |

This gun is available in Olympic Trap, Double Trap, Skeet, Sporting, and American (Single) Trap Combo versions. The last of these models has interchangeable single and over-and-under double-barrels. The height of the barrel rib of the MX10 can be adjusted to change the centre of aim.

## *Perazzi MX11L Olympic*

**TECHNICAL DETAILS**

| Gauge/calibre | : 12 |
|---|---|
| Chamber length | : 70mm (2³/₄in) or 76mm (3in) |
| Number of barrels | : double-barrels over-and-under |
| Action | : breech-loading |
| Locking | : barrel-block locking |
| Trigger | single trigger, removable trigger |
| Weight | : 3.1–3.5kg (6lb 13oz–7lb 11oz) |
| Length | : 104–130cm (41–51³/₁₆in) |
| Barrel length | : 68–86cm (26³/₄–33⁷/₈in) |
| Ejector | : automatic |
| Choke | interchangeable chokes |
| Sight | 11mm (⁹/₃₂in) wide ventilated rib and bead |
| Safety | : sliding safety catch on neck of stock |

**CHARACTERISTICS**

| — material | : steel |
|---|---|
| — finish | : blued |
| — stock | : walnut stock, with pistol-grip and adjustable comb |

This gun is available in Olympic Trap, Double Trap, Skeet, Sporting, and American (Single) Trap Combo versions. The last of these models has interchangeable single and over-and-under double-barrels.

## *Perazzi MX12 Game*

**TECHNICAL DETAILS**

| Gauge/calibre | : 12, 20, 28, or .410 |
|---|---|

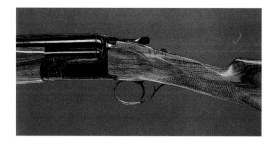

Chamber length    : 70mm (2³/₄in) or 76mm (3in)
Number of barrels : double-barrels over-and-under
Action            : breech-loading
Locking           : barrel-block locking
Trigger             single trigger
Weight            : 3.2–3.3kg (7lb–7lb 4oz)
Length            : 112–114cm (44¹/₈–44⁷/₈in)
Barrel length     : 68 or 70cm (26³/₄ or 27¹/₂in)
Ejector           : automatic
Choke               interchangeable chokes
Sight             : 7mm (⁹/₃₂in) wide ventilated rib and bead
Safety            : sliding safety catch on neck of stock, also barrel
                    selector

**CHARACTERISTICS**
— material        : steel
— finish          : blued or blued barrels and bare metal action
— stock           : walnut stock: straight English or with pistol-grip

This gun is available in the following versions:

– MX12 Game in 12 gauge with fixed trigger
– MX12/20 in 20 gauge with fixed trigger
– MX12/28 in 28 gauge with fixed trigger
– MX12/410 in .410 gauge with fixed trigger

## *Perazzi MX1 American Single Trap Combo*

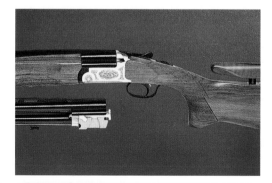

**TECHNICAL DETAILS**
Gauge/calibre    : 12

Chamber length    : 76mm (3in)
Number of barrels : single-barrel
Action            : breech-loading
Locking           : barrel-block locking
Trigger             single trigger, removable trigger, barrel selector
                    behind trigger
Weight            : 3.7–3.9kg (8lb 2¹/₄oz–8lb 9¹/₄oz)
Length            : 118–129cm (46¹/₂–50³/₄in)
Barrel length     : 75–86cm (29¹/₂–33⁷/₈in)
Ejector           : automatic
Choke               interchangeable chokes
Sight             : 11mm (⁷/₁₆in) wide raised ventilated rib and bead
Safety            : sliding safety catch on neck of stock

**CHARACTERISTICS**
— material        : steel
— finish          : blued (MX14) or blued barrels and bare metal
                    action (MX14L)
— stock           : walnut stock with pistol-grip and adjustable comb

This gun is supplied with an interchangeable double-barrel over-and-under barrel set.

## *Perazzi MX15L Single Trap*

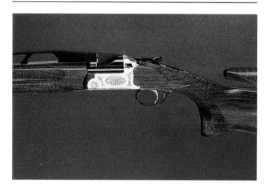

**TECHNICAL DETAILS**
Gauge/calibre    : 12
Chamber length    : 76mm (3in)
Number of barrels : single-barrel
Action            : breech-loading
Locking           : barrel-block locking
Trigger             single trigger, removable trigger
Weight            : 3.7–3.9kg (8lb 2¹/₄oz–8lb 9¹/₄oz)
Length            : 124 or 129cm (48³/₄ or 50³/₄in)
Barrel length     : 81 or 86cm (32 or 33⁷/₈in)
Ejector           : automatic
Choke               interchangeable chokes
Sight             : 11mm (⁷/₁₆in) wide raised ventilated rib and bead
Safety            : sliding safety catch on neck of stock

**CHARACTERISTICS**
— material        : steel

| | |
|---|---|
| – finish | : blued (MX15) or blued barrels and bare metal action (MX15L) |
| – stock | : walnut stock with pistol-grip and adjustable comb |

The height of the barrel rib of the MX15 is adjustable to vary the centre of aim.

## Perazzi TMX Special Single Trap

### TECHNICAL DETAILS
| | |
|---|---|
| Gauge/calibre | : 12 |
| Chamber length | : 76mm (3in) |
| Number of barrels | : single-barrel |
| Action | : breech-loading |
| Locking | : barrel-block locking |
| Trigger | single trigger, removable trigger |
| Weight | : 3.7–3.9kg (8lb 2¹/₄oz–8lb 9¹/₄oz) |
| Length | : 124 or 129cm (48³/₄ or 50³/₄in) |
| Barrel length | : 81 or 86cm (32 or 33⁷/₈in) |
| Ejector | : automatic |
| Choke | interchangeable chokes |
| Sight | 11mm (⁷/₁₆in) wide raised ventilated rib and bead |
| Safety | : sliding safety catch on neck of stock |

### CHARACTERISTICS
| | |
|---|---|
| – material | : steel |
| – finish | : blued |
| – stock | : walnut stock with pistol-grip and adjustable comb |

# Powell & Son Gunmakers Ltd.

The name of William Powell has been associated for almost two hundred years with the making of traditional English shotguns.

The company is based in Birmingham, England.

William Powell and Joseph Simmons established the company in 1802.

Today the business is run by David and Peter Powell, descendants of the founder and still makes traditional shotguns by hand.

It is possible to buy a Powell gun from stock but the majority are made specifically to customer's preferences.

There are also Powell cartridges in gauges 12 and 20. Besides guns, the Powell company also sell yachting clothing and accessories plus superb secure gun cabinets, hidden within walnut bookcases.

## Powell No. 1 Side-lock

### TECHNICAL DETAILS
| | |
|---|---|
| Gauge/calibre | : 12, 16, or 20 |
| Chamber length | : 2¹/₂in (63.5mm) or 2³/₄in (70mm) |
| Number of barrels | : double-barrels side-by-side |
| Action | : breech-loading, self-breeching |
| Locking | : double barrel-block locking |
| Trigger | twin triggers |
| Weight | : 6lb 9¹/₂ oz (3kg) |
| Length | : 45in (114.5cm) |
| Barrel length | : 28in (71cm) |
| Ejector | : automatic |
| Choke | to choice |
| Sight | bead |
| Safety | : sliding safety catch on neck of stock |

### CHARACTERISTICS
| | |
|---|---|
| – material | : steel |
| – finish | : blued, bare metal action with engraved side-lock plates, side-locks can be removed by hand |
| – stock | : straight English stock of walnut, or specially-selected walnut stock, with pistol-grip |

This gun can be supplied as a single gun,

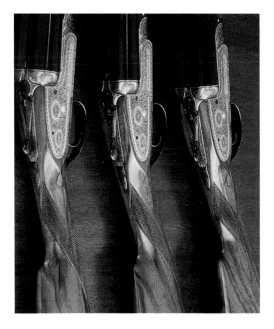

pair, or trio in a leather gun case with consecutive serial numbers (see illustration).

## Powell Heritage No. 1 Side-lock

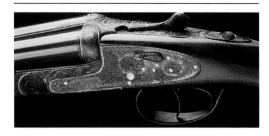

**TECHNICAL DETAILS**
| | |
|---|---|
| Gauge/calibre | : 12, 16, or 20 |
| Chamber length | : 2¹/₂in (63.5mm) or 2³/₄in (70mm) |
| Number of barrels | : double-barrels side-by-side |
| Action | : breech-loading, self-breeching |
| Locking | : double barrel-block locking |
| Trigger | twin triggers |
| Weight | : 6lb 9¹/₂oz (3kg) |
| Length | : 45in (114.5cm) |
| Barrel length | : 28in (71cm) |
| Ejector | : automatic |
| Choke | to choice |
| Sight | bead |
| Safety | : sliding safety catch on neck of stock |

**CHARACTERISTICS**
| | |
|---|---|
| — material | : steel |
| — finish | : blued, bare metal action with engraved side-lock plates, side-locks can be removed by hand |
| — stock | : straight English stock of walnut, or specially-selected walnut stock, with pistol-grip |

## Powell Heritage No. 2 Side-lock

**TECHNICAL DETAILS**
| | |
|---|---|
| Gauge/calibre | : 12, 16, or 20 |
| Chamber length | : 2¹/₂in (63.5mm) or 2³/₄in (70mm) |
| Number of barrels | : double-barrels side-by-side |
| Action | : breech-loading |
| Locking | : double barrel-block locking |
| Trigger | twin triggers |
| Weight | : 6lb 9¹/₂oz (3kg) |
| Length | : 45in (114.5cm) |
| Barrel length | : 28in (71cm) |
| Ejector | : automatic |
| Choke | to choice |
| Sight | bead |
| Safety | : sliding safety catch on neck of stock |

**CHARACTERISTICS**
| | |
|---|---|
| — material | : steel |
| — finish | : blued, bare metal action with engraved side-lock plates, side-locks can be removed by hand |
| — stock | : straight English stock of walnut, or specially-selected walnut stock, with pistol-grip |

## Powell No. 3

**TECHNICAL DETAILS**
| | |
|---|---|
| Gauge/calibre | : 12, 16, or 20 |
| Chamber length | : 2¹/₂in (63.5mm) or 2³/₄in (70mm) |
| Number of barrels | : double-barrels side-by-side |
| Action | : breech-loading |

| | |
|---|---|
| Locking | : double barrel-block locking |
| Trigger | twin triggers |
| Weight | : approx. 6lb 9¹/₂ oz (3kg) |
| Length | : to choice |
| Barrel length | : to choice |
| Ejector | : to choice |
| Choke | to choice |
| Sight | bead |
| Safety | : sliding safety catch on neck of stock |

**CHARACTERISTICS**

| | |
|---|---|
| — material | : steel |
| — finish | : blued, bare metal action with engravings of hunting motifs |
| — stock | : straight English stock of walnut |

# Remington

Eliphalet Remington, (known as Lite) founded E. Remington in Illion, New York State, in 1825.

His son Philo joined the company in 1844, and following the death of Lite in 1961, Phil was joined by his brothers Samuel and Eliphalet III and the company name was changed to E. Remington & Sons. During the American Civil War, Remington produced large numbers of military weapons. Afterwards, the company switched over to making hunting and sporting guns.

After the death of Samuel Remington in 1880, the company went into decline and even bankruptcy in 1886. Two businessmen, Marcellus Hartley of the Union Metallic Cartridge Company and Thomas Bennett, son-in-law of the famous Oliver Winchester purchased the company for $200,000 and changed the name to Remington Arms Company. After Hartley died, he was succeeded by his 21-year-old son Marcy Hartley Dodge.

A Danish technical specialist, J.D. Pedersen was employed in 1907 and he developed Remington's first pump-action shotgun. In 1912, the company was merged with Hartley Dodge's other company, the Union Cartridge Company. World War I created a huge demand for firearms At first Remington hired a car factory to produce Enfield rifles but this capacity was soon too small. This was because, among other reasons, the company received an order from Russia for 1,000,000 rifles and 100,000,000 cartridges. The business was moved to Bridgeport, Connecticut where 25 new factory buildings were rapidly built.

Production soared to 5,000 rifles and 2.5 million cartridges per day. After the fall of Tsar Nicholas II in the Russian Revolution, the new government cancelled the order, leaving Remington with 750,000 rifles on their hands. These were mainly sold at a loss to France, who passed them on to the White Russians. The peace in 1918 caused a large drop in orders. Remington was forced to switch over to sporting and hunting guns and also the manufacture of cash registers.

A new company head, Charles Davis, took over in 1933 and the Remington company bought the Peters Cartridge Company in 1936. During World War II Remington switched to production for the forces and in 1943 employed 82,000 people.

The company has formed a part of the Du-Pont group since 1980 and is still based in Bridgeport, Connecticut but also in Wilmington, Delaware.

## Remington 11-97 Premier Light Contour

**TECHNICAL DETAILS**

| | |
|---|---|
| Gauge/calibre | : 12 |
| Chamber length | : 3in (76mm) |
| Number of barrels | : single-barrel |
| Magazine | : tubular magazine for 2–5 cartridges |
| Action | : semi-automatic (gas-pressure operated) |
| Locking | : falling block locking |
| Trigger | single trigger |
| Weight | : 7lb 8oz–7lb 11oz (3.4–3.5kg) |
| Length | : 46¹/₂–50¹/₂in (118–128cm) |
| Barrel length | : 26, 28, or 30in (66, 71, or 76cm) |
| Ejector | : extractor |
| Choke | Remington interchangeable choke set |
| Sight | ventilated rib and bead |

| Safety | : push-button safety catch at rear of trigger guard |

**CHARACTERISTICS**
| — material | : steel |
| — finish | : blued |
| — stock | : walnut stock, with pistol-grip |

This gun is also available in a left-handed version.

## Remington 11-87 Premier Sporting Clays

**TECHNICAL DETAILS**
| Gauge/calibre | : 12 |
| Chamber length | : 3in (76mm) |
| Number of barrels | : single-barrel |
| Magazine | : tubular magazine for 2–5 cartridges |
| Action | : semi-automatic (gas-pressure operated) |
| Locking | : falling block locking |
| Trigger | single trigger |
| Weight | : 7lb 8oz (3.4kg) |
| Length | : 48$^1$/$_2$in (123.2cm) |
| Barrel length | : 28in (71cm) |
| Ejector | : extractor |
| Choke | Remington interchangeable choke set |
| Sight | 8mm ($^5$/$_{16}$in) wide ventilated rib and bead |
| Safety | : push-button safety catch at rear of trigger guard |

**CHARACTERISTICS**
| — material | : steel |
| — finish | : blued |
| — stock | : walnut stock, with pistol-grip |

The same gun is also available as an 11/87 Premier SC-NP with nickel-plated action body. Both guns are also available in left-handed versions.

## Remington 11-87 Special Purpose Deer

**TECHNICAL DETAILS**
| Gauge/calibre | : 12 |
| Chamber length | : 3in (76mm) |
| Number of barrels | : single-barrel |
| Magazine | : tubular magazine for 2–5 cartridges |
| Action | : semi-automatic (gas-pressure operated) |
| Locking | . falling block locking |
| Trigger | single trigger |
| Weight | : 8lb (3.6kg) |

| Length | : 40$^1$/$_2$in (103cm) |
| Barrel length | : 20in (50.8cm) |
| Ejector | : extractor |
| Choke | not applicable, rifled barrel |
| Sight | none; mounting for telescopic sight |
| Safety | : push-button safety catch at rear of trigger guard |

**CHARACTERISTICS**
| — material | : steel |
| — finish | : matt black |
| — stock | : black plastic stock, with pistol-grip |

## Remington 11-87 Special Turkey Real Tree Extra

**TECHNICAL DETAILS**
| Gauge/calibre | : 12 |
| Chamber length | : 3in (76mm) |
| Number of barrels | : single-barrel |
| Magazine | : tubular magazine for 2–5 cartridges |
| Action | : semi-automatic (gas-pressure operated) |
| Locking | : falling block locking |
| Trigger | single trigger |
| Weight | : 8lb (3.6kg) |
| Length | : 41in (104cm) |
| Barrel length | : 21in (50.8cm) |
| Ejector | : extractor |
| Choke | Remington interchangeable choke set |
| Sight | ventilated barrel rib and bead |
| Safety | : push-button safety catch at rear of trigger guard |

**CHARACTERISTICS**
| — material | : steel |
| — finish | : matt coating with tree and leaf motifs |
| — stock | : plastic stock with tree and leaf motifs and pistol-grip |

This gun is not suitable for use with a shotgun certificate in the United Kingdom because the length of barrel is less than the minimum of 24in (61cm). The magazine capacity is restricted to 2 cartridges in a number of European countries including the United Kingdom.

## Remington 11-96 Euro Lightweight

**TECHNICAL DETAILS**

| | |
|---|---|
| Gauge/calibre | : 12 |
| Chamber length | : 3in (76mm) |
| Number of barrels | : single-barrel |
| Magazine | : tubular magazine for 2–5 cartridges |
| Action | : semi-automatic (gas-pressure operated) |
| Locking | : falling block locking |
| Trigger | single trigger |
| Weight | : 7lb or 7lb 4oz (3.2–3.4kg) |
| Length | : 46 or 48in (116 or 122cm) |
| Barrel length | : 26 or 28in (66 or 71cm) |
| Ejector | : extractor |
| Choke | Remington interchangeable choke set |
| Sight | 6mm ($^3/_8$in) wide ventilated rib with bead |
| Safety | : push-button safety catch at rear of trigger guard |

**CHARACTERISTICS**

| | |
|---|---|
| — material | : steel |
| — finish | : blued |
| — stock | : walnut stock, with pistol-grip |

## Remington 90-T Trap

**TECHNICAL DETAILS**

| | |
|---|---|
| Gauge/calibre | : 12 |
| Chamber length | : 3in (76mm) |

| | |
|---|---|
| Number of barrels | : single-barrel |
| Action | : breech-loading |
| Locking | : barrel-block locking |
| Trigger | single trigger |
| Weight | : 8lb 12oz (4kg) |
| Length | : 51in (129.5cm) |
| Barrel length | : 34in (86.4cm) |
| Ejector | : automatic |
| Choke | fixed full choke |
| Sight | ventilated rib with bead |
| Safety | : sliding safety catch on neck of stock |

**CHARACTERISTICS**

| | |
|---|---|
| — material | : steel |
| — finish | : blued |
| — stock | : walnut stock, with pistol-grip |

## Remington 396 Skeet

**TECHNICAL DETAILS**

| | |
|---|---|
| Gauge/calibre | : 12 |
| Chamber length | : 3in (76mm) |
| Number of barrels | : double-barrels over-and-under |
| Action | : breech-loading |
| Locking | : barrel-block locking |
| Trigger | single trigger |
| Weight | : 7lb 4oz or 7lb 8oz (3.3 or 3.4kg) |
| Length | : 45 or 47in (114.3 or 119.4cm) |
| Barrel length | : 28 or 30in (71 or 76cm) |
| Ejector | : automatic |
| Choke | Remington interchangeable choke set |
| Sight | 10mm ($^7/_{16}$ in) wide ventilated rib with bead |
| Safety | : sliding safety catch on neck of stock |

**CHARACTERISTICS**

| | |
|---|---|
| — material | : steel |
| — finish | : blued barrels, engraved bare metal action and side-plates (no side-lock) |
| — stock | : walnut stock, with pistol-grip |

## Remington 396 Sporting

**TECHNICAL DETAILS**

| | |
|---|---|
| Gauge/calibre | : 12 |
| Chamber length | : 3in (76mm) |

Number of barrels : double-barrels over-and-under with compensator vents
Action : breech-loading
Locking : barrel-block locking
Trigger single trigger
Weight : 7lb 4oz or 7lb 8oz (3.3 or 3.4kg)
Length : 45 or 47in (114.3 or 119.4cm)
Barrel length : 28 or 30in (71 or 76cm)
Ejector : automatic
Choke Remington interchangeable choke set
Sight 10mm ($^7/_{16}$in) wide ventilated rib with bead
Safety : sliding safety catch on neck of stock
Choke : Rem chokewisselset

**CHARACTERISTICS**
— material : steel
— finish : blued barrels, engraved bare metal action and side-plates (no side-lock)
— stock : walnut stock, with pistol-grip

## *Remington 870 Express*

**TECHNICAL DETAILS**
Gauge/calibre : 12, 20, 28, or .410
Chamber length : 3in (76mm)
Number of barrels : single-barrel
Magazine : tubular magazine for 2–5 cartridges
Action : pump-action
Locking : falling block locking
Trigger single trigger
Weight : 6lb–7lb 8oz (2.7–3.4kg)
Length : 41$^1/_2$–48$^1/_2$in (105.4–123.2cm)
Barrel length : 21–28in (53–71cm)
Ejector : extractor
Choke Remington interchangeable choke set
Sight ventilated rib with bead
Safety : push-button safety catch at rear of trigger guard

**CHARACTERISTICS**
— material : steel
— finish : blued
— stock : walnut stock, with pistol-grip

## *Remington 870 SPS Camo*

**TECHNICAL DETAILS**
Gauge/calibre : 12
Chamber length : 3in (76mm)
Number of barrels : single-barrel
Magazine : tubular magazine for 2–5 cartridges
Action : pump-action
Locking : falling block locking
Trigger single trigger
Weight : 7lb 4oz (3.3kg)
Length : 46$^1/_2$in (118cm)
Barrel length : 26in (66cm)
Ejector : extractor
Choke Remington interchangeable choke set
Sight ventilated rib with bead
Safety : push-button safety catch at rear of trigger guard

**CHARACTERISTICS**
— material : steel
— finish : special "Mossy Oak" colour camouflage coating
— stock : synthetic stock with pistol-grip in camouflage colours

## *Remington 870 Special Purpose Turkey Real Tree Extra*

**TECHNICAL DETAILS**
Gauge/calibre : 12
Chamber length : 3in (76mm)
Number of barrels : single-barrel
Magazine : tubular magazine for 2–5 cartridges
Action : pump-action
Locking : falling block locking
Trigger single trigger
Weight : 7lb (3.2kg)
Length : 41$^1/_2$in (105.4cm)
Barrel length : 21in (53cm)
Ejector : extractor
Choke Remington interchangeable choke set
Sight ventilated rib with bead
Safety : push-button safety catch at rear of trigger guard

**CHARACTERISTICS**
— material : steel

| | |
|---|---|
| – finish | : matt-finish special tree and leaf motif coating |
| – stock | : plastic stock with pistol-grip with tree and leaf motifs |

The length of the barrel of this gun is less than the minimum 24in (61cm) required for a shotgun certificate in the United Kingdom.

Magazines must also be restricted to 2 cartridges in the United Kingdom and some other European countries.

## *Remington 870 Wingmaster*

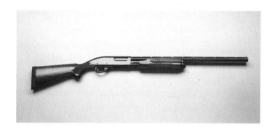

### TECHNICAL DETAILS
| | |
|---|---|
| Gauge/calibre | : 12 or 20 |
| Chamber length | : 3in (76mm) |
| Number of barrels | : single-barrel |
| Magazine | : tubular magazine for 2–5 cartridges |
| Action | : pump-action |
| Locking | : falling block locking |
| Trigger | single trigger |
| Weight | : 6lb 8oz–8lb (3–3.6kg) |
| Length | : 46$^1$/$_2$–50$^1$/$_2$ in (118–128.3cm) |
| Barrel length | : 26, 28, or 30in (66, 71, or 76cm) |
| Ejector | : extractor |
| Choke | Remington interchangeable choke set |
| Sight | ventilated rib with bead |
| Safety | : push-button safety catch at rear of trigger guard |

### CHARACTERISTICS
| | |
|---|---|
| – material | : steel |
| – finish | : blued |
| – stock | : walnut stock, with pistol-grip |

## *Remington 1100 Special Field*

### TECHNICAL DETAILS
| | |
|---|---|
| Gauge/calibre | : 12 or 20 |
| Chamber length | : 3in (76mm) |
| Number of barrels | : single-barrel |
| Magazine | : tubular magazine for 2–5 cartridges |
| Action | : semi-automatic (gas-pressure operated) |
| Locking | : falling block locking |
| Trigger | single trigger |
| Weight | : 6lb 8oz–7lb 4oz (3–3.3kg) |
| Length | : 43$^1$/$_2$ in (110cm) |
| Barrel length | : 23$^5$/$_8$in (60cm) |
| Ejector | : extractor |
| Choke | Remington interchangeable choke set |
| Sight | ventilated rib with bead |
| Safety | : push-button safety catch at rear of trigger guard |

### CHARACTERISTICS
| | |
|---|---|
| – material | : steel |
| – finish | : blued |
| – stock | : straight English stock of walnut stock |

## *Remington SP-10 Magnum Camo*

### TECHNICAL DETAILS
| | |
|---|---|
| Gauge/calibre | : 10 |
| Chamber length | : 3$^1$/$_2$in (89mm) |
| Number of barrels | : single-barrel |
| Magazine | : tubular magazine for 2–4 cartridges |
| Action | : semi-automatic (gas-pressure operated) |
| Locking | : falling block locking |
| Trigger | single trigger |
| Weight | : 10lb (4.5kg) |
| Length | : 43$^1$/$_2$ in (110cm) |
| Barrel length | : 23in (58.4cm) |
| Ejector | : extractor |
| Choke | Remington interchangeable choke set |
| Sight | ventilated rib with bead |
| Safety | : push-button safety catch at rear of trigger guard |

### CHARACTERISTICS
| | |
|---|---|
| – material | : steel |
| – finish | : special Mossy Oak camouflage colour coating |
| – stock | : synthetic stock with pistol-grip in camouflage colours |

This type of gun is widely used for shooting wild turkey in the USA. The barrel also falls under the minimum required of 24in (61cm). Similar restrictions apply in certain other European countries. Gauge 10 is banned in some European countries.

# Rigby

The firm of John Rigby & Co. (Gunsmiths) Ltd. was established in 1735 and has therefore been in existence for more than 260 years. At first the business was in Dublin but it moved to London in 1865 when John Rigby was appointed Superintendent of the Royal Arms Factory at Enfield.

Rigby is famous for double-barrelled Magnum-Express rifles in .450 Cordite, .416 Rigby, .577 Nitro, and even .600 Nitro Express. These guns were specially made for shooting big game in Africa and Asia. Professional hunters throughout the entire world rate these guns most highly.

The value of Rigby guns is greatly because they are hand made. The price of a side-by-side shotgun starts at £22,000 and can be as high as £100,000 for a pair of matching guns in a leather case with additional barrels and gold inlaid engraving of choice.

The Rigby Company hold the Royal warrant as suppliers to Her Majesty The Queen. Traditional Rigby side-lock side-by-side shotguns are not mere guns, rather they are collectors objects or even works of art.

Rigby shotguns are only made by hand, which is why the delivery time of one and a half to two year. It is difficult to supply technical data regarding chokes, lengths, etc. These can only be given for guns already made. When customers acquires Rigby guns they are not only taking possession of a gun but also an investment of great beauty.

## Rigby 10

### TECHNICAL DETAILS

| | |
|---|---|
| Gauge/calibre | : 10 (Magnum) |
| Chamber length | : 3¹/₂in (89mm) |
| Number of barrels | : double-barrels side-by-side |
| Action | : breech-loading |
| Locking | : double barrel-block locking |
| Trigger | twin triggers |
| Weight | : approx. 6lb 13oz (3.1kg) |
| Length | : approx. 44in (112cm) |
| Barrel length | : approx. 28in (71cm) |
| Ejector | : automatic |
| Choke | to choice |
| Sight | bead (see remark) |

| | |
|---|---|
| Safety | : sliding safety catch on neck of stock |

### CHARACTERISTICS

| | |
|---|---|
| — material | : steel |
| — finish | : blued barrels, tempered action with hand engraving of side-lock plates to choice |
| — stock | : stock of specially-selected English walnut |

This gun is only available to order and delivery is 1¹/₂–2 years. It is supplied with interchangeable barrel set. In the illustration, the rifled barrels with Express folding sight can be seen. The rifle calibre is to choice. This type of gun is popular for shooting wild turkey in the United States. Some other European countries do not permit the use of 10 gauge for hunting. The gun cannot be held on a United Kingdom shotgun certificate if fitted with the optional rifled barrel.
☜

## Rigby 12 Pair

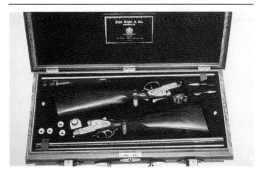

### TECHNICAL DETAILS

| | |
|---|---|
| Gauge/calibre | : 12 |
| Chamber length | : 2³/₄in (70mm) |
| Number of barrels | : double-barrels side-by-side |
| Action | : breech-loading |
| Locking | : double barrel-block locking |
| Trigger | twin triggers |
| Weight | : approx. 6lb 13oz (3.1kg) |
| Length | : approx. 44in (112cm) |
| Barrel length | : approx. 20in (71cm) |
| Ejector | : automatic |

Choke          to choice
Sight          bead
Safety         : sliding safety catch on neck of stock

**CHARACTERISTICS**
— material      : steel
— finish        : blued barrels, tempered action with hand engrav-
                  ing of side-lock plates to choice
— stock         : stock of specially-selected English walnut: straight
                  English or with pistol-grip to choice

A pair of these guns have side-lock plates
engraved with pheasants and gun dogs. The
guns are supplied in a leather gun case. A
pair of these guns are only available to order
and delivery is 1¹/₂–2 years.

## *Rigby 12 Pair External Hammers*

**TECHNICAL DETAILS**
Gauge/calibre    : 12
Chamber length   : 2³/₄in (70mm)
Number of barrels : double-barrels side-by-side
Action           : breech-loading
Locking          : double barrel-block locking
Trigger          twin triggers
Weight           : approx. 6lb 13oz (3.1kg)
Length           : approx. 44in (112cm)
Barrel length    : approx. 28in (71cm)
Ejector          : automatic
Choke            to choice
Sight            bead
Safety           : sliding safety catch on neck of stock

**CHARACTERISTICS**
— material      : steel
— finish        : blued barrels, tempered action with hand engrav-
                  ing of side-lock plates to choice
— stock         : stock of specially-selected English walnut: straight
                  English or with pistol-grip to choice

This exceptional gun is one of a pair of
matching guns. The gold inlaid figure "2"
seen on the barrel rib of the gun in the illustration denotes this is the second gun of the
pair. These guns are supplied in a leather gun
case, are only available to order, and delivery
is 1¹/₂–2 years.

## *Rigby 20*

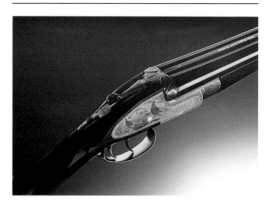

**TECHNICAL DETAILS**
Gauge/calibre    : 20
Chamber length   : 3in (76mm)
Number of barrels : double-barrels side-by-side
Action           : breech-loading
Locking          : double barrel-block locking
Trigger          twin triggers
Weight           : approx. 6lb 13oz (3.1kg)
Length           : approx. 44in (112cm)
Barrel length    : approx. 28in (71cm)
Ejector          : automatic
Choke            to choice
Sight            bead
Safety           : sliding safety catch on neck of stock

**CHARACTERISTICS**
— material      : steel
— finish        : blued barrels, tempered action with hand engrav-
                  ing of side-lock plates to choice
— stock         : stock of specially-selected English walnut: straight
                  English or with pistol-grip to choice

This gun is only available to order; delivery
is 1¹/₂–2 years.

## Rigby Standard

**TECHNICAL DETAILS**

Gauge/calibre : 12
Chamber length : 2³/₄in (70mm)
Number of barrels : double-barrels side-by-side
Action : breech-loading
Locking : double barrel-block locking
Trigger twin triggers
Weight : approx. 6lb 13oz (3.1kg)
Length : approx. 44in (112cm)
Barrel length : approx. 28in (71cm)
Ejector : automatic
Choke to choice
Sight bead
Safety : sliding safety catch on neck of stock

**CHARACTERISTICS**

— material : steel
— finish : blued barrels, tempered action with hand engraving of side-lock plates to choice
— stock : stock of specially-selected English walnut: straight English or with pistol-grip to choice

This gun is only available to order; delivery is 1¹/₂–2 years.

# Rizzini

There are two different arms factories bearing the Rizzini name in the little town of Marcheno in the Italian Brescia region. Both firms have an old family tradition as gunmakers. Different family members went their own way earlier in the twentieth century. The Rizzini Battista gun factory chose the ultra modern route with computer controlled machining but the craftsmanship of the company remains high in accordance with the gunmaking traditions of Brescia.
All shotguns are tested to 1200 bar. Virtually all their shotguns have interchangeable chokes. Guns can be supplied with fixed chokes at extra cost.

## Rizzini Argo

**TECHNICAL DETAILS**

Gauge/calibre : 12 or 16
Chamber length : 70mm (2³/₄in) or 76mm (3in)
Number of barrels : double-barrels over-and-under
Action : breech-loading
Locking : barrel-block locking
Trigger single trigger
Weight : 3.05–3.15kg. (6lb 11¹/₄oz–6lb 14³/₄oz)
Length : 113 or 116cm (44¹/₂ or 45⁵/₈in)
Barrel length : 67 or 70cm (26³/₈ or 27¹/₂in)
Ejector : automatic
Choke ³/₄ and full, or ¹/₄ and ³/₄
Sight 7mm (⁹/₃₂in) ventilated rib and bead
Safety : sliding safety catch on neck of stock

**CHARACTERISTICS**

— material : steel
— finish : blued barrels, nickel-chrome steel action with engravings of birds on side-plates (no side-lock)
— stock : walnut stock, with pistol-grip

Illustrated from top to bottom: Rizzini Argo and Rizzini Omnium.

## Rizzini Artemis 12/16

## TECHNICAL DETAILS

Gauge/calibre : 12 or 16
Chamber length : 70mm (2³/₄in) or 76mm (3in)
Number of barrels : double-barrels over-and-under
Action : breech-loading
Locking : barrel-block locking
Trigger single trigger
Weight : 3.05kg. (6lb 11¹/₄oz)
Length : 113 or 116cm (44¹/₂ or 45⁵/₈in)
Barrel length : 67 or 70cm (26³/₈ or 27¹/₂ in)
Ejector : automatic
Choke ³/₄ and full, or ¹/₄ and ³/₄
Sight 7mm (⁹/₃₂in) ventilated rib and bead
Safety : sliding safety catch on neck of stock

## CHARACTERISTICS

— material : steel
— finish : blued barrels, nickel-chrome steel action with engravings of birds on side-plates (no side-lock)
— stock : walnut stock, with pistol-grip

Illustrated from top to bottom: Rizzini Artemis and Rizzini Aurum.

## Rizzini Artemis 20/28/410

## TECHNICAL DETAILS

Gauge/calibre : 20, 28, or .410
Chamber length : 65 (2¹/₂in), 70mm (2³/₄in), or 76mm (3in)
Number of barrels : double-barrels over-and-under
Action : breech-loading
Locking : barrel-block locking
Trigger single trigger
Weight : 2.5–2.7kg. (5lb 8oz—6lb)
Length : 113 or 116cm (44¹/₂ or 45⁵/₈in)
Barrel length : 67 or 70cm (26³/₈ or 27¹/₂in)
Ejector : automatic
Choke ³/₄ and full; interchangeable chokes in 20 gauge
Sight 6mm (³/₈in) ventilated rib with bead
Safety : sliding safety catch on neck of stock

## CHARACTERISTICS

— material : steel
— finish : blued barrels, nickel-chrome steel action with engravings of birds on side-plates (no side-lock)
— stock : walnut stock, with pistol-grip

Illustrated from top to bottom: Rizzini Artemis and Rizzini Aurum.

## Rizzini Artemis EL

## TECHNICAL DETAILS

Gauge/calibre : 12, 20, 28, or .410
Chamber length : 65 (2¹/₂in), 70mm (2³/₄in), or 76mm (3in)
Number of barrels : double-barrels over-and-under
Action : breech-loading
Locking : barrel-block locking
Trigger single trigger
Weight : 2.5–3.05kg. (5lb 8oz—6lb 11¹/₄oz)
Length : 113 or 116cm (44¹/₂ or 45⁵/₈in)
Barrel length : 67 or 70cm (26³/₈ or 27¹/₂in)
Ejector : automatic
Choke ³/₄ and full; or interchangeable chokes
Sight 7mm (⁹/₃₂in) ventilated rib and bead
Safety : sliding safety catch on neck of stock

## CHARACTERISTICS

— material : steel
— finish : blued barrels, nickel-chrome steel action with hand engraved designs of birds on side-plates (no side-lock)
— stock : special grade walnut stock, with pistol-grip

## Rizzini Aurum

## TECHNICAL DETAILS

Gauge/calibre : 12, 16, 20, 28, or .410
Chamber length : 65 (2¹/₂in), 70mm (2³/₄in), or 76mm (3in)
Number of barrels : double-barrels over-and-under
Action : breech-loading
Locking : barrel-block locking
Trigger single trigger
Weight : 2.5–3.kg. (5lb 8oz—6lb 9¹/₂oz)
Length : 112–116cm (44¹/₈–45⁵/₈in)
Barrel length : 67 or 70cm (26³/₈ or 27¹/₂in)

| | |
|---|---|
| Ejector | : automatic |
| Choke | $^3/_4$ and full; or interchangeable chokes |
| Sight | 7mm ($^9/_{32}$ in) ventilated rib and bead |
| Safety | : sliding safety catch on neck of stock |

**CHARACTERISTICS**

| | |
|---|---|
| — material | : steel |
| — finish | : blued barrels, nickel-chrome steel action with engravings of birds on side-plates (no side-lock) |
| — stock | : walnut stock, with pistol-grip |

Illustrated from top to bottom:
Rizzini Aurum and Rizzini Artemis.

## *Rizzini Aurum Slug*

**TECHNICAL DETAILS**

| | |
|---|---|
| Gauge/calibre | : 12 or 16 |
| Chamber length | : 70mm ($2^3/_4$in), or 76mm (3in) |
| Number of barrels | : double-barrels over-and-under |
| Action | : breech-loading |
| Locking | : barrel-block locking |
| Trigger | single trigger |
| Weight | : 2.9kg. (6lb 6oz) |
| Length | : 108cm ($42^1/_2$in) |
| Barrel length | : 62cm ($24^3/_8$in) |
| Ejector | : automatic |
| Choke | cylindrical (both barrels) |
| Sight | 9mm ($^9/_{32}$in) ventilated rib and bead |
| Safety | : sliding safety catch on neck of stock |

**CHARACTERISTICS**

| | |
|---|---|
| — material | : steel |

| | |
|---|---|
| — finish | : blued |
| — stock | : walnut stock, with pistol-grip |

## *Rizzini Express 90*

**TECHNICAL DETAILS**

| | |
|---|---|
| Gauge/calibre | : see below |
| Chamber length | : not applicable |
| Number of barrels | : double-barrels over-and-under |
| Action | : breech-loading |
| Locking | : barrel-block locking |
| Trigger | single trigger |
| Weight | : 3.1–3.6kg. (6lb 13oz–7lb $14^3/_{10}$oz) |
| Length | : 104cm (41in) |
| Barrel length | : 60cm ($23^5/_8$in) |
| Ejector | : automatic |
| Choke | not applicable, rifled barrels |
| Sight | notched sight and bead; mount for telescopic sight |
| Safety | : sliding safety catch on neck of stock |

**CHARACTERISTICS**

| | |
|---|---|
| — material | : steel |
| — finish | : blued barrels, bare metal engraved action |
| — stock | : walnut stock, with pistol-grip |

Available calibres: 6.5x55, .270 Win., 7x57R, .30-06 Spr., .308 Win., 8x57 JRS, 9.3x74R, .444 Marlin.
Illustrated from top to bottom: Express 92, 90L, and 90.

## *Rizzini Express 90L*

**TECHNICAL DETAILS**

| | |
|---|---|
| Gauge/calibre | : see below |
| Chamber length | : not applicable |
| Number of barrels | : double-barrels over-and-under |
| Action | : breech-loading |
| Locking | : barrel-block locking |
| Trigger | single trigger |
| Weight | : 3.1–3.6kg. (6lb 13oz–7lb $14^3/_{10}$oz) |
| Length | : 104cm (41in) |
| Barrel length | : 60cm ($23^5/_8$in) |
| Ejector | : automatic |
| Choke | not applicable, rifled barrels |
| Sight | notched sight and bead; mount for telescopic sight |

| Safety | : sliding safety catch on neck of stock |

## CHARACTERISTICS
| — material | : steel |
| — finish | : blued barrels, tempered and engraved action |
| — stock | : walnut stock, with pistol-grip |

Available calibres: 6.5x55, .270 Win., 7x57R, .30-06 Spr., .308 Win., 8x57 JRS, 9.3x74R, .444 Marlin.
Illustrated from top to bottom: Express 92, 90L, and 90.

## Rizzini Express 92

### TECHNICAL DETAILS
| Gauge/calibre | : see below |
| Chamber length | : not applicable |
| Number of barrels | : double-barrels over-and-under |
| Action | : breech-loading |
| Locking | : barrel-block locking |
| Trigger | single trigger |
| Weight | : 3.1–3.6kg. (6lb 13oz–7lb 14³/₄oz) |
| Length | : 104cm (41in) |
| Barrel length | : 60cm (23⁵/₈in) |
| Ejector | : automatic |
| Choke | not applicable, rifled barrels |
| Sight | notched sight and bead; mount for telescopic sight |
| Safety | : sliding safety catch on neck of stock |

### CHARACTERISTICS
| — material | : steel |
| — finish | : blued barrels, tempered action with engraving on side-plates (no side-lock) |
| — stock | : walnut stock, with pistol-grip |

Available calibres: 6.5x55, .270 Win., 7x57R, .30-06 Spr., .308 Win., 8x57 JRS, 9.3x74R, .444 Marlin.
Illustrated from top to bottom: Express 92, 90L, and 90.

## Rizzini MC

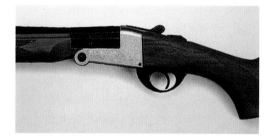

### TECHNICAL DETAILS
| Gauge/calibre | : 12, 16, 20, 24, 28, 32, or .410 |
| Chamber length | : 70mm (2³/₄in), or 76mm (3in) |

| Number of barrels | : single-barrel |
| Action | : breech-loading |
| Locking | : barrel-block locking |
| Trigger | single trigger |
| Weight | : 2.2kg. (4lb 13¹/₂oz) |
| Length | : 116cm (45⁵/₈in) |
| Barrel length | : 70cm (27¹/₂in) |
| Ejector | : automatic |
| Choke | full |
| Sight | 6mm (³/₈in) ventilated rib with bead |
| Safety | : sliding safety catch on neck of stock |

### CHARACTERISTICS
| — material | : steel |
| — finish | : blued barrels, nickel-chrome steel action with floral engravings and light alloy trigger guard |
| — stock | : hardwood stock, with pistol-grip |

## Rizzini Omnium

### TECHNICAL DETAILS
| Gauge/calibre | : 12, 16, 20, 28, or .410 |
| Chamber length | : 65 (2¹/₂in), 70mm (2³/₄in), or 76mm (3in) |
| Number of barrels | : double-barrels over-and-under |
| Action | : breech-loading |
| Locking | : barrel-block locking |
| Trigger | single trigger |
| Weight | : 2.5–3.kg. (5lb 8oz–6lb 9¹/₂oz) |
| Length | : 112–116cm (44¹/₈–45⁵/₈in) |
| Barrel length | : 67 or 70cm (26³/₈ or 27¹/₂in) |
| Ejector | : automatic |
| Choke | ³/₄ and full, ¹/₄ and ³/₄, or interchangeable chokes |
| Sight | 7mm (⁹/₃₂in) ventilated rib and bead |
| Safety | : sliding safety catch on neck of stock |

### CHARACTERISTICS
| — material | : steel |
| — finish | : blued barrels, nickel-chrome steel action with engravings of pheasant |
| — stock | : walnut stock, with pistol-grip |

## Rizzini Premier

### TECHNICAL DETAILS
| Gauge/calibre | : 12 or 20 |

Chamber length : 70mm (2³/₄in) or 76mm (3in)
Number of barrels : double-barrels over-and-under
Action : breech-loading
Locking : barrel-block locking
Trigger single trigger
Weight : 3.2–3.7kg. (7lb–8lb 2¹/₄oz)
Length : 112–119cm (44¹/₈–46⁷/₈in)
Barrel length : Trap: 75cm (29¹/₂in)
Skeet:67 or 71cm (26³/₈ or 28in)
Sporting: 71 or 75cm (28 or 29¹/₂in)
Ejector : automatic
Choke interchangeable chokes
Sight 10mm (⁷/₁₆in) ventilated rib with bead
Safety : sliding safety catch on neck of stock

### CHARACTERISTICS
— material : steel
— finish : blued
— stock : walnut stock, with pistol-grip
〰

## Rizzini S780 EM (Economy Model)

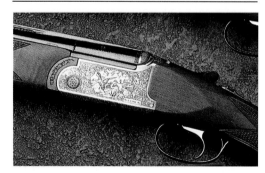

### TECHNICAL DETAILS
Gauge/calibre : 12, 16, 20, 28, or .410
Chamber length : 65 (2¹/₂in), 70mm (2³/₄in), or 76mm (3in)
Number of barrels : double-barrels over-and-under
Action : breech-loading
Locking : barrel-block locking
Trigger single trigger
Weight : 2.5–3.kg. (5lb 8oz–6lb 9¹/₂oz)
Length : 111–116cm (39³/₄–45¹/₄in)
Barrel length : 67 or 70cm (26³/₈ or 27¹/₂in)
Ejector : automatic

Choke : ¹/₂ and full, ¹/₄ and ³/₄
Sight 7mm (⁹/₃₂in) ventilated rib and bead
Safety : sliding safety catch on neck of stock

### CHARACTERISTICS
— material : steel
— finish : blued barrels, nickel-chrome steel action with hunting motif
— stock : walnut stock, with pistol-grip
〰

## Rizzini S780 EM Slug (Economy Model)

### TECHNICAL DETAILS
Gauge/calibre : 12 or 16
Chamber length : 70mm (2³/₄in), or 76mm (3in)
Number of barrels : double-barrels over-and-under
Action : breech-loading
Locking : barrel-block locking
Trigger single trigger
Weight : 2.9kg. (6lb 6oz)
Length : 106cm (41³/₄in)
Barrel length : 62cm (24³/₈in)
Ejector : automatic
Choke cylindrical (both barrels)
Sight 9mm (⁹/₃₂in) ventilated rib and bead
Safety : sliding safety catch on neck of stock

### CHARACTERISTICS
— material : steel
— finish : blued barrels, nickel-chrome steel with hunting motif
— stock : walnut stock, with pistol-grip
〰

## Rizzini S780 EMEL (Deluxe Model)

## TECHNICAL DETAILS

Gauge/calibre : 12
Chamber length : 70mm (2³/₄in), or 76mm (3in)
Number of barrels : double-barrels over-and-under
Action : breech-loading
Locking : barrel-block locking
Trigger : single trigger
Weight : 3.kg. (6lb 9¹/₂oz)
Length : 111 or 114cm (39³/₄—44⁷/₈in)
Barrel length : 67 or 70cm (26³/₈ or 27¹/₂in)
Ejector : automatic
Choke : ¹/₂ and full, ¹/₄ and ³/₄
Sight : 7mm (⁹/₃₂in) ventilated rib and bead
Safety : sliding safety catch on neck of stock

## CHARACTERISTICS

— material : steel
— finish : blued barrels, nickel-chrome steel action with hand-engraved hunting motif
— stock : stock of selected stock, with pistol-grip

This gun can be supplied in a luxury leather gun case.

## *Rizzini S780 EML*

## TECHNICAL DETAILS

Gauge/calibre : 12 or 16
Chamber length : 70mm (2³/₄in), or 76mm (3in)
Number of barrels : double-barrels over-and-under
Action : breech-loading
Locking : barrel-block locking
Trigger : single trigger
Weight : 3.kg. (6lb 9¹/₂oz)
Length : 111 or 114cm (39³/₄—44⁷/₈in)
Barrel length : 67 or 70cm (26³/₈ or 27¹/₂ in)
Ejector : automatic
Choke : ¹/₂ and full, ¹/₄ and ³/₄
Sight : 7mm (⁹/₃₂in) ventilated rib and bead
Safety : sliding safety catch on neck of stock

## CHARACTERISTICS

— material : steel
— finish : blued barrels, nickel-chrome steel action with hunting scene
— stock : stock of special walnut, with pistol-grip

## *Rizzini S780 N (Standard Model)*

## TECHNICAL DETAILS

Gauge/calibre : 12 or 16
Chamber length : 70mm (2³/₄in), or 76mm (3in)
Number of barrels : double-barrels over-and-under
Action : breech-loading
Locking : barrel-block locking
Trigger : single trigger
Weight : 2.9kg. (6lb 6oz)
Length : 111 or 114cm (39³/₄—44⁷/₈in)
Barrel length : 67 or 70cm (26³/₈ or 27¹/₂in)
Ejector : automatic
Choke : ¹/₂ and full, ¹/₄ and ³/₄
Sight : 7mm (⁹/₃₂in) ventilated rib and bead
Safety : sliding safety catch on neck of stock

## CHARACTERISTICS

— material : steel
— finish : blued barrels, nickel-chrome steel action with hunting motif
— stock : walnut stock, with pistol-grip

## *Rizzini S780 Skeet*

## TECHNICAL DETAILS

Gauge/calibre : 12
Chamber length : 70mm (2³/₄in)
Number of barrels : double-barrels over-and-under
Action : breech-loading
Locking : barrel-block locking
Trigger : single trigger
Weight : 3.2kg. (7lb)

| | |
|---|---|
| Length | : 111 or 115cm (39³/₄–45¹/₄in) |
| Barrel length | : 67 or 70cm (26³/₈ or 27¹/₂in) |
| Ejector | : automatic |
| Choke | interchangeable chokes |
| Sight | 10mm (⁷/₁₆in) ventilated rib with bead |
| Safety | : sliding safety catch on neck of stock |

**CHARACTERISTICS**

| | |
|---|---|
| — material | : steel |
| — finish | : blued barrels, nickel-chrome steel action decorated with floral designs and clay pigeon motifs |
| — stock | : walnut stock, with pistol-grip |

🐓

## *Rizzini S780 Sporting*

**TECHNICAL DETAILS**

| | |
|---|---|
| Gauge/calibre | : 12 |
| Chamber length | : 70mm (2³/₄in) |
| Number of barrels | : double-barrels over-and-under |
| Action | : breech-loading |
| Locking | : barrel-block locking |
| Trigger | single trigger |
| Weight | : 3.3kg. (7lb 4oz) |
| Length | : 115–119cm (45¹/₄–46⁷/₈in) |
| Barrel length | : 71 or 75cm (28 or 29¹/₂in) |
| Ejector | : automatic |
| Choke | interchangeable chokes |
| Sight | 10mm (⁷/₁₆in) ventilated rib with bead |
| Safety | : sliding safety catch on neck of stock |

**CHARACTERISTICS**

| | |
|---|---|
| — material | : steel |
| — finish | : blued barrels, nickel-chrome steel action with floral decoration |
| — stock | : walnut stock, with pistol-grip |

🐓

## *Rizzini S780 Trap*

**TECHNICAL DETAILS**

| | |
|---|---|
| Gauge/calibre | : 12 |
| Chamber length | : 70mm (2³/₄in) |
| Number of barrels | : double-barrels over-and-under |
| Action | : breech-loading |
| Locking | : barrel-block locking |
| Trigger | single trigger |

| | |
|---|---|
| Weight | : 3.7kg. (8lb 2¹/₄oz) |
| Length | : 122cm (48in) |
| Barrel length | : 75cm (29¹/₂in) |
| Ejector | : automatic |
| Choke | interchangeable chokes |
| Sight | 11mm (⁷/₁₆in) ventilated rib and bead |
| Safety | : sliding safety catch on neck of stock |

**CHARACTERISTICS**

| | |
|---|---|
| — material | : steel |
| — finish | : blued barrels, nickel-chrome steel action |
| — stock | : walnut stock, with pistol-grip |

🐓

## *Rizzini S782 EMEL (Deluxe Model)*

**TECHNICAL DETAILS**

| | |
|---|---|
| Gauge/calibre | : 12 or 16 |
| Chamber length | : 70mm (2³/₄in), or 76mm (3in) |
| Number of barrels | : double-barrels over-and-under |
| Action | : breech-loading |
| Locking | : barrel-block locking |
| Trigger | single trigger |
| Weight | : 3.05kg (6lb 11¹/₄oz) |
| Length | : 111 or 114cm (39³/₄ 44³/₄in) |
| Barrel length | : 67 or 70cm (26³/₈ or 27¹/₂in) |

| | |
|---|---|
| Ejector | : automatic |
| Choke | : $^1/_2$ and full, $^1/_4$ and $^3/_4$, or interchangeable chokes |
| Sight | : 7mm ($^9/_{32}$in) ventilated rib and bead |
| Safety | : sliding safety catch on neck of stock |

**CHARACTERISTICS**

| | |
|---|---|
| – material | : steel |
| – finish | : blued barrels, nickel-chrome steel action with hand engraved and gold inlaid hunting scenes on side-lock plates |
| – stock | : stock of selected walnut, with pistol-grip |

This gun can be supplied with a luxury leather gun case.

## *Rizzini S782 EML*

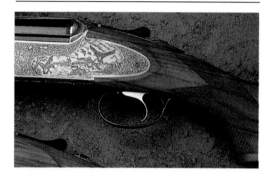

**TECHNICAL DETAILS**

| | |
|---|---|
| Gauge/calibre | : 12 or 16 |
| Chamber length | : 70mm ($2^3/_4$in), or 76mm (3in) |
| Number of barrels | : double-barrels over-and-under |
| Action | : breech-loading |
| Locking | : barrel-block locking |
| Trigger | : single trigger |
| Weight | : 3.05kg. (6lb 11$^1/_4$oz) |
| Length | : 111 or 114cm (39$^3/_4$–44$^7/_8$in) |
| Barrel length | : 67 or 70cm (26$^3/_8$ or 27$^1/_2$in) |
| Ejector | : automatic |
| Choke | : $^1/_2$ and full, $^1/_4$ and $^3/_4$ |
| Sight | : 7mm ($^9/_{32}$in) ventilated rib and bead |
| Safety | : sliding safety catch on neck of stock |

**CHARACTERISTICS**

| | |
|---|---|
| – material | : steel |
| – finish | : blued barrels, nickel-chrome steel action with hunting scenes on side-lock plates |
| – stock | : stock of selected walnut, with pistol-grip |

## *Rizzini S790 EL Trap/Skeet/Sporting*

**TECHNICAL DETAILS**

| | |
|---|---|
| Gauge/calibre | : 12 |
| Chamber length | : 70mm ($2^3/_4$in) |
| Number of barrels | : double-barrels over-and-under |
| Action | : breech-loading |

| | |
|---|---|
| Locking | : barrel-block locking |
| Trigger | : single trigger |
| Weight | : 3.7kg. (8lb 2$^1/_4$oz) |
| Length | : 118 or 122cm (46$^1/_2$–48in) |
| Barrel length | : 71 or 75cm (28 or 29$^1/_2$in) |
| Ejector | : automatic |
| Choke | : interchangeable chokes |
| Sight | : 10mm ($^7/_{16}$in) ventilated rib with bead |
| Safety | : sliding safety catch on neck of stock |

**CHARACTERISTICS**

| | |
|---|---|
| – material | : steel |
| – finish | : blued barrels, nickel-chrome steel action with gold inlaid engraving of clay pigeons |
| – stock | : stock of selected walnut, with pistol-grip |

## *Rizzini S790 EMEL*

**TECHNICAL DETAILS**

| | |
|---|---|
| Gauge/calibre | : 20, 28, or .410 |
| Chamber length | : 65mm (2$^1/_2$in), 70mm (2$^3/_4$in), or 76mm (3in) |
| Number of barrels | : double-barrels over-and-under |
| Action | : breech-loading |
| Locking | : barrel-block locking |
| Trigger | : single trigger |
| Weight | : 2.5–2.7kg. (5lb 8oz–6lb) |
| Length | : 113 or 116cm (44$^1/_2$ or 45$^5/_8$in) |
| Barrel length | : 67 or 70cm (26$^3/_8$ or 27$^1/_2$ in) |
| Ejector | : automatic |
| Choke | : $^1/_2$ and full, or $^1/_4$ and $^3/_4$ |
| Sight | : 6mm ($^3/_8$in) ventilated rib with bead |
| Safety | : sliding safety catch on neck of stock |

- material : steel
- finish : blued barrels, nickel-chrome steel action with hand engraved monogram
- stock : stock of specially-selected walnut, with pistol-grip

This gun can be supplied with an exclusive leather gun case.

## Rizzini S792 EMEL

| | |
|---|---|
| Weight | : 3.7kg. (8lb 2$^1$/$_4$oz) |
| Length | : 122cm (48in) |
| Barrel length | : 75cm (29$^1$/$_2$ in) |
| Ejector | : automatic |
| Choke | : $^1$/$_2$ and full or interchangeable chokes |
| Sight | : 10mm ($^7$/$_{16}$ in) ventilated rib with bead |
| Safety | : sliding safety catch on neck of stock |

**CHARACTERISTICS**
- material : steel
- finish : blued barrels, nickel-chrome steel action with side-lock plates
- stock : stock of specially-selected walnut, with pistol-grip

**TECHNICAL DETAILS**
| | |
|---|---|
| Gauge/calibre | : 20, 28, or .410 |
| Chamber length | : 65mm (2$^1$/$_2$in), 70mm (2$^3$/$_4$in), or 76mm (3in) |
| Number of barrels | : double-barrels over-and-under |
| Action | : breech-loading |
| Locking | : barrel-block locking |
| Trigger | single trigger |
| Weight | : 2.5–2.7kg. (5lb 8oz–6lb) |
| Length | : 113 or 116cm (44$^1$/$_2$ or 45$^5$/$_8$in) |
| Barrel length | : 67 or 70cm (26$^3$/$_8$ or 27$^1$/$_2$in) |
| Ejector | : automatic |
| Choke | : $^1$/$_2$ and full, or $^1$/$_4$ and $^3$/$_4$ |
| Sight | : 6mm ($^3$/$_8$in) ventilated rib with bead |
| Safety | : sliding safety catch on neck of stock |

**CHARACTERISTICS**
- material : steel
- finish : blued barrels, nickel-chrome steel action with hand engraved hunting motifs on side-lock plates
- stock : stock of specially-selected walnut: straight English or with pistol-grip to choice

This gun can be supplied with an exclusive leather gun case.

## Rizzini S2000 Trap

**TECHNICAL DETAILS**
| | |
|---|---|
| Gauge/calibre | : 12 |
| Chamber length | : 70mm (2$^3$/$_4$in) |
| Number of barrels | : double-barrels over-and-under |
| Action | : breech-loading |
| locking | : barrel-block locking |
| Trigger | single trigger |

# Rottweil/Dynamit Nobel

The famous chemist Alfred Nobel founded Alfred Nobel & Co. near Hamburg, Germany, in 1865. Initially, the company solely made the Dynamite explosive that Nobel had invented.

Subsequently other products were added such as munitions, plastics, and firearms. The company merged with RWS (the Rheinisch-Westfälischen Sprengstoff-Fabriken) in 1931. The company produced a wide range of rifle and shotgun cartridges under the RWS name. The brand name Rottweil originates from the town of that name in the Black Forest where shotgun cartridges were made for Dynamit Nobel.

The name later became used for a range of shotguns of the highest quality. Another company within the group is Geco, a contraction of Genschow & Co., who used to make pistol and revolver ammunition.

Dynamit Nobel is now a multinational concern with about 13,000 employees in many subsidiary companies. The Rottweil Paragon is the showpiece of the company. The gun can be regarded as a do-it-yourself kit, since all the essential parts can easily be changed by the owner.

Typical of the parts that can be changed are a range of alternative trigger groups, 11 different barrels, 9 types of stock, and 6 choices of fore-end. This enables one gun to be used for a range of different sporting activities.

## *Rottweil 90*

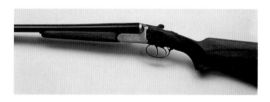

**TECHNICAL DETAILS**
Gauge/calibre     : 12
Chamber length    : 70mm (2³/₄in)
Number of barrels : double-barrels side-by-side
Action            : breech-loading
Locking           : double barrel-block locking
Trigger             twin triggers
Weight            : 3.2kg. (7lb)
Length            : 113cm (44¹/₂ in)
Barrel length     : 71cm (28in)
Ejector           : extractor only
Choke              ¹/₂ and full
Sight              low rib with bead
Safety            : sliding safety catch on neck of stock and barrel
                    selector

**CHARACTERISTICS**
— material        : steel
— finish          : blued barrels, bare metal action
— stock           : walnut stock, with pistol-grip

The Type DF 90E of this model has ejectors.

## *Rottweil 92*

**TECHNICAL DETAILS**
Gauge/calibre     : 12

Chamber length    : 70mm (2³/₄in)
Number of barrels : double-barrels side-by-side
Action            : breech-loading
Locking           : quadruple barrel-block locking
Trigger             single trigger
Weight            : 3kg (6lb 9¹/₂oz)
Length            : 114cm (44⁷/₈in)
Barrel length     : 71cm (28in)
Ejector           : automatic
Choke              ¹/₂ and full
Sight              low rib with bead
Safety            : sliding safety catch on neck of stock and barrel
                    selector

**CHARACTERISTICS**
— material        : steel
— finish          : blued
— stock           : walnut stock, with pistol-grip
〰

## *Rottweil 94 SE*

**TECHNICAL DETAILS**
Gauge/calibre     : 12
Chamber length    : 70mm (2³/₄in)
Number of barrels : double-barrels side-by-side
Action            : breech-loading
Locking           : double barrel-block locking
Trigger             twin trigger
Weight            : 3.2kg (7lb)
Length            : 113cm (44¹/₂in)
Barrel length     : 71cm (28in)
Ejector           : automatic
Choke              ¹/₂ and full
Sight              low rib with bead
Safety            : sliding safety catch on neck of stock and barrel
                    selector

**CHARACTERISTICS**
— material        : steel
— finish          : blued barrels, bare metal action with floral engravings on side-lock plates
— stock           : straight English stock of walnut
〰

## *Rottweil 96 SE*

## TECHNICAL DETAILS

Gauge/calibre    : 12 or 20
Chamber length    : 70mm (2³/₄in) or 76mm (3in) for 20 gauge
Number of barrels : double-barrels side-by-side
Action    : breech-loading
Locking    : double barrel-block locking
Trigger    twin trigger
Weight    : 20 gauge: 2.9kg (6lb 6oz) 12 gauge: 3.2kg (7lb)
Length    : 118cm (46¹/₂in)
Barrel length    : 71cm (28in)
Ejector    : automatic
Choke    ¹/₂ and full
Sight    low rib with bead
Safety    : sliding safety catch on neck of stock and barrel selector

## CHARACTERISTICS

— material    : steel
— finish    : blued barrels, bare metal action with hand-engraved floral motifs on side-lock plates
— stock    : straight English stock of walnut

## Rottweil 500

## TECHNICAL DETAILS

Gauge/calibre    : 12
Chamber length    : 70mm (2³/₄in)
Number of barrels : double-barrels over-and-under
Action    : breech-loading
Locking    : locking lugs in upper barrel with transverse locking in breech
Trigger    single trigger
Weight    : 3.1kg (6lb 13oz)
Length    : 114cm (44⁷/₈in)
Barrel length    : 71cm (28in)
Ejector    : extractor only
Choke    ¹/₂ and full
Sight    7mm (⁹/₃₂in) ventilated rib and bead
Safety    : sliding safety catch on neck of stock; barrel selector in top of trigger

## CHARACTERISTICS

— material    : steel
— finish    : blued barrels, bare metal action
— stock    : hardwood stock with pistol-grip

## Rottweil Model 500 LX

## TECHNICAL DETAILS

Gauge/calibre    : 12
Chamber length    : 70mm (2³/₄in)

## TECHNICAL DETAILS (right column)

Number of barrels : double-barrels over-and-under
Action    : breech-loading
Locking    : locking lugs in upper barrel with transverse locking in breech
Trigger    single trigger
Weight    : 3.1kg (6lb 13oz)
Length    : 114cm (44⁷/₈in)
Barrel length    : 71cm (28in)
Ejector    : extractor only
Choke    ¹/₂ and full
Sight    7mm (⁹/₃₂ in) ventilated rib and bead
Safety    : sliding safety catch on neck of stock; barrel selector in top of trigger

## CHARACTERISTICS

— material    : steel
— finish    : blued barrels, bare metal action
— stock    : walnut stock with pistol-grip

## Rottweil 600

## TECHNICAL DETAILS

Gauge/calibre    : 12
Chamber length    : 70mm (2³/₄in)
Number of barrels : double-barrels over-and-under
Action    : breech-loading
Locking    : double barrel-block locking
Trigger    single trigger
Weight    : 3.1kg (6lb 13oz)
Length    : 114cm (44⁷/₈in)
Barrel length    : 71cm (28in)
Ejector    : extractor only
Choke    ¹/₂ and full
Sight    7mm (⁹/₃₂ in) ventilated rib and bead
Safety    : sliding safety catch on neck of stock; barrel selector in top of trigger

## CHARACTERISTICS

— material    : steel

| | |
|---|---|
| – finish | : blued, no ejector |
| – stock | : hardwood stock with pistol-grip or straight English stock |

## Rottweil 700 AL Lightweight

**TECHNICAL DETAILS**

| | |
|---|---|
| Gauge/calibre | : 12 |
| Chamber length | : 70mm (2³/₄in) |
| Number of barrels | : double-barrels over-and-under |
| Action | : breech-loading |
| Locking | : double barrel-block locking |
| Trigger | single trigger |
| Weight | : 2.5kg (5lb 8oz) |
| Length | : 105cm (41in) |
| Barrel length | : 61cm (24in) |
| Ejector | : automatic |
| Choke | ¹/₄ and ³/₄ |
| Sight | 7mm (⁹/₃₂in) ventilated rib and bead |
| Safety | : sliding safety catch on neck of stock; barrel selector in top of trigger |

**CHARACTERISTICS**

| | |
|---|---|
| – material | : steel |
| – finish | : blued |
| – stock | : walnut stock with pistol-grip |

## Rottweil 770 Hunter

**TECHNICAL DETAILS**

| | |
|---|---|
| Gauge/calibre | : 12 |
| Chamber length | : 70mm (2³/₄in) |
| Number of barrels | : double-barrels over-and-under |
| Action | : breech-loading |
| Locking | : double barrel-block locking |
| Trigger | single trigger |
| Weight | : 3.1kg (6lb 13oz) |
| Length | : 114cm (44⁷/₈in) |

| | |
|---|---|
| Barrel length | : 71cm (28in) |
| Ejector | : automatic |
| Choke | ¹/₂ and full |
| Sight | 7mm (⁹/₃₂in) ventilated rib and bead |
| Safety | : sliding safety catch on neck of stock; barrel selector in top of trigger |

**CHARACTERISTICS**

| | |
|---|---|
| – material | : steel |
| – finish | : blued barrels, bare metal action |
| – stock | : walnut stock with pistol-grip |

## Rottweil 770 Jagd-AL Lightweight

**TECHNICAL DETAILS**

| | |
|---|---|
| Gauge/calibre | : 12 |
| Chamber length | : 70mm (2³/₄in) |
| Number of barrels | : double-barrels over-and-under |
| Action | : breech-loading |
| Locking | : double barrel-block locking |
| Trigger | single trigger |
| Weight | : 2.6kg (5lb 11³/₄oz) |
| Length | : 111cm (43³/₄in) |
| Barrel length | : 68cm (26³/₄in) |
| Ejector | : automatic |
| Choke | ¹/₂ and full |
| Sight | 7mm (⁹/₃₂in) ventilated rib and bead |
| Safety | : sliding safety catch on neck of stock; barrel selector in top of trigger |

**CHARACTERISTICS**

| | |
|---|---|
| – material | : steel barrels, light alloy action |
| – finish | : blued barrels, bare metal lock plate in action |
| – stock | : walnut stock with pistol-grip |

## Rottweil Paragon

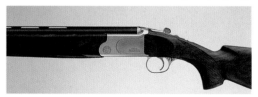

**TECHNICAL DETAILS**

| | |
|---|---|
| Gauge/calibre | : 12 |
| Chamber length | : 70mm (2³/₄in) |
| Number of barrels | : double-barrels over-and-under |

| | |
|---|---|
| Action | : breech-loading |
| Locking | : self-locating locking lugs that grip in recesses either side of the bottom barrel |
| Trigger | single trigger |
| Weight | : 3.3–3.8kg (7lb 9$^1$/$_2$oz–8lb 5$^3$/$_4$oz) |
| Length | : 107–124cm (42$^1$/$_8$–48$^3$/$_4$in) |
| Barrel length | : 70–86cm (27$^1$/$_2$–33$^3$/$_4$in): 11 different barrels available |
| Ejector | : automatic; can be disengaged |
| Choke | fixed chokes to choice of interchangeable chokes |
| Sight | with or without ventilated rib |
| Safety | : sliding safety catch on neck of stock; barrel selector in rear of trigger |

**CHARACTERISTICS**
| | |
|---|---|
| — material | : steel |
| — finish | : blued barrels, bare metal action |
| — stock | : walnut stock with pistol-grip; 9 different stocks and 6 different fore-ends |

## *Rottweil Pump Standard*

**TECHNICAL DETAILS**
| | |
|---|---|
| Gauge/calibre | : 12 |
| Chamber length | : 70mm (2$^3$/$_4$in) or 76mm (3in) |
| Number of barrels | : single-barrel |
| Magazine | : tubular magazine for 2, 6 (70mm) or 5 (76mm) cartridges |
| Action | : pump-action |
| Locking | : rotating lock |
| Trigger | single trigger |
| Weight | : 3kg (6lb 9$^1$/$_2$oz) |
| Length | : 127cm (50in) |
| Barrel length | : 71cm (28in) |
| Ejector | : extractor |
| Choke | interchangeable chokes |
| Sight | ventilated rib with bead |
| Safety | : push-button safety catch in front of trigger guard |

**CHARACTERISTICS**
| | |
|---|---|
| — material | : steel barrel, light alloy casing |
| — finish | : matt blued |
| — stock | : walnut stock with pistol-grip |

## *Rottweil Pump PSG/8*

**TECHNICAL DETAILS**
| | |
|---|---|
| Gauge/calibre | : 12 |
| Chamber length | : 70mm (2$^3$/$_4$in) 76mm (3in) |

| | |
|---|---|
| Number of barrels | : single-barrel |
| Magazine | : tubular magazine for 2, 8 (70mm) or 7 (76mm) cartridges |
| Action | : pump-action |
| Locking | : rotating lock |
| Trigger | single trigger |
| Weight | : 3kg (6lb 9$^1$/$_2$oz) |
| Length | : 106cm (41$^3$/$_4$in) |
| Barrel length | : 50cm (19$^3$/$_4$in) |
| Ejector | : extractor |
| Choke | cylindrical |
| Sight | bead |
| Safety | : push-button safety catch in front of trigger guard |

**CHARACTERISTICS**
| | |
|---|---|
| — material | : steel barrel, light alloy casing |
| — finish | : matt black |
| — stock | : walnut stock with pistol-grip |

This shotgun cannot be issued with a shotgun certificate in the United Kingdom because the barrel is shorter than the 24in (61cm) minimum length required. Similar restrictions apply in certain European countries.

# Ruger

Sturm, Ruger & Company Inc. was started in 1948 by William Batterman Ruger and Alexander M. Sturm. Between them, they rented a shed in Southport, Connecticut, and established a modest workshop for small-weapons. Ruger had gained his experience at the state arsenal, the Springfield Armory and at the armaments manufacturer Auto-Ordnance which made the Tommy-gun sub-machine gun. Their first product was a small-calibre pistol that was introduced in 1949. After the death of Sturm in an aircraft crash, William (Bill) Ruger continued in business on his own. Up to 1959, Ruger was best known for a wide range of revolvers. The first rifle design was introduced in 1959. It was a semi-automatic carbine in .44 Magnum calibre. In 1964 the company built a new factory in Newport, New Hampshire. The Ruger No. 1 single-shot rifle went into production in the new plant in 1967. Until this time, single-shot weapons were rather looked down upon. Those available were mainly inexpensive breech-loading firearms for hunting small game. Ruger himself was an admirer of heavy single-shot English rifles such as those of Alexander Henry. He considered that such a concept was also suitable for the North American market. The respected maker of stocks, Leonard Brownell, was taken on to design attractive stocks for this type of rifle and he became the technical manager of the Newport factory. The No. 1 rifle was a great success. A subsequent rifle was the model 77 introduced in 1968. This was a bolt-action repeating rifle with a stock designed by Brownell. This classic rifle was most unusual for its time. In 1974, Ruger developed an automatic army carbine, the Mini-14 for .223 Rem. calibre that was followed the next year by a civilian version. At first glance, the Mini-14 looks like a cross between the M1-Garand rifle and the Winchester .30-M1 carbine. Ruger introduced their first 20 gauge shotgun in 1977 because Ruger considered most customers preferred the size to 12 gauge. He appears to have estimated the US market very accurately. It was not until 1982 that Ruger also introduced a 12 gauge shotgun.

## Ruger Red Label KRL-1227

**TECHNICAL DETAILS**

| | |
|---|---|
| Gauge/calibre | : 12 |
| Chamber length | : 3in (76mm) |
| Number of barrels | : double-barrels over-and-under |
| Action | : breech-loading |
| Locking | : locking lugs on either side of bottom barrel |
| Trigger | single trigger |
| Weight | : 8lb (3.6kg) |
| Length | : 45in (114.3cm) |
| Barrel length | : 28 (71cm) |
| Ejector | : automatic |
| Choke | interchangeable chokes |
| Sight | ventilated rib with bead |
| Safety | : safety catch on neck of stock; automatic safety after breaking gun |

**CHARACTERISTICS**

| | |
|---|---|
| – material | : steel barrels, stainless steel action |
| – finish | : blued barrels, bare metal action |
| – stock | : walnut stock with pistol-grip |

## Ruger Red Label KRL-2030

**TECHNICAL DETAILS**

| | |
|---|---|
| Gauge/calibre | : 20 |
| Chamber length | : 3in (76mm) |
| Number of barrels | : double-barrels over-and-under |
| Action | : breech-loading |
| Locking | : locking lugs on either side of bottom barrel |
| Trigger | single trigger |
| Weight | : 7lb 4oz (3.3kg) |
| Length | : 45in (114.3cm) |
| Barrel length | : 28 (71cm) |
| Ejector | : automatic |
| Choke | interchangeable chokes |
| Sight | ventilated rib with bead |
| Safety | : safety catch on neck of stock; automatic safety after breaking gun |

**CHARACTERISTICS**

| | |
|---|---|
| – material | : steel barrels, stainless steel action |
| – finish | : blued barrels, bare metal action |
| – stock | : walnut stock with pistol-grip |

## Ruger Red Label KRL-2826

**TECHNICAL DETAILS**

| | |
|---|---|
| Gauge/calibre | : 28 |
| Chamber length | : 2³/₄in (70mm) |
| Number of barrels | : double-barrels over-and-under |
| Action | : breech-loading |
| Locking | : locking lugs on either side of bottom barrel |
| Trigger | single trigger |
| Weight | : 6lb (2.7kg) |
| Length | : 43in (109.2cm) |
| Barrel length | : 26 (66cm) |
| Ejector | : automatic |
| Choke | interchangeable chokes |
| Sight | ventilated rib with bead |
| Safety | : safety catch on neck of stock; automatic safety after breaking gun |

**CHARACTERISTICS**
— material : steel barrels, stainless steel action
— finish : blued barrels, bare metal action
— stock : walnut stock with pistol-grip

**CHARACTERISTICS**
— material : steel barrels, stainless steel action
— finish : blued barrels, bare metal action
— stock : straight English stock of walnut

## *Ruger Red Label KRL-2827*

## *Ruger Red Label KRLS-2029*

**TECHNICAL DETAILS**

| | |
|---|---|
| Gauge/calibre | : 28 |
| Chamber length | : 2³/₄in (70mm) |
| Number of barrels | : double-barrels over-and-under |
| Action | : breech-loading |
| Locking | : locking lugs on either side of bottom barrel |
| Trigger | single trigger |
| Weight | : 6lb 2¹/₂ oz (2.8kg) |
| Length | : 45in (144.3cm) |
| Barrel length | : 28 (71cm) |
| Ejector | : automatic |
| Choke | interchangeable chokes |
| Sight | ventilated rib with bead |
| Safety | : safety catch on neck of stock; automatic safety after breaking gun |

**TECHNICAL DETAILS**

| | |
|---|---|
| Gauge/calibre | : 20 |
| Chamber length | : 3in (76mm) |
| Number of barrels | : double-barrels over-and-under |
| Action | : breech-loading |
| Locking | : locking lugs on either side of bottom barrel |
| Trigger | single trigger |
| Weight | : 6lb 12oz (3.1kg) |
| Length | : 43in (109.2cm) |
| Barrel length | : 26 (66cm) |
| Ejector | : automatic |
| Choke | interchangeable chokes |
| Sight | ventilated rib with bead |
| Safety | : safety catch on neck of stock; automatic safety after breaking gun |

**CHARACTERISTICS**
— material : steel barrels, stainless steel action
— finish : blued barrels, bare metal action
— stock : walnut stock with pistol-grip

**CHARACTERISTICS**
— material : steel barrels, stainless steel action
— finish : blued barrels, bare metal action
— stock : straight English stock of walnut

## *Ruger Red Label KRLS-1226*

## *Ruger Sporting Clays KRL-1236*

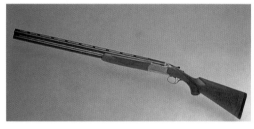

**TECHNICAL DETAILS**

| | |
|---|---|
| Gauge/calibre | : 12 |
| Chamber length | : 3in (76mm) |
| Number of barrels | : double-barrels over-and-under |
| Action | : breech-loading |
| Locking | : locking lugs on either side of bottom barrel |
| Trigger | single trigger |
| Weight | : 7lb 8oz (3.4kg) |
| Length | : 43in (109.2cm) |
| Barrel length | : 26 (66cm) |
| Ejector | : automatic |
| Choke | interchangeable chokes |
| Sight | ventilated rib with bead |
| Safety | : safety catch on neck of stock; automatic safety after breaking gun |

**TECHNICAL DETAILS**

| | |
|---|---|
| Gauge/calibre | : 12 |
| Chamber length | : 3in (76mm) |
| Number of barrels | : double-barrels over-and-under |
| Action | : breech-loading |
| Locking | : locking lugs on either side of bottom barrel |
| Trigger | single trigger |
| Weight | : 7lb 12oz (3.5kg) |
| Length | : 47in (119.4cm) |
| Barrel length | : 30 (76cm) |
| Ejector | : automatic |
| Choke | interchangeable chokes |

Sight          ventilated rib with bead
Safety        : safety catch on neck of stock; automatic safety after breaking gun

**CHARACTERISTICS**
- material    : steel barrels, stainless steel action
- finish       : blued barrels, bare metal action
- stock       : walnut stock, with pistol-grip

## Ruger KRL-2036 Sporting Clays

**TECHNICAL DETAILS**
Gauge/calibre    : 20
Chamber length   : 3in (76mm)
Number of barrels : double-barrels over-and-under
Action         : breech-loading
Locking       : locking lugs on either side of bottom barrel
Trigger        single trigger
Weight        : 7lb (3.2kg)
Length        : 47in (119.4cm)
Barrel length    : 30 (76cm)
Ejector       : automatic
Choke        interchangeable chokes
Sight         ventilated rib with bead
Safety       : safety catch on neck of stock; automatic safety after breaking gun

**CHARACTERISTICS**
- material    : steel barrels, stainless steel action
- finish       : blued barrels, bare metal action
- stock       : walnut stock, with pistol-grip

## Ruger KWS-1226

**TECHNICAL DETAILS**
Gauge/calibre    : 12
Chamber length   : 3in (76mm)
Number of barrels : double-barrels over-and-under
Action         : breech-loading
Locking       : locking lugs on either side of bottom barrel
Trigger        single trigger
Weight        : 7lb 12oz (3.5kg)
Length        : 43in (109.2cm)

---

Barrel length    : 26 (66cm)
Ejector       : automatic
Choke        interchangeable chokes
Sight         ventilated rib with bead
Safety       : safety catch on neck of stock; automatic safety after breaking gun

**CHARACTERISTICS**
- material    : steel barrels, stainless steel action
- finish       : blued barrels, bare metal action with decorative grooves
- stock       : walnut stock, with pistol-grip

## Ruger KWS-1227 Woodside

**TECHNICAL DETAILS**
Gauge/calibre    : 12
Chamber length   : 3in (76mm)
Number of barrels : double-barrels over-and-under
Action         : breech-loading
Locking       : locking lugs on either side of bottom barrel
Trigger        single trigger
Weight        : 8lb (3.6kg)
Length        : 45in (114.3cm)
Barrel length    : 28 (71cm)
Ejector       : automatic
Choke        interchangeable chokes
Sight         ventilated rib with bead
Safety       : safety catch on neck of stock; automatic safety after breaking gun

**CHARACTERISTICS**
- material    : steel barrels, stainless steel action
- finish       : blued barrels, bare metal action with decorative grooves
- stock       : walnut stock, with pistol-grip

## Ruger KWS-1236 Woodside

**TECHNICAL DETAILS**
Gauge/calibre    : 12
Chamber length   : 3in (76mm)
Number of barrels : double-barrels over-and-under
Action         : breech-loading

| | |
|---|---|
| Locking | : locking lugs on either side of bottom barrel |
| Trigger | single trigger |
| Weight | : 7lb 12oz (3.5kg) |
| Length | : 47in (119.4cm) |
| Barrel length | : 30 (76cm) |
| Ejector | : automatic |
| Choke | interchangeable chokes |
| Sight | ventilated rib with bead |
| Safety | : safety catch on neck of stock; automatic safety after breaking gun |

**CHARACTERISTICS**

| | |
|---|---|
| — material | : steel barrels, stainless steel action |
| — finish | : blued barrels, bare metal action with decorative grooves |
| — stock | : walnut stock, with pistol-grip |

# Sauer

The history of the German Sauer & Sohn goes back to 1751. The firm was established in the German town of Suhl, in Thuringia where it originally made army rifles, such as the 1871 model.

Sauer decided to switch over to making hunting guns in 1870 and introduced their first triple-barrelled gun around 1900. Between 1913 and 1945, Sauer's production capacity was turned over to serve the army.

After World War II, the eastern part of Germany was occupied by Russian troops and the German Democratic Republic was formed, otherwise known as East Germany. This was the end of the original company. The new J.P. Sauer & Sohn was established in Eckenförde in 1951, in Schleswig-Holstein. The new company's first product was a side-by-side shotgun. This proved successful and the number of employees doubled within two years. Sauer brought out the first West German triple-barrelled gun in 1953 and these guns were followed by many other models. Sauer also produced a number of types of revolver for export, based on the Colt Single Action Army revolver. A total of 310,000 of these were made for the North American market.

Sauer was looking for a working partnership with one of the larger arms manufacturers by the 1970's and in 1972, the company entered into an agreement with Colt which led to Sauer guns being sold under the Colt-Sauer name in America. Sauer also made

agreements with FFV of Sweden and FN Herstal in Belgium.

In 1973, the company developed a relationship with the Swiss SIG concern. SIG wanted a arms maker for new models of pistol they had developed. This led in 1976 to the SIG-Sauer range of pistols. The range of hunting guns was expanded in 1984 with Franchi shotguns, marketed under the Sauer-Franchi name.

## *Sauer 3000 Drilling (triple-barrelled)*

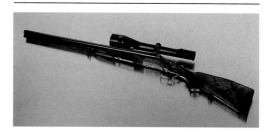

**TECHNICAL DETAILS**

| | |
|---|---|
| Gauge/calibre | : see below |
| Chamber length | : smooth-bore barrels: 2³/₄in (70mm) |
| Number of barrels | : 2 smooth-bore barrels above and 1 rifle barrel under |
| Action | : breech-loading |
| Locking | : Greener transverse and double barrel-block locking locking |
| Trigger | twin triggers |
| Weight | : 3–3.3kg (6lb 9¹/₂ oz–7lb 4oz) |
| Length | : 106.5cm (41⁷/₈in) |
| Barrel length | : 63.5cm (25) |
| Ejector | : extractors |
| Choke | smooth-bore barrels: ¹/₂ and full |
| Sight | folding sight and bead; mounting for telescopic sight |
| Safety | : safety catch on neck of stock; cocking mechanism for rifle barrel, barrel selector in left-hand side of stock above the triggers, load indicator on top of action |

**CHARACTERISTICS**

| | |
|---|---|
| — material | : steel |
| — finish | : blued barrels, engraved bare metal action |
| — stock | : walnut stock, with cheek plate and pistol-grip |

Available calibres/gauges (smooth-bore): 12 or 16; (rifle): .243 Win., 6.5x57R, 7x57R, 7x65R, .30-06 Spr., 9.3x74R. The 3000 deluxe model has a magazine for rifle cartridges in the bottom of the stock.

## *Sauer-Franchi Diplomat*

**TECHNICAL DETAILS**

| | |
|---|---|
| Gauge/calibre | : 12 |
| Chamber length | : 70mm (2³/₄in) |
| Number of barrels | : double-barrels over-and-under |

| Action | : breech-loading |
|---|---|
| Locking | : barrel-block locking |
| Trigger | single or twin triggers |
| Weight | : 3.1kg (6lb 13oz) |
| Length | : 114cm (44⁷/₈in) |
| Barrel length | : 71cm (28) |
| Ejector | : automatic |
| Choke | full and ¹/₂, ¹/₄ and ³/₄, or interchangeable chokes |
| Sight | 10mm (7/16in) wide ventilated rib with bead |
| Safety | : safety catch on neck of stock |

**CHARACTERISTICS**

| – material | : steel |
|---|---|
| – finish | : blued barrels, bare metal action with decorative engraving in the English manner |
| – stock | : stock of specially-walnut, with pistol-grip |

### Sauer-Franchi Favorit

**TECHNICAL DETAILS**

| Gauge/calibre | : 12 |
|---|---|
| Chamber length | : 70mm (2³/₄in) |
| Number of barrels | : double-barrels over-and-under |
| Action | : breech-loading |
| Locking | : barrel-block locking |
| Trigger | single or twin triggers |
| Weight | : 3.1kg (6lb 13oz) |
| Length | : 114cm (44⁷/₈in) |
| Barrel length | : 71cm (28) |
| Ejector | : automatic |
| Choke | full and ¹/₂, ¹/₄ and ³/₄, or interchangeable chokes |
| Sight | 10mm (⁷/₁₆in) wide ventilated rib with bead |
| Safety | : safety catch on neck of stock |

**CHARACTERISTICS**

| – material | : steel |
|---|---|
| – finish | : blued barrels, bare metal action with decorative engraving |
| – stock | : walnut stock, with pistol-grip |

Special barrel-extending interchangeable chokes for trap shooting are available for this gun. The barrel length is then 76cm (30in)

## Savage

Savage Arms Inc. has a long history of making arms. In 1993, the business had been in existence for 130 years. This American company was founded by Arthur William Savage in Westfield, Massachusetts, where it is still based today, in the weapon industry enclave surrounding the town of Springfield. The company's logo – an Indian head – was first used at the beginning of the twentieth century. In 1901, Savage supplied guns to Cheyenne Indians for them to use for hunting in their Wyoming reservation in return for the Indians promoting Savage rifles at Wild West shows that were very popular at that time.

Savage was the first American maker in 1920, with their 1920 Hi-Power, to introduce a rifle for the .250-3000 and .300 Savage calibres. The latter of these calibres was specially developed for the company by Charles Newton. During World War II, the production of sporting arms more or less stopped. Virtually the entire capacity of Savage was given over to making Browning machineguns. The Savage model 99 has remained the most successful gun brought out by the company. It has been produced in a range of calibres and versions, indicated by letters after the model number. A special commemorative 88CE model was introduced in 1995 to mark the centenary of the original model 99 in 1895. Savage won the annual award of the American Firearms Industry in 1996 for this gun. In 1997, Savage introduced two bolt-action shotguns: model 210F Master Shot Slug Gun, with rifled grooves for slugs and a similar model 210 FT, single-barrel shotgun.

### Savage 24F Combination gun

**TECHNICAL DETAILS**

| Gauge/calibre | : see below |
|---|---|
| Chamber length | : 3in (76mm) |

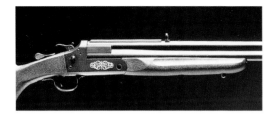

| | |
|---|---|
| Number of barrels | : double-barrels over-and-under |
| Action | : breech-loading |
| Locking | : barrel-block locking |
| Trigger | single trigger |
| Weight | : 8lb (3.6kg) |
| Length | : 40½ in (103cm) |
| Barrel length | : 24in (61cm) |
| Ejector | : extractor |
| Choke | interchangeable chokes for smooth-bore barrel |
| Sight | notched sight with bead; suitable for mounting telescopic sight |
| Safety | : push-button safety catch below cock and barrel selector |

### CHARACTERISTICS

| | |
|---|---|
| — material | : steel |
| — finish | : matt black |
| — stock | : black plastic stock, with pistol-grip |

Available calibres/gauges (bottom barrel): 12, combined with .22 Hornet, .223 Rem., or (bottom barrel): 20, combined with .22LR, .22 Hornet, .223 Rem., or .30-30 Win.

## Savage 210F Master Shot Slug

### TECHNICAL DETAILS

| | |
|---|---|
| Gauge/calibre | : see below |
| Chamber length | : 3in (76mm) |
| Number of barrels | : single-barrel |
| Magazine | : fixed magazine for 3 cartridges |
| Action | : bolt-action |
| Locking | : 3-lugs locking |
| Trigger | single trigger |
| Weight | : 7lb 8oz (3.4kg) |
| Length | : 43½ in (111cm) |
| Barrel length | : 24in (61cm) |
| Ejector | : extractor in bolt head |
| Choke | not applicable; rifled barrel |
| Sight | none; suitable for mounting telescopic sight |
| Safety | : safety catch on right of bolt |

### CHARACTERISTICS

| | |
|---|---|
| — material | : steel |
| — finish | : blued |
| — stock | : black plastic stock, with pistol-grip |

## Savage 210FT Master Shot Turkey Shotgun

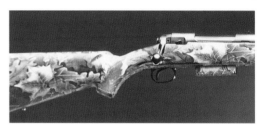

### TECHNICAL DETAILS

| | |
|---|---|
| Gauge/calibre | : 12 |
| Chamber length | : 3in (76mm) |
| Number of barrels | : single-barrel |
| Magazine | : fixed magazine for 3 cartridges |
| Action | : bolt-action |
| Locking | : 3-lugs locking |
| Trigger | single trigger |
| Weight | : 7lb 8oz (3.4kg) |
| Length | : 43½ in (111cm) |
| Barrel length | : 24in (61cm) |
| Ejector | : extractor in bolt head |
| Choke | long distance full choke |
| Sight | notched and bead |
| Safety | : safety catch on right of bolt |

### CHARACTERISTICS

| | |
|---|---|
| — material | : steel |
| — finish | : blued |
| — stock | : black plastic stock, with pistol-grip in leaf motif camouflage colours |

# Simson/Suhl

The master gunsmith Franz Jäger from Suhl in Germany was granted a patent in 1906 on a new type of breech-operating action. Until World War II, a number of different rifles were made using this action, under the name Simson-Jäger. After the war, the system was further improved. An unusual feature of this action is that it remains uncocked when it has been opened, loaded and re-closed. Cocking of the firing pin and trigger tumbler does not occur until a cocking lever on the neck of the stock is operated. If no shot is fired, the weapon can be uncocked again silently by moving the sliding lever forwards again. The trigger-pressure can be adjusted in three steps.

The Simson Superleicht (extremely light) is available with ten different types of engraving and in two versions, depending on the choice of rifle calibre.

## Simson Superleicht (extremely light) Combination gun

### TECHNICAL DETAILS

| | |
|---|---|
| Gauge/calibre | : see below |
| Chamber length | : 76mm (3in) |
| Number of barrels | : double-barrels over-and-under |
| Action | : breech-loading |
| Locking | : double barrel-block locking with extra upper lug |
| Trigger | twin triggers |
| Weight | : 2.3–2.8kg (5lb–5lb 2½ oz) |
| Length | : 115–120cm (45¼–47¼ in) |
| Barrel length | : 66–71cm (26–28in) |
| Ejector | : extractor |
| Choke | to choice |
| Sight | fixed notch and bead: special swivel mount for telescopic sight |
| Safety | : automatic safety after breaking gun; slider for cocking rifle barrel |

### CHARACTERISTICS

| | |
|---|---|
| — material | : steel |
| — finish | : blue barrels, bare metal action with choice of engravings |
| — stock | : stock of specially-selected walnut, with pistol-grip and cheek plate |

Available calibres/gauges (smooth-bore): 20/76; (rifle): .22 Hornet, .223 Rem., 5.6x50RM, 5.6x52R; model SL-II: 6.5x62R Frères, .243 Win., 6.5x57R, 6.5x65R, 7x57R, 7x65R, .308 Win., .30-06 Spr., .30R Blaser, 8x57 IRS, 8x76RS, 9.3x74R.

# Thompson/Center

The Thompson/Center Arms Company Inc. was established in 1964. Warren Center, who developed the Thompson/Center Contender single-shot pistol, already had a major background as a weapons specialist.

During his military service at the time of World War II, he worked in Ordnance, which is a government department that manages the government procurement of weapons. After the war, he was a gunsmith in Dallas, Texas but he suddenly decided to return to the area where he was born in Massachusetts, where he set up his own weapons workshop.

In 1954, he was employed by the Iver Johnson weapon factory for which he developed several revolvers. In 1959, he started his own business with Elton Whiting, making single-shot pistols. In 1963, he was head of development of the well-known firm of Harrington & Richardson and in that year, he developed a prototype breech-loading single-shot pistol for which his employer had no interest.

In 1964, he came into contact with Kenneth William Thompson. Together, they decided to produce this pistol. He became a director of the K. W. Thompson Tool Company and in 1965 both directors established the Thompson/Center Arms Company. The Thompson/Center pistol was introduced in 1967.

It was not until 1985 that the company brought out a carbine version of the Thompson/Center pistol in 9 different calibres. A new rifle, the Encore, was introduced in 1997. All Thompson/Center weapons are equipped with a unique safety switch on the head of the hammer. This permits the firing pin to be switched between centre- or rim-fire but it also allows the firing pin to be completely withdrawn so that the weapon cannot be fired.

## Thompson Contender Carbine

## TECHNICAL DETAILS

Calibre : .410
Chamber length : 3in (76mm)
Number of barrels : single-barrel
Action : breech-loading
Locking : barrel-block on bottom of breech
Weight : 5lb 5oz (2.4kg)
Trigger : single trigger
Length : 34³/₄in (88.3cm)
Barrel length : 21in (53.3cm)
Ejector : extractor only
Choke : full choke tube
Sight : ventilated rib and bead
Safety : firing pin point on hammer can be withdrawn, closing safety, trigger blocked when breech is opened

## CHARACTERISTICS

— material : steel
— finish : blued
— stock : walnut stock, with pistol-grip

This gun cannot be held on a shotgun certificate in the United Kingdom because its barrel is shorter than the minimum 24in (61cm) required. Similar restrictions apply in certain other European countries.

# Ugartechea

The name Ugartechea does not sound particularly Spanish but it is a Spanish company, based in Eibar, in the north of the Spanish Basque country. Eibar is a centre for arms manufacture and there is a national proof house for testing guns based in the town. The proof mark of Eibar closely resembles that of Ugartechea, an armour helmet and shield. The company was founded in 1922 by Juan Iriondo Echeverria. Since its founding, the company has solely produced side-by-side shotguns for international sale. Armas Ugartechea has managed to combine craftsmanship with modern production techniques. The company's guns are exported to other European countries, but chiefly to North and South America.

### Ugartechea 30/30 EX

## TECHNICAL DETAILS

Calibre : 12, 16, 20, 28, or .410
Chamber length : 70mm (2³/₄in); 76mm (3in) for 20 gauge
Number of barrels : double-barrels side-by-side
Action : breech-loading
Locking : barrel-block locking
Trigger : twin triggers
Weight : 3.1–3.3kg (6lb 13oz–7lb 4oz)
Length : 109–114cm (42⁷/₈–44⁷/₈in)
Barrel length : 66, 69, or 71cm (26, 27¹/₈ or 28in)
Ejector : extractor (model 30) or ejector (30EX)
Choke : ¹/₄ and ³/₄, ¹/₂ and full, ¹/₄ and ³/₄, or ³/₄ and full
Sight : bead
Safety : sliding safety-catch on neck of stock

## CHARACTERISTICS

— material : steel
— finish : blued barrels, tempered action
— stock : walnut stock, straight English or with pistol-grip to choice

This gun is also produced for the North American market in gauge 10 Magnum for 3¹/₂ in (89mm) chambers with 32in (81cm) barrels.

## Ugartechea 40/40 EX

### TECHNICAL DETAILS
| | |
|---|---|
| Calibre | : 12, 16, 20, 28, or .410 |
| Chamber length | : 70mm (2³/₄in); 76mm (3in) for 20 gauge |
| Number of barrels | : double-barrels side-by-side |
| Action | : breech-loading |
| Locking | : barrel-block locking |
| Trigger | : twin triggers |
| Weight | : 3.1–3.3kg (6lb 13oz–7lb 4oz) |
| Length | : 109–114cm (42⁷/₈–44⁷/₈in) |
| Barrel length | : 66, 69, or 71cm (26, 27¹/₈ or 28in) |
| Ejector | : extractor (model 40) or ejector (40EX) |
| Choke | : ¹/₄ and ³/₄, ¹/₂ and full, ¹/₄ and ¹/₂, or ³/₄ and full |
| Sight | : bead |
| Safety | : sliding safety-catch on neck of stock |

### CHARACTERISTICS
| | |
|---|---|
| — material | : steel |
| — finish | : blued barrels, lightly engraved bare metal action |
| — stock | : walnut stock, straight English or with pistol-grip to choice |

## Ugartechea 75 / 75-EX

### TECHNICAL DETAILS
| | |
|---|---|
| Calibre | : 12, 16, or 20 |
| Chamber length | : 70mm (2³/₄in); 76mm (3in) for 20 gauge |
| Number of barrels | : double-barrels side-by-side |
| Action | : breech-loading |
| Locking | : barrel-block locking |
| Trigger | : twin triggers |

| | |
|---|---|
| Weight | : 3.1–3.3kg (6lb 13oz–7lb 4oz) |
| Length | : 109–114cm (42⁷/₈–44⁷/₈ in) |
| Barrel length | : 66, 69, or 71cm (26, 27¹/₈ or 28in) |
| Ejector | : extractor or ejector (Milano-EX) |
| Choke | : ¹/₄ and ³/₄, ¹/₂ and full, ¹/₄ and ¹/₂, or ³/₄ and full |
| Sight | : bead |
| Safety | : sliding safety-catch on neck of stock |

### CHARACTERISTICS
| | |
|---|---|
| — material | : steel |
| — finish | : blued barrels, bare metal action with floral engraving on side-lock plates |
| — stock | : straight English walnut stock |

## Ugartechea 110

### TECHNICAL DETAILS
| | |
|---|---|
| Calibre | : 12, 16, 20, 28, or .410 |
| Chamber length | : 70mm (2³/₄in); 76mm (3in) for 20 gauge |
| Number of barrels | : double-barrels side-by-side |
| Action | : breech-loading |
| Locking | : barrel-block locking |
| Trigger | : twin triggers |
| Weight | : 3.1–3.3kg (6lb 13oz–7lb 4oz) |
| Length | : 109–114cm (42⁷/₈–44⁷/₈in) |
| Barrel length | : 66, 69, or 71cm (26, 27¹/₈ or 28in) |
| Ejector | : automatic |
| Choke | : ¹/₄ and ³/₄, ¹/₂ and full, ¹/₄ and ¹/₂, or ³/₄ and full |
| Sight | : bead |
| Safety | : sliding safety-catch on neck of stock, gas vents in underside of barrel block |

### CHARACTERISTICS
| | |
|---|---|
| — material | : steel |
| — finish | : blued barrels, bare metal action with Arabesque engraving of side-lock plates |
| — stock | : walnut stock, straight English or with pistol-grip to choice |

## Ugartechea 116

### TECHNICAL DETAILS
| | |
|---|---|
| Calibre | : 12, 16, 20, 28, or .410 |
| Chamber length | : 70mm (2³/₄in); 76mm (3in) for 20 gauge |
| Number of barrels | : double-barrels side-by-side |

Action           : breech-loading
Locking          : barrel-block locking
Trigger          : twin triggers
Weight           : 3.1–3.3kg (6lb 13oz–7lb 4oz)
Length           : 112–116cm (44¹/₈–45³/₄in)
Barrel length    : 66, 69, or 71cm (26, 27¹/₈ or 28in)
Ejector          : automatic
Choke            : ¹/₄ and ³/₄, ¹/₂ and full, ¹/₄ and ¹/₂, or ³/₄ and full
Sight            : bead
Safety           : sliding safety-catch on neck of stock, gas vents in underside of barrel block

## CHARACTERISTICS

— material        : steel
— finish          : blued barrels, bare metal action with Arabesque engraving of side-lock plates
— stock           : walnut stock, straight English or with pistol-grip to choice

## Ugartechea 119

**TECHNICAL DETAILS**

Calibre          : 12, 16, 20, 28, or .410
Chamber length   : 70mm (2³/₄in); 76mm (3in) for 20 gauge
Number of barrels : double-barrels side-by-side
Action           : breech-loading
Locking          : barrel-block locking
Trigger          : twin triggers
Weight           : 3.1–3.3kg (6lb 13oz–7lb 4oz)
Length           : 112–116cm (44¹/₈–45¹/₄in)
Barrel length    : 66, 69, or 71cm (26, 27¹/₈ or 28in)

Ejector          : automatic
Choke            : ¹/₄ and ³/₄, ¹/₂ and full, ¹/₄ and ¹/₂, or ³/₄ and full
Sight            : bead
Safety           : sliding safety-catch on neck of stock, gas vents in underside of barrel block

## CHARACTERISTICS

— material        : steel
— finish          : blued barrels, bare metal action with Arabesque engraving of side-lock plates
— stock           : walnut stock, straight English or with pistol-grip to choice

## Ugartechea 1000

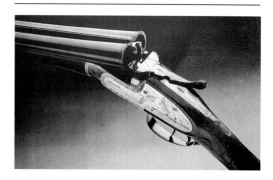

**TECHNICAL DETAILS**

Calibre          : 12, 16, or 20
Chamber length   : 70mm (2³/₄in); 76mm (3in) for 20 gauge
Number of barrels : double-barrels side-by-side
Action           : breech-loading
Locking          : barrel-block locking
Trigger          : twin triggers
Weight           : 3.1–3.3kg (6lb 13oz–7lb 4oz)
Length           : 112–116cm (44¹/₈–45³/₄in)
Barrel length    : 66, 69, or 71cm (26, 27¹/₈ or 28in)
Ejector          : automatic
Choke            : ¹/₄ and ³/₄, ¹/₂ and full, ¹/₄ and ¹/₂, or ³/₄ and full
Sight            : bead
Safety           : sliding safety-catch on neck of stock, gas vents in underside of barrel block

## CHARACTERISTICS

— material        : steel
— finish          : blued barrels, bare metal action with Arabesque engraving of side-lock plates
— stock           : walnut stock, straight English or with pistol-grip to choice

## Ugartechea 1030

**TECHNICAL DETAILS**

Calibre          : 12, 16, or 20
Chamber length   : 70mm (2³/₄in); 76mm (3in) for 20 gauge
Number of barrels : double-barrels side-by-side
Action           : breech-loading

| | |
|---|---|
| Locking | : barrel-block locking |
| Trigger | : twin triggers |
| Weight | : 3.1–3.3kg (6lb 13oz–7lb 4oz) |
| Length | : 112–116cm (44¹/₈–45³/₄in) |
| Barrel length | : 66, 69, or 71cm (26, 27¹/₈ or 28in) |
| Ejector | : automatic |
| Choke | : ¹/₄ and ³/₄, ¹/₂ and full, ¹/₄ and ¹/₂, or ³/₄ and full |
| Sight | : bead |
| Safety | : sliding safety-catch on neck of stock, gas vents in underside of barrel block |

**CHARACTERISTICS**
- material : steel
- finish : blued barrels, tempered action with Arabesque engraving of side-lock plates
- stock : walnut stock, straight English or with pistol-grip to choice

# Ugartechea 1042

**TECHNICAL DETAILS**

| | |
|---|---|
| Calibre | : 12, 16, or 20 |
| Chamber length | : 70mm (2³/₄in); 76mm (3in) for 20 gauge |
| Number of barrels | : double-barrels side-by-side |
| Action | : breech-loading |
| Locking | : barrel-block locking |
| Trigger | : twin triggers |
| Weight | : 3.1–3.3kg (6lb 13oz–7lb 4oz) |
| Length | : 112–116cm (44¹/₈–45³/₄in) |
| Barrel length | : 66, 69, or 71cm (26, 77¹/₈ or 28in) |
| Ejector | : automatic |
| Choke | : ¹/₄ and ³/₄, ¹/₂ and full, ¹/₄ and ¹/₂, or ³/₄ and full |

| | |
|---|---|
| Sight | : bead |
| Safety | : sliding safety-catch on neck of stock, gas vents in underside of barrel block |

**CHARACTERISTICS**
- material : steel
- finish : blued barrels, bare metal action with decorative engraving of side-lock plates
- stock : walnut stock, straight English or with half or full pistol-grip to choice

# Ugartechea BR-1

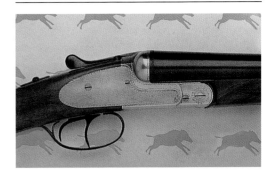

**TECHNICAL DETAILS**

| | |
|---|---|
| Calibre | : 12 |
| Chamber length | : 70mm (2³/₄in) |
| Number of barrels | : double-barrels side-by-side |
| Action | : breech-loading |
| Locking | : barrel-block locking |
| Trigger | : twin triggers |
| Weight | : 3.1–3.3kg (6lb 13oz–7lb 4oz) |
| Length | : 109–114cm (42⁷/₈–44⁷/₈in) |
| Barrel length | : 66, 69, or 71cm (26, 27¹/₈ or 28in) |
| Ejector | : extractor |
| Choke | : ¹/₂ and ¹/₂ |
| Sight | : bead |
| Safety | : sliding safety-catch on neck of stock |

**CHARACTERISTICS**
- material : steel
- finish : blued barrels, bare metal action with side-lock plates
- stock : straight English stock of walnut

# Ugartechea Jabali

**TECHNICAL DETAILS**

| | |
|---|---|
| Calibre | : 12 |
| Chamber length | : 70mm (2³/₄in) |
| Number of barrels | : double-barrels side-by-side |
| Action | : breech-loading |
| Locking | : barrel-block locking |
| Trigger | : twin triggers |
| Weight | : 3.2kg (7lb) |
| Length | : 106cm (41³/₄in) |

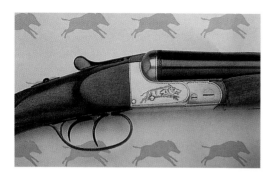

Barrel length : 63.5cm (25in)
Ejector : extractor
Choke : ¹/₄ and ¹/₄
Sight : notch and bead
Safety : sliding safety-catch on neck of stock

### CHARACTERISTICS
— material : steel
— finish : blued barrels, bare metal action with hunting motifs
— stock : walnut stock, with pistol-grip

This model is also available as Jabali EX with automatic ejectors. This gun is mainly intended for use with slugs.

### *Ugartechea Milano*

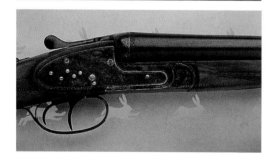

### TECHNICAL DETAILS
Calibre : 12, 16, or 20
Chamber length : 70mm (2³/₄in), 76mm (3in) for 20 gauge
Number of barrels : double-barrels side-by-side
Action : breech-loading
Locking : barrel-block locking
Trigger : twin triggers
Weight : 3.1–3.3kg (6lb 13oz–7lb 4oz)
Length : 109–114cm (42⁷/₈–44⁷/₈in)
Barrel length : 66, 69, or 71cm (26, 27⁷/₈ or 28in)
Ejector : extractor or ejector (Milano-EX)
Choke : ¹/₄ and ³/₄, ¹/₂ and full, ¹/₄ and ¹/₂, or ³/₄ and full
Sight : bead
Safety : sliding safety-catch on neck of stock

### CHARACTERISTICS
— material : steel
— finish : blued barrels, tempered action with side-lock plates
— stock : straight English stock of walnut

## Verney-Carron

**Verney-Carron**

This French company is located in that part of France surrounding Saint-Etienne at the foot of the Pyrenees. It has been a typical family business since its foundation in 1820. The company has a wide range of hunting shotguns and rifles.

The shotguns consist of a number of basic models and variants. The Super-9 range comprises six different versions, sub-divided into classic, luxury and extra luxury versions. The extra luxe d'or versions are decorated with golden animal figures.

Each model is available with a choice of straight English stock or with a pistol-grip. The Super-9 shotgun has traditional locking with a split barrel-block beneath breech block. Other models include the Sagittaire shotguns and Express rifles, plus AGO and ARC semi-automatic shotguns, and PAX pump-action shotguns.

The Sagittaire has double pin locking which is similar to that of Beretta. Verney-Carron also have a range of traditional side-by-side guns names Jubile and Jet.

The locking of the side-by-side guns is quite unusual. In addition to the barrel-block lock , the guns also have a pin lock in the centre between the pair of barrels.

### *Verney-Carron A.G.O. Luxe Magnum*

### TECHNICAL DETAILS
Calibre : 12

Chamber length   : 76mm (3in)
Number of barrels : single-barrel
Magazine         : tubular magazine for 2 cartridges
Action           : semi-automatic (gas-pressure operated)
Locking          : falling-block locking
Trigger          : single trigger
Weight           : 3.15kg (6lb 14³/₄oz)
Length           : 115–125cm (45³/₈–49³/₈in)
Barrel length    : 61 or 71cm (24 or 28in)
Ejector          : automatic
Choke            : Chokinox or Poly-Choke interchangeable chokes
Sight            : ventilated rib and bead
Safety           : push-button safety-catch in rear or trigger guard

**CHARACTERISTICS**

— material   : light alloy casing, steel barrels
— finish     : blued with bare metal sides to action body
— stock      : walnut stock, with pistol-grip

## Verney-Carron A.R.C. Luxor

**TECHNICAL DETAILS**

Calibre          : 12 or 20
Chamber length   : 70mm (2³/₄in)
Number of barrels : single-barrel
Magazine         : tubular magazine for 2 cartridges
Action           : semi-automatic
Locking          : inertia locking
Trigger          : single trigger
Weight           : 2.6kg (5lb 11¹/₂ oz) for 20 gauge to 3kg (6lb 9¹/₂ oz)
Length           : 115–130cm (45³/₈–51¹/₄in)
Barrel length    : 61, 66, 71, or 76cm (24. 26, 28, or 30in)
Ejector          : automatic
Choke            : Chokinox or Poly-Choke interchangeable chokes
Sight            : ventilated rib and bead
Safety           : push-button safety-catch in rear or trigger guard

**CHARACTERISTICS**

— material   : light alloy casing, steel barrels
— finish     : blued with bare metal sides to action body
— stock      : walnut stock, with pistol-grip

Model ARC Luxor Gros Gibier is available with a 61cm (24in) rifled barrel for use with slugs.

## Verney-Carron A.R.C. Super Leger

**TECHNICAL DETAILS**

Calibre          : 12
Chamber length   : 70mm (2³/₄in)
Number of barrels : single-barrel
Magazine         : tubular magazine for 2 cartridges
Action           : semi-automatic
Locking          : inertia locking
Trigger          : single trigger
Weight           : 3kg (6lb 9¹/₂oz)
Length           : 115 or 120cm (45³/₈–47¹/₄in)
Barrel length    : 61 or 66cm (24 or 26in)
Ejector          : automatic
Choke            : Chokinox interchangeable chokes
Sight            : ventilated rib and bead
Safety           : push-button safety-catch in rear or trigger guard

**CHARACTERISTICS**

— material   : light alloy casing, steel barrels
— finish     : blued with bare metal sides to action body
— stock      : walnut stock, with pistol-grip

## Verney-Carron J.E.T.

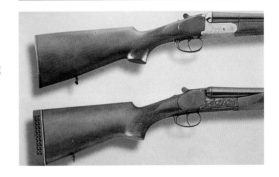

**TECHNICAL DETAILS**

Calibre          : 12 or 16
Chamber length   : 70mm (2³/₄in)
Number of barrels : double-barrels side-by-side
Action           : breech-loading
Locking          : barrel block and pin locking
Trigger          : twin triggers
Weight           : 3kg (6lb 9¹/₂oz)

| | |
|---|---|
| Length | : 113cm (44½ in) |
| Barrel length | : 70 or 80cm (27½ or 31½ in) |
| Ejector | : extractor only |
| Choke | : full and ½ |
| Sight | : bead |
| Safety | : sliding safety-catch on neck of stock |

**CHARACTERISTICS**

| | |
|---|---|
| — material | : steel |
| — finish | : blued barrels, with bare metal or tempered action |
| — stock | : hardwood, with pistol-grip |

The Rustic and Canardouze (with 80cm barrel) versions of the JET are illustrated.

## Verney-Carron Jubile

**TECHNICAL DETAILS**

| | |
|---|---|
| Calibre | : 12 |
| Chamber length | : 70mm (2¾ in) |
| Number of barrels | : double-barrels side-by-side |
| Action | : breech-loading |
| Locking | : barrel block and pin locking |
| Trigger | : twin triggers |
| Weight | : 2.95–3kg (6lb 8oz–6lb 9½ oz) |
| Length | : 108 or 113cm (42½ or 44½ in) |
| Barrel length | : 66 or 71cm (26 or 28in) |
| Ejector | : automatic |
| Choke | : ¼ and ¾ |
| Sight | : bead |
| Safety | : sliding safety-catch on neck of stock |

**CHARACTERISTICS**

| | |
|---|---|
| — material | : steel |
| — finish | : blued barrels, bare metal action |
| — stock | : walnut stock, with pistol-grip |

## Verney-Carron P.A.X. Magnum

**TECHNICAL DETAILS**

| | |
|---|---|
| Calibre | : 12 |
| Chamber length | : 76mm (3in) |
| Number of barrels | : single-barrel |
| Magazine | : tubular magazine for 2 or 5 cartridges |
| Action | : pump-action |

| | |
|---|---|
| Locking | : falling block locking |
| Trigger | : single trigger |
| Weight | : 3kg (6lb 9½ oz) |
| Length | : 113 or 126cm (44½ in or 49⅝ in) |
| Barrel length | : 66 or 71cm (26 or 28in) |
| Ejector | : automatic |
| Choke | : cylindrical |
| Sight | : adjustable notched sight and bead |
| Safety | : safety-catch at front of trigger guard |

**CHARACTERISTICS**

| | |
|---|---|
| — material | : light alloy casing, steel barrel |
| — finish | : matt black |
| — stock | : black plastic |

The Sous-Bois (with 61cm barrel) and Special Canard (76cm) barrel are illustrated.

## Verney-Carron R.E.X. Magnum

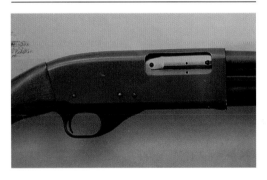

**TECHNICAL DETAILS**

| | |
|---|---|
| Calibre | : 12 |
| Chamber length | : 76mm (3in) |
| Number of barrels | : single-barrel |
| Magazine | : tubular magazine for 2 or 4 cartridges |
| Action | : pump-action |
| Locking | : falling block locking |
| Trigger | : single trigger |
| Weight | : 3.5kg (7lb 11oz) |
| Length | : 113cm (44½ in) |
| Barrel length | : 61cm (24in) |
| Ejector | : automatic |
| Choke | : cylindrical |

Sight   : bead
Safety   : safety-catch at front of trigger guard

**CHARACTERISTICS**
- material  : light alloy casing, steel barrel
- finish   : matt black
- stock   : hardwood stock, with pistol-grip

## *Verney-Carron Sagittaire*

**TECHNICAL DETAILS**
Calibre    : 12
Chamber length : 70mm (2³/₄in)
Number of barrels : double-barrels over-and-under
Action    : breech-loading
Locking    : double pin locking
Trigger    : single or twin triggers to choice
Weight    : 2.7–2.9kg (6lb–6lb 6oz)
Length    : 106 or 111cm (41³/₄ or 43³/₄in)
Barrel length  : 66 or 71cm (26 or 28in)
Ejector    : automatic or extractor only
Choke    : fixed chokes or Chokinox interchangeable chokes
Sight     : wide ventilated rib and bead
Safety    : automatic safety, selector above trigger in trigger guard

**CHARACTERISTICS**
- material  : steel
- finish   : blued barrels, bare metal action with hunting engravings
- stock   : walnut stock, with pistol-grip

## *Verney-Carron Sagittaire Mallette Trio*

**TECHNICAL DETAILS**
Calibre    : 12 (see below)
Chamber length : 70mm (2³/₄in)
Number of barrels : double-barrels over-and-under
Action    : breech-loading
Locking    : double pin locking
Trigger    : single or twin triggers to choice
Weight    : 2.9–3.1kg (6lb 6oz–6lb 13oz)
Length    : 106–111cm (41³/₄–43³/₄in)
Barrel length  : 66 or 71cm (26 or 28in)
Ejector    : automatic

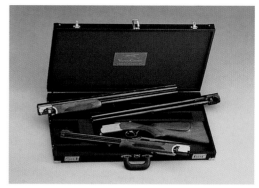

Choke    : fixed chokes or Chokinox interchangeable chokes
Sight     : wide ventilated rib and bead
Safety    : automatic safety, selector above trigger in trigger guard

**CHARACTERISTICS**
- material  : steel
- finish   : blued barrels, bare metal action with hunting engravings
- stock   : walnut stock, with pistol-grip

This gun is supplied in a luxury leather gun case with 3 barrel sets: gauge 12 (66cm), and 71cm); and as a double-barrel Express rifle for calibres 7x65R, 8x57 JRS, or 9.3x74R.

## *Verney-Carron S.I.X. Supercharge Magnum*

**TECHNICAL DETAILS**
Calibre    : 12 or 20
Chamber length : 76mm (3in)
Number of barrels : double-barrels over-and-under
Action    : breech-loading
Locking    : barrel-block locking
Trigger    : twin triggers
Weight    : 2.8–3.2kg (6lb 2³/₄oz–7lb)
Length    : 117 or 122cm (46¹/₈ or 48in)
Barrel length  : 70 or 76cm (27¹/₂ or 29⁷/₈in)
Ejector    : automatic or extractor only
Choke    : fixed chokes to choice or interchangeable chokes
Sight     : ventilated rib and bead
Safety    : sliding safety-catch on neck of stock

**CHARACTERISTICS**
- material  : steel

| | |
|---|---|
| – finish | : blued barrels, bare metal action |
| – stock | : walnut stock, with pistol-grip |

## Verney-Carron Super 9 Fulgur Side-lock

**TECHNICAL DETAILS**

| | |
|---|---|
| Calibre | : 12 |
| Chamber length | : 70mm (2³/₄in) |
| Number of barrels | : double-barrels over-and-under |
| Action | : breech-loading |
| Locking | : barrel-block locking |
| Trigger | : single or twin triggers to choice |
| Weight | : 2.7–2.9kg (6lb–6lb 6oz) |
| Length | : 111–116cm (43³/₄–45⁵/₈in) |
| Barrel length | : 71 or 76cm (28 or 29⁷/₈in) |
| Ejector | : automatic |
| Choke | : fixed chokes to choice or Chokinox interchangeable chokes |
| Sight | : wide ventilated rib and bead |
| Safety | : sliding safety-catch on neck of stock |

**CHARACTERISTICS**

| | |
|---|---|
| – material | : steel |
| – finish | : blued barrels, bare metal action engraved with hunting motifs on side-lock plates |
| – stock | : walnut stock, with pistol-grip |

## Verney-Carron Super 9 Grand Becassier

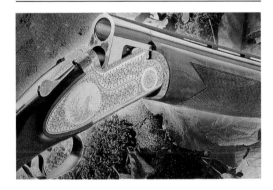

**TECHNICAL DETAILS**

| | |
|---|---|
| Calibre | : 12 |
| Chamber length | : 70mm (2³/₄in) |
| Number of barrels | : double-barrels over-and-under |
| Action | : breech loading |
| Locking | : barrel-block locking |
| Trigger | : single or twin triggers to choice |

| | |
|---|---|
| Weight | : 2.7kg (6lb) |
| Length | : 101cm (39³/₄in) |
| Barrel length | : 61cm (24in) |
| Ejector | : automatic |
| Choke | : fixed chokes to choice or Chokinox interchangeable chokes |
| Sight | : wide ventilated rib and bead |
| Safety | : sliding safety-catch on neck of stock |

**CHARACTERISTICS**

| | |
|---|---|
| – material | : steel |
| – finish | : blued barrels, bare metal action with or without side-lock plates, engraved with hunting motifs |
| – stock | : walnut: choice of straight English stock or pistol-grip |

The bottom barrel is rifled for use with slugs.

## Verney-Carron Super 9 Plume Side-lock

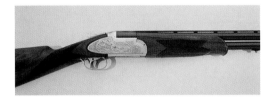

**TECHNICAL DETAILS**

| | |
|---|---|
| Calibre | : 12 |
| Chamber length | : 70mm (2³/₄in) |
| Number of barrels | : double-barrels over-and-under |
| Action | : breech-loading |
| Locking | : barrel-block locking |
| Trigger | : single or twin triggers to choice |
| Weight | : 2.7–2.9kg (6lb–6lb 6oz) |
| Length | : 106–111cm (41³/₄–43³/₄in) |
| Barrel length | : 66–71cm (26–28in) |
| Ejector | : automatic |
| Choke | : fixed, to choice or Chokinox interchangeable chokes |
| Sight | : wide ventilated rib and bead |
| Safety | : sliding safety-catch on neck of stock |

**CHARACTERISTICS**

| | |
|---|---|
| – material | : steel |
| – finish | : blued barrels, bare metal action and side-lock plates, engraved with hunting motifs |
| – stock | : walnut: choice of straight English stock or pistol-grip |

## Verney-Carron Super 9 Super Leger

**TECHNICAL DETAILS**

| | |
|---|---|
| Calibre | : 12 |
| Chamber length | : 70mm (2³/₄in) |
| Number of barrels | : double-barrels over-and-under |
| Action | : breech-loading |
| Locking | : barrel-block locking |
| Trigger | : single or twin triggers to choice |

| Weight | : 2.6kg |
|---|---|
| Length | : 106cm (41in³/₄) |
| Barrel length | : 66cm (26in) |
| Ejector | : automatic |
| Choke | : fixed chokes to choice or Chokinox interchangeable chokes |
| Sight | : wide ventilated rib and bead |
| Safety | : sliding safety-catch on neck of stock |

**CHARACTERISTICS**

| — material | : steel |
|---|---|
| — finish | : blued barrels, bare metal engraved with hunting motifs |
| — stock | : straight English stock of walnut |

## Verney-Carron Super 9 de Tir

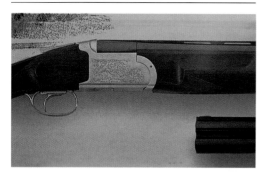

**TECHNICAL DETAILS**

| Calibre | : 12 |
|---|---|
| Chamber length | : 70mm (2³/₄in) |
| Number of barrels | : double-barrels over-and-under |
| Action | : breech-loading |
| Locking | : barrel-block locking |
| Trigger | : single or twin triggers to choice |
| Weight | : 2.9kg (6lb 6oz) |
| Length | : 111–116cm (43³/₄–45⁵/₈in) |
| Barrel length | : 71 or 76cm (28 or 29⁷/₈in) |
| Ejector | : automatic |
| Choke | : fixed, to choice or Chokinox interchangeable chokes |
| Sight | : 12mm (⁷/₁₆ in) wide ventilated rib with bead |
| Safety | : sliding safety-catch on neck of stock |

**CHARACTERISTICS**

| — material | : steel |
|---|---|
| — finish | : blued barrels, bare metal action engraved with hunting motifs |
| — stock | : walnut stock, with pistol-grip |

Verney-Carron has two models of this gun: Trap (76cm/30in barrels) and Parcours de Chasse or Sporting Clays (71cm/28in barrels).

# Weatherby

3100 El Camino Real, Atascadero, CA 93422
(805) 466-1767

Weatherby, which is one of America's best-known gunmakers, celebrated fifty years in business in 1995. The legendary Roy Weatherby founded his business in 1945 and in about 1947 he experimented with a range of cartridges. At that time the tendency was to develop large calibre hunting cartridges which consequently had a lower velocity. Roy Weatherby looked at the matter from the opposite direction. He considered small calibres with a high velocity would be more effective. The first Weatherby Magnums were based on the .300 Holland & Holland Magnum cartridge. These were the .257, the .270, and the .300 Weatherby Magnum cartridges. He started a small gun shop in South Gate, California and built his own rifles, based on Mauser and Mauser/FN systems. His very powerful super Magnum rifles attracted the attention of weapons experts such as Elmer Keith and Jack O'Connor. In about 1955, Weatherby developed further Magnum calibres, such as the .358 Weatherby Magnum, and the .460 Weatherby Magnum that were more powerful than any other cartridge at that time. In 1957, he brought out his own weapon system, the Weatherby 58 rifle that was to become the Mark V. The Mark V is still the foundation of the Weatherby company. He developed a special nine lug locking mechanism for this rifle to withstand the extremely high gas-pressures of his new calibres. Because of the nine lugs, the bolt only needs to rotate through 54 degrees; this was exceptional at that time. In the area of marketing, a concept barely heard of at that time, Weatherby was gifted. He was able to interest influential people in his rifles such as John Wayne, Gary Cooper, and Roy Rogers, but also the former US president George Bush, and General Norman Schwarzkopf. The Weatherby company has grown considerably since its beginnings and it is currently based at Atascadera in California. The Weatherby family still manage the firm. Most Weatherby designed guns used to be made in Japan but in 1993, Weatherby decided to make his guns in the USA. The guns are now made by Saco Defense Inc. of Saco, in Maine. All Weatherby shotguns are equipped with interchangeable screw-in chokes. Weatherby shotguns are not only of excellent technical quality, they also have a wide range of sporting uses, thanks to the multichoke sets. The stainless steel chokes are of course suitable for use with steel shot.

## Weatherby Athena Grade IV Field

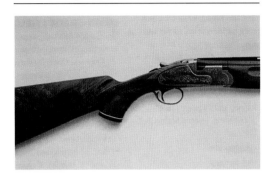

**TECHNICAL DETAILS**
Calibre : 12 or 20
Chamber length : 3in (76mm)
Number of barrels : double-barrels over-and-under
Action : breech-loading
Locking : Kersten locking
Trigger : single trigger
Weight : 6lb 8oz–8lb (2.9–3.6kg)
Length : 43 or 45in (109 or 114cm)
Barrel length : 26 or 28in (66 or 71cm)
Ejector : automatic
Choke : multichoke
Sight : ventilated rib with bead
Safety : sliding safety-catch on neck of stock, barrel selector in upper trigger guard

**CHARACTERISTICS**
— material : steel
— finish : blued barrels, nitrate grey action engraved with floral motifs
— stock : specially-selected American walnut

## Weatherby Athena Grade V Classic Field

**TECHNICAL DETAILS**
Calibre : 12 or 20
Chamber length : 3in (76mm)
Number of barrels : double-barrels over-and-under
Action : breech-loading
Locking : Kersten locking
Trigger : single trigger
Weight : 6lb 8oz–8lb (2.9–3.6kg)
Length : 43 or 45in (109 or 114cm)
Barrel length : 26 or 28in (66 or 71cm)
Ejector : automatic
Choke : multichoke
Sight : ventilated rib with bead
Safety : sliding safety-catch on neck of stock, barrel selector in upper trigger guard

**CHARACTERISTICS**
— material : steel
— finish : blued barrels, nitrate grey engraved action
— stock : specially-selected American walnut

## Weatherby Orion Grade I Field

**TECHNICAL DETAILS**
Calibre : 12 or 20
Chamber length : 3in (76mm)
Number of barrels : double-barrels over-and-under
Action : breech-loading
Locking : Kersten locking
Trigger : single trigger
Weight : 6lb 8oz–8lb (2.9–3.6kg)
Length : 43, 45, or 47in (109, 114, or 119cm)
Barrel length : 26, 28, or 30in (66, 71, or 76cm)
Ejector : automatic
Choke : multichoke
Sight : ventilated rib with bead
Safety : sliding safety-catch on neck of stock, barrel selector in upper trigger guard

**CHARACTERISTICS**
— material : steel
— finish : blued
— stock : specially-selected American walnut

## Weatherby Orion Grade II Classic Sporting

**TECHNICAL DETAILS**
Calibre : 12
Chamber length : 3in (76mm)

| Number of barrels | : double-barrels over-and-under |
| Action | : breech-loading |
| Locking | : Kersten locking |
| Trigger | : single trigger |
| Weight | : 7lb 8oz—8lb (3.4—3.6kg) |
| Length | : 45 or 47in (114 or 119cm) |
| Barrel length | : 28 or 30in (71 or 76cm) |
| Ejector | : automatic |
| Choke | : multichoke |
| Sight | : ventilated rib with bead |
| Safety | : sliding safety-catch on neck of stock, barrel selector in upper trigger guard |

**CHARACTERISTICS**

| — material | : steel |
| — finish | : blued barrels, nitrate grey action |
| — stock | : specially-selected American walnut |

## *Weatherby Orion Grade II Sporting*

**TECHNICAL DETAILS**

| Calibre | : 12 |
| Chamber length | : 3in (76mm) |
| Number of barrels | : double-barrels over-and-under |
| Action | : breech-loading |
| Locking | : Kersten locking |
| Trigger | : single trigger |
| Weight | : 7lb 8oz—8lb (3.4—3.6kg) |
| Length | : 45 or 47in (114 or 119cm) |
| Barrel length | : 28 or 30in (71 or 76cm) |
| Ejector | : automatic |
| Choke | : multichoke |
| Sight | : ventilated rib with bead |

| Safety | : sliding safety-catch on neck of stock, barrel selector in upper trigger guard |

**CHARACTERISTICS**

| — material | : steel |
| — finish | : blued barrels, nitrate grey action |
| — stock | : specially-selected American walnut |

## *Weatherby Orion Grade III Classic Field*

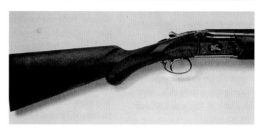

**TECHNICAL DETAILS**

| Calibre | : 12 or 20 |
| Chamber length | : 3in (76mm) |
| Number of barrels | : double-barrels over-and-under |
| Action | : breech-loading |
| Locking | : Kersten locking |
| Trigger | : single trigger |
| Weight | : 6lb 8oz—8lb (2.9—3.6kg) |
| Length | : 43 or 45in (109 or 114cm) |
| Barrel length | : 26 or 28in (66 or 71cm) |
| Ejector | : automatic |
| Choke | : multichoke |
| Sight | : ventilated rib with bead |
| Safety | : sliding safety-catch on neck of stock, barrel selector in upper trigger guard |

**CHARACTERISTICS**

| — material | : steel |
| — finish | : blued barrels, nitrate grey engraved action engraved with gold inlaid hunting motifs |
| — stock | : specially-selected American walnut |

# Westley Richards

The English family firm of Westley Richards was established in Birmingham in 1812 and set-up a branch in London's Bond Street in 1814.

A well known sporting figure, William Bishop, was taken on as manager. When Bishop retired, the firm sold the London shop to Malcolm Lyell, owner of Holland & Holland, the gunmakers. John Deeley and William Anson, inventors of the Anson & Deeley action were directors of Westley Richards when they patented their inven-

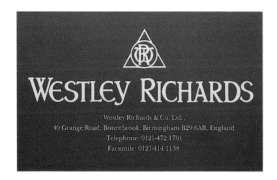

**WESTLEY RICHARDS**

Westley Richards & Co. Ltd.,
40 Grange Road, Bournbrook, Birmingham B29 6AR, England.
Telephone: 0121-472 1701
Facsimile: 0121-414 1138.

## Westley Richards Side-lock

tion. During World War I, the company switched to production for the war effort. In 1918 when Westley Richards returned to making sporting guns, the company was forced to slim down considerably. When World War II started the company could not raise sufficient capital and the company went into voluntary liquidation. The company was purchased by army Captain E.D. Barclay who put much of the production capacity to making harpoons and tools. This was not sufficiently profitable and Barclay sold his shares in 1957 to an industrialist, Walter Clode, who is still the company's managing director. From this time on Westley Richards did not look back as part of a group making guns of the highest quality. The success is largely due to Clode combining modern production techniques with hand crafted skills. Every gun is an individual piece of craftsmanship. This is reflected in the company's slogan: "British is Best," and in the prices.

The cheapest rifle, based on the bolt-action Mauser, has a basic price of £5,750, with the cheapest shotgun being £18,000. Westley Richards build traditional English side-by-side shotguns and double-Express rifles. The rifles have heavy calibres, such as .458 Win. Mag., and .500 Nitro Express but smaller calibres are also available. If desired, customers can have a customised leather gun case for about £1,350.

The guns illustrated serve merely as an indication because Westley Richards guns are made to the customer's individual requirements and only after the client has personally visited the gunmakers.

**TECHNICAL DETAILS**

| | |
|---|---|
| Calibre | : to choice: all shotgun gauges |
| Chamber length | : to choice |
| Number of barrels | : double-barrels side-by-side |
| Action | : breech-loading |
| Locking | : barrel-block locking |
| Trigger | : twin triggers |
| Weight | : 6lb 8oz–7lb 11oz (2.9–3.5kg) |
| Length | : 42$^1/_2$–49$^5/_8$in (108–126cm) |
| Barrel length | : 24–32in (61–81cm) |
| Ejector | : to choice |
| Choke | : fixed chokes to choice |
| Sight | : bead |
| Safety | : sliding safety-catch on neck of stock |

**CHARACTERISTICS**

| | |
|---|---|
| – material | : steel |
| – finish | : blued, blued barrels and tempered action, or blued barrels and bare metal action; with choice of engraving |
| – stock | : specially-selected walnut: straight English stock or with pistol-grip |

## Westley Richards William Bishop Side-lock

**TECHNICAL DETAILS**

| | |
|---|---|
| Calibre | : to choice: all shotgun gauges |
| Chamber length | : to choice |
| Number of barrels | : double barrels side-by-side |
| Action | : breech-loading |

| Locking | : barrel-block locking |
|---|---|
| Trigger | : twin triggers |
| Weight | : 6lb 8oz–7lb 11oz (2.9–3.5kg) |
| Length | : 42½–49⅝in (108–126cm) |
| Barrel length | : 24–32in (61–81cm) |
| Ejector | : to choice |
| Choke | : fixed chokes to choice |
| Sight | : bead |
| Safety | : sliding safety-catch on neck of stock |

**CHARACTERISTICS**

| – material | : steel |
|---|---|
| – finish | : blued, blued barrels and tempered action, or blued barrels and bare metal action; with choice of engraving |
| – stock | : straight English stock of specially-selected walnut |

The guns shown form one of a pair (identical guns numbered 1 and 2). The normal price for such a pair is about £42,000, excluding the customised leather gun case. The engraving of the side-lock plates is hand executed.

⌣

# Winchester

In 1855, Horace Smith, Daniel B. Wesson, and C.C. Palmer set up the Volcanic Repeating Arms Company. One of the shareholders of the company was Oliver F. Winchester, a clothing manufacturer from New Haven, Connecticut.

The company produced the Volcanic lever-action repeating rifle. In 1857, Winchester became the largest shareholder and the company name was first changed to New Haven Arms Company and then ten years later to Winchester Repeating Arms Company.

In addition to the famous lever-action repeating rifle, Winchester also produced both shotguns and bolt-action rifles for hunting. During 1917–1918, Winchester switched most of its production capacity to producing the US Rifle Model 1917, in .30-06 Springfield calibre. At the start of World War II, Winchester developed the famous .30-M1 carbine of which the company itself made 818,000. This weapon was made

under licence until the end of the war by many other companies, including Inland, Underwood, Quality Hardware & Machinery Corp., Rock-Ola, Saginaw, Irwin-Pedersen, National Poster Meter, Standard Products, and IBM. More than 6,000,000 were made during the war. Winchester was also closely involved with the production of the M1-Garand army rifle.

From about 1970 onwards, Winchester had a number of shotguns made in Japan. The 101 range, including the Super Grades, was introduced by Winchester in 1972.

A deluxe version, the Grand European, was brought out in 1981. Currently, Winchester has a limited range of shotguns based on the 1300 pump-action which they supply in numerous versions. Virtually all of these guns are equipped with Winchoke interchangeable choke sets.

The locking mechanism is a bolt with rotating bolt head with four locking lugs. The 1300 range includes "deer guns" for use (in the US) with slugs with both smooth-bore and rifled barrels. The 1300 Field range is for shooting smaller game and wildfowl. Finally, the Defender range are riot-guns: short firearms with a fixed stock or with only a pistol-grip. Winchester no longer make or sell breech-loading shotguns. The current name of the company is the US Repeating Arms Company Inc. It is part of the Olin group.

## *Winchester Model 23*

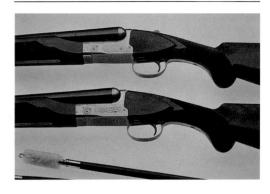

**TECHNICAL DETAILS**

| Calibre | : 12 or 20 |
|---|---|
| Chamber length | : 3in (76mm) |
| Number of barrels | : double-barrels side-by-side |
| Action | : breech-loading |
| Locking | : barrel-block locking |
| Trigger | : single trigger |

| Weight | : 6lb 9³/₄oz–7lb 8oz (3–3.4kg) |
|---|---|
| Length | : 44¹/₈ or 44⁷/₈in (112 or 114cm) |
| Barrel length | : 27¹/₈ or 28in (69 or 71cm) |
| Ejector | : automatic |
| Choke | : fixed: ¹/₂ and full, or Winchoke interchangeable choke set |
| Sight | : bead |
| Safety | : sliding safety-catch on neck of stock |

### CHARACTERISTICS

| — material | : steel |
|---|---|
| — finish | : blued barrels, bare metal decoratively engraved action |
| — stock | : walnut stock, with pistol-grip  |

## Winchester 101

### TECHNICAL DETAILS

| Calibre | : 12 or 20 |
|---|---|
| Chamber length | : 2³/₄in (70mm) or 3in (76mm) |
| Number of barrels | : double-barrels over-and-under |
| Action | : breech-loading |
| Locking | : barrel-block locking |
| Trigger | : single trigger |
| Weight | : 6lb 6oz–7lb (2.9–3.2kg) |
| Length | : 43³/₄ or 44⁷/₈in (111 or 114cm) |
| Barrel length | : 27¹/₈ or 28in (69 or 71cm) |
| Ejector | : automatic |
| Choke | : fixed: ¹/₂ and full, ¹/₄ and ¹/₂ , or ³/₄ and ¹/₄ |
| Sight | : ventilated barrel rib and bead |
| Safety | : sliding safety-catch on neck of stock |

### CHARACTERISTICS

| — material | : steel or light alloy action(lightweight version) |
|---|---|
| — finish | : blued barrels, bare metal engraved action |
| — stock | : walnut stock, with pistol-grip |

Illustrated from top to bottom are 101 Grand European and 101 Lightweight.

## Winchester 1300 Deer Black Shadow

### TECHNICAL DETAILS

| Calibre | : 12 |
|---|---|

| Chamber length | : 3in (76mm) |
|---|---|
| Number of barrels | : single-barrel |
| Magazine | : 2 or 5 cartridges |
| Action | : pump-action |
| Locking | : rotating locking |
| Trigger | : single trigger |
| Weight | : 7lb (3.2kg) |
| Length | : 42¹/₂in (108cm) |
| Barrel length | : 22in (55.9cm) |
| Ejector | : extractor |
| Choke | : cylindrical (for slugs) |
| Sight | : adjustable notched sight and bead |
| Safety | : push-button safety-catch at front of trigger guard |

### CHARACTERISTICS

| — material | : steel |
|---|---|
| — finish | : matt black protective coating |
| — stock | : plastic stock, with pistol-grip |

Illustrated from top to bottom are: 1300 Deer Camo and Deer Black Shadow. Only rifles held by permit holders may be used to shoot deer in the United Kingdom. This gun cannot be held on a shotgun certificate in the United Kingdom because its barrel is less than 24in (61cm) long. Similar restrictions apply in certain other European countries.

## Winchester 1300 Deer Camo

### TECHNICAL DETAILS

| Calibre | : 12 |
|---|---|
| Chamber length | : 3in (76mm) |
| Number of barrels | : single-barrel |
| Magazine | : 2 or 5 cartridges |
| Action | : pump-action |
| Locking | : rotating locking |
| Trigger | : single trigger |
| Weight | : 7lb (3.2kg) |
| Length | : 42¹/₂in (108cm) |
| Barrel length | : 22in (55.9cm) |
| Ejector | : extractor |
| Choke | : cylindrical (for slugs) |
| Sight | : adjustable notched sight and bead |
| Safety | : push-button safety-catch at front of trigger guard |

## CHARACTERISTICS

— material : steel
— finish : protective coating in camouflage colours
— stock : plastic stock, with pistol-grip

Illustrated from top to bottom are: 1300 Deer Camo and Deer Black Shadow. Only rifles held by permit holders may be used to shoot deer in the United Kingdom. This gun cannot be held on a shotgun certificate in the United Kingdom because its barrel is less than 24in (61cm) long. Similar restrictions apply in certain other European countries.

## Winchester 1300 Deer Ranger

### TECHNICAL DETAILS

| | |
|---|---|
| Calibre | : 12 |
| Chamber length | : 3in (76mm) |
| Number of barrels | : single-barrel |
| Magazine | : 2 or 5 cartridges |
| Action | : pump-action |
| Locking | : rotating locking |
| Trigger | : single trigger |
| Weight | : 7lb (3.2kg) |
| Length | : 42¹/₂ in (108cm) |
| Barrel length | : 22in (55.9cm) |
| Ejector | : extractor |
| Choke | : cylindrical (for slugs) |
| Sight | : adjustable notched sight and bead |
| Safety | : push-button safety-catch at front of trigger guard |

### CHARACTERISTICS

| | |
|---|---|
| — material | : steel |
| — finish | : matt black action body, blued barrel |
| — stock | : hardwood stock, with pistol-grip |

Illustrated from top to bottom are: 1300 Deer Rifled and Deer Ranger. Only rifles held by permit holders may be used to shoot deer in the United Kingdom.
This gun cannot be held on a shotgun certificate in the United Kingdom because its barrel is less than 24in (61cm) long. Similar

restrictions apply in certain other European countries.

## Winchester 1300 Deer Rifled

### TECHNICAL DETAILS

| | |
|---|---|
| Calibre | : 12 |
| Chamber length | : 3in (76mm) |
| Number of barrels | : single-barrel |
| Magazine | : 2 or 5 cartridges |
| Action | : pump-action |
| Locking | : rotating locking |
| Trigger | : single trigger |
| Weight | : 7lb 4oz (3.3kg) |
| Length | : 42¹/₂ in (108cm) rifled barrel |
| Barrel length | : 22in (55.9cm) |
| Ejector | : extractor |
| Choke | : cylindrical (for slugs) |
| Sight | : adjustable notched sight and bead |
| Safety | : push-button safety-catch at front of trigger guard |

### CHARACTERISTICS

| | |
|---|---|
| — material | : steel |
| — finish | : protective matt black coating |
| — stock | : walnut stock, with pistol-grip |

Illustrated from top to bottom are: 1300 Deer Rifled and Deer Ranger.

 ◉

## Winchester 1300 Field

### TECHNICAL DETAILS

| | |
|---|---|
| Calibre | : 12 |
| Chamber length | : 3in (76mm) |
| Number of barrels | : single-barrel |
| Magazine | : 2 or 5 cartridges |
| Action | : pump-action |
| Locking | : rotating locking |
| Trigger | : single trigger |
| Weight | : 7lb 4oz (3.3kg) |
| Length | : 46¹/₂ or 48¹/₂ in (118 or 123cm) |
| Barrel length | : 26 or 28in (66 or 71cm) |
| Ejector | : extractor |
| Choke | : Winchoke interchangeable chokes |
| Sight | : ventilated rib and bead |
| Safety | : push-button safety-catch at front of trigger guard |

## CHARACTERISTICS
- material : steel
- finish : blued
- stock : walnut stock, with pistol-grip

🕊️

# Winchester Diamondgrade Skeet

## TECHNICAL DETAILS
| | |
|---|---|
| Calibre | : 12 |
| Chamber length | : 2³/₄in (70mm) |
| Number of barrels | : double-barrels over-and-under |
| Action | : breech-loading |
| Locking | : barrel-block locking |
| Trigger | : single trigger |
| Weight | : 7lb 4oz–7lb 11oz (3.3–3.5kg) |
| Length | : 44¹/₈–44⁷/₈in (112 or 114cm) |
| Barrel length | : 27¹/₈–28in (69 or 71cm) |
| Ejector | : automatic |
| Choke | : double Skeet or Winchoke interchangeable chokes |
| Sight | : ventilated rib and bead |
| Safety | : sliding safety-catch on neck of stock |

## CHARACTERISTICS
- material : steel
- finish : blued barrels, engraved bare metal action
- stock : stock of selected walnut, with pistol-grip

Illustrated from top to bottom: Diamond Grade Skeet with compensator vents in barrel; Super Grade Skeet, and Diamond Grade with interchangeable chokes.

🕊️

# Winchester Diamondgrade Trap

## TECHNICAL DETAILS
| | |
|---|---|
| Calibre | : 12 |
| Chamber length | : 2³/₄in (70mm) |
| Number of barrels | : double-barrels over-and-under |
| Action | : breech-loading |
| Locking | : barrel-block locking |
| Trigger | : single trigger |
| Weight | : 8lb–8lb 13oz (3.6–4kg) |
| Length | : 47¹/₄in (120cm) |
| Barrel length | : 30in (76cm) |
| Ejector | : automatic |

| | |
|---|---|
| Choke | : Winchoke interchangeable chokes |
| Sight | : ventilated rib and bead |
| Safety | : sliding safety-catch on neck of stock |

## CHARACTERISTICS
- material : steel
- finish : blued barrels, engraved bare metal action
- stock : stock of selected walnut, with pistol-grip

🐓

# Winchester Supergrade Combi

## TECHNICAL DETAILS
| | |
|---|---|
| Calibre | : see below |
| Chamber length | : smooth-bore: 3in (76mm) |
| Number of barrels | : double-barrels over-and-under |
| Action | : breech-loading |
| Locking | : barrel-block locking |
| Trigger | : single trigger |
| Weight | : 8lb (3.6kg) |
| Length | : 42¹/₄in (107cm) |
| Barrel length | : 25in (63.5cm) |
| Ejector | : extractor |
| Choke | : upper barrel with Winchoke interchangeable chokes |
| Sight | : folding sight and bead; mounting for telescopic sight |
| Safety | : sliding safety-catch on neck of stock |

## CHARACTERISTICS
- material : steel
- finish : blued barrels, engraved bare metal action
- stock : walnut stock, with pistol-grip and cheek plate

Available calibres/gauges (upper smooth-bore barrel): 12; (bottom barrel): 5.6x57R, 7x65R,

.30-06 Spr., .300 Win. Mag., 9.3x74R. 7x65R, .30-06 Springf., .300 Win. Mag., 9,3x74R.
🕊

## Winchester Supergrade Lightweight

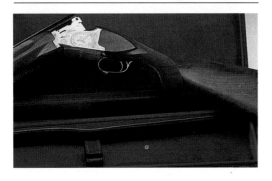

**TECHNICAL DETAILS**

| | |
|---|---|
| Calibre | : 12 or 20 |
| Chamber length | : 3in (76mm) |
| Number of barrels | : double-barrels over-and-under |
| Action | : breech-loading |
| Locking | : barrel-block locking |
| Trigger | : single trigger |
| Weight | : 6lb 6oz (2.9kg) |
| Length | : 43³/₄in (111cm) |
| Barrel length | : 27¹/₈ in (69cm) |
| Ejector | : automatic |
| Choke | : Winchoke interchangeable chokes |
| Sight | : ventilated rib and bead |
| Safety | : sliding safety-catch on neck of stock |

**CHARACTERISTICS**

| | |
|---|---|
| — material | : steel barrels, light alloy action |
| — finish | : blued barrels, engraved bare metal action |
| — stock | : walnut stock, with pistol-grip |

🕊

# Zabala Hermanos

Zabala Hermanos is established in the village of Elgueta, close to the industrial city of Eibar in the northern Spanish Basque region, on the Bay of Biscay. Zabala Hermanos, or Zabala Brothers, started as a family business in 1932 to make shotguns. These were initially made for the domestic market but later the guns began to be exported to North and South America and then to elsewhere in Europe. Some Zabala models are sold in North America under the American Arms brand name. Zabala has a wide range of shotguns: both traditional side-by-side guns and modern over-and-under Trap and Skeet guns. Spanish guns did not enjoy a good reputation at the end of the nineteenth century, thanks largely to the use of insufficiently hard steel. Such matters are now very much a thing of the past.

The quality of finish is excellent and the prices are modest. Pre-1980 side-by-side guns had barrel-block locking combined with Greener locking.

Old models that collectors still come across include the 219-A and 180 single-barrel breech-loading guns, 212 with Greener locking, and 226 with removable side-lock plates. The modern side-by-side guns are all equipped with double barrel-block locking. The external hammer side-by-side gun, 211-deluxe is a fine example of craftsmanship.

## Zabala 211-Luxe

**TECHNICAL DETAILS**

| | |
|---|---|
| Calibre | : 12 |
| Chamber length | : 70mm (2³/₄in) |
| Number of barrels | : double-barrels side-by-side |
| Action | : breech-loading |
| Locking | : double barrel-block locking |
| Trigger | : twin triggers |
| Weight | : 3kg (6lb 9¹/₂oz) |
| Length | : 112cm (44¹/₈ in) |
| Barrel length | : 70cm (27¹/₂ in) |
| Ejector | : extractor |
| Choke | : to choice |
| Sight | : bead |
| Safety | : half-cock of external hammer |

**CHARACTERISTICS**

| | |
|---|---|
| — material | : chrome-molybdenum steel |
| — finish | : blued barrels, bare metal action with Arabesque engraving |
| — stock | : walnut stock, with pistol-grip |

# Zabala 213

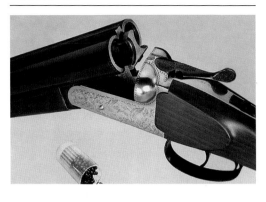

## TECHNICAL DETAILS

| | |
|---|---|
| Calibre | : 12, 16, 20, 28, or .410 |
| Chamber length | : 70mm (2³/₄in) |
| Number of barrels | : double-barrels side-by-side |
| Action | : breech-loading |
| Locking | : double barrel-block locking |
| Trigger | : twin triggers (Anson & Deeley action) |
| Weight | : 3.1kg (6lb 13oz) |
| Length | : 115cm (45³/₈ in) |
| Barrel length | : 71cm (28in) |
| Ejector | : extractor or automatic to choice |
| Choke | : to choice |
| Sight | : bead |
| Safety | : sliding safety catch on neck of stock |

## CHARACTERISTICS

| | |
|---|---|
| — material | : chrome-molybdenum steel |
| — finish | : blued barrels, bare metal action with engraving of hunting motifs |
| — stock | : walnut stock, with pistol-grip |

## Zabala 213 Magnum

## TECHNICAL DETAILS

| | |
|---|---|
| Calibre | : 10, 12, or 20 |
| Chamber length | : gauge 10: 89mm (3¹/₂in) 12 & 20: 76mm (3in) |
| Number of barrels | : double-barrels side-by-side |
| Action | : breech-loading |
| Locking | : double barrel-block locking |
| Trigger | : twin triggers |

## Zabala 222 Side-lock

| | |
|---|---|
| Weight | : 3.1–3.3kg (6lb 13oz–7lb 4oz) |
| Length | : 115, 120, or 127cm (45³/₈, 47¹/₄, or 50in) |
| Barrel length | : 70, 75, or 82cm (27¹/₂, 29¹/₂, or 32¹/₄in) |
| Ejector | : extractor or automatic ejector |
| Choke | : to choice |
| Sight | : bead |
| Safety | : sliding safety catch on neck of stock |

## CHARACTERISTICS

| | |
|---|---|
| — material | : chrome-molybdenum steel |
| — finish | : blued barrels, bare metal action with engraving of hunting motifs |
| — stock | : walnut stock, with pistol-grip and rubber recoil shock absorber |

Some European countries other than the United Kingdom do not permit the use of 10 gauge.

## Zabala 222 Side-lock

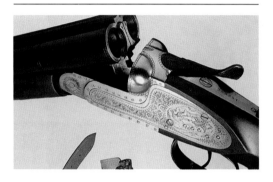

## TECHNICAL DETAILS

| | |
|---|---|
| Calibre | : 12 |
| Chamber length | : 70mm (2³/₄in) |
| Number of barrels | : double-barrels side-by-side |
| Action | : breech-loading |
| Locking | : double barrel-block locking |
| Trigger | : twin triggers |
| Weight | : 3.1–3.2kg (6lb 13oz–7lb) |
| Length | : 115 or 120cm (45³/₈ or 47¹/₄in) |
| Barrel length | : 71 or 76cm (28 or 30in) |
| Ejector | : extractor or automatic ejector |
| Choke | : to choice |
| Sight | : bead |
| Safety | : sliding safety catch on neck of stock |

## CHARACTERISTICS

| | |
|---|---|
| — material | : chrome-molybdenum steel |
| — finish | : blued barrels, bare metal action with engraving of hunting motifs on side-lock plates |
| — stock | : straight English stock, or with pistol-grip |

## Zabala Model 326-P Side-lock

## TECHNICAL DETAILS

| | |
|---|---|
| Calibre | : 12 |

Chamber length  : 70mm (2³/₄in)
Number of barrels : double-barrels side-by-side
Action      : breech-loading
Locking     : double barrel-block locking
Trigger     : twin triggers
Weight      : 3.1–3.2kg (6lb 13oz–7lb)
Length      : 115 or 120cm (45³/₈ or 47¹/₄in)
Barrel length  : 71 or 76cm (28 or 30in)
Ejector     : extractor or automatic ejector
Choke      : to choice
Sight      : bead
Safety      : sliding safety catch on neck of stock

CHARACTERISTICS
— material    : chrome-molybdenum steel
— finish     : blued barrels, bare metal action with decorative
          engraving on side-lock plates
— stock     : straight English stock, or with pistol-grip

# Zabala Berri

TECHNICAL DETAILS
Calibre     : 12, 16, or 20
Chamber length  : 70mm (2³/₄in)
Number of barrels : double-barrels side-by-side
Action      : breech-loading
Locking     : double barrel-block locking
Trigger     : single trigger (Anson & Deeley action)
Weight      : 3.1–3.3kg (6lb 13oz–7lb 4oz)
Length      : 115, 120, or 125cm (45³/₈, 47¹/₄, or 49¹/₄in)
Barrel length  : 71, 76, or 81cm (28, 30, or 32in)

Ejector     : extractor or automatic ejector
Choke      : to choice
Sight      : bead
Safety      : sliding safety catch on neck of stock

CHARACTERISTICS
— material    : chrome-molybdenum steel
— finish     : blued barrels, bare metal action
— stock     : straight English stock of walnut, or with pistol-grip

# Zabala Kestrel

TECHNICAL DETAILS
Calibre     : 12, 16, 20, 28, or .410
Chamber length  : 70mm (2³/₄in)
Number of barrels : double-barrels side-by-side
Action      : breech-loading
Locking     : double barrel-block locking
Trigger     : twin triggers (Anson & Deeley action)
Weight      : 3.1–3.3kg (6lb 13oz–7lb 4oz)
Length      : 120 or 125cm (47¹/₄ or 49¹/₄in)
Barrel length  : 76 or 81cm (30 or 32in)
Ejector     : extractor or automatic ejector
Choke      : to choice
Sight      : bead
Safety      : sliding safety catch on neck of stock

CHARACTERISTICS
— material    : chrome-molybdenum steel
— finish     : blued barrels, bare metal action
— stock     : straight English stock of walnut

# Zabala Sporting

TECHNICAL DETAILS
Calibre     : 12
Chamber length  : 70mm (2³/₄in) or 76mm (3in)
Number of barrels : double-barrels side-by-side
Action      : breech-loading
Locking     : double barrel-block locking
Trigger     : single trigger
Weight      : 3.1–3.3kg (6lb 13oz–7lb 4oz)
Length      : 115 or 120cm (45³/₈ or 47¹/₄in)
Barrel length  : 71 or 76cm (28 or 30in)

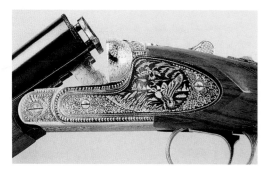

| | |
|---|---|
| Ejector | : extractor |
| Choke | : fixed chokes to choice |
| Sight | : bead |
| Safety | : sliding safety catch on neck of stock |

### CHARACTERISTICS

| | |
|---|---|
| — material | : chrome-molybdenum steel |
| — finish | : blued barrels, bare metal action with decorative side-lock plates |
| — stock | : walnut stock, with pistol-grip |

## Zabala Sporting Inter-Choke

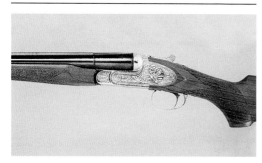

### TECHNICAL DETAILS

| | |
|---|---|
| Calibre | : 12 |
| Chamber length | : 70mm (2³/₄in) or 76mm (3in) |
| Number of barrels | : double-barrels side-by-side |
| Action | : breech-loading |
| Locking | : double barrel-block locking |
| Trigger | : single trigger |
| Weight | : 3.1–3.3kg (6lb 13oz–7lb 4oz) |
| Length | : 115 or 120cm (45³/₈ or 47¹/₄ in) |
| Barrel length | : 71 or 76cm (28 or 30in) |
| Ejector | : extractor |
| Choke | : interchangeable chokes with 5 choke tubes |
| Sight | : bead |
| Safety | : sliding safety catch on neck of stock |

### CHARACTERISTICS

| | |
|---|---|
| — material | : chrome-molybdenum steel |
| — finish | : blued barrels, bare metal action with decorative side-lock plates |
| — stock | : walnut stock, with pistol-grip |

## Zabala Suprema

### TECHNICAL DETAILS

| | |
|---|---|
| Calibre | : 12 |
| Chamber length | : 76mm (3in) |
| Number of barrels | : double-barrels over-and-under |
| Action | : breech-loading |
| Locking | : double barrel-block locking |
| Trigger | : single trigger |
| Weight | : 3.1–3.3kg (6lb 13oz–7lb 4oz) |
| Length | : 115 or 120cm (45³/₈ or 47¹/₄ in) |
| Barrel length | : 71 or 76cm (28 or 30in) |
| Ejector | : automatic |
| Choke | : interchangeable chokes with 5 choke tubes |
| Sight | : ventilated rib and bead |
| Safety | : sliding safety catch on neck of stock |

### CHARACTERISTICS

| | |
|---|---|
| — material | : chrome-molybdenum steel |
| — finish | : blued barrels, bare metal action |
| — stock | : walnut stock, with pistol-grip |

The barrels of this gun are tested to 1,200 bar.

## Zabala Vencedor Side-lock

### TECHNICAL DETAILS

| | |
|---|---|
| Calibre | : 12, 16, or 20 |
| Chamber length | : 70mm (2³/₄ in) |

Number of barrels : double-barrels side-by-side
Action : breech-loading
Locking : double barrel-block locking
Trigger : twin triggers
Weight : 3.1–3.3kg (6lb 13oz–7lb 4oz)
Length : 115 or 120cm (45³/₈ or 47¹/₄ in)
Barrel length : 71 or 76cm (28 or 30in)
Ejector : extractor or automatic ejector
Choke : interchangeable chokes with 5 choke tubes
Sight : bead
Safety : sliding safety catch on neck of stock

**CHARACTERISTICS**

— material : chrome-molybdenum steel
— finish : blued barrels, bare metal action with Arabesque engraving of side-lock plates
— stock : straight English stock of walnut

# Zabala Vencedor-Luxe Side-lock

**TECHNICAL DETAILS**

Calibre : 12, 20, 28, or .410
Chamber length : 70mm (2³/₄ in) or 76mm (3in) for gauges 20 and .410
Number of barrels : double-barrels side-by-side
Action : breech-loading
Locking : double barrel-block locking
Trigger : twin triggers
Weight : 3.1–3.3kg (6lb 13oz–7lb 4oz)
Length : 115 or 120cm (45³/₈ or 47¹/₄in)
Barrel length : 71 or 76cm (28 or 30in)
Ejector : extractor or automatic ejector
Choke : to choice
Sight : bead
Safety : sliding safety catch on neck of stock

**CHARACTERISTICS**

— material : chrome-molybdenum steel
— finish : blued barrels, bare metal action with floral motif engraving of side-lock plates
— stock : straight English stock of walnut

The barrels of this gun are tested to 1,200 bar.

# Zabala XL-90 Inter-Choke

**TECHNICAL DETAILS**

Calibre : 12, 16, or 20
Chamber length : 70mm (2³/₄in) or 76mm (3in)
Number of barrels : double-barrels over-and-under
Action : breech-loading
Locking : barrel-block locking
Trigger : single trigger
Weight : 3.2–3.4kg (7lb–7lb 8oz)
Length : 110, 115 or 120cm (43¹/₄, 45³/₈ or 47¹/₄in)
Barrel length : 66, 71 or 76cm (26, 28 or 30in)
Ejector : automatic
Choke : set of 5 interchangeable chokes
Sight : ventilated rib with bead
Safety : sliding safety catch on neck of stock

**CHARACTERISTICS**

— material : chrome-molybdenum steel
— finish : blued barrels, bare metal action
— stock : walnut stock, with pistol-grip

The barrels of this gun are tested to 1,200 bar.

# Zabala XL-90 Inter-Choke Recorridos

**TECHNICAL DETAILS**

Calibre : 12
Chamber length : 70mm (2³/₄in)

Number of barrels : double-barrels over-and-under
Action : breech-loading
Locking : barrel-block locking
Trigger : single trigger
Weight : 3.2–3.4kg (7lb–7lb 8oz)
Length : 110, 115, 120, or 125cm (43¼, 45⅜, 47¼, or 49¼ in)
Barrel length : 66, 71, 76, or 81cm (26, 28, 30, or 32in)
Ejector : automatic
Choke : set of 5 interchangeable chokes
Sight : ventilated rib with bead
Safety : sliding safety catch on neck of stock

**CHARACTERISTICS**

— material : chrome-molybdenum steel
— finish : blued barrels, bare metal action
— stock : walnut stock, with pistol-grip

The barrels of this gun are tested to 1,200 bar.

## *Zabala XL-90 Trap*

**TECHNICAL DETAILS**

Calibre : 12
Chamber length : 70mm (2¾in)
Number of barrels : double-barrels over-and-under
Action : breech-loading
Locking : barrel-block locking
Trigger : single trigger
Weight : 3.4kg (7lb 8oz)
Length : 120cm (47¼ in)
Barrel length : 76cm (30in)
Ejector : automatic
Choke : set of 5 interchangeable chokes
Sight : ventilated rib with bead
Safety : sliding safety catch on neck of stock

**CHARACTERISTICS**

— material : chrome-molybdenum steel
— finish : blued barrels, bare metal action
— stock : walnut stock, with pistol-grip

The barrels of this gun are tested to 1,200 bar.

## *Zabala XL-92 Inter-Choke Deluxe*

**TECHNICAL DETAILS**

Calibre : 12
Chamber length : 70mm (2¾in)
Number of barrels : double-barrels over-and-under
Action : breech-loading
Locking : barrel-block locking
Trigger : single trigger
Weight : 3.2–3.4kg (7lb–7lb 8oz)
Length : 115 or 120cm (45⅜ or 47¼in)
Barrel length : 71 or 76cm (28 or 30in)
Ejector : automatic
Choke : set of 5 interchangeable chokes
Sight : ventilated rib with bead
Safety : sliding safety catch on neck of stock

**CHARACTERISTICS**

— material : chrome-molybdenum steel
— finish : blued barrels, bare metal action with hunting motifs engraved on decorative side-lock plates
— stock : walnut stock, with pistol-grip and rubber recoil shock absorber

The barrels of this gun are tested to 1,200 bar.

# Angelo Zoli

The firm of Angelo Zoli should not be confused with the company of Antonio Zoli, which is also based in the Brescia region of Italy. Angelo Zoli was a typical family business making an outstanding range of shotguns and also making guns for other companies. Zoli made the Regency shotgun for Weatherby and also made the Rottweil 650 for the German company. Angelo Zoli also made replica guns, such as the Kentucky black powder rifle in calibres .45 and .50 and also the Zouave rifle in calibre .58. Shotguns by Angelo Zoli were produced from chrome-molybdenum steel and the inside of the barrels was given a tough chromium coating. All Angelo Zoli shotguns were proved to 1,200 bar in the proof house at Gardone. The company ceased making guns some ten years ago but because there are many of these guns in use by both game and sporting shots throughout Europe, they have been included in this book.

## Angelo Zoli Airone combination gun

### TECHNICAL DETAILS

| | |
|---|---|
| Calibre | : see below |
| Chamber length | : smooth-bore: 70mm (2³/₄in) |
| Number of barrels | : double-barrels over-and-under |
| Action | : breech-loading |
| Locking | : barrel-block locking |
| Trigger | : twin triggers (front trigger with pre-set) |
| Weight | : approx. 3.1kg (6lb 13oz) |
| Length | : 108cm (42¹/₂ in) |
| Barrel length | : 62cm (24³/₄in) |
| Ejector | : extractor only |
| Choke | : smooth-bore barrel: full |
| Sight | : folding sight and bead |
| Safety | : sliding safety catch on neck of stock, dropped-gun safety |

### CHARACTERISTICS

| | |
|---|---|
| — material | : steel |
| — finish | : blued barrels, bare metal action with engraved extension plates (no side-lock) |
| — stock | : walnut stock, with pistol-grip |

Available calibres/gauges (smooth-bore): 12; (rifle): 5.6x57R, 6.5x57R, 6.5x68R, 7x57R, 7x65R. An interchangeable barrel set of double smooth-bore barrels was also available for this gun. Illustrated from top to bottom

are: Zoli Condor, Zoli Saint George combination gun, and Zoli Airone. The company of Angelo Zoli ceased production in the 1980's.

## Angelo Zoli Athena Side-lock external hammers

### TECHNICAL DETAILS

| | |
|---|---|
| Calibre | : 12 or 20 |
| Chamber length | : 70mm (2³/₄ in) |
| Number of barrels | : double-barrels side-by-side |
| Action | : breech-loading |
| Locking | : double barrel-block locking with additional locking lug |
| Trigger | : twin triggers |
| Weight | : 3.1kg (6lb 13oz) |
| Length | : 113 or 116cm (44¹/₂ or 45⁵/₈ in) |
| Barrel length | : 68 or 70cm (26³/₄ or 27¹/₂in) |
| Ejector | : automatic |
| Choke | : full and ¹/₂, or ³/₄ and ¹/₄ |
| Sight | : bead |
| Safety | : half-cock of external hammers |

### CHARACTERISTICS

| | |
|---|---|
| — materiaal | : staal |
| — uitvoering | : geblauwde lopen, blanke bascule met gegraveerde zijslotplaten |
| — kolf | : walnotenhouten Engelse kolf |

When produced, this gun was only made to order. Illustrated from top to bottom are: Zoli Edward and Zoli Athena. The company of Angelo Zoli ceased production in the 1980's.

## Angelo Zoli Brescia Armi

### TECHNICAL DETAILS

| | |
|---|---|
| Calibre | : 12 |
| Chamber length | : 70mm (2³/₄in) |
| Number of barrels | : double-barrels over-and-under |
| Action | : breech-loading |
| Locking | : double Purdy locking |
| Trigger | : single or twin triggers |
| Weight | : 3.2kg (7lb) |

| Length | : 114cm (44$^7$/$_8$in) |
| Barrel length | : 70cm (27$^1$/$_2$ in) |
| Ejector | : automatic or extractor only |
| Choke | : $^3$/$_4$ and $^1$/$_4$ |
| Sight | : ventilated rib and bead |
| Safety | : sliding safety-catch on neck of stock |

### CHARACTERISTICS
| — material | : steel |
| — finish | : blued barrels, engraved bare metal action |
| — stock | : walnut stock, with pistol-grip |

The company of Angelo Zoli ceased production in the 1980's.

## Angelo Zoli Condor combination gun

### TECHNICAL DETAILS
| Calibre | : see below |
| Chamber length | : smooth-bore: 70mm (2$^3$/$_4$in) |
| Number of barrels | : double-barrels over-and-under |
| Action | : breech-loading |
| Locking | : barrel-block locking |
| Trigger | : twin triggers (front trigger with pre-set) |
| Weight | : approx. 3.1kg (6lb 13oz) |
| Length | : 108cm (42$^1$/$_2$in) |
| Barrel length | : 62cm (24$^3$/$_8$ in) |
| Ejector | : extractor only |
| Choke | : smooth bore barrels: full |
| Sight | : folding sight and bead |
| Safety | : sliding safety catch on neck of stock, dropped-gun safety |

### CHARACTERISTICS
| — materiaal | : staal |
| — uitvoering | : geblauwde lopen, blanke, gegraveerde bascule |
| — kolf | : walnotenhouten kolf, met pistoolgreep |

Available calibres/gauges (smooth-bore): 12; (rifle): 5.6x57R, 6.5x57R, 6.5x68R, 7x57R, 7x65R. An interchangeable barrel set of double smooth-bore barrels was also available for this gun. Illustrated from top to bottom are: Zoli Condor, Zoli Saint George combination gun, and Zoli Airone. The company of Angelo Zoli ceased production in the 1980's.

## Angelo Zoli Daino

### TECHNICAL DETAILS
| Calibre | : 12, 16, 20, 24, 28, or .410 |
| Chamber length | : 70mm (2$^3$/$_4$in) |
| Number of barrels | : single-barrel |
| Action | : breech-loading |
| Locking | : locking lugs with locking catch at front of trigger guard |
| Trigger | : single trigger |
| Weight | : 1.6kg (3lb 8$^1$/$_4$oz) |
| Length | : 115cm (45$^1$/$_4$in) |
| Barrel length | : 70cm (27$^1$/$_2$ in) |
| Ejector | : extractor |
| Choke | : $^1$/$_4$ |
| Sight | : bead |
| Safety | : sliding safety-catch on neck of stock |

### CHARACTERISTICS
| — material | : steel barrels, light alloy action |
| — finish | : blued barrels, engraved bare metal action |
| — stock | : hardwood stock, with pistol-grip |

The company of Angelo Zoli ceased production in the 1980's.

## Angelo Zoli Edward Side-lock

### TECHNICAL DETAILS
| Calibre | : 12 or 20 |

Chamber length : 70mm (2³/₄ in)
Number of barrels : double-barrels side-by-side
Action : breech-loading
Locking : double barrel-block locking
Trigger : single trigger
Weight : 3kg (6lb 9¹/₂ oz)
Length : 113 or 116cm (44¹/₂ or 45⁵/₈ in)
Barrel length : 68 or 70cm (26³/₄ or 27¹/₂in)
Ejector : automatic
Choke : full and ¹/₂, or ³/₄ and ¹/₄
Sight : bead
Safety : sliding safety-catch on neck of stock

**CHARACTERISTICS**
— material : steel
— finish : blued barrels, bare metal action with engraved side-lock plates
— stock : straight English stock of walnut

Illustrated from top to bottom: Zoli Edward and Zoli Athena. The company of Angelo Zoli ceased production in the 1980's.

## Angelo Zoli Saint George Caccia

**TECHNICAL DETAILS**
Calibre : 12
Chamber length : 70mm (2³/₄ in)
Number of barrels : double-barrels over-and-under
Action : breech-loading
Locking : double barrel-block locking with additional upper lug
Trigger : single trigger

Weight : 3.1–3.2kg (6lb 13oz–7lb)
Length : 111 or 114cm (43³/₄ or 44⁷/₈in)
Barrel length : 68 or 71cm (26³/₄ or 28in)
Ejector : extractor or ejector
Choke : ³/₄ and ¹/₄ (71cm/28in); full and ¹/₂ (68cm/26 in)
Sight : ventilated rib and bead
Safety : sliding safety-catch on neck of stock

**CHARACTERISTICS**
— material : steel
— finish : blued barrels, bare metal action with decorative engraving
— stock : walnut stock, with pistol-grip

Illustrated from top to bottom: Zoli Saint George, LS model, Maremma model, and Caccia model. The company of Angelo Zoli ceased production in the 1980's.

## Angelo Zoli Saint George combination gun

**TECHNICAL DETAILS**
Calibre : see below
Chamber length : smooth-bore: 70mm (2³/₄ in)
Number of barrels : double-barrels over-and-under
Action : breech-loading
Locking : barrel-block locking
Trigger : twin triggers (front trigger with pre-set)
Weight : approx. 3.1kg (6lb 13oz)
Length : 108cm (42¹/₂in)
Barrel length : 62cm (24³/₈ in)
Ejector : extractor only
Choke : smooth-bore barrel: full
Sight : folding sight and bead, sp. mount for telesc. sight
Safety : sliding safety catch on neck of stock, dropped-gun safety

**CHARACTERISTICS**
— material : steel
— finish : blued barrels, engraved bare metal action
— stock : walnut stock, with pistol-grip

Available calibres/gauges (smooth-bore): 12; (rifle): 5.6x57R, 6.5x57R, 6.5x68R, 7x57R,

7x65R. An interchangeable barrel set of double smooth-bore barrels was also available for this gun. Illustrated from top to bottom are: Zoli Condor, Zoli Saint George combination gun, and Zoli Airone. The company of Angelo Zoli ceased production in the 1980's.

## Angelo Zoli Saint George LS

**TECHNICAL DETAILS**

Calibre : 12
Chamber length : 70mm (2¾/4 in)
Number of barrels : double-barrels over-and-under
Action : breech-loading
Locking : double barrel-block locking with additional upper lug
Trigger : single trigger
Weight : 3.1–3.2kg (6lb 13oz–7lb)
Length : 111 or 114cm (43¾/4 or 44⅞/8 in)
Barrel length : 68 or 71cm (26¾/4 or 28in)
Ejector : extractor or ejector to choice
Choke : ¾/4 and ¼/4 (71cm/28in); full and (68cm/26in)
Sight : ventilated rib and bead
Safety : sliding safety-catch on neck of stock

**CHARACTERISTICS**

— material : steel
— finish : blued barrels, bare metal action with decorative engraved extension plates (no side-lock)
— stock : walnut stock, with pistol-grip

Illustrated from top to bottom: Zoli Saint George, LS model, Maremma model, and Caccia model. The company of Angelo Zoli ceased production in the 1980's.

## Angelo Zoli Saint George Maremma

**TECHNICAL DETAILS**

Calibre : 12
Chamber length : 70mm (2¾/4 in)
Number of barrels : double-barrels over-and-under
Action : breech-loading

Locking : double barrel-block locking with additional upper lug
Trigger : twin triggers
Weight : 3kg (6lb 9½/2 oz)
Length : 110cm (43¼/4 in)
Barrel length : 60cm (23⅝/8 in)
Ejector : automatic
Choke : cylindrical and full
Sight : raised rib, folding sight and bead
Safety : sliding safety-catch on neck of stock

**CHARACTERISTICS**

— material : steel
— finish : blued barrels, bare metal action with decorative engraving
— stock : walnut stock, with pistol-grip

Illustrated from top to bottom: Zoli Saint George, LS model, Maremma model, and Caccia model. The company of Angelo Zoli ceased production in the 1980's.

## Angelo Zoli Saint George Trap or Skeet

**TECHNICAL DETAILS**

Calibre : 12
Chamber length : 70mm (2¾/4 in)
Number of barrels : double-barrels over-and-under
Action : breech-loading
Locking : double barrel-block locking with additional upper lugs
Trigger : single trigger

| | |
|---|---|
| Weight | : 3.4kg (7lb 8oz) |
| Length | : 117cm (46in) |
| Barrel length | : 74cm (29⅛ in) |
| Ejector | : automatic |
| Choke | : trap or skeet |
| Sight | : 10mm (⁷/₁₆ in) wide ventilated rib with bead |
| Safety | : sliding safety-catch on neck of stock |

**CHARACTERISTICS**

| | |
|---|---|
| — material | : steel |
| — finish | : blued barrels, bare metal action with decorative engraving of side-plate extension (no side-lock) |
| — stock | : stock of specially-selected walnut, with pistol-grip |

The company of Angelo Zoli ceased production in the 1980's.

# Zoli

The history of the Italian arms maker Zoli stretches back to the Middle-Ages. It is known that early in the fifteenth century the Zoli family were making blunderbuss-type weapons as a kind of home industry for small principalities in Italy and surrounding countries. Many families throughout this region continued to make weapons by hand on a small scale until well after the Industrial Revolution,. It is known that Giovanni Zoli was making locking mechanisms for firearms in 1867. A fine example of his handicraft is the marvellous front-loading pistol that is displayed in the present-day Zoli factory. Antonio Zoli, who founded Antonio Zoli S.p.a. was born in 1905. His father, Giuseppe Zoli had a small workshop for weapons in Magno di Valtrompia. Prior to World War II, Antonio Zoli worked as a gunsmith for various weapon manufacturers in the region. In October 1945, he decided to set up his own business with his sons. At first they made double-barrelled shotguns but their range was later increased to include Express rifles and bolt-action rifles. The third generation of the family since the company was formed is now engaged in the business. The family is justly proud that they carry on the traditions established by the old craftsmen but with the latest technology.

## Zoli Ariete M1-M2

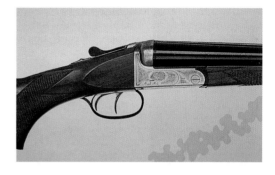

**TECHNICAL DETAILS**

| | |
|---|---|
| Calibre | : 12 |
| Chamber length | : 70mm (2¾ in) |
| Number of barrels | : double-barrels side-by-side |
| Action | : breech-loading |
| Locking | : double barrel-block locking |
| Trigger | : twin triggers |
| Weight | : 3–3.1kg (6lb 9½ oz–6lb 13oz) |
| Length | : 113 or 117cm (44½ or 46⅛ in) |
| Barrel length | : 67 or 71cm (26⅛ or 28in) |
| Ejector | : extractor (M1), ejector (M2) |
| Choke | : full and ½, or ¾ and ¼ |
| Sight | : bead |
| Safety | : sliding safety-catch on neck of stock |

**CHARACTERISTICS**

| | |
|---|---|
| — material | : steel |
| — finish | : blued barrels, bare metal action with engraving |
| — stock | : walnut stock, with pistol-grip |

## Zoli Ariete M3

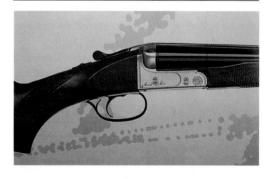

**TECHNICAL DETAILS**

| | |
|---|---|
| Calibre | : 12 |
| Chamber length | : 70mm (2¾ in) |
| Number of barrels | : double-barrels side-by-side |
| Action | : breech-loading |
| Locking | : double barrel-block locking |
| Trigger | : twin triggers |
| Weight | : 3–3.1kg (6lb 9½ oz–6lb 13oz) |
| Length | : 113 or 117cm (44½ or 46⅛ in) |

| Barrel length | : 67 or 71cm (26$^1$/$_8$ or 28in) |
| Ejector | : automatic |
| Choke | : full and $^1$/$_2$, or $^3$/$_4$ and $^1$/$_4$ |
| Sight | : bead |
| Safety | : sliding safety-catch on neck of stock |

### CHARACTERISTICS

| — material | : steel |
| — finish | : blued barrels, bare metal action |
| — stock | : walnut stock, with pistol-grip |

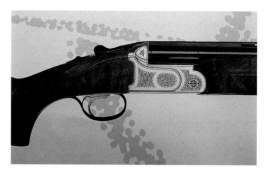

## *Zoli Combinato RT*

| Chamber length | : 70mm (2$^3$/$_4$ in) |
| Number of barrels | : double-barrels side-by-side |
| Action | : breech-loading |
| Locking | : double barrel-block locking |
| Trigger | : single adjustable trigger |
| Weight | : 3.1–3.3kg (6lb 13oz–6lb 4oz) |
| Length | : 115 or 120cm (45$^1$/$_4$ or 47$^1$/$_4$in) |
| Barrel length | : 71 or 75cm (28 or 29$^1$/$_2$ in) |
| Ejector | : automatic |
| Choke | : $^3$/$_4$ and full, or double skeet |
| Sight | : ventilated rib and bead |
| Safety | : sliding safety-catch on neck of stock |

### CHARACTERISTICS

| — material | : steel |
| — finish | : blued barrels, bare metal engraved action |
| — stock | : stock of selected walnut, with pistol-grip |

## *Zoli Empire*

### TECHNICAL DETAILS

| Calibre | : smooth-bore: 12, 16, or 20; rifle: see below |
| Chamber length | : smooth-bore: 70mm (2$^3$/$_4$ in) or 76mm (3in) |
| Number of barrels | : double-barrels over-and-under |
| Action | : breech-loading |
| Locking | : double barrel-block locking |
| Trigger | : twin triggers, front with pre-set |
| Weight | : 3.2–3.4kg (7lb–7lb 8oz) |
| Length | : 106 or 110cm (41$^3$/$_4$ or 43$^3$/$_4$ in) |
| Barrel length | : 60 or 65cm (23$^5$/$_8$ or 23$^5$/$_8$ in) () |
| Ejector | : extractor only |
| Choke | : interchangeable chokes for smooth-bore barrel |
| Sight | : folding sight and mount for telescopic sight |
| Safety | : sliding safety-catch on neck of stock, dropped-gun safety |

### CHARACTERISTICS

| — material | : steel |
| — finish | : blued barrels, bare metal engraved action |
| — stock | : walnut stock, with pistol-grip |

Available rifle calibres: .22 Hornet, .222 Rem., 5.6x50R, 5.6x57R, .243 Win., 6.5x57R, 6.5x68S, .270 Win., 7x65R, .308 Win., .30-06 Spr., 9.3x74R. Interchangeable double rifled, double smooth-bore, or smooth-bore/rifle barrels in any combination of gauge and calibre are available for this gun.

## *Zoli Elite Trap of Skeet*

### TECHNICAL DETAILS

| Calibre | : 12 or 20 (for Trap) |

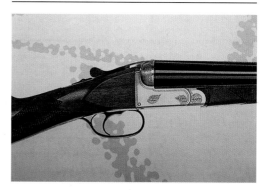

### TECHNICAL DETAILS

| Calibre | : 12 or 20 (for Trap) |
| Chamber length | : 70mm (2$^3$/$_4$ in) 76mm (3in) for 20 gauge |
| Number of barrels | : double-barrels side-by-side |
| Action | : breech-loading |
| Locking | : double barrel-block locking |
| Trigger | : single or twin triggers |
| Weight | : 3–3.1kg (6lb 9$^1$/$_2$ oz–6lb 13oz) |
| Length | : 113 or 117cm (44$^1$/$_2$ or 46$^1$/$_8$ in) |
| Barrel length | : 67 or 71cm (26$^1$/$_8$ or 28in) |
| Ejector | : automatic |
| Choke | : full and $^1$/$_2$, or $^3$/$_4$ and $^1$/$_4$ |

| Sight | : bead |
| Safety | : sliding safety-catch on neck of stock |

**CHARACTERISTICS**
| — material | : steel |
| — finish | : blued barrels, bare metal action |
| — stock | : straight English stock of selected walnut |

## Zoli Exclusive Trap of Skeet

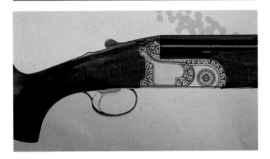

**TECHNICAL DETAILS**
| Calibre | : 12 or 20 (for Trap) |
| Chamber length | : 70mm (2³/₄ in) |
| Number of barrels | : double-barrels over-and-under |
| Action | : breech-loading |
| Locking | : double barrel-block locking |
| Trigger | : single adjustable trigger |
| Weight | : 3.1–3.3kg (6lb 13oz—6lb 4oz) |
| Length | : 115 or 120cm (45¹/₄ or 47¹/₄ in) |
| Barrel length | : 71 or 75cm (28 or 29¹/₂ in) |
| Ejector | : automatic |
| Choke | : ¹/₂ and full, or double skeet |
| Sight | : ventilated rib and bead |
| Safety | : sliding safety-catch on neck of stock |

**CHARACTERISTICS**
| — material | : steel |
| — finish | : blued barrels, bare metal action with outline engraving |
| — stock | : stock of selected walnut, with pistol-grip |

## Zoli Express

**TECHNICAL DETAILS**
| Calibre | : see below |
| Chamber length | : not applicable |
| Number of barrels | : double-barrels over-and-under |

| Action | : breech-loading |
| Locking | : double barrel-block locking |
| Trigger | : twin triggers; front trigger pre-set |
| Weight | : 3.3–3.45kg (6lb 13oz—7lb 9oz) |
| Length | : 106cm (41³/₄ in) |
| Barrel length | : 60cm (23⁵/₈ in) |
| Ejector | : automatic or extractor |
| Choke | : not applicable; rifled barrels |
| Sight | : fold-down sight and bead |
| Safety | : sliding safety-catch on neck of stock |

**CHARACTERISTICS**
| — material | : steel |
| — finish | : blued barrels, bare metal engraved action |
| — stock | : walnut stock, with pistol-grip and cheek plate |

Available calibres: 7x65R, .30-06 Spr., .308
Win., 8x57 JRS, 9.3x74R.

## Zoli Express EL

**TECHNICAL DETAILS**
| Calibre | : see below |
| Chamber length | : not applicable |
| Number of barrels | : double-barrels over-and-under |
| Action | : breech-loading |
| Locking | : double barrel-block locking |
| Trigger | : twin triggers; front trigger pre-set |
| Weight | : 3.3–3.45kg (6lb 13oz—7lb 9oz) |
| Length | : 106cm (41³/₄in) |
| Barrel length | : 60cm (23⁵/₈ in) |
| Ejector | : automatic or extractor |
| Choke | : not applicable; rifled barrels |
| Sight | : fold-down sight and bead |
| Safety | : sliding safety-catch on neck of stock |

**CHARACTERISTICS**
| — material | : steel |
| — finish | : blued barrels, bare metal engraved action |
| — stock | : walnut stock, with pistol-grip and cheek plate |

Available calibres: 7x65R, .30-06 Spr., .308
Win., 8x57 JRS, 9.3x74R. Interchangeable
barrels in various calibres are available for
this double-barrelled rifle.

## Zoli Falcon

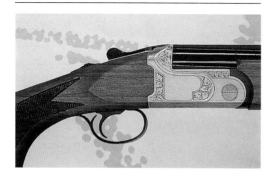

**TECHNICAL DETAILS**

| | |
|---|---|
| Calibre | : 12 or 20 |
| Chamber length | : 70mm (2³/₄ in) or 76mm (3in) for 20 gauge |
| Number of barrels | : double-barrels over-and-under |
| Action | : breech-loading |
| Locking | : double barrel-block locking |
| Trigger | : single trigger |
| Weight | : 3.1–3.3kg (6lb 13oz–6lb 4oz) |
| Length | : 111 or 115cm (43³/₄ or 45¹/₄ in) |
| Barrel length | : 67 or 71cm (26³/₈ or 28in) |
| Ejector | : automatic |
| Choke | : full and ¹/₂, or ³/₄ and full, or Falcon EMSC interchangeable chokes |
| Sight | : ventilated rib and bead |
| Safety | : sliding safety-catch on neck of stock |

**CHARACTERISTICS**

| | |
|---|---|
| — material | : steel |
| — finish | : blued barrels, bare metal engraved action |
| — stock | : walnut stock, with pistol-grip |

## Zoli Falcon Super

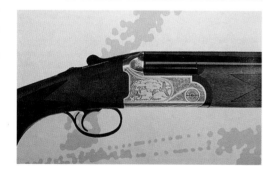

**TECHNICAL DETAILS**

| | |
|---|---|
| Calibre | : 12 or 20 |
| Chamber length | : 70mm (2³/₄ in) or 76mm (3in) for 20 gauge |
| Number of barrels | : double-barrels over-and-under |
| Action | : breech-loading |
| Locking | : double barrel-block locking |
| Trigger | : single trigger |
| Weight | : 3.1–3.3kg (6lb 13oz–6lb 4oz) |

| | |
|---|---|
| Length | : 111 or 115cm (43³/₄ or 45¹/₄ in) |
| Barrel length | : 67 or 71cm (26³/₈ or 28in) |
| Ejector | : automatic |
| Choke | : full and ¹/₂, or ³/₄ and full, or Falcon Super EMSC interchangeable chokes |
| Sight | : ventilated rib and bead |
| Safety | : sliding safety-catch on neck of stock |

**CHARACTERISTICS**

| | |
|---|---|
| — material | : steel |
| — finish | : blued barrels, bare metal action engraved with hunting motifs |
| — stock | : stock of selected walnut, with pistol-grip  |

## Zoli Gazzella

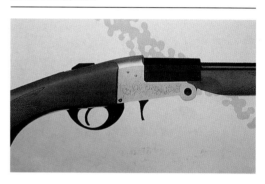

**TECHNICAL DETAILS**

| | |
|---|---|
| Calibre | : 12, 16, 20, 24, 28, or .410 |
| Chamber length | : 70mm (2³/₄ in) |
| Number of barrels | : single-barrel |
| Action | : breech-loading |
| Locking | : lug locking with locking lever in front of trigger guard |
| Trigger | : single trigger |
| Weight | : 1.6–1.8kg (3lb 8¹/₄ oz–3lb 15³/₄ oz) |
| Length | : 115–125cm (45¹/₄–49¹/₄ in) |
| Barrel length | : 70, 76, or 81cm (27¹/₂, 30, or 31⁷/₈ in) |
| Ejector | : extractor |
| Choke | : ¹/₄ |
| Sight | : bead |
| Safety | : sliding safety-catch on neck of stock |

**CHARACTERISTICS**

| | |
|---|---|
| — material | : steel barrel, light alloy action |
| — finish | : blued barrels, bare metal action |
| — stock | : hardwood stock, with pistol-grip |

## Zoli GM8 Pump-action

**TECHNICAL DETAILS**

| | |
|---|---|
| Calibre | : 12 |
| Chamber length | : 76mm (3in) |
| Number of barrels | : single-barrel |
| Magazine | : 2 or 8 cartridges |
| Action | : pump action |
| Locking | : falling block locking |

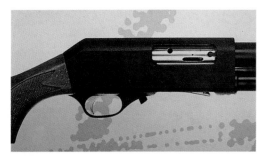

| | |
|---|---|
| Trigger | : single trigger |
| Weight | : 3.4kg (7lb 8oz) |
| Length | : 101cm (39¾ in) |
| Barrel length | : 50cm (19¾ in) |
| Ejector | : extractor |
| Choke | : cylindrical |
| Sight | : bead |
| Safety | : push-button safety-catch at rear of trigger guard |

**CHARACTERISTICS**

| | |
|---|---|
| — material | : steel |
| — finish | : matt black |
| — stock | : hardwood stock, with pistol-grip |

This gun cannot be held on a shotgun certificate in the United Kingdom because its barrel is shorter than the minimum 24in (61cm) required. Similar restrictions apply in certain other European countries.

## Zoli LX 95

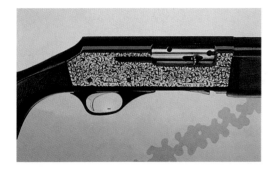

**TECHNICAL DETAILS**

| | |
|---|---|
| Calibre | : 12 |
| Chamber length | : 76mm (3in) |
| Number of barrels | : single-barrel |
| Magazine | : 2 or 6 cartridges |
| Action | : semi-automatic |
| Locking | : falling block locking |
| Trigger | : single trigger |
| Weight | : 3.3kg (7lb 4oz) |
| Length | : 121cm (47⅝ in) |

| | |
|---|---|
| Barrel length | : 71cm (28in) |
| Ejector | : extractor |
| Choke | : interchangeable chokes |
| Sight | : ventilated rib and bead |
| Safety | : push-button safety-catch at rear of trigger guard |

**CHARACTERISTICS**

| | |
|---|---|
| — material | : steel barrel, light alloy action body |
| — finish | : blued with floral motifs on action body |
| — stock | : hardwood stock, with pistol-grip |

## Zoli MG 92 Drilling (triple-barrels)

**TECHNICAL DETAILS**

| | |
|---|---|
| Calibre | : smooth-bore: 12; rifle: see below |
| Chamber length | : smooth bore: 70mm (2¾ in) |
| Number of barrels | : triple-barrelled |
| Action | : breech-loading |
| Locking | : barrel-block locking |
| Trigger | : twin triggers, front trigger with pre-set |
| Weight | : 3.3–3.45kg (7lb 4oz–7lb 9oz) |
| Length | : 106cm (41¾ in) |
| Barrel length | : 60cm (23⅝ in) |
| Ejector | : extractor only |
| Choke | : right-hand barrel: ½, left-hand barrel: full |
| Sight | : fold-down sight and mount for telescopic sight |
| Safety | : sliding safety-catch on neck of stock, rifle barrel can be disengaged |

**CHARACTERISTICS**

| | |
|---|---|
| — material | : steel |
| — finish | : blued barrels, bare metal action with Arabesque engraving |
| — stock | : walnut stock and fore-end |

Available rifle calibres: 6.5x57R, 7x65R, .30-06 Spr., 9.3x74R.

## Zoli MG 92 EL Drilling

## TECHNICAL DETAILS

| | |
|---|---|
| Calibre | : smooth-bore: 12; rifle: see below |
| Chamber length | : smooth bore: 70mm (2³/₄ in) |
| Number of barrels | : triple-barrelled |
| Action | : breech-loading |
| Locking | : barrel-block locking |
| Trigger | : twin triggers, front trigger with pre-set |
| Weight | : 3.3–3.45kg (7lb 4oz–7lb 9oz) |
| Length | : 106cm (41³/₄ in) |
| Barrel length | : 60cm (23⁵/₈ in) |
| Ejector | : extractor only |
| Choke | : right-hand barrel: ¹/₂, left-hand barrel: full |
| Sight | : fold-down sight and mount for telescopic sight |
| Safety | : sliding safety-catch on neck of stock, rifle barrel can be disengaged |

## CHARACTERISTICS

| | |
|---|---|
| — material | : steel |
| — finish | : blued barrels, bare metal action with Arabesque engraving |
| — stock | : stock and fore-end of specially-selected walnut |

Available rifle calibres: .222Rem., 6.5x55, 6.5x57R, 7x57R, 7x65R, 8x57 JRS, .30-06 Spr., 9.3x74R.

# Zoli Ritmo E

## TECHNICAL DETAILS

| | |
|---|---|
| Calibre | : 12 or 20 |
| Chamber length | : 70mm (2³/₄ in) or 76mm (3in) for 20 gauge |
| Number of barrels | : double-barrels over-and-under |
| Action | : breech-loading |
| Locking | : double barrel-block locking |
| Trigger | : single or twin triggers (Ritmo-ES) |
| Weight | : 2.9–3.1kg (6lb 6oz–6lb 13oz) |
| Length | : 111 or 115cm (43³/₄ or 45¹/₄ in) |
| Barrel length | : 67 or 71cm (26³/₈ or 28in) |
| Ejector | : automatic |
| Choke | : full and ¹/₂, or ³/₄ and full, or interchangeable chokes (Ritmo EMSC) |
| Sight | : ventilated rib and bead |
| Safety | : sliding safety-catch on neck of stock |

## CHARACTERISTICS

| | |
|---|---|
| — material | : steel barrels, light-alloy action |

---

| | |
|---|---|
| — finish | : blued barrels, bare metal engraved action |
| — stock | : walnut stock, with pistol-grip |

# Zoli Ritmo S

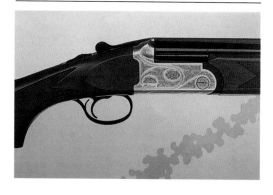

## TECHNICAL DETAILS

| | |
|---|---|
| Calibre | : 12 or 20 |
| Chamber length | : 70mm (2³/₄ in) or 76mm (3in) for 20 gauge |
| Number of barrels | : double-barrels over-and-under |
| Action | : breech-loading |
| Locking | : double barrel-block locking |
| Trigger | : single or twin triggers (Ritmo-SX) |
| Weight | : 3.1–3.3kg (6lb 13oz–7lb 4oz) |
| Length | : 111 or 115cm (43³/₄ or 45¹/₄ in) |
| Barrel length | : 67 or 71cm (26³/₈ or 28in) |
| Ejector | : extractor |
| Choke | : full and ¹/₂, or ³/₄ and full, or interchangeable chokes (Ritmo SMSC) |
| Sight | : ventilated rib and bead |
| Safety | : sliding safety-catch on neck of stock |

## CHARACTERISTICS

| | |
|---|---|
| — material | : steel |
| — finish | : blued barrels, bare metal engraved action |
| — stock | : walnut stock, with pistol-grip |

# Zoli Safari

## TECHNICAL DETAILS

| | |
|---|---|
| Calibre | : smooth-bore: 12, 16, or 20; rifle: see below |
| Chamber length | : smooth bore: 70mm or 76mm (3in) for 20 gauge |

| | |
|---|---|
| Number of barrels | : double-barrels over-and-under |
| Action | : breech-loading |
| Locking | : double barrel-block locking |
| Trigger | : twin triggers, front trigger with pre-set |
| Weight | : 3.2–3.4kg (7lb–7lb 8oz) |
| Length | : 106 or 110cm (41³/₄–43¹/₄ in) |
| Barrel length | : 60 or 65cm (23⁵/₈–25⁵/₈ in) |
| Ejector | : extractor only |
| Choke | : interchangeable chokes for smooth-bore barrel |
| Sight | : fold-down sight and mount for telescopic sight |
| Safety | : sliding safety-catch on neck of stock, dropped-gun safety |

### CHARACTERISTICS

| | |
|---|---|
| — material | : steel |
| — finish | : blued barrels, bare metal action with engraved false side-plates (no side-lock) |
| — stock | : walnut stock, with pistol-grip |

Available rifle calibres: .22 Hornet, .222 Rem.,5.6x50R, 5.6x57R, .243 Win., 6.5x57R, 6.5x68S, .270 Win., 7x65R, .308 Win., .30-06 Spr., 9.3x74R.

## Zoli Silver Fox

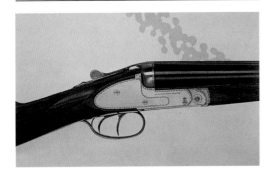

### TECHNICAL DETAILS

| | |
|---|---|
| Calibre | : 12 or 20 |
| Chamber length | : 70mm (2³/₄ in) or 76mm (3in) for 20 gauge |
| Number of barrels | : double-barrels side-by-side |
| Action | : breech-loading |
| Locking | : double barrel-block locking |
| Trigger | : single or twin triggers |
| Weight | : 3–3.1kg (6lb 9¹/₂ oz–6lb 13oz) |
| Length | : 113 or 117cm (44¹/₂ or 46in) |
| Barrel length | : 67 or 71cm (26³/₈ or 28in) |
| Ejector | : automatic |
| Choke | : full and ¹/₂, or ³/₄ and ¹/₄ |
| Sight | : bead |
| Safety | : sliding safety-catch on neck of stock |

### CHARACTERISTICS

| | |
|---|---|
| — material | : steel |
| — finish | : blued barrels, bare metal action with extended plates (no side-lock) |
| — stock | : straight English stock of selected walnut |

## Zoli Slug-gun

### TECHNICAL DETAILS

| | |
|---|---|
| Calibre | : 12 |
| Chamber length | : 76mm (3in) |
| Number of barrels | : double-barrels over-and-under |
| Action | : breech-loading |
| Locking | : double barrel-block locking |
| Trigger | : single or twin triggers |
| Weight | : 3.2g (7lb) |
| Length | : 110cm (44¹/₄in) |
| Barrel length | : 60cm (23⁵/₈ in) |
| Ejector | : to choice |
| Choke | : cylindrical and full |
| Sight | : raised rib, folding sight and bead |
| Safety | : sliding safety-catch with barrel selector on neck of stock |

### CHARACTERISTICS

| | |
|---|---|
| — material | : steel |
| — finish | : blued barrels, bare metal action with decorative engraving |
| — stock | : walnut stock, with pistol-grip |

## Zoli Solitaire

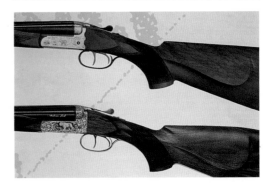

### TECHNICAL DETAILS

| | |
|---|---|
| Calibre | : 7x65R, 8x57 JRS, 9.3x74R |
| Chamber length | : not applicable |
| Number of barrels | : double-barrels side-by-side |
| Action | : breech-loading |

| Locking | : double barrel-block locking |
|---|---|
| Trigger | : twin triggers; front trigger pre-set |
| Weight | : 3.3–3.45kg (6lb 13oz–7lb 9oz) |
| Length | : 106cm (41³/₄ in) |
| Barrel length | : 60cm (23⁵/₈ in) |
| Ejector | : automatic |
| Choke | : not applicable; rifled barrels |
| Sight | : fold-down sight, bead and mount for telesc. sight |
| Safety | : sliding safety-catch on neck of stock, load indicator on action |

### CHARACTERISTICS
| — material | : steel |
|---|---|
| — finish | : blued barrels, bare metal engraved action |
| — stock | : walnut stock, with pistol-grip and cheek plate |

Illustrated from top to bottom: Solitaire and Solitaire EL.

## Zoli Sport Z-92

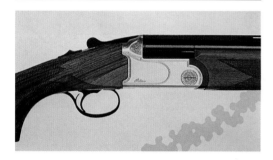

### TECHNICAL DETAILS
| Calibre | : 12 |
|---|---|
| Chamber length | : 70mm (2³/₄ in) |
| Number of barrels | : double-barrels over-and-under |
| Action | : breech-loading |
| Locking | : double barrel-block locking |
| Trigger | : single trigger |
| Weight | : 3.3kg (7lb 4oz) |
| Length | : 115cm (45¹/₄in) |
| Barrel length | : 71cm (28in) |
| Ejector | : automatic |
| Choke | : ³/₄ and ¹/₄, or interchangeable chokes |
| Sight | : ventilated rib and bead |
| Safety | : sliding safety-catch on neck of stock |

### CHARACTERISTICS
| — material | : steel |
|---|---|
| — finish | : blued barrels, bare metal action |
| — stock | : walnut stock, with pistol-grip |

## Zoli Super Express E3-XELL

### TECHNICAL DETAILS
| Calibre | : smooth-bore: 20 |
|---|---|
| Chamber length | : smooth-bore: 76mm (3in) |

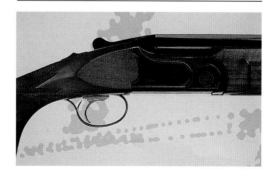

| Number of barrels | : double-barrels over-and-under |
|---|---|
| Action | : breech-loading |
| Locking | : barrel-block locking |
| Trigger | : twin triggers |
| Weight | : approx. 3.1kg (6lb 13oz) |
| Length | : 106cm (41³/₄in) |
| Barrel length | : 60cm (23⁵/₈ in) |
| Ejector | : automatic |
| Choke | : interchangeable chokes for smooth-bore barrel |
| Sight | : fold-down sight and mount for telescopic sight |
| Safety | : sliding safety-catch on neck of stock, dropped-gun safety |

### CHARACTERISTICS
| — material | : steel |
|---|---|
| — finish | : blued barrels, bare metal action with engraved side-plates (no side-lock) |
| — stock | : walnut stock, with pistol-grip |

Available rifle calibres: .222 Rem., .222 Rem. Mag., 5.6x50R Mag, 5.6x57R, .243 Win., .270 Win., 6.5x55, 6.5x57R, 6.5x68, 7x65R, .308 Win., .30-06 Spr., 9.3x74R. Interchangeable double rifled, double smooth-bore, or smooth-bore/rifle barrels in any combination of gauge and calibre are available for this gun.

## Zoli Trap Z-92 / Skeet Z-92

### TECHNICAL DETAILS
| Calibre | : 12 or 20 (for Trap) |
|---|---|
| Chamber length | : 70mm (2³/₄ in) |
| Number of barrels | : double-barrels over-and-under |

| Action | : breech-loading |
|---|---|
| Locking | : double barrel-block locking |
| Trigger | : single trigger |
| Weight | : 3—3.2kg (6lb 9$^1$/$_2$ oz—7lb) |
| Length | : 115 or 120cm (45$^1$/$_4$ or 47$^1$/$_4$ in) |
| Barrel length | : 71 or 75cm (28 or 29$^1$/$_2$ in) |
| Ejector | : automatic |
| Choke | : $^1$/$_2$ and full, or double skeet |
| Sight | : ventilated rib and bead |
| Safety | : sliding safety-catch on neck of stock |

**CHARACTERISTICS**

| — material | : steel barrels, light-alloy action |
|---|---|
| — finish | : blued |
| — stock | : walnut stock, with pistol-grip |

## *Zoli Vulcano Record Side-lock*

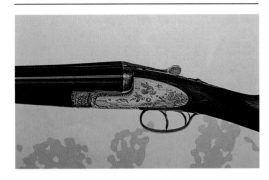

**TECHNICAL DETAILS**

| Calibre | : 12 |
|---|---|
| Chamber length | : 70mm (2$^3$/$_4$ in) |
| Number of barrels | : double-barrels side-by-side |
| Action | : breech-loading |
| Locking | : double barrel-block locking |
| Trigger | : single or twin triggers |
| Weight | : 2.9—3.1kg (6lb 6oz—6lb 9$^1$/$_2$ oz) |
| Length | : 113 or 117cm (44$^1$/$_2$ or 46in) |
| Barrel length | : 67 or 71cm (26$^3$/$_8$ or 28in) |
| Ejector | : to choice |
| Choke | : full and $^1$/$_2$, or $^3$/$_4$ and $^1$/$_4$ |
| Sight | : bead |
| Safety | : sliding safety-catch on neck of stock |

**CHARACTERISTICS**

| — material | : steel |
|---|---|
| — finish | : blued barrels, bare metal action with side-lock plates engraved to choice |
| — stock | : straight English stock of selected walnut |

## *Zoli White Diamond*

**TECHNICAL DETAILS**

| Calibre | : 12 or 20 |
|---|---|
| Chamber length | : 70mm (2$^3$/$_4$ in) or 76mm (3in) for 20 gauge |
| Number of barrels | : double-barrels over-and-under |

| Action | : breech-loading |
|---|---|
| Locking | : double barrel-block locking |
| Trigger | : single or twin triggers to choice |
| Weight | : 3—3.3kg (6lb 9$^1$/$_2$ oz—7lb 4oz) |
| Length | : 111—121cm (43$^3$/$_4$ or 47$^5$/$_8$in) |
| Barrel length | : 67, 71 or 75cm (26$^3$/$_8$, 28 or 29$^1$/$_2$ in) |
| Ejector | : to choice |
| Choke | : interchangeable chokes |
| Sight | : ventilated rib and bead |
| Safety | : sliding safety-catch on neck of stock |

**CHARACTERISTICS**

| — material | : steel |
|---|---|
| — finish | : blued barrels, bare metal with choice of engraving for side-plates (no side-lock) |
| — stock | : specially-selected walnut stock: straight English or with pistol-grip to choice |

## *Zoli Z-95 Combination gun*

**TECHNICAL DETAILS**

| Calibre | : see below |
|---|---|
| Chamber length | : smooth-bore: 70mm (2$^3$/$_4$ in) |
| Number of barrels | : double-barrels over-and-under |
| Action | : breech-loading |
| Locking | : barrel-block locking |
| Trigger | : twin triggers |
| Weight | : approx. 3.1kg (6lb 13oz) |
| Length | : 106cm (41$^3$/$_4$ in) |
| Barrel length | : 60—65cm (23$^5$/$_8$—25$^5$/$_8$ in): 60cm to calibre 5.6; 65cm from .243 Win. |
| Ejector | : extractor only |
| Choke | : interchangeable chokes for smooth-bore barrel |
| Sight | : fold-down sight and mount for telescopic sight |
| Safety | : sliding safety-catch on neck of stock, dropped-gun safety |

## CHARACTERISTICS

- material : steel
- finish : blued barrels, bare metal engraved action
- stock : walnut stock and fore-end

Available gauges/calibres (smooth-bore): 12 or 16; (rifle): .222 Rem., 5.6x50R Mag, .243 Win., 6.5x57R, 7x57R, 7x65R, 7x64, 8x57 IRS, .308 Win., .30-06 Spr., 9.3x74R. Interchangeable double rifled, double smooth-bore, or smooth-bore/rifle barrels in any combination of gauge and calibre are available for this gun.

| | |
|---|---|
| Chamber length | : smooth-bore: 70mm (2³/₄ in) |
| Number of barrels | : double-barrels over-and-under |
| Action | : breech-loading |
| Locking | : barrel-block locking |
| Trigger | : twin triggers |
| Weight | : approx. 3.2kg (7lb) |
| Length | : 106cm (41³/₄ in) |
| Barrel length | : 65cm (25⁵/₈ in) |
| Ejector | : extractor only |
| Choke | : interchangeable chokes for smooth-bore barrel |
| Sight | : fold-down sight and mount for telescopic sight |
| Safety | : sliding safety-catch on neck of stock, dropped-gun safety |

## Zoli Z-95 Deluxe Combination gun

## TECHNICAL DETAILS

Calibre : smooth-bore 12; rifle: see below

## CHARACTERISTICS

- material : steel
- finish : blued barrels, bare metal engraved action
- stock : stock and fore-end of specially-selected walnut

Available calibres: 12 or 16; .243 Win., 6.5x57R, 7x57R, 7x65R, 7x64, 8x57 IRS, .308 Win., .30-06 Spr., 9.3x74R. Interchangeable double rifled, double smooth-bore, or smooth-bore/rifle barrels in any combination of gauge and calibre are available for this gun.

# Acknowledgements

*The author and publisher wish to thank those individuals and companies whose help was invaluable in the preparation of this book. They are listed in alphabetical order.*

AKAH: Albrecht Kind GmbH & Co., Germany; American Arms Inc., N. Kansas City, USA; Armscor/KBI Inc., Harrisburg USA; Armtech, Heerlen, The Netherlands; Arrieta S. L., Elgoibar, Spain; A.S.I. Publishers, Lelystad, The Netherlands; Baikal/lzhevsky Mekhanichesky Zavod, Izhevsk, Russia; Benelli Armi SA, Urbino, Italy; Pietro Beretta, Gardone V.T., Italy; Bernardelli, Gardone V.T., Italy; Blaser Jagdwaffen GmbH, Isny im Allgau, Germany; Browning Inc., Morgan, USA; Browning S.A., Herstal, Belgium; Chapuis, Saint Bonnet 1e Chateaux, France; Colt's Manufacturing Company Inc., Hartford, USA; Connecticut Shotgun Mfg. (A.H. Fox), New Britain, USA; Consorio Armaioli Bresciani, Italy; Cosmi Americo & Figlio snc., Ancona, Italy; CZ-Cesksa Zbrojovka A.s., Uhersky Brod, Czech Republic; Dakota Arms Inc., Sturgis, USA; Dynamit Nobel, Troisdorf, Germany; Fabarm S.p.A., Travagliato/Brescia, Italy; FAIR Techni-Mec Snc. di Isidor Rizzini & C., Marcheno/Brescia, Italy; Fanzoj GmbH, Ferlach, Austria; Armi Ferlib di Libero, Gardone V.T., Italy; Granger/S.A.R.L., St. Etienne, France; FN-Browning S.A. Herstal, Belgium; Franchi S.p.A., Brescia, Italy; Frankonia Jagd, Würzburg, Germany; Gaucher Armes S.A., St. Etienne, France; Harrington & Richardson 1871 Inc., Gardner, USA; Hege/Zeughaus GmbH, Überlingen, Germany; Friedrich Wilhelm Heym GmbH & Co. KG, Münnerstadt, Germany; Helmut Hofmann GmbH, Mellrichstadt, Germany; IGA/E.R. Amantino & Cia Ltda (IGA Shotgun Division), Veranopolis, Brazil; Izhevsky Mekanichesky Zavod/-Baika1, Izhevsk, Russia; KBI Inc./Armscor, Harrisburg, USA; Eduard Kettner, Cologne, Germany; Albrecht Kind GmbH & Co., Gummersbach-Hunstig, Germany; Krieghoff Gun Co., U1m, Germany; Lanber/Comlanber S.A., Zaldibar (Vicaya), Spain; Laurona Armas Eibar S.a.l., Eibar, Spain; Lebeau-Courally, Liège, Belgium; Ljutic Industries Inc., Yakima, USA; Magnum Research Inc, Minneapolis, USA; MagTech/CBC Ribeirao Pires, Sao Paulo, Brazil; Marlin Firearms Co., New Haven, USA; Marocchi S.p.A., Zanano di Sarezzo/Brescia, Italy; Merkel/Jagd & Sportwaffen Suhl GmbH, Suhl, Germany; Mitchell Arms Inc., Santa Ana, USA; O.F. Mossberg & Sons Inc., North Haven, USA; New England Firearms, Gardner, USA; Norinco/Norconia GmbH, Rottendorf, Germany; Armi Perazzi S.p.a., Botticino Mattina/Brescia, Italy; Powell & Son (Gunmakers) Ltd., Birmingham, United Kingdom; Remington Arms Company Inc., Wilmington/DE, USA; John Rigby & Co., London, United Kingdom; Battista Rizzini, Marcheno/Brescia, Italy; Ruger/Sturm, Ruger & Company Inc, Southport, CT, USA; S.A.R.L. G. Granger, St. Etienne. France; Savage Arms Inc., Westfield MA, USA; The Magnum Broederschap shooting association, Nieuwpoort, The Netherlands; De Zwarte Tulp shooting association, Brandwijk, The Netherlands; South Holland marksman's association, Nieuwpoort, The Netherlands; Simson-Suhl, Suhler Jagd & Sportwaffen GmbH, Suhl, Germany; Stoeger Industries, Wayne NJ, USA; Sturm, Ruger & Company Inc, Southport CT, USA; Thormpson/Center Arms, Rochester, New Hampshire, USA; Ugartechea S.A., Eibar, Spain; De Valken gun shop, Gouda, The Netherlands, (owner of the Breton and Darne shotguns featured); Verney-Carron, St. Etienne. France; Weatherby, Atlascaldero, CA, USA; Westley Richards & Co., Birmingham, United Kingdom; Winchester/US Repeating Arms Company Inc., Morgan, Utah, USA; Wischo Jagd & Sportwaffen GmbH & Co. Erlangen, Germany; Hermanos Zabala S.A., Eibar, Spain; Angelo Zoli Fabbrica D'Armi, Gardone VT/Brescia, Italy; Antonio Zoli Fabbrica D'Armi, Gardone VT/ Brescia, Italy; and those others who I may have overlooked. My special thanks to my wife Annelies Hartink, whose editing of my text was invaluable and who ensured I could write this book undisturbed by intrusions.

The publishers wish to thank the following for their help in the preparation of the English version of this book: The British Deer Society and its chairman, Michael Squire; the gun room at Holland & Holland, London; Reg Homard, The Lewes Gunshop, Lewes; Firearms Licensing Officer, Sussex Police.

# Useful Internal Pages

American Firearms Industry Index:
http://www.amfire.com

Armtech-The Netherlands/Belgium:
http://www.limburg.nl/armtech

Arrieta, Aya, Chapuis, Fox, Gazalan,
Gunshop, Merkel:
http://www.gunshop.com

Baikal Russian guns:
http://www.mehzavod.ru/catalog

Benelli:
http://www.benelli.it/english

Beretta:
http://www.beretta.it

Bismuth Cartridge Company:
http://www.bismuth-notox.com

Blaser:
http://home.t-online.de/home/
   blaser.jagdwaffen

Browning Arms Company:
http://www.browning.com

CZ/Ceska Zbrojovka:
http://www.czub.cz

Dakota Arms:
http://www.dakotaarms.com

Double-barrel shotguns and combination
guns useer group (BBS):
http://gunshop.com/HyperNews

FAIR Techni-Mec I. Rizzini:
http://www.studionet.it/Re Emilio Rizzini

Ferlib:
http://www. ivtnet. it/ferlib

GunHoo GunPages Central:
http://www.gunsgunsguns.com/gunhoo

Gunindex:
http://www.gunindex.com

HIS-Rifles & Shotguns:
http://www.ford-info.com/his/sshot gun.htm

Hunting in foreign countries:
http://www.huntinfo.com

Krieghoff:
http://www.halkguns.com

Lanber/Comlanber:
http://www.ilinks.net/~jnystrom/lanber

Marlin firearms:
http://www.marlin-firearms.com

Marocchi:
http://www.precision-sales.com/marocchi

Mossberg:
http://www.mossberg.com

Perazzi:
http://www.shootingsports.com/perazzi

Rebo gun books:
http://www.rebo-publishers.com

Ruger (Sturm & Ruger):
http://www.ruger-firearms.com

Russian guns:
http://www.izhmash.ru

Shooting sports:
http://www.shootingsports.com

Verney-Carron:
http://www.verney-carron.com

Vihtavuori:
http://www.vihtavuori.fi

Winchster/U.S. Repeating Arms:
http://www.winchester.com

# Useful addresses

**British Assn. for Shooting & Conservation**
Marford Mill, Rossett, Wrexham LL12 0HL
01244 573000
E mail: enq@basc.demon.co.uk
Internet: http://www.basc.org.uk

**British Deer Society**
Burgate Manor, Fordingbridge, Hampshire
SP6 1EF
01425 655434
E mail: info@bds.hq@dial.pipex.com
Internet:
http://dialspace.dial.pipex.com/british-deer-society-hq/

**British Shooting Sports Council**
PO Box 11, Bexhill-on-Sea, East Sussex,
TN40 1ZZ
01424 217031

**Clay Pigeon Shooting Association**
Earlstrees Court, Earlstrees Road, Corby,
Northampstonshire NN17 4AX
01536 443566
E mail: info@cpsa.co.uk
Internet: http://www.cpsa.co.uk/

**Countryside Alliance/British Field Sports
Society**
The Old Town Hall, 367 Kennington Road,
London SE11 4PT
0171 582 5432
E mail: info@bfss.org
Internat: http://www.bfss.org

**Game Conservancy Trust**
Fordingbridge, Hampshire, SP6 1EF
01425 652381
E mail: game-conservancy@ukonline.co.uk
Internet: http://www.game-conservancy.
org.uk

**Gun Trade Association**
PO Box 7, Evesham WR11 6AN
01386 443304

**The Shooting Gazette**
2 West Street, Bourne, Lincolnshire PE10
9NE
01778 393747
E mail: CountryPursuits@compuserve.com
Internet:
http://www.countrypursuits.co.uk/sg.htm

# Bibliography

*Title*

| | |
|---|---|
| *Alles over Geweren* (Everything about Guns) | Achard/Solar/Rebo |
| *Alles over Jachtgeweren* (Everything about Shotguns) | Berton/Solar/Rebo |
| *Armas* (Arms) | Hobby Press SA |
| *Deutches Waffen Journal* (German Arms Journal) | Schwend Verlag |
| *Encyclopedia of Rifles & Carbines* | Hartink, Rebo |
| *Exploded Long Gun Drawings* | H.A Murtz |
| *Feuerwaffen für Sammler* (Firearms for collectors) | Steinwedel |
| *Firearms* | Myatt |
| *Firearms Assembly/Disassembly* | Gun Digest |
| *Firearms History* | Hogg |
| *Frankonia Jagd catalogue* | Frankonia Jagd |
| *Gewehre, Pistolen und Revolver* (Rifles, Pistols and Revolvers) | Müller |
| *Guns* | Publishers Development Guns & Ammo |
| *Gun Annual* | Modern Day Periodicals |
| *Gun Digest* | DBI Books Inc. |
| *Gun Parts No. 21* | Gun Parts Corp. |
| *Guns & Gunsmiths* | North & Hogg |
| *Guns Illustrated* | DBI Books Inc. |
| *Gun Journal* | Charlton Publishing Inc. |
| *Guns & Shooting* | Aceville Publishing Ltd |
| *Guns of the World* | Tanner and others |
| *Gun World* | Gallant Charger Publishers |
| *Handboek voor de herlader* (handbook for reloaders) | ASI/Hartink |
| *Internationles Waffen Magazin* (International Arms Magazine) | Füssli Verlag |
| *Internationles Waffen Spiegel* (International Arms Mirror) | Civil Arms Verlag |
| *Kaliber* (Calibre) | Magnum Publishers |
| *Kettner catalogue* | E. Kettner |
| *Man/Magnum* | SA Man 1982 (Pty) Ltd. |
| *Modern Shotgun, The, volumes 1–3* | Burrard |
| *Nederlandse Jager (de)* (The Dutch Hunter) | KNJV (Royal Dutch Hunters Association) |
| *Pleasure of Guns* | Rosa & May |
| *Sam* | NVTU De Schakel |
| *Sam* | SI Publications |
| *Schusswaffen tunen und testen* (Tuning and Testing Firearms) | Heymann |
| *Schweizer Waffen Magazin* (Swiss Arms magazine) | Orell Füssli Verlag |
| *Shooter's Bible* | Stoeger Publishing Co. |
| *Shooting Times* | PJS Publishing Inc. |
| *Shotgun Digest* | Lewis/DBI Books |
| *Visier* (Sights) | Pietsch & Scholten |
| *Waffen Digest* (Arms Digest) | Motorbuch Verlag |
| *Waffen Lexicon* (Lexicon of Arms) | Lampel & Mahrholdt |
| *Waffen Revue* (Arms Revue) | Schwend Verlag |
| *Waffen Sammeln* (Collecting Arms) | König & Hugo |
| *WM Waffenmarkt Jahrbuch* (Arms market Yearbook) | GFI Verlag GmbH |

# Index

*Lebeau- Courally Versailles Trio*

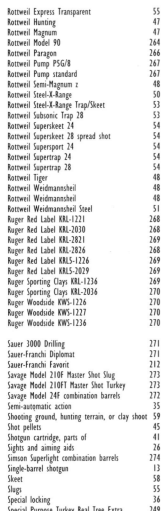

*Rizzini model S790 EL Sport*